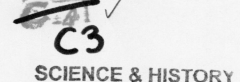

ANALYZING
CONCEPTS
IN
SOCIAL SCIENCE

ANALYZING CONCEPTS IN SOCIAL SCIENCE

SCIENCE, IDEOLOGY, AND VALUE
VOLUME I

Abraham Edel

Transaction Books
New Brunswick, New Jersey

Library of Congress Catalog Number: 76-50327
ISBN: 0-87855-143-3 (cloth)
Printed in the United States of America

Library of Congress Cataloging in Publication Data

Edel, Abraham, 1908-
    Analyzing concepts in social science.

    (His Science, ideology, and value; v. 1)
    Includes index.
    1. Social sciences.   2. Concepts.   3. Social
values.   I. Title.
H33.E3 vol. 1 [H61]   300'.1s [300'.1'8]   76-50327
ISBN 0-87855-143-3

For Matthew and Deborah

CONTENTS

PREFACE

To reread one's own papers written over four decades is an interesting and instructive experience. Unnoticed unities, relations, and lines of development almost pop out in the process. Earlier papers take on fresh appearance when looked at in terms of their intellectual offspring, and later papers acquire a character of culmination. Lessons about methods of inquiry begin to emerge as one wonders what the papers would have been like had later ideas been present at the outset. In one of the fashionable dialects, this would, I take it, be seen as a process of self-transcendence—the self-reflecting on itself as object from a more exalted meta-standpoint. In plainer language, it is simply learning from intellectual experience, which does not differ from learning generally. Such lessons are not private, but can be shared as hypotheses for sharpening thought. I am grateful to Professor Irving Horowitz, who proposed a collection of this sort, for making this learning possible. I have benefited for many years from his incisive insight in the social analysis of ideas.

The papers selected for inclusion in these two volumes are organized around two central problems that have played a vital role in the study of human affairs in the twentieth century: methods of analyzing concepts, and the relation of fact and value. (They cannot of course be kept wholly apart since the role of values in ideas—most glaring in ideological thought—is itself an important issue.) Conflicts over how to analyze concepts have been widespread and have reflected the diversity of schools in both philosophy and social science. Their effects on the work of social scientists have been immediate and profound. The issue over the separation of fact and value, with its attempt to establish a neutral social science aloof from social commitments, has reverberated through social theory as well as social practice. (I shall argue that it has always been a program, in fact an unachievable one, not an

ix

unavoidable metaphysics.) The first volume includes case studies in the analysis of concepts from different fields of the inquiry into human ways, as well as theoretical explorations of different phases of the problems of analysis. The second volume both addresses the fact-value dichotomy from different angles and includes papers on special applications in practical judgment.

I should like to thank those who have given permission for the republication of a number of the papers previously published or originally designed for special conferences. Individual acknowledgement is to be found on the acknowledgements page. My indebtedness to friends and colleagues whose writings and discussion played an enormous part at various times in the original preparation of these papers and in their criticism is, of course, too general and too widespread to allow more than this wholesale expression of gratitude.

The two volumes are dedicated to my son, Matthew, and my daughter, Deborah. Both are practitioners in the fields under consideration: the one contributing in his professional work as economist to combining the methods of economics, anthropology, and history; the other in her professional work in special education, particularly concerned with the kinds of values involved in furthering individual self-development.

Volume 1 begins with a long introductory essay written for the volume which provides a philosophic overview of the conflicts of methods of analysis. It presents a sense of the diversity and the way this diversity may best be regarded if we are to have helpful cooperation, rather than an internecine strife of schools. The next part consists of papers written at various times that analyze specific concepts in somewhat different ways for different purposes. The final part gathers papers that have discussed the theory of ideas and the character of ideology, some in reference to general problems, some in relation to particular fields.

I have not attempted, for the most part, to bring the older studies up to date, in the sense of replacing earlier references to work in social science with later ones. It seemed to me that the methodological points could be made with either, so that there was no need to add the labors of fresh exploration for such a diversity of topics. I have also not attempted to note changes of view or emphasis in my own outlook on the contents of the papers. Instead, I have added some remarks at the beginning of each paper, characterizing its context and the kind of analysis I was doing at the time (in relation to the study of types in the introductory essay), and have suggested further directions that could be followed if analyses of more comprehensive variety were to be employed. In this sense, the lessons of the overview are exhibited in a measure of self-criticism.

A. E.

ACKNOWLEDGEMENTS

"The Theory of Social Classes: A Logical Analysis" was originally published in the *Marxist Quarterly*, April-June 1937, pp. 237-52.

"The Concept of the Unconscious: Some Analytic Preliminaries" was originally published in *Philosophy of Science* 31 (1964): 18-32.

"Some Reflections on the Concept of Human Rights" was originally published in *Human Rights: AMINTAPHIL I*, ed. Ervin H. Pollack (Buffalo: Jay Stewart, 1971), pp. 1-23. The volume consists of papers presented at the second plenary meeting of the American Section of the International Association for Philosophy of Law and Social Philosophy (AMINTAPHIL).

"The Meaning of Human Dignity" is part of "Humanist Ethics and the Meaning of Human Dignity," in *Moral Problems in Contemporary Society, Essays in Humanistic Ethics*, ed. Paul Kurtz (Englewood Cliffs, N.J.: Prentice-Hall, 1969), pp. 227-40. The section used here is from pages 231-40.

"The Place of Respect for Persons in Moral Philosophy" is reprinted by permission of The Cleveland State University, Cleveland, Ohio, from *Philosophy in Context*, Volume 3, 1974, pp. 23-32. Copyright © 1974.

"Power as an Organizing Concept in Social Theory" was originally published in *Science and Society* (Fall 1952): 346-51, as a review of *Power and Society*, by Harold D. Lasswell and Abraham Kaplan.

"The Concept of Levels in Social Theory" was originally published in *Symposium on Sociological Theory*, ed. Llewellyn Gross (Evanston, Ill.: Row, Peterson, 1959), pp. 167-95.

ANALYZING CONCEPTS IN SOCIAL SCIENCE

Introduction
Modes of Analysis: A Philosophic Overview

The nature of analysis has been a perennial theme in philosophy since the days when Socrates first began to explore ideas by asking people what they meant by justice, piety, courage, beauty, and knowledge. It has become a controversial concept at the hands of recent philosophical schools that have been polarized as analytic and antianalytic philosophy. Meanwhile, all through the ages, logicians and epistemologists have worked away at problems of definition, meaning, and—to invoke the title of Peirce's best-known essay—how to make our ideas clear. The social scientist has not concerned himself much with these controversies—not even to explore, to any marked degree, the social bases of philosophical schools. But he has had a constant stake in their products. For one thing, social scientists have been not only consumers of the usual philosophical and ordinary concepts, but frequent creators of technical ones. In the earlier part of our century, for example, an advanced discipline like economics long had a full storehouse of technical ideas—capital, labor, rent, profit, free market, and others—which economists proceeded to manipulate in spunout systems. Political theory, lacking comparable manipulative possibilities, seemed almost resigned to asking definitional questions: what is the state, authority, power, democracy, and so forth, not to speak of traditional notions of liberty and equality. In due course, political theorists ventured on freshly-constructed concepts like totalitarianism. Sociology inherited definitional questions about community, association, and class; sociologists worried about how to analyze groups and experimented by con-

1

structing ideal types. Anthropology, avidly adding to its mountains of descriptive data, took its time about articulating the changes in the structure of institutional concepts that its materials clearly called for. Psychology, on its nonphysiological side, kept struggling with concepts of instinct, intelligence, and personality. When it wearied of "what is ...?" questions, it still continued to answer them implicitly by the way it set up its research. It was obvious enough in all the social sciences that questions of definition and conceptual analysis were either the alpha or the omega of inquiry: as alpha, they laid down the field and prescribed the method of investigation; as omega, they incorporated the systematic answers of discovery.

The social sciences thus had definite links to philosophical theories of proper procedure in definition and analysis, even when they were not explicitly marked out. This became startlingly clear once in a while when a philosophic method of analyzing concepts rose to dizzying heights and embarked on a career of dominance in social science itself. Thus the winds of operationalism swept through psychology and sociology in the 1930s and reenforced existing behaviorial trends. An operationalism (more positivistic than pragmatic) is still entrenched in many a province of social theory and practice. Phenomenological analysis has beaten a few paths into behavioral and social science, with blood-curdling antipositivist slogans. Even ordinary language analysis has turned up recently in surprising contexts of social theory, to suggest that the social scientist will get further by inquiry into what people say rather than by seeking explanations along physical science models.

Different conceptions of analysis lie at the heart of differences in philosophical schools. It is quite likely that new philosophical schools take their rise when a new methodology of dealing with concepts comes to the fore. Should the social scientist become thoroughly conscious of this, he would be less likely to fall victim to the methodological conflicts on the philosophical scene. Instead, he could welcome their rich variety and, ignoring the frenzied controversy in which they were generated, simply appropriate what he found useful for his own work. A workshop stocked with many different tools is, in general, better prepared than one relying on a single instrument! His motto might well be: TOOLS, NOT SCHOOLS.

This chapter provides a philosophic overview of many of the kinds of analysis that have appeared on the philosophic scene, past and present. Indeed, the history of methods in philosophy reveals a whole range of modes of analysis, and a general sketch helps dig out the presuppositions of the different ones. If we pay attention to the contexts in which they arose, the purposes they served, the assumptions that guided their demands, and their conceptions of results to be achieved, we can better understand where they can be usefully employed and where they may become obstacles to scientific and philosophic advance. Recognizing a variety in modes of analysis can help avoid slavishness in methodology and perhaps see how a creative treatment of concepts may be possible.

Such an overview could, in a more extended study, even begin to reckon with what is at stake in the conflicts of philosophical schools. But our present purpose is more limited—simply an invitation to emancipation in the treatment of concepts in social science.

I

Analysis roughly refers to a way of thinking reflectively, but the adjectives employed with it do not all go in the same direction. *Economic analysis* and *political analysis* mean analysis of economic and political materials, as biblical analysis means analysis of the biblical writings. But Socratic analysis does not mean analysis of Socrates, but rather the *mode of analysis* he carried on, while *ordinary language analysis* does mean analysis of ordinary linguistic usage, and it is a formidable mode of analysis today. This variation suggests that no sharp line can be drawn between a way of reflecting and cultivation of a given *area,* if it be broad enough and important enough. For example, if *symbolic analysis* were taken to signify a mode of analyzing, it could still mean the analysis of symbols. Its rank as a mode would come from the assumption that symbols play an important part in all areas of inquiry, and therefore, a way of analyzing symbols constitutes, at the same time, a way of analyzing various areas of specific materials. We may think of a mode of analysis, therefore, as a way of analyzing or dealing with concepts in the effort to understand them and learn how to use them, which has taken shape as a stable, more or less systematic form of reflection promising significant results.

Casting our overview in a historical form, though with wide historical spaces and great historical leaps, we may begin with

Socratic analysis, the earliest and most perennial type, whose innocent charm has enabled it to survive the comings and goings of many other modes.

Socratic analysis takes place in dialogue generated by the question, "What is X?" It hopes both to clarify our meaning in talking about X and to bring into focus the object or reality talked about. (There is thus no special need to distinguish the linguistic from the material aspect in its operation.) Take, for example, the first answer given in Plato's *Republic* to the question, "What is justice?" The proposal is that justice consists in telling the truth and paying one's debts. Says Socrates: should one return a borrowed weapon to a lender who has meanwhile gone mad? From a horrified negative response he concludes that not every debt should be paid. Therefore, justice cannot be simply telling the truth and paying one's debts.

Note how much is packed away in this brief application of the method. In general form it is dialectical: there is a proposed answer to the question; a discrepancy or counter-instance is suggested; the speaker must then offer a new proposal or refine his old one in order to remove a possible contradiction. If the speaker had refused to accept the counter-instance—if he had said the weapon should be returned to the madman because it was his, since justice required paying every debt—then he would have maintained consistency but at the price of accepting the consequences of his stand. The method thus involves an act of voluntary acceptance. All participants in dialogue recognize that no one can rest on a contradiction or meet it with a shrug, but the burden of decision at each point falls on the speaker who proposed the answer. In this sense, the method is libertarian: it does not put down or charge wrongness, but calls for the growth of ideas in the mind of the speaker. Just as Socrates' mother had been a midwife, so he thought of himself as a midwife of ideas in others, not as a begetter or imposer of doctrine. In the *Republic*, another speaker takes up the example given: he shifts the answer from the concrete paying of a debt to the more abstract giving of *what is due* (and to a madman no weapon is due). The argument now moves in search of a formula for what is due.

With regard to form of results envisaged from use of the method, Socrates imposes two stern criteria. The result must be *general*, and it must convey what is *essential*, not some accidental concomitant of the essential nor even some consequent attribute following from the essence. The requirement of generality is usually Socrates' first lesson. In the early dialogues, first answers tend to give examples or point to particular instances. "What is courage?" is answered by "sticking to one's post and not retreating," and similarly, a particular act for piety, an object for beauty, and so on. Socrates shows how analysis of each concept requires comparison of different instances to which it applies. For example, is not the soldier equally courageous who obeys an order to retreat even though he wants to stick to his post? Comparison leads beyond examples to a general formula. The second requirement, that of essentiality, is more difficult. In the *Euthyphro* (which asks "What is piety?"), after learning the lesson of generality, Euthyphro comes up with the proposed answer that piety is what is pleasing to the gods. Socrates wants to know whether conduct is pious because it is pleasing to the gods or pleasing to the gods because it is pious. If the latter, piety involves a good which is compelling to gods and men alike. To ascertain this good would give an essential answer, as against a consequential or an accidental one. Socrates seems committed to the view that there is a kind of rational or systematic order to be found in analyzing a concept, not just a conglomeration of acts or objects or properties.

Later methodological argument shows that much theory is packed away here. Why should the analysis of a concept move toward generalization? Can we grasp the concept of, say, dictatorship better by a general formula, or by reading a case history (or even a novel) of Nazi Germany? Perhaps comparison would be necessary to separate the irrelevant—in Italy there was a fascist dictatorship without the racial laws. Comparison moves us to generalizing and toward theory-formation. But some moderns might want to move instead toward deriving "pure cases" or "ideal types," or toward seeking understanding in a kind of feeling-intuition in the face of the clear example, or working toward "ideographic" as contrasted with "nomothetic" methods (presenting the individual in a global way as against looking for formulae). Some have even thought that if analysis is pinned to generality, analysis may not be the best way to understand concepts!

Again, there has been considerable modern controversy over whether the unity of a concept may not be historical, rather than rational or normative. In the *Euthyphro* example, perhaps there would turn out to be no essence of piety to furnish a norm for the affective reactions; the gods might be purely capricious in their pleasurings and the only answer to what piety is might be an empirical-historical-statistical account of their responses. Parallel to this contrast are such modern controversies in legal theory as the following. Should we say something is property because it is protected by law or is it protected by law because it is property? Is an act a crime because it is punished under the criminal law or is it punished because it is a crime? It usually depends on whether there is a rational or systematic order in what is protected or what is punished, or even in what ought to be protected or ought to be punished. Perhaps protection and punishment are to be understood as social mechanisms to be used wherever it is socially useful to use them (rather than alternative mechanisms), and the kinds of reasons for using them have been too diverse and too complex to be compressed into a general formula. Something like this is involved in the philosophical underpinnings of the legal realists in the twentieth century, and not surprisingly, their mode of analysis is historical-pragmatic rather than a search for essences in unpacking concepts.

Whatever Socrates thought, Plato appears to have believed that the Socratic method would end up with basic intellectual truths—sufficient to guide the reconstruction of individual and social life. The great analytic modes of ancient and medieval times were dominated by this Platonic elaboration of Socratic analysis. The goal of the method became standardized: to achieve a rational insight into basic ideas and basic truths. Different emphases followed from the combination of different psychological theories of thinking with different attitudes to the empirical and the material. Thus an Aristotle or an Aquinas rendered the method more self-consciously systematic. Aristotle started particular analyses with a more clearly-located base in common beliefs—gathering general views, linguistic uses, theories of eminent persons as well as prevailing opinions—so that this resultant analysis achieved a more comprehensive as well as a more consistent outcome. With a greater respect than Plato for the empirical base of knowledge and the role of sense-experience, Aristotle was alert to the inductive process whereby particulars lined up to shape a general concept in the mind. Aquinas's analytic method was especially acute in reconciling differences in the list of arguments that he marshalled on a topic at the outset of an inquiry.

In the history of thought, the ancient analytic modes settled down, with considerable loss of their richness, into a scholastic *rationalistic essentialism*. A concept has *a* correct analysis which the mind can grasp after the skirmishing is finished and the inductive contribution is made. The correct analysis reveals a general structure. This outlook maintained itself even into modern times, long after its scholastic base had gone. Thus in the field of human affairs, an analysis of "society" is said to give us the necessary and sufficient features to characterize a collection of people as a society. So too for "state," "democracy," "class," "capitalism," "intelligence," "personality," "family," and so on. Each has its essence and essential marks; knowledge in a field ends with these in the order of learning and begins with these in the order of further deductive or empirical investigation. We may, of course, argue about the correctness of the analysis. For example, is "democracy" to be analyzed in terms of a formula of rule by the people or only by popular checks on representatives? Does it involve a concept of the will of the people or a concept of the general good? Also, a belief about the essence of the family may be corrected by a wider range of experience, showing a less adequate definition to have been based on, say, purely European data. But the confidence that there is a correct analysis to yield a real structure remains unimpaired.

II

As the mathematical model became dominant and the older biological model receded, emphasis shifted from looking for an overall structure dominating the detailed operations of a field, to breaking up the larger concept into elementary units so that the whole could be understood in step-by-step construction from those units. This mode was strengthened by the resurgence of the ancient atomism in physics. With the triumph of physics in Galileo and Newton, what we may think of as *element analysis* became the fundamental mode for all understanding. The "natural" direction of understanding an idea was to break it up into its parts and see what tied the parts together.

Analysis in the empiricist tradition flowered entirely in this way in the seventeenth and eighteenth centuries. It was the other face of the coin of empiricist psychology. Since John Locke would have it that our ideas trooped into the mind as elementary sensations, each preserved as an ideational copy in the mind and associated as they were in our experience, the understanding of a complex idea came from separating its parts and seeing how each was derived and what experience brought them together.

Take, for example, Hume's famous (or notorious) analysis of the idea of *cause*. Gone are any intellectual principles of sufficient reason or any general conceptions of force. He wants to know simply what are the elementary components in the complex idea when we say that *A causes B*. We have an idea of *A*, an idea of *B*, an idea of succession, an idea of regularity, and an idea of necessity. The governing rule is to trace an idea to its original impression (Hume's word for the Lockean sensation). We have no trouble with the first four ideas. *A* and *B* correspond to a complex of associated experiences. Succession also reflects an experience. Regularity reflects the accumulated trend of experience. But necessity is no more than a feeling. We find no impression or set of impressions to which it corresponds. It is thus, Hume concludes, merely the expression of the customary in our experience.

Hume's analysis—we are not concerned with its evaluation, which has troubled philosophers of science to our time—was of course momentous. It read necessity out of nature, made the discovery of causal laws an empirical matter and so begat probabilism, and turned the very concept of scientific law from a governing necessity of nature into inductively ascertained habits in experience. Our concern here is with the mode of analysis and its type: a concept is understood by breaking it up into its parts and seeing how these parts correspond to experienced elements and experienced relations in the course of human experience.

It is perhaps already clear that a psychological theory of experiencing is itself integral to this way of analyzing and, indeed, partially constitutive of it. For the mode tends in different directions as the psychology changes. If experience is seen primarily as a collection of sensations, the empiricist element analysis goes one way. If experience is taken to be directly of gestalt structures, the analysis goes another way. If experience is thought to be given variable form by our purposes and needs and there is no privileged "given," analysis takes still another turn. Of course, one may call for a presuppositionless description of experience prior to any psychological inquiry, but this may itself turn out to involve assumptions in the psychology thereafter generated. Nothing in our suggestion about the relation of psychology and mode of analysis tells us which comes first. Indeed, a well-entrenched psychology may beget a mode of analysis which in later generations loses the sense of its origins and thinks of itself as begotten straight from the mind of Zeus. It may then impose its criteria on the growth of psychology itself.

That the mode of analysis resting on the empiricist psychology took over the growing sciences of man in the late eighteenth century and continued throughout the nineteenth is commonplace. The basic program was to trace the laws of the operation of the mind and its states of consciousness (ideas, sentiments, desires) and derive, corroborating by experience where possible, their consequences in economic and political life, as well as for morality and social policy. Such was the intellectual program of a broadly conceived utilitarianism, and it guided economic, political, and moral sciences. It hoped that as men became aware of the laws governing their own operations they could improve their pursuit of well-being.

The further career of the derivatives of empiricist element analysis belongs to the twentieth century—to the kinds of analysis carried out by Bertrand Russell and by logical positivism. Before that, however, we must look at the great sweep of temporally-oriented modes of analysis that characterized the middle and late nineteenth century.

III

With the emergence of history as a modern discipline and the development of evolutionary theory, temporally-oriented modes of analysis were worked out. To understand a concept, it was maintained, one had to know how it developed. Concepts have hidden histories packed away in them, residual layers that have present effects, but are unintelligible without a knowledge of their past. Eventually, as the different social sciences themselves have contributed to a knowledge of man and his ways, there have arisen mature forms of what is often called *genetic analysis*.

Genetic analysis has been disparaged as mere "psychologism" or "sociologism," even as committing the "genetic fallacy" of substituting a causal history of an idea for the idea itself. This will be discussed in detail below in the paper on "Context and Content in the Theory of Ideas." It is true, of course, that many subsidiary and now discarded notions of the nature and path of development governed the analysis of concepts at various periods. For example, there were assumptions, as in Herbert Spencer, that what is later must always be more complex, or hidden evaluations that the later form is always the better. Too often, the analyst's own day was taken to be the acme of civilization. Even in the 1920s, a political theorist could write a book on the state, in which the functions exercised in a liberal democratic society were described as the very nature of the state reaching its mature form of development. Thus any attempt to extend governmental regulation over business could be seen as regression to an earlier stage. While this was a kind of genetic analysis, it remained limited to the ancient picture of development—from seed to perfect ending in adult form. It took no advantage of the evolutionary conceptions in which are included changes of form over time, intervening variations and consolidation of new forms (new species), selective processes in terms of the needs of existent forms and the extent to which they are satisfied by chance variations (as in natural selection), and so on. Such a fuller genetic mode of analysis applied to the concept of the state would give a quite different view. It would be more consonant with the changing character of political institutions in a world of vast economic and social transformations where no ideal terminus is anticipated.

Just as different forms of empiricist element analysis were rooted in different psychologies, so different forms of genetic analysis reflected either a theory of biological evolution, or a theory of history or the lessons of anthropology and sociology or sometimes the results of a depth psychology. Genetic analysis is concerned not with any concepts in themselves, for it denies that they have an isolated self-enclosed meaning. It deals with concepts as ideas operative in the lives of individuals, cultures and societies, historical continuities and changes. And so some forms of genetic analysis work out techniques for seeing how an idea grows, is transformed, is influential as well as influenced. The idea may be related to parts of the cultural pattern, to needs and desires in individual life, or to stages of historical development of the society. Such analyses, when they go beyond merely causal accounts, tend to become *functional analyses;* that is, studies of the way the idea operates to justify, support, give shape to, and help determine application to the institutions and cultural forms of the society at that period of its development. Functional analyses will embody the presuppositions of the social sciences of the period. For example, at one time the functionalism will be pluralistic: ideas are related to special trends, whether in religion or economics or intellectual production. At another time an overall functionalism will prevail, in which to understand the idea requires a total view of the cultural pattern with all institutions and cultural symbols reenforcing a unified scheme. Thus the analysis of, say, moral ideas takes quite different forms in Marx or Durkheim or Weber, even though all are, in one sense or another, doing genetic analysis. When genetic modes of analysis combine causal, functional, and developmental components in a complex pattern, we may have one or another type of *evolutionary mode*.

Take, for example, a broad concept like education. It could be analyzed in terms of the growth of the ideal of an educated person and consist in showing how different elements were added at different times. This mode would differ from an element analysis only by spreading the components over time—in one age the intellectual components constituted the major part of learning, in a second age sentiment became important, in a third age technical abilities, and finally we have the ideal of an all-round educated and cultivated person. In an expanded genetic mode, attention would be paid at least also to the causal picture—why the first age concentrated solely on the intellect, and so on. In a still more complex mode, the functional aspect would become central—what needs, personal and social, were being served by the elements as they were added (an obvious example: the addition of technical competence geared to the rising demands of industry). But the functional does not have to be merely external; the very meaning of the intellectual component undergoes change as it moves from the contemplation of eternal necessities to the generalized knowledge-basis of power and control, and the subjects included in education are shifted from logic and metaphysics to the growing physical sciences. In a still more complex analytic mode, evolutionary types come into play. A full picture of the social basis of education is demanded, showing intimate interaction of ideal and content with the diversity of needs and their interrelations, thus including both aspects of social demand and human aspiration. Nothing less, it is felt, would give an understanding of the concept of education—or for that matter of any complex social concept in current use.

The most formidable type of genetic analysis on the academic scene was the *dialectical analysis* associated, though in different forms, with Hegel and Marx. It combined the genetic and functional character with a totalistic view insisting on the reckoning of an idea in full relation to the whole movement of world development. Its basic tendency in relation to social science may be expressed briefly as follows. To understand an idea, one must put it into context. But its context is wider than is usually thought. The narrowest context is the play of ideas with which it is associated, but dominant themes in the idea themselves reflect the whole state of the culture in all aspects of social life, for the culture itself has a patterned unity. One cannot stop here, however, because the patterned unity of a culture reflects its stage in the development of mankind, and of the total world in which man is set. But even all this is not enough, since it is so far only past-oriented. The world is constantly developing, though there is an order in its development. Each point in its development reflects its past, but is pregnant with the future. Every stage thus has an inner conflict, so that to understand what is going on involves grasping the direction of movement and the interplay of forces. Hence, to understand an idea is to see its place in the interdependent dialectical whole, including the direction of change and the role the idea will play.

I have given this oversimplified version (ignoring differences between Hegel and Marx) to concentrate on the type of analysis. In its totalistic character, there is probably nothing like it as a projected analytic method until we come to attempts at systems analysis today. And this, as we know, is an effort forced upon practice because the application of knowledge to prediction and control in human affairs requires the cooperation of all the sciences, as well as, of course, data from all over the globe. Today no economist, for example, would dream of reckoning the state of the American economy simply in terms of trends in America alone. He has to know all about resources, currents, and trends (political and ideological as well as economic) throughout the whole world. The proponents of dialectical analysis maintained that the world has always been like that, so that a full account at any point would have had to include the relative temporary isolation of parts of the totality from vital influence at that point (and the grounds for that isolation). The dialectical materialists made a point of contrasting dialectical analysis with the *metaphysical* mode of thought, characterizing the latter as one that turned an abstracted or isolated phase of the totality into an "essence" and expected to predict for real processes from it alone.

In some respects, the impact of dialectical analysis has been taken for granted. We no longer expect political science to furnish us formulae for the nature of the state without reference to either the development of political forms or their varying economic context at different times. Nor in the light of sociological and anthropological evidence of varied and changing familial forms do we expect to understand the family at a given time without examining its institutional interlockings and the way its multiple functions are being carried out through other institutional channels at a given stage of social development. We keep our eyes on the working of the whole and on the constant feedback of what is happening on the changing character of the whole. Perhaps the most striking influence in the popular mind toward a dialectical mode has come with the pressure of ecological problems in recent times, for in this area the effect of (almost) everything, including mankind, upon everything else has to be kept in mind. The changing structure of the whole has to be monitored constantly in the light of the totality of changing knowledge, if things are not to get out of hand.

There are many areas, however, especially where values and morality impinge, in which dialectical analysis is kept at more than arm's length. There still are, for example, large-scale attempts to give an essential and eternal formula for justice that will govern institutional formation and reorientation, without seeing it as expressive of the needs and problems generated in the total interactions of the period, nor even as tapping invariant interests over all historical periods. The justification of dialectical analysis in such areas, as of any analytic mode, cannot thus be taken for granted. It has to prove its utility for each area—to invoke Francis Bacon's criteria—by studies that yield both fruit and light.

The multiplicity of analytic modes of the genetic type, we may note again here, should not embarrass a contemporary social scientist. He needs to have a refined rather than a controversial sharpening of each—not in the spirit of deciding whether it is right or wrong, but in that of fashioning intellectual instruments for possible use, just as model building anticipates alternative models. Which genetic mode is useful for what purpose and how genetic modes compare in serviceability to other modes will then be left to an evaluation based on the experience of the sciences.

IV

The analytic aftermath of the evolutionary naturalization of man was a psychology of thinking that, while broadly empiricist, supplanted the Lockean. This was the view of activist man in William James's psychology, in which stress falls on the character of man's consciousness as constantly constructional, and on the role of needs and purposes in attending and governing the path of comparison—the selective observation of similarity and difference—and so the very root of concept formation. In Jamesian pragmatism, and more explicitly in Deweyan instrumentalism, concepts are intellectual instruments for solving problems in the flux of life. They give shape to awareness and direct its formulation of inquiry. The result is a forward-looking attitude in which analytic emphasis falls on the promise that an idea carries.

For pragmatism, generally, the meaning of an idea is to be found in the differences it makes in experience. A *pragmatic analysis* of a concept thus looks forward to consequences in human purposes and their fulfillment or frustration. It embodies a functional view of the very idea of ideas. In its Peircean form, this mode of analysis has an almost laboratory character: to seek the meaning of an idea is to ask what kind of experiments it would point to. In James's philosophy, it became a way of facing the unknown, and consolidating the lessons of experience, not as hardened dogma, but being attentive to the possibilities of novelty and creativity. In Dewey's social perspective, it became a persistent way of evaluating men's institutions and forms of thought by relating the ideas to the directions that institutions operated in human life and the consequences of their operation on human well-being and the quality of life. For Dewey, meanings were inherently social, not merely productive of social effects. Throughout the pragmatic philosophers, in spite of different stresses, the mode of analysis was uniform and constant: the meaning of a concept is to be found in its practical consequences. To understand an idea is to see how it works out.

Pragmatic analysis was thus set against the older metaphysical modes with their assumption of essence and fixity. Its focus was on the succession of particular situations, not upon getting away from the particular real into some realm of universality and eternity. Appreciative of the changing contexts of human life and the changes that men make in their world, it kept a firm grip on the purposive element in all consciousness and all activity. Later pragmatism especially underscored the transactional and the feedback character of experience. The evaluative attitude was seen to permeate all thinking and all action. Pragmatism never fell victim to the sharp dichotomy of fact and value that beset so many other, even later, schools of philosophic thought.

Pragmatic analysis obviously affected the social sciences markedly. In economics, it turned theory from abstract classical systems deducing human economic behavior from the psychology of the economic man, to empirical study of the functioning of economic institutions. Similarly, in sociology and politics, it focused on translating abstract statements about the character and aims of groups into the study of interactions among people in groups; for example, it stimulated the study of pressure groups in politics. In moral science, it continued, on the whole, the liberal reformist tradition of utilitarianism. In law, the pragmatic mode found clear application in legal realism, which saw the meaning of legal rules in the practical terms of action in courts and legal agencies. Sometimes it took a narrow form, as in Justice Holmes's suggestion that we look at law from the bad man's point of view, in which law becomes in effect a price list tagged to the commission of particular acts. But a pragmatic approach could also be an evaluative summons to bring empirical knowledge into legal judgment, to reckon in terms of effects on human life. In education, the pragmatic mode turned interest to the growth of individuality in each child and evaluation of educational institutions. In morals, it brought rules and duties before the critical bar of consequences in experience, and analyzed ethical concepts as methods for guiding decision in contexts of moral conflict and hesitation, rather than as eternal verities to be conformed with in inner struggle and anguish. The history of pragmatism is itself an imposing illustration of the way in which a mode of analysis not merely presupposes a whole psychological outlook, but can become a massive instrument for reconstructing the way in which problems are discerned and approached.

V

The note of triumphant modernity in Russell, in logical positivism and in their derivatives, came from the fact that they thought themselves to be capturing the latest revolutionary advances in physics, mathematics, and mathematical logic. It was quite inevitable that new modes of analysis should be offered reflecting the intellectual ferment or capitalizing on its revolutionary fervor.

Russell's *logical analysis* inspired decades of work on the philosophical frontier. It went after ideas that had been traditional sources of obscurantism, in the sense of begetting mysterious entities and assumptions, and reduced them to known elements in the clear light of day. The ideas ranged all the way from logical concepts such as *implication* or *the,* and metaphysical concepts such as *determinism* or *matter* or *mind,* to moral concepts of *right* and *good* and social concepts of *power.* When he called on philosophers to substitute logical constructions for inferred entities, he gave them stirring models to follow. For example, there is his famous theory of descriptions analyzing the notion of *the so-and-so*. When we say, "Scott is the author of *Waverly*," all we mean is that there is an x that is Scott, that x wrote *Waverly*, and that if any y wrote *Waverly*, then y is identical with x. The apparently mysterious idea of uniqueness was translated into the already clarified language of symbolic logic. Similarly, the mysterious idea of *number* with which Plato and Augustine had conjured turned simply into constructed sets: number is the class of all specific numbers, and a specific number, say *two*, is the class of all classes similar to (that is, capable of being put into a one-one relation with) a given class (say, my hands). Again, in the domain of physical objects, mindful of the perennial controversies about matter, Russell at one point tried to work out a translation of statements about physical objects into statements about sense-data; in other intellectual experiments, he treated statements about matter as statements about classes of events.

The degree of success of a Russellian analysis was always controversial, even when it involved the most precise logical breakup into elements. There was always the question whether some other analysis could not serve equally well, and whether the analysis fell short of depicting fully the material analyzed. Nevertheless, philosophical questions seemed to be brought to a new level, so that there was usually a sense of a great leap forward. Yet, after all, as a mode of analysis there was little new. It was a skillful use of the old rationalistic element analysis, on the one hand, and Humean empiricist element analysis, on the other. Once it got beyond logical issues, there was almost invariably the appeal to sense data in the Lockean heritage. Looking back, the conclusion is unavoidable that the Russellian mode of analysis got its novelty from the context in which it was carried out—the new ideas in logic and the theory of science—as well as from Russell's own skill.

The more grandiose exploitation of the new ideas came in the mode of analysis of neo-positivism or, as it came to be called in its development, logical positivism or logical empiricism. It was a much more self-conscious effort to combine the new logical power and the empirical interpretation of ideas into a method of doing philosophy. It shifted from philosophical talk about objects and the real world to analyzing the language (or systems of ideas) in terms of which different disciplines talked about the world. It developed the sharp distinction (implicit in Hume and explicit in Kant) between the *analytic* and the *synthetic*, the former ultimately seen as expressing a rule of language and the latter as an empirical assertion. Hence, all the mysterious principles of the intellect, all a priori truths, all intuitive principles, had to take sides: either they were formal or conventional rules of language to be justified by their utility, or else they were disguised empirical generalizations to be unmasked and brought before the bar of experience.

The characteristic task of logical positivism was then to carry out a logical reconstruction of the language of discipline after discipline—of logic, of physics, of psychology, of social science, of ethics, and so on. Some of its familiar slogans were comments on this effort. "Metaphysics is bad grammar" meant that traditional metaphysical quandaries about the nature of reality were pseudo-problems and would be dissolved when it was seen that they were merely confusions in the use of language. "Ethical statements are meaningless" meant that they were nonfactual and incapable of empirical verification, and that when the syntax of an ethical utterance was worked out it would turn out to be an imperative, an optative, or an expletive utterance and so not strictly true or false. The militant tone of the movement came from such slogans. But underlying them was the verifiability theory of meaning, that the meaning of an idea lay in the way in which one would verify assertions in which it appeared. Meaning (for empirical sentences) is the mode of verification. This fundamental tenet moved clearly in the same direction as pragmatism, and logical empiricism later discovered this affinity. But it had a more limited character than pragmatism had shown. Perhaps this was because pragmatism usually worked in the area of common experience, in which purposes and values were directly present guiding influences, whereas logical positivism did its work in the milieu of the advanced physical sciences, in which purposes and values had been pushed out to a standardized set of aims for the scientific enterprise as a whole and so were ignored in the day-to-day analytic labors. We shall see the importance of this difference in considering operationalism below.

In working out its mode of analysis, positivism had great strengths and great weaknesses. It was bold in its constructive power, not being fearful of creating formal systems. Sometimes this promised more than it performed, for so much effort went into constructing a system that little energy was left for showing its fruitful applicability. Especially enlightening, however, was its development of logical methods for doing important specific tasks, or at least getting concrete work under way to replace loose general ideas. For example, there was Neurath's effort to work out the detail of reducing one system to another; or Carnap's study of reduction-modes of defining (which might relate psychological to physical statements without reducing psychology to physics); or the latter's attempt to distinguish different kinds of probability statements; or the exchange of Schlick, Neurath, and others working out the nature of protocol statements (those used as verifying statements in different disciplines); or Reichenbach's and Frank's analyses of general physical ideas.

On the side of weaknesses it has been noted by subsequent modes of linguistic analysis that positivism, in its admiration for reconstruction, tended to disparage ordinary language whose ambiguities it appreciated but whose subtleties it overlooked. More serious perhaps was a lack of self-consciousness about its own psychological presuppositions. Perhaps because it was analyzing the language of science, it acted as though its philosophical discipline was *prior* to the results of the sciences and in no way dependent on the kinds of results produced by the sciences. Thus it failed to appreciate the interaction of science and method itself, treating analysis as a pure and autonomous discipline depending on logical tools alone. Yet one had only to look at its theory of meaning—the principle of verifiability—to see its Lockean derivation; for it often took that principle to require the translation of the meaning of an idea into the observations or reported sensory experiences by which it was tested. And there was little attempt, in such appeal to sense-data, to bring its method in line with contemporary psychological research on sensation and perception. Again, the positivist analysis fell readily into a set of dogmas about the sharp separation from one another of logic, fact, and value, which seems to reflect nothing so much as the old faculty psychology that sharply separated thinking, sensing, and feeling. When logical positivism entered into partnership with pragmatism in America, one might have expected a major corrective, since pragmatism, as we have seen, was never without the sense of governing purposes in human consciousness and human knowledge. But on the whole, the several "dogmas of empiricism" stood in the way, especially when positivism had made the transition from the bad boy of philosophy to an orthodoxy.

VI

The influence of positivism in the psychological and social sciences came importantly in the form of *operationalism*. It is worth digressing briefly to see how its mode of analysis itself operated in a sweeping program. The classic source, at least in America, was P.W. Bridgman's *The Logic of Modern Physics* (1927), which appeared to show how the scientific revolution rested on a persistent and strict use of operationalist method, that is, of equating concepts with the operations by which the concepts are applied.

Actually, Bridgman's detailed discussion can be seen to involve three separate themes which could lead in different directions. The first theme was simply that a concept without any operations at all was meaningless; that is, operations are a necessary condition for meaning. The second theme was that where different operations were employed, the concepts were different. The third theme went all the way and *equated* the concept with its operations; operations were both necessary and sufficient for meaning.

The first thesis was a broadly-wielded weapon. Ideas of absolute motion or absolute simultaneity were declared meaningless because any mode of deciding whether a thing was moving involved a frame of reference to other things, and any judgment of simultaneity involved using some process to clock it. We should not ask whether the ultimate standard for a meter was itself "really" one meter long, but should recognize that it was being *adopted* as an operation for judgments of length. The general impact of this thesis was salutary since it pressed for specification of how an idea could be tested rather than merely talked about. But in the not-too-long run it had to be relaxed a bit. There were respectable scientific ideas that could not point to direct operations at the time they were used, but could lead to consequences with respect to other ideas that had operational interpretation. For example, the notion of the kinetic energy of a single molecule in a gas might have no testable operation at one stage of scientific work, but that of the mean kinetic energy of all the molecules in a confined space might be testable by effects on a thermometer. Again, mathematical constructions like the square root of two would not have directly testable consequences if we spoke of a length exactly conforming to it (since actual measurement would yield a definite rational magnitude) but there would be consequences in mathematical manipulation. Operations thus were broadened in several directions. For one thing, they could not be limited to actual operations, but would include possible or conceived operations. (The positivists had used the narrower criterion in early formulations when they said that statements about the other side of the moon were meaningless because we had no way of actually testing them.) Again, the operations had to be construed as public, not private. (Bridgman, in a later book, had argued that a man's saying to himself that he will die is meaningless, because there are no tests by which *he* can tell that he is dead.)

The second thesis was particularly fruitful in showing that ideas associated with different operations might really be covering a conceptual mixture. Intelligence, for which all sorts of tests were used—some involving reading, some arithmetical computation, some social sensitivity—might not be a single concept if the results diverged; it would be better to break it up into intelligence$_1$, intelligence$_2$, and so forth. Even a single test scored on two different points (for example, accuracy and speed of performance) might be combining different abilities, so that the superior score of one group over another might imply nothing more than, say, that an urban environment had accentuated their speed of doing things. The very meaning of a general idea like intelligence depended, therefore, on achieved empirical correlations. Bridgman went further, inspired perhaps by his own work on critical points in gases under high pressure, and called attention to the fact that the correlations could change under changes in the conditions of application. For example, length tested by the surveyor's use of light could coincide with length tested by a yardstick for small distances, but because of the curvature of the earth they need not coincide as the distance measured became greater. Hence, one could not ride freely even on accepted operations without persistent and continual attention to conditions.

While the second thesis functioned admirably to ensure empirical responsibility for theoretical ideas, the third turned out to have a profoundly antitheoretical bent. This was evident in the example of intelligence cited, when some psychologists at a certain point threw up their hands with a sigh of relief and stopped probing into the meaning of intelligence because, they said, intelligence is simply what the intelligence tests test. (A similar move led some political scientists to abandon the attempt to work out a more satisfactory conception of democracy and to dismiss issues of capitalism and socialism, and even of fascism, as unoperational.) Bridgman himself pointed out that to say that intelligence is what the tests test implies the repeated application of the test and the finding that the results have the property of a *what*; in fact, the situation here is one of spiral approximation. Nevertheless, to see what is involved in this process carries us much further into theory than the view of concepts as synonymous with operations had suggested. For, even with respect to apparently simple operations, analysis would show a reliance on theory; for example, the equality of weights as measured by a balance presupposes the theory of torques, and of forces generally, in the construction of the balance. And improvement in the operations, as in the measurement of length for a thousandth of an inch, is a highly theoretical business. In the long run, philosophers of science, even when positivistic in outlook, came to realize that operationalism gave too simplistic a picture of the interrelation of theory, operations, and results. Thus, the concept could not be equated with the operations alone.

Equally important was the failure to keep in steady view the purposes for which the underlying inquiry was instituted and to recognize their role in guiding the direction of operational selection and refinement. (This basic lesson of pragmatism was neglected, we noted above, even at the time when positivism and pragmatism were moving together in America.) The general history of the concept of intelligence is instructive again on this point. Intelligence tests were originally developed to distinguish those who could not do school work from those who were for other reasons (emotional, lack of effort) not doing it well and might hope to be improved. Thus the purpose of the tests was to guide educational work for a given type of school curriculum and a given type of school atmosphere. Testing was extended in World War I for military placement and then to make judgments about whole populations. A new branch of psychology thus grew up with the aim of coming to understand "the nature of intelligence." But there was also the practical aim of sorting out those who could be expected to do well in the kinds of jobs for which it was assumed that school work prepared people. Since no general theory of intelligence emerged, the inquiry stayed with the tests (though there were attempts to sort out a general factor in the test results). It was assumed that in predicting school success they predicted the whole subsequent work success. This did not inhibit new kinds of tests being offered, even off the beaten track, but they had to run the gauntlet of showing they correlated well; that is, they would do the grading job the older tests were doing. But there was little systematic reckoning with whether education itself was undergoing change, and how far doing well in school work under the changed conditions meant doing well in subsequent jobs. Neither of these questions, in spite of the great social transformations over half a century as well as the development of almost universal education, had much impact in test refinement. A few voices were raised to suggest that the older tests did not tap creativity and persistent long-range effort—characteristics increasingly important in a complex society—and some work was done in testing along these lines. But the bulk of testing seemed to go on grading, without worrying about what it was grading for and for what ends. Recent controversies about race and intelligence have brought these issues to a head and seem likely to prompt a more thorough reconsideration of tests in a fuller purposive as well as theoretical setting. Comparable lessons can probably be learned for the critique of traditional tests of democracy in our changed world, where socialist societies have been added to capitalist societies and numerous intermediate forms have emerged, and for criteria of a sound economy in a world increasingly affected by multinational corporations, as well as by intensified economic interaction on a global scale.

Whether, in the long run, operationalism paid too high a price of exaggerated empiricism for expelling obscurantism from the social sciences is a question for historians of science to settle. But this reckoning applies only to its generalization as a philosophy. Its permanent contribution as a mode of analysis was to show how far the empirical penetrated into the conceptual and its very structure. If we add to this the converse recognition of the penetration of theory into the empirical, and the pragmatic recognition of the penetration of the purposive into both theory and experience, the ground is well laid for reconsidering the traditional dogmas of empiricism.

VII

Somewhere in the late 1940s and early 1950s in Anglo-American philosophy, the positivist mode of analysis was overshadowed by what has been variously called "Oxford analysis," "British analysis," or "ordinary language analysis." Opponents of the whole "analytic movement" often did not notice the difference because they were too busy attacking "linguistic analysis," which the two modes had in common. Even partisans of one or another of the linguistic trends tended to bring them together in writing of the glorious revolution in twentieth century philosophy.

From a close view of the transition, the ordinary language mode of analysis (I shall use this term even though it does not quite cover the whole complex group) differed on basic points from the logical reconstruction of the positivists. The root difference lay in attitude to ordinary language. The positivists, as well as Russell, saw ordinary language as embodying the accumulated errors of the past, or as misleading philosophy into a merely everyday view of the world. Thus Russell often complained that the subject-predicate structure of ordinary language not only made us talk of the world as things with qualities stuck to them, but hindered the development of a powerful logic of relations. Even Wittgenstein in his early work—before he became the father of a new analytic mode—thought in terms of an ideal language whose structure would mirror the structure of the world. Hence a logical reconstruction would look to a technical language as superior to the ordinary language, as the body of science was superior to ordinary beliefs. Ordinary language analysts, on the contrary, have the highest respect for ordinary language. It embodies, writes J.L. Austin, the accumulated wisdom of human beings, it is constantly tested in practical communication, and it includes the most subtle distinctions. We would do much better to philosophize in its terms than in abstractions that override differences. Austin's own essays on "A Plea for Excuses" and again on "Ifs and Cans" (both to be found in his *Philosophical Papers,* edited by Urmson and Warnock) are excellent illustrations. Instead of approaching a general problem of free will and producing variants on traditional moves, he breaks open the question by the detailed study of the extremely varied sorts of things we say and accept as excusing our behavior, and by seeing what conditions we admit in the myriad ways we use "if" and "can."

The numerous insights that ordinary language analysis brought to many areas could have readily been accepted by the positivists as burrowing among the phenomena preparatory to systematization. But ordinary language analysis took the initiative and launched a counterattack on formalization itself. Perhaps the clearest statement of this is to be seen when Ryle carries the attack into the shrine of positivism—logic itself. Formal logic, says Ryle (writing on "Formal and Informal Logic" in his *Dilemmas*) is merely the extreme case of rigidly drilling a few terms ("and," "or," "not," "if-then") to march in strict order. It does not allow these words to get out of line and show their richness. An informal logic would recognize that every word has its patterns of use—variegated but definite—and they can be tracked down by analyzing ordinary uses in different contexts. Such a mode of analysis does not aim at formalization because the field does not admit of it. It is unavoidably context-bound.

The generally pluralistic attitude underlying the ordinary language mode is readily seen when it analyzes the functions of utterances. For example, in moral discourse, where the positivist mode had taken moral terms to be expressive or emotive, the ordinary language mode simply traced the variety of functions: moral utterances serve to guide, give advice, direct, grade, persuade, warn, encourage, promulgate rules, and so on. Even one single term such as "ought" can have different functions; for example, in "I ought" it prescribes, in "they ought" it evaluates. The attempt to set up a formal logic overriding context—as in deontic logics of "ought" with basic definitions and theorems— would be to simply compound the errors by violating context-differentiation and to ignore inevitable pluralism.

In general, the ordinary language attitude to ordinary language is reminiscent of the traditional British lawyer's veneration of the Common Law. Legal understanding is taken to require steeping oneself in the detail of cases; neither legal concepts nor principles can be understood abstractly. To attempt a formal codification is a mistake. Wisdom is embedded in the full historical development and the multitude of distinctions that will be found by those who immerse themselves in that development.

Perhaps the only view completely shared by the positivist and ordinary language modes is that many an impasse comes from linguistic difficulties. But whereas the positivists thought it was produced by the looseness of ordinary expressions and turned toward formalization, the ordinary language analysts think that ordinary language itself provides a therapy to dissolve the impasse. In general, this ordinary language concern tends to overlook the sources of many an impasse in language change and the problems of adjusting language to changed scientific knowledge. Take, for example, the familiar epistemological problem of whether we "really see" a distant object when we are dependent on physical stimuli coming from it. It is true that we get into a quandary involving the meaning of both "real" and "see" in the case where we now "see" a star which has long gone out of existence. But the resolution of this problem may lie less in a linguistic therapy than in recognizing that our ordinary use of the term is geared to a situation of immediate and close observation and was generalized on the assumption that the velocity of light was infinite, so that all situations would be immediate and close. The discovery that light has a finite velocity made conceivable a situation in which the object seen could be destroyed in a time less than it took the light to reach the observer. A more detailed attention to the physical processes of perception, attentive to changed physical beliefs, would therefore be the way to resolve the quandary and provide a basis for reconstructing the language of perception, if necessary.

A serious difference between positivist and ordinary language modes, which only became clear as the latter movement developed, is that the ordinary language mode was never really committed to the dogmas of the sharp separation of logic and fact, and fact and value. These would be quandaries that came from oversweeping abstract use of concepts. Nevertheless it did not wholly emancipate itself from the value-fact dichotomy. (This is a question we cannot pursue here, but which will bulk large in Volume 2.)

Perhaps the distinctive character of the ordinary language analysis has become clear from this extended contrast with the positivist mode. It remains enclosed within a linguistic approach, but with its own special attitudes. A full evaluation would, of course, be another matter. Some of its implications have become apparent in recent extension into what is, in effect, an offensive in the social sciences. It is claimed that the social sciences go astray when they use physical science models, rather than think in terms of the language of *action*. This language, which is extensively explored in the ordinary language mode, involves quite different ways of looking at human beings. While some advocates look to the promise of deeper understanding by such procedures, critics see it as simply hemming the social sciences within the traditional categories of the old-fashioned view of man. Thus the attitude to language change—whether ordinary language embodies the past, while technical languages may express advances in knowledge before they are assimilated into ordinary language—becomes a vital problem.

VIII

Roughly parallel in time to the rise of ordinary language analysis in the Anglo-American world was the emergence in public view of the phenomenological movement on the European continent. Grounded in the technical work of Husserl and his followers, it had increasingly wide influence in psychology, psychiatry, and the social sciences, as well as in philosophy. It also created an atmospheric effect in which some of its general lessons began to be urged without necessarily having direct relation to its special doctrine.

Phenomenology is not generally cast as a mode of analyzing concepts. It is more likely to be set the task of revealing the essential structure of the experiential world. But it is not difficult to draw its lessons for dealing with ideas, our limited aim here, and to indicate them as injunctions for *phenomenological analysis*.

This mode does not send the analyst to the consequences of the idea in pragmatic fashion, to the sensory verification in positivist fashion, to the context of linguistic use in ordinary language fashion, nor even to contexts of genetic development. Instead, it calls for the phenomenological analysis of direct experience, without presuppositions. There are two important warnings associated with this injunction. The first is that the experience be viewed from the standpoint of the experiencer, not from that of an observer studying the other person's experience and experiencing. The behaviorist may think he has captured the subject's experience in reporting the subject's differential behavior, but he has missed all the inner content. Phenomenological analysis is the analysis of subjectivity, in contrast with a natural science way of studying human beings. The second warning is to remain concentrated on the experience and not to slip down the bypaths of physical reduction or psychological association. In technical terms, phenomenological analysis at the outset *brackets* these other fields and remains presuppositionless in its description of direct experience. Take the obvious case of experienced colors. Let them first be described as they occur in the visual field, not as the effects of a given range of wavelengths, nor in terms of association, as for example red with revolution or black with death. Of course the description is not limited to the more obvious qualities. In fact, the strength of the method comes from its sensitive description of the more subtle properties. It may, for example, differentiate the color as shaped surface and as thin film. It may even, while rejecting the associations with red and black, discern their descriptive properties of *rousing* and *somber*. But these qualities are not to be construed as psychological effects, any more than the analysis is concerned with cultural uses; for example, one culture may use black for mourning ceremonies while another makes it a symbol of rejoicing since the enemy has been killed. The basic injunction then is to stay within the field and describe it thoroughly as the field of the experiencer's beholding, not to label it and hurry away to physics and psychology.

To insist on a thorough description, with all the subtle differentiation it reveals, is of course consonant with many different analytic modes. But making it the starting point in an age where dominant scientific trends were either physical or where they used a mechanistic associationist psychology or a behaviorist model was bound to have far-reaching effects. For one thing, it restored a respect for the field of direct experience as a legitimate scientific focus in the study of human beings, both as individuals and in social life. It had long been recognized that—to take the study of the emotions—a physiological psychology had so far furnished only the gross physical conditions of the emotions and not differentiating conditions for such varied forms as anger, indignation, wrath, resentment, and the rest. Description of the latter set was more likely to be found in novels than in scientific texts. Santayana (in *Reason in Science)*, writing in the first decade of the twentieth century, distinguished physiological psychology from "literary psychology," with only the former regarded as scientific. But the situation changed when phenomenologically-influenced branches of psychology, such as Gestalt psychology, studied the properties of the visual field without raising issues about where the color might "really" be (whether in the physical world or the mind) or whether observed foreground-background shifts were forms of "illusion," and at the same time without invoking the physical bases and the current theories of psychological construction through association. Again, in psychiatric work, the phenomenological emphasis sought a fuller picture of the patient's world, rather than labelling his processes in terms of an established diagnosis. For example, when he reports what a gloomy day it is (though in fact the sun is shining brightly), it is not disposed of as simply projection of his inner state. If he reports feeling guilty, it is important to know more intimately what the experience is, whether he sees it as disobeying an authority, or being somehow unclean, or violating his own commitments. Again, in moral theory, one has only to reflect on the way pleasure and pain have been treated as isolated self-contained units (tempting one to a Benthamite measuring of quantities) to see what a richer theory might come from a fully differentiated description of being pleased and being pained. An analysis of the actually different experiences of pleasure—such as the sense of release of tension, the sense of gratification, the sense of successful performance, and so on—may even suggest that when we get to a psychological reckoning of these phenomena, their differences may turn out more important than any presumed common physiological basis or their generic classification as pleasures.

The guiding rule in all such phenomenological description is to focus on the object of experience or the field of experience. This is prompted by the doctrine of *intentionality* that the phenomenological approach built on from Brentano—that every psychic act is directed to an object, so that the understanding of the experience from the experiencer's standpoint is to be found in the focus on the object. This is taken to hold even when we begin to study experiential acts; they now enter the field of our beholding, so that we must always distinguish between the self or signs pointing to a self in the field and any talk of a self presupposed as underlying the field.

In the sciences of man, phenomenological analysis thus insists that descriptions of the human life field bring understanding by showing us the structure of *meanings* of the participants. To ask for the meaning of ideas or concepts is to look for the meanings in experience of the people involved in our common social world. The refinement of description carries us imperceptibly into the specification of meaning. This has important bearings—for example, for social psychology in its study of attitudes, for sociology in its use of concepts about group relations, in history for its use of concepts over changing temporal stretches. While behavioral studies of attitudes are often content with concepts framed in terms of similar behavior, for example discrimination in housing or employment, the phenomenological mode will want to know whether the discriminatory attitude involves seeing the object as a dangerous rival, a sinister influence, a pushing upstart, or any of a large set of properties which, once the differentiation is made, can even be seen to point to different proposals for tackling the social problems. Again, when the sociologist talks of customs, or of community, it is important to discern whether custom is seen as the dead weight of the past or the distilled wisdom of experience or merely the statistically preponderant way of doing something, and whether community is felt as a kind of consolidated self or a helpful milieu for individual effort, or a setting for bargaining to avoid the war of all against all. Again, in historical study, does a concept such as usury used in different historical periods mean the same in each? Karl Duncker, for example, argued (in an article on "Ethical Relativity" in Mind, 1939) that usury was condemned when it was seen as charging high interest to those who borrowed out of need for purposes of consumption, whereas it was acceptable when seen as sharing in the profits of those who borrowed for investment. Incidentally, the moral issue of relativity is helped by such analysis, for while at first people seem to have simply changed moral attitude to the same act, phenomenological analysis shows that they really have different moral attitudes to different acts. The relation of value and meaning here is like that in the controversy over abortion: the advocate does not see the embryo as a human person, the opponent does.

The search for meanings is not an enterprise subsequent to the phenomenological description. It is rather an intuitive revelation of essence in the analysis of experience. We need not enter here into controversies within phenomenology itself as to how to interpret notions of essence finding. But there is little dispute about the state of the essences when found: they are part of the structure of the real. It is interesting to compare the positivist and phenomenological approach at this point. The positivist tends to take a conventionalist view of essences: they are constructions fashioned out of linguistic materials and empty in the sense of analytic. To say they apply or do not apply to a designated part of existence is a synthetic assertion to be tested empirically. As in model building, alternatives are possible, and the basic issue, once models are constructed, is which is useful for what. The phenomenologist analyzing the essence finds it to be a part of the structure of the experienced real, in the case of social concepts the social reality. But the reality is self-contained, not dependent on anything beyond the experience intuited. Alternative concepts are simply different intuitive essences. There is no outside critique possible about the correctness of the intuition. This kind of self-evidence is very much like the one G.E. Moore made central in his commonsense analysis: to regard something as self-evident is to say that it needs no evidence, not that intuition furnishes a special kind of evidence. Moore's analysis in many respects resembles the phenomenological one.

The realistic terminology, though used, may be misleading in the case of phenomenology. For reality is subjectivity, and so the outcome has often been that phenomenology is a gateway to idealism, sometimes of a Berkeleyan sort. By contrast, the harder scientific views today, when they employ phenomenological modes, do so chiefly for the descriptive richness noted above. When the description is over they remove the brackets placed around the natural and the psychological. Thus Wolfgang Köhler, having used phenomenological description and analysis in the manner of Gestalt psychology, thereafter raises hypotheses about the isomorphism of the phenomenological field as analyzed and the electrical patterns of the brain. Or Erich Fromm, having distinguished phenomenologically the different kinds of pleasure experience noted above, raises questions about their correlation with different kinds of psychological development depicted in psychoanalytical dynamic terms. Similarly, the psychiatrist who has used the phenomenological mode to get the fullest insight into his patient's world may go on thereafter to diagnose the illness not in phenomenological terms alone (as the disintegration of a phenomenological structure), but in terms of a theory of psychic development in which the organic, depth-psychological, environmental-cultural, and phenomenological may be integrated in a complex way.

Only the philosophers or scientists who have made a total outlook of phenomenology never remove the brackets. Every fresh question that is asked is absorbed into a phenomenological question. Every attempt to go beyond the phenomenological field is translated into a search for signs in the field that point in an outward direction, or properties in the field that tempt a belief in an independent external world. Even the traditional scientist's work is given a phenomenological reinterpretation, when he is not bedevilled in dealing with man by dualistic, mechanistic, and naturalistic seductions. The assumption is that the structure of the real social world can be successfully grasped in phenomenological terms.

The problems of psychology and social science that such a view will find most troublesome are clearly those of variety and change in the phenomenological field itself. For it tries to understand them without appeal to genetic-developmental or institutional-functional accounts, and often without allowing an appeal to concepts of causality in human affairs. Occasionally, the view denies variety in the structure of experience by assuming that phenomenological analysis can achieve a "pure case" in analyzing experience. But the very concept of a pure case is one that contains the essential features without distracting elements, and there are no criteria to tell us when the case we set up is pure. Hence, the assumption of a pure case is either straight postulation of structure, or an indirect and question-begging assumption that we have an invariant structure. Similar problems arise for change as for variety: once we admit the possibility of change in the phenomenological field of human experience, to deny that we have to go beyond the field to find an explanation can be offered as a program, but only some success in explanation will make it even partially credible.

If we put aside the broader theses and consider only phenomenological analysis as a mode of dealing with ideas, its rich appeal to experience has a salutary role where a psychological or social behaviorism has overnarrowed the methods of social science, or where a mechanistic model has been dogmatically imposed. But in serving as a corrective, it may be quite compatible with many of the modes it has attacked as naturalistic. So far, phenomenological analysis has made out a case for joining the Analytic Club, not for taking it over.

IX

Let us pause to look over the fence at what had been going on in the well-tilled gardens of logical inquiry during all this time. For works on logic not only covered the formal structure of deduction, but traditionally along with induction (theory of knowledge of matters of fact) dealt with definition. And as we saw at the outset, to define our concepts was long regarded as the beginning and the end of reflection in social science.

Definition had always been a stress point in logical theory because it is the place where an inquiry into the meaning of concepts produces the "essence," and in the notion of essence there is a confrontation of different kinds of metaphysical outlooks. The main struggle was between an essentialist realism that spoke of essences in things and a conventionalist nominalism that took defining to be merely setting up conventions or marking stipulations (arbitrary in nature) about the use of words. It is worth noting that a parallel struggle was taking place in the theory of classification about whether there are correct and privileged classifications or whether all classification is merely an arbitrary setting-up of pigeonholes for our own special purposes.

This was particularly acute in biology over the notion of species—whether it indicates a real structure in nature or our arbitrary shuffling around of specimens into a man-made order.

By the mid-twentieth century, one began to find in logic texts a set of types of definition: the *nominal* which simply equates symbols, one being a shorthand for the other; more generally, the *stipulative* or conventional decision on the use of a term; the *denotative* or *ostensive* or *extensional*, which either points to an instance or lines up the existent members of the class; and the *real* or *structural* or *theoretical*. This last was the heir of the essentialist outlook. It was usually given an empirical interpretation. It presupposed either the extension of the class term or a set of acknowledged properties of the class members; these constituted the material by reference to which correctness of the definition would be checked. The definition itself would be carrying out one of several tasks. It could be giving a general formula that was empirically correct. It could be revising a previous definition in terms of the newer results of the relevant science (as "matter" might be redefined in terms of fresh discoveries of physical particles). Or it could be giving an analysis of the predesignated properties in a systematic formula adequate for explaining them. Whether one takes a particular metaphysical interpretation of the result is indifferent. For example, some biologists, unwilling to think of a species as simply an arbitrary convenience in classification, attempt to see a species as a discovered continuity in nature over time. The interest underlying it may be arbitrary, but the result expressed in the classification is not. Thus if the underlying interest in mammalian classification is in reflecting the evolutionary development of the animal forms, the definition of a particular species would reflect a historically correct account.

Several tendencies contributed to the contemporary broadening of the theory of definition. One was the revival of a very old interest that is found in Aristotle's *Topics* (alongside his formal account of definition in the *Posterior Analytics*)—the practical effort to work out specific techniques for discerning and removing ambiguities. For example, if a word has two opposites, it has two meanings: the opposite of "clear" is "rough" in the case of the skin and "confused" in the case of an argument. This tradition has a long history, though often in the theory of rhetoric rather than in the more formal theory of logic. Again, in the ordinary language mode of analysis, the general slogan, "Don't ask for the meaning, ask for the use," pointed to analysis of varieties of contexts for the use of the term, and as we saw above, it did not expect an ultimately unified account in a single definition.

A parallel broadening of definition came out of attempts in the last hundred years to analyze the way terms functioned in the sciences. The most fruitful development here for the theory of definition was to be found in mathematics, where it was precipitated by the development of alternative geometries and the separation of pure from interpreted and applied systems. Thus "point" in a particular geometry, it was realized, need not necessarily have a prior and external meaning, and in any case, it was irrelevant; what "a Euclidean point" meant was formulated by the Euclidean postulates—a point was what satisfied the postulates with respect to that term. This notion of "implicit definition" was criticized by those who argued that different interpretations could satisfy the same postulate set, so that the implicit definition could at best be partial. But the general idea that clarification of a term comes from the wider system in which it occurs rather than in a fragmentary equivalence of two sets of words (the right-hand side giving the precisely necessary and sufficient conditions for the left-hand side) encouraged a broadened notion in definition. After all, why define "definition" by an ideal that is rarely attained?

Another tendency, therefore, was to relax the notion of definition itself, or to see it as simply one case of the wider effort at specification of meaning. Attention was turned once more to different processes by which clarification is brought about rather than to the structure of the finished product. (The contrast of process-product was a hard-worked one in these discussions.) Thus clarification could start with a paradigm instance or clear case of the use of a term (sometimes compared to a peak in a mountain range) and then look for the complex convergence of properties in it. The next step would be to study each of these properties in its fuller range where it appeared, even without the remainder of the cluster. (Max Black gave the name of "range definition" to some such procedure, in his "Definition, Presupposition, and Assertion" in his *Problems of Analysis,* 1954.) For example, *charisma* could be "defined" in this way by starting with a number of clear instances, recognizing the converging properties of *spellbinding* and *authoritative leadership,* and going on to study authority along its full range, even where the spellbinding is in doubt. We might eventually, armed with the results, make finer distinctions in the original cases and specify the precise type of psychological dominance-submission relation that is associated with spellbinding. And so on in the direction of other associated properties.

A further and more systematic broadening of the theory of definition came in the study of signs and symbols as a whole, generally called *semiotic*. Here is where such distinctions were offered as *syntactic* (the rules relating the symbols), *semantic* (the rules relating symbol and object), and *pragmatic* (the rules relating symbol and user). Operations, for example, thus constituted one type of semantic rules, and the laws of deduction (transformation rules) a type of syntactic rules. The general effect was to throw open the whole area of language as symbolic behavior to all kinds of study.

In brief, the position has almost been reached where, while not everything is possible, there is ample room in the theory of definition for creating new modes of clarification. This relaxes the hold that the modes of defining appropriate to the advanced disciplines of mathematics and physics have had on the psychological and social sciences. These types of definition still remain as possible instruments of clarification for the other disciplines, but not as the only ones required.

The kind of definition or clarificatory technique to be employed is, therefore, relative to the state of the given field, the extent of controversy about the factual assumptions incorporated into the definition, and the kinds of aims that govern the inquiry. For example, take the extreme controversy that once characterized political theory about the definition of "the state." Proposals were found as varied as, "The state is an organization of society to provide the necessary external conditions of the good life," and "The state is the executive arm of the ruling class in a society to keep the lower classes under control." Now obviously the first was specifying a function to be carried out by the organization; a great deal rested on the reference to "external" conditions, which forbade the state to put its hand on "internal" or cultural matters of the spirit. (It could provide for defense and work against depressions, but not dictate to religion or conscience.) The second definition was historically oriented, implying that the state had arisen and operated in an exploitative, repressive way. And these were only two in a whole host of varying definitions, emanating from different social philosophies, different theories of history, different moral programs. Under these conditions, the definitional policy most appropriate might be a limited stipulative one which took out programmatic functions and controversies over historical development and allowed them to be formulated independently. For example, the state could be defined as the organization of society which established a monopoly of armed force. Historical views about how the force has been used might then differ and be explored in historical study. Policy decisions about functions to be supported by this force could also differ and could be argued for directly in normative terms. Some indecision would, of course, remain about whether one should speak of the state existing in earlier societies when force was not monopolized in one organization. These cases would have to be dealt with as either nonstate societies or as precursor-state forms. The limited stipulative definition would, at that point, be encouraging detailed historical study of "the rise of the state."

Where the controversies and underlying purposes cannot be so sharply brought into focus, a definitory process could well include an *explanatory preamble*. For example, given the innumerable definitions of "personality" in psychology, one might abandon defining and stake a domain of inquiry by listing the phenomena that invite the creation of a possibly unified domain. Thus the preamble could point to functions that get performed in the life of an individual, as diverse as the scheduling of activity in daily life, the ordering of values for preferential choice among activities, and the standardization of typical roles in the development of the individual. "Personality" would then be construed as a pattern of ordering in such activities of the individual. Obviously, a specific characterization of "personality" would then embody a specific psychological theory of development which would show what kind of unity was expected in the functions listed and why. It might also be necessary to specify whether certain value-interests governed the definition. For example, "personality" is sometimes defined as what distinguishes one individual from another, which obviously focuses the inquiry on individual differences rather than simply type of order. A definition that allowed all people in a society to have the same personality would be a different one, although it could be supplemented by a separate definition of "a given individual's personality" which was inherently differentiating him from others.

There are other concepts in social science which are better clarified not in terms of a generalized property or set of properties, but by including a stage-parameter whether indicative of range or extent or temporal development. For example, "democracy" has often been defined in terms of operations of popular decision. But as new techniques of decision are utilized as the size of the society increases (e.g., representation instead of town meeting), the definition will differentiate for group size, though some generalized aims might carry through all, even if not themselves sufficient conditions for the presence of a democratic form. Again, in areas in which there are well-defined historical or temporal stages of development—for example, "capitalism" relative to different stages in the development of industrial forms, or "maturity" relative to different stages in the individual's psychological development—the stage reference might well be incorporated in the definition, associated with specific modes that were "capitalistic" or "mature" at that stage.

In general, in the light of such developments in the theory of definition, it would be well for definition in social science to substitute an explanation of problems, purposes, and established knowledge for speculative hypotheses or hoped-for results, and to substitute a sense of the relevance of different definitional modes for the rather voluntaristic pronouncements of meaning so often found in the history of its many disciplines.

X

The remark just made about the open and creative mood in the theory of definition should obviously carry over to the theory of analysis. At least it suggests looking around for what new modes of analysis may be in the offing, or what older, hitherto subdued modes may be gathering strength, perhaps even in the end what new directions may be desirable. A rapid glance at prospects is warranted.

Kant engaged in "transcendental deduction" or, in general, used a transcendental method which consisted of looking for presuppositions to make sense of what is said or held as belief. Take, for example, his analysis of free will. We say to someone, "You ought not to have done this," which presupposes that he could have acted otherwise. Hence, moral judgment presupposes the meaningfulness of the attribution of free will. Many criticisms have been offered of Kant's procedure. Some say that his kind of presupposition is nothing more than an implication or logical deduction from the belief, and so cannot act as the basis of a different kind of method. Others reduce it to a search for a hypothesis from which the belief follows, and so point out that

Kant jumps too quickly to one among possible presuppositions, as if it alone were possible. For example, deterministic philosophies could grant that the moral judgment presupposes "he could have acted otherwise" but might offer a different analysis of the latter under determinist assumptions.

Some philosophers—R.G. Collingwood is perhaps the clearest case—take *presupposition* in a very distinctive sense, as concepts and principles that enter into our very asking of questions so that a search for presuppositions is required if we are to understand the kinds of answers that are suggested and elaborated in a given age. In a view of such a sort, every age is, so to speak, wrapped in its own presuppositions. The ancient concept of *phusis,* usually translated "nature" entered into the pivotal question, "What is the nature of things?" so that all the different philosophical schools were answering the same question. If we take this nature to be a hidden essence or power, like a primitive *mana,* we offer one interpretation of early Greek philosophy; if we take it to be a modern search for systematic laws, we take quite a different interpretation. Similarly, in reading early modern writers, we come across—even in Descartes—the assumption that the effect cannot be greater in power than the cause. If we track down this assumption, it proves to rest eventually on the whole view of God the creator as containing all perfection, so that nothing issuing from God can contain the same full strength and perfection. Only then can we realize why the evolutionary and postevolutionary idea of emergence, that is with wholly new forms coming into existence, could not easily have been offered in medieval and early modern times as a way of looking at change. Such fascinating intellectual case studies make attractive the view that the search for presuppositions, as affecting the questions asked in philosophy and science, should be given a central place among analytic modes.

In recent times, considerable attention has been given to analyzing the notion of presupposition in the attempt to pin it down and distinguish it from kindred notions, as well as to study the relations of what is presupposed to what presupposes it. In ordinary language analysis, distinctions have been drawn between what is *assumed,* what is *implied,* what is *contextually implied,* and what is *presupposed.* An assumption would be a premise from which (with others) the assertion at issue could be deduced. An implication would be a further assertion deducible from the original one. A contextual implication would be something we could read from the context of the assertion—for example, a person who says "It is raining" can normally be taken to believe it is raining; a person who says "X is a conservative, not a reactionary" usually believes an important distinction can be drawn between the two concepts. A presupposition is a precondition for the assertion being either true or false. For example, to say, "The absent member of this committee will decide the issue for or against the motion," takes for granted both that the present members are evenly divided and that the absent member is alive; now while the former is entailed by the statement, the latter would be treated as a presupposition without which the statement does not in that context make sense, rather than its being false. (This view, it should be pointed out, has been the subject of considerable controversy.)

In addition to such treatment in ordinary language analysis, there have been some attempts to work out a strict formalization for the relation of "presupposes" to yield a "presupposition logic."

In spite of all these interesting developments that center around the notion of presupposition, it does not appear likely that a systematic mode of "presuppositional analysis" will emerge. For one thing, there appear to be no rules to specify how to look for a presupposition—it is rather a matter of *insight*. This is not, however, a fatal objection, for insight is involved in all modes. Even the well-specified rules of deduction do not tell us, given a set of axioms or postulates, what theorems to derive from them. And even Socratic analysis and ordinary language analysis involve an uncanny insight in spotting precisely the counterinstance that will cause most trouble and bring most light. A formidable objection to regarding the search for presuppositions as heading up into a fresh mode is that such a search is involved in practically all analysis, whatever its kind. Indeed, it is a great part of the business of philosophy as such. (In the present chapter we have, in fact, been looking for the presuppositions of all the modes and of the schools that crystallized about them.) But perhaps the most serious difficulty is that no systematic body of procedures or method of inquiry has been established. If one develops, it will be worth thinking about a new "presuppositional mode of analysis." Until then, the phenomena show simply the importance of looking for presuppositions, not the existence of a distinct analytic mode.

Two other areas in which one suspects an aspiration toward the status of new modes of analysis are *hermeneutics* and *structuralism*, both of which are on the verge of operating as philosophical schools. Yet their insights are clearer if we pay attention not to these aspirations but to their roots in specific techniques. Thus hermeneutics starts in the study of different kinds of interpretation and compares the shape that interpretation takes in different fields. Legal interpretation, biblical interpretation, psychoanalytic interpretation, religious symbolic interpretation, even divination—all can be grist in its mill. What kinds of unity and contrast can be found in such a study? The "book of nature" was thought by Galileo to be written in the language of mathematics. Perhaps some of its pages—especially the book of human nature—are written in a different language to which hermeneutics as a study might offer the key. Or again, in the case of structuralism in its contemporary ascent, there are the root structural phenomena inviting comparison: patterns in culture, gestalts in psychology, ego structures in psychoanalysis, depth grammars in linguistics, organic systems in biology, ecological systems, and so on. Let go the controversial issues of native versus developed structures in the apparently variegated phenomena. Perhaps the lessons of the search for structure will help balance the varieties of elementaristic analysis we noted as we went along.

There is nothing to prevent enthusiasts and partisans of emerging and allegedly emerging modes from hoping and speculating and analogizing. But until systematic results and successes are in fact consolidated, a partisan can but press his work and an observer can but wait.

As for desirable directions in which one would like to see analytic modes developed, one suggestion emerges from our study, although it points less to a new special mode of analysis than to an aspect all modes would do well to consider. In most cases, analysis starts as an attempt to clarify ideas that we already have. But as genetic analysis makes clear, ideas have a history and have come to take the shape they have at the moment when we look into them. And what is more, especially as the pace of change increases in all phases of contemporary life, we may expect ideas also to undergo transformation. Analysis in such a context, therefore, becomes constructive as well as clarificatory. It would be misleading to suggest new modes to be labelled "reconstructive analysis" or "speculative analysis" or to compare its tasks to model building which fashions alternative models for trying out. It is rather that the reconstructive aspect can be expected to become increasingly prominent where change and direction become more imperative. In that case, instead of asking what ideas have meant, we might ask, in the light of what they have meant, what they should come to mean in the time ahead of us.

XI

Such then is our sketch of analytic modes seen in a philosophic overview. Note how different they look set in context from the way they have often been posed—as the *only* way to analyze ideas if you are to achieve clarity. But, in fact, no one is set off from the influences of knowledge of the day, the play of philosophical ideas of the day, and the central problems and purposes of its time. But each, in turn, has its effect on the continuum of advancing method.

Can we generalize about analysis as a whole? Not really. For the basic phenomenon is, as just suggested, reflective thinking which operates with knowledge, with purposes, within contexts of assumed theory, and with logical weapons corresponding to the state of development of logic.

Can we work out a systematic classification of modes of analysis? Why not, for after all, they constitute an area of human activity in which classificatory schemes can be tried out, though how far they are useful is a separate empirical matter. For example, we could try classifying on a temporal orientation. Historical and genetic modes are past-oriented, seeking understanding in terms of the growth of the ideas; contextual-linguistic modes are present-oriented in their concern with the existent pattern of usage; pragmatic and logical reconstruction modes are more future-oriented. Again, we could classify by type of outcome of the analysis—formal, informal, or something in between such as a network type. And this is only a beginning for an area that has not been systematically studied in this way.

Can we offer criteria for the evaluation of modes ? Certainly they all bring some type of increased clarity to concepts. With particular purposes in mind, the different temporal orientations might have different utilities. We might evaluate the modes according to their assumptions about language, about logic, about the psychology of experience; some would be simplistic, some might be out of date, some more comprehensive than others. We might evaluate along a scale of technical complexity and suitability, but probably no general value scale would result—it would depend on the tasks we had in mind. Another direction might be the social use of a mode in its historical context; for example, whether it served as an ideology, or shut out inquiry in important matters. In this sense, some analytic modes have been attacked as conservative in allowing only answers pertinent to past forms and so diverting reconstruction.

Finally, what would be a sound policy for social science today toward modes of analysis? Certainly it must be careful not to narrow analysis of concepts to one current popular model. But should it aim at a synthesis of modes? Or should it simply become thoroughly acquainted with the variety and regard them as an armory or a workshop with many weapons and many tools to be used where they can best do the particular jobs? A synthesis would be fine if it were possible, but it does not yet seem available, and if one were offered at this point, there might be fears of its dogmatic character, when knowledge and logic are rapidly advancing and have still so far to go. Perhaps the inventory of tools is a better analogy.

Take, for comparison, the situation that existed in political theory when the arguments about the basis of political authority consisted in a dispute about whether it rested on power, on consent, or on reason. How much better the situation became when these three theories were turned into possible types of authority systems and the political scientists tried to depict pure types of power societies, consent societies, and rational societies. How much better even than that when one asked: what part of existent societies rests on each of these elements and what forms do they take? Still better, what are the causes of these phenomena in existent forms, what functions do they serve, what conditions in human life make what mixtures necessary, or desirable, with what overall human goals about quality of life? Perhaps the controversies over modes of analysis are destined for a similar career.

This is not the end. The social scientist, for his own protection and the development of his field, should not merely become aware of different modes, to be able to invoke them when and where he needs them, but should be ready to try out new modes and bring his results in using them to test their utility. Perhaps this is a perennial area of interdisciplinary cooperation between philosophy and social science. But philosophy itself will not be well served by a social science that is philosophically slavish and looks to philosophy as a monarch to dictate the latest analytic mode. Social science will be served even less so.

Part 1

Case Studies in the Analysis of Social Concepts

1. The Theory of Social Classes: A Logical Analysis

This paper is the earliest in the volume, written in the mid 1930s. It is carried out in the spirit of the then-rising logical positivism—note the neutral analytic stance at the outset, the eager separation of the factual and valuational, and the central emphasis on the logical reconstruction of current theories and claims to show how verification and empirical decision would be possible. The paper does not bring out the pragmatic aspect—the purposes governing selection of a framework for discussing classes. Nor does it treat the genetic-historical aspect—the importance of the issue at that time and what was at stake in the different ways in which it was dealt with. There is a touch here and there of a search for presuppositions, but not a persistent inquiry in that direction.

The contrast between the tone of the paper and the hectic social context of the time is startling in retrospect. But there is no doubt in my mind of its underlying aim. These were the days of the early New Deal, the rise of the labor movement in the CIO, the intellectual conflicts of Marxists and liberals. All were overshadowed by the rise of fascism and the need for a united battle against it. Could liberal and Marxist thinkers, then so active on the social scene, be brought together, not simply by agreeing on a common limited defense objective, but by clarifying the terms of their conflict so that the search for evidence rather than ideological tumult or victories by surreptitious definition could become the common focus? In this sense, the paper had a very definite social aim.

The specific framework developed for class theory is still of value. In its terms, a great deal of the work that went on subsequently in

American sociology—for example, Lloyd Warner's scheme of classes from upper-upper to lower-lower and the controversies that centered around whether there really were classes in the United States—can be seen as an attempted empirical mapping of consciousness in different American groupings. It did not concern itself with prediction of what would happen to that consciousness as economic-social changes took place. (It constituted a kind of social phenomenological description.) Meanwhile, Marxian argument about whether the intellectuals constituted a stratum rather than a class reflected the problem of refining the notion of "role played in the processes of production"—perhaps the impact of social change in the character of production with the growth of greater participation by science and technology. On the American scene, the theory of classes was soon derailed into the theoretical conflicts over "power" (see Chapter 7).

One of the major tasks of the philosopher being the examination of the conditions of meaning, it follows that in social matters part of his role will be to analyze the conditions of meaningfulness of propositions asserted in that domain. Thus with regard to the theory of social classes, he must analyze propositions in which the term "class" occurs and any other terms frequently found in conjunction with it: for example, "dominant" in the expression "dominant class," "important," "basic," "fundamental" in such assertions as that a certain social division is "the most important, basic, or fundamental one." Two warnings, however, are necessary. First, there is no initial guarantee that these assertions are meaningful; it is the task of philosophic analysis to indicate the types of conditions by satisfying which they are meaningful. Second, insofar as the analysis of the meaning of any particular assertion reveals certain assumptions about matters of fact or judgments of value, the philosopher alone cannot determine the truth of the former, nor does he have to hold the latter. If he is a social philosopher, he may be interested in identifying himself with a movement or age or group whose values he will try to make clear and consistent, and so too he may hold opinions on matters of economics, psychology, and so forth but he must distinguish these opinions and these values from the logically prior analysis of meaning.

In this paper, I propose to attempt such an analysis of the notion of social classes, to consider some alternative analyses, and finally to review at length possible meanings of the term "fundamental" as it occurs in propositions about classes. I have selected the notion of classes as an illustration because of the frequency of its occurrence in propositions about social change, in the explanation of cultural traits, and in the descriptions of particular societies.

I

The logician defines a class as a group of individuals, each having certain properties, in virtue of which they are said to be members of the class. Thus, logically, all that is required to divide men into classes is to state some property of differentiation; for example men are divided into the class blue-eyed and non-blue-eyed; that is, any individual man will either have blue eyes or will not, thereby being a member of one class or of the other. The fundamental division or basis of division may be any characteristic: spatial, physical, biological, psychological, social, imaginative, or what you will.

In the domain of the social, the basis of division may be any social characteristic. The division may be into contradictories or contraries, for example, into Catholics and non-Catholics or into Catholics and Protestants. Empirically in any particular society these may coincide; thus all the non-Catholics in some country might actually be Protestants. We must distinguish the theoretical possibility of a third alternative from the empirical question of whether there is one actualized and the still further question if there is one possible but not one actualized, whether in the special circumstances of that case one could or could not probably develop. Thus New Zealand might have a division into the social classes of Maori and White, if in fact certain social consequences follow from it; but though Yellow might be a third possible alternative, rigid immigration laws might prevent its actual development.

A priori, any division into classes might have or come to have social consequences in any society, that is, be the basis of different social behavior on the part of men. Jewish parentage in Germany today [in the 1930s], color in America, the type of work one engages in in Russia, epileptic tendencies among the Chukchee in Siberia as requisite for shamanship, are the bases of social divisions in that the people who possess or do not possess these marks behave or are behaved towards differently. Why these marks rather than others become the bases of such divisions is a question for historical and cultural analysis, in which there may be both necessary and accidental elements. An example of a necessary element might be a division on the basis of strength in a militarist society. The necessity, of course, is hypothetical.

In approaching any particular society, therefore, one may discover a mass of such divisions which are found to have social consequences. From this point of view, one would tend to say that there are many class divisions, and that the same man might fall in different classes with different fellow members in each. The tradition in social science, however, has been against such a use of the term and for its specialized application; for example, it has at times been fashionable to deny that there are classes in the United States. Some have therefore employed the term "groups" or "groupings" to designate the fact that many social divisions can be made in a society and that the same individuals may not fall together on the same side in them all. The term "class" would then indicate the fact that a great many social divisions resulted in the almost identical set of men falling on the same side in each division. A. F. Bentley, in his *The Process of Government*, presents such a view:

> A third line of distinction has to do with the extent to which interest groupings are consolidated in different classes in the community. We can use the word class, holding fast to the essential elements of its popular meaning, to describe any set of groupings so consolidated in a particular set of persons as to make that set of persons, as a whole, come into opposition in a great majority of their activities to one or more other classes which are likewise sets of persons, embodying similarly consolidated grouping.[1]

And again, "Hereditary membership is one of the tests that is used in making such distinctions for special investigations, and the possession of special legal privileges is another test. But even without hereditary affiliation and without formal advantages in law, there may be a solidification of interest in fixed forms such as to justify the use of the general term class, as opposed to the freer groupings out of which class phenomena crystallize themselves."[2] Karl Marx seems to hold a kindred view at times, as when he says in *The Eighteenth Brumaire of Louis Bonaparte*:

> In so far as millions of families live in economic circumstances which distinguish their mode of life, their interests

and their culture, from those of other classes, and make them more or less hostile to other classes, these peasant families form a class. But in so far as the tie between the peasants is merely one of propinquity, and in so far as the identity of their interests has failed to find expression in a community, in a national association, or in a political organization, these peasant families do not form a class.[3]

He has, however, added the notion of economic circumstances as distinguishing the mode of life and so forth which must be separately explored.

For the rest who hold such a view of *class*, the emphasis lies upon a set of men who have *a chief or preponderant or most important part* of their social activity similar among themselves and different from and opposed to that of another set. The terms in this account require clarification. By "social activity" is meant any actions which are either social in themselves or have social consequences. "Opposed to" may have broadly two meanings:

1. "Activity A is opposed to activity B" may mean that the occurrence and successful exercise of A interferes directly or indirectly with the occurrence and successful exercise of B. Thus my occupying a specified seat interferes with your doing so, and my playing the radio may interfere with your sleeping. More indirectly, the activity of someone in a neighboring apartment may interfere with my activity in writing a philosophical paper, if the walls are thin, though it need not if they were soundproof.

2. If we take "activity" in the fuller sense in which it includes also the ends of the action, then "Activity A is opposed to activity B" may mean that involved in either is a cluster of desires or aims for the sake of which the action is taking place, and that these aims are directly or indirectly thwarted in part or in whole by the other activity. Thus your locking the door would be opposed to my going out of the room, and a merger is likewise opposed to the activity of the employees whose hours and wages will be reduced. More indirectly, A's luxury would be thought opposed to B's activity as a worker aiming at a good standard of living by one who saw it as the waste of part of a finite total of labor which might have been otherwise devoted; it would not be

thought opposed to *B*'s activity by one who argued that luxury provides employment.

It follows in both senses of opposition that the fact that one activity is opposed to another must be shown from any or all of (1) the nature of the activities; (2) the goals or ends or aims of the actors; (3) the empirical circumstances of the system of situations in which the actors find themselves and in which their activities occur. The importance of (3) is seen in cases where a kind of action on the part of one man is opposed to the very same kind of action on the part of another, for example, occupancy of a limited supply of land. Since the activities involved in its occupancy by one man would not include the fact that it was limited, it follows that the nature of the activities abstractly stated is insufficient to determine whether they are opposed.

This is the analysis for the opposition of two activities. How two sets of men can have a chief or preponderant or most important part of their social activities opposed to one another depends, of course, on the meaning assigned to such terms as "chief" or "preponderant" or "most important." These difficult notions we shall examine soon. Meanwhile, for brevity's sake let us agree to call the type of view we have been considering the *consolidated-groupings* theory.

A second type of theory of classes, at present very prevalent, seems quite different from this, though the two types are not contradictory and given certain interpretations might, for special cases, coincide. The essence of this theory is the selection of some social relation or activity as the basis of division into classes, on the ground that it is more fundamental than other activities or relations or differences. Which basis is selected depends, of course, upon the opinions of the advocate. St. Augustine distinguished the damned and the saved, whose class or "city" would be manifested, no doubt, in the morality of their conduct. Occupational bases are frequent, the skilled and the unskilled, the farmer and commercial classes, the city and country folk, and so forth. Most prominent now is the Marxist emphasis on the objective role that men play in the processes of economic production, crystallized in the opposition of the bourgeoisie and the proletariat. What concerns us here is the meaning any or all of these theories assign to the notion of *fundamental* or *important*, because if they be asked why that particular basis has been selected by them for division into classes rather than any of the other possibilities (e.g., in addition to those mentioned, religion, language, nationality, race, sex), the answer will invariably be that in some sense this particular division is more important than the rest. Let us call this type of theory the *importance-selection* theory. It is essentially monistic in this domain, though not necessarily absolutistic. To deny this type of theory would be equivalent to denying that in some context, or some culture, or in general, one division was more fundamental than any other.

Though both the consolidated-groupings theory and the importance-selection theory use such notions as chief or preponderant part, important, fundamental, and basic, they do not necessarily mean them in the same sense. In fact, the approaches may be distinctly different, and our task for most of the remainder of this paper is to clarify the diverse senses. The consolidated-groupings theory has in mind as the extreme form or ideal type of class division a caste system in which (to paint the ideal with a free brush) the different castes might have different religions or different roles in the same religion, different languages or dialects, different economic or social roles and privileges, different or specialized cultural sets of interests, and different racial or physical characteristics. This would be the case if (hypothetically) one set of men in a country were white, Christian, employers, and English speaking, and the other set were black, pagan, workers, and Bantu speaking. There would be in each a strong sense of its separateness and its internal cohesion. Now classes would be relative approximations to this ideal type, differing in degree. Bentley's definition which we quoted above spoke of coming into opposition "in a great majority of their activities," but our analysis of "opposition of activities" showed some of the difficulties involved, since the types of activity did not even have to be different to get opposition. Obviously then according to this theory, not mere opposition, but consolidated large-scale opposition lining up diversities in activities of all kinds on opposing sides constitutes a class division. To understand the meaning of "a great majority" or "a chief or preponderant part" becomes, therefore, all the more imperative. Is it merely numerical? Then there is no evaluation of the components, and variant styles of music will have the same weight as economic differences. How far is the separation of strands to continue? Is art one basis or can it be divided into difference in painting, in sculpture, in music, and so forth. Obviously, there is as yet no classification and evaluation of the component parts of social activity sufficiently precise to render adequately the numerical assessment which this theory requires.

There are, however, ways out for the theory. It might reject such attempts and interpret "a major part" as enough diversities lined up to bring about a general hostility, an internal cohesion, and a feeling of separateness. The mark of class division, therefore, would be the consciousness and action in the consciousness of class division. This is an entirely consistent definition. It need give no general account of what precise factors in a culture or how many would bring this consciousness. This might vary in different epochs and cultures with temperament, sensitivity, social conditions, and so forth. There might indeed be no general account. Swift's Lilliputians divided on the question whether the egg should be opened at the big end or the little end. Hobbes says of his own day (and it is true enough of ours) that if there followed different consequences to personal interest from any proposition in Euclid it would be the basis of fiery disputation and struggle. There need be no attempt to predict for all the future and conjecture for all the past. Wherever any factors are sufficient by their diversity to develop class consciousness and unity of action, classes result.

The consolidated-groupings theory, when worked out consistently in this way, defines classes in terms of consciousness of mutual interest so that people will act together against others. The psychological phenomenon is clear enough in the nationalism of our day as it is found among the mass of the sincerely patriotic in any country. No doubt the feeling of solidarity and of separateness and the notion of acting as a group themselves require more careful analysis, but having no space for it here I will take their understanding for granted and leave them in the hands of the social psychologist. It follows from this interpretation of the theory, for instance, that as long as a man feels himself allied with different people for different ends and acts accordingly—with his employer religiously, his skilled fellow-worker economically, his age group culturally, and so forth—he is not a member of any one class.

Another interpretation of the consolidated-groupings theory leads in another direction. If one holding it still refuses to treat it as we have done, the only alternative is to propose some mode of evaluation of social activities so that we should be able to say what constituted "a major part of their activities" to a group of men, if not that about which they had a certain type of feeling and acted in a certain unison. This mode of evaluation need not consist in a fixed classification and universal hierarchy of aspects of social activity. Any single aspect might be differently evaluated in different cultures, but there would have to be some rule of evaluation in each. We would have to know how to tell, even though the people in the group might not feel closely united, that they were really one class because they had so-and-so many or such-and-such interests or activities in common, and in opposition to the other group. We should then be able to tell them that they were members of a certain class even if they did not realize it because our rule would determine the importance of some as against other of their activities, and those would be the unifying activities. This is the only way in which an objective position, rather than one emphasizing consciousness of unity and separateness, could be worked out on the consolidated-groupings theory. If this were done, however, it is obvious that the emphasis would no longer be on the consolidation of groupings, but on the fact that those special groupings as distinct from the rest were more fundamental, basic, or important. The theory would thus differ little from what we called an importance-selection theory, except perhaps in that it stressed two or three rather than one or two social activities or relations. Our next task, therefore, is to examine the notion of fundamental, basic, or important in this type of theory, remembering that its essential characteristic is the selection of some social activities as the basis of class distinction because they are declared to be *objectively* fundamental; that is, a man belongs to a certain class whether he is conscious of it or not. On this interpretation too, when it was said that there were no classes in the United States, it was meant that no one social activity was more fundamental than any of a number of others in which people variously engaged, in whatever relevant sense fundamental might here be taken.

I shall try soon to distinguish four different senses of the term. Before that, however, in order that our illustration may be more concrete, let us review briefly a few of the bases of division which different theories call fundamental:

1. St. Augustine uses the distinction of the elect and the damned; some of the Protestant schools which later believed in predestination held to the same basis as fundamental for the division of classes. Since there was obviously no ready access to

the deity's selection, the basis on which human beings made the classification was a moral one. The type of conduct which characterized a man acted as evidence of his class: for example, serenity, self-denial, chastity, charity, and so forth.

2. Some social scientists have stressed the urban-rural division as a fundamental cleavage in any country. The particular basis on which this distinction is made is variously stated—in terms of numbers, agglomeration, occupation, and so forth. Thus J. M. Williams, in *Our Rural Heritage*, seems to begin with rural as meaning agricultural and below a certain density of population.[4] Scott E.W. Bedford, in his *Readings in Urban Sociology*, says the term "cities" is to be used in the book as centers of population of more than 100,000.[5] Adna F. Weber's *The Growth of Cities in the 19th Century* discusses methods of definition, rejects agglomeration by itself as a suitable basis of distinction, and settles finally on numbers.[6] Frederic C. Howe's *The City, the Hope of Democracy* distinguishes an urban aggregation from a city. A world's fair is not a city; there must be united purpose and a definite ideal. "When in addition to self-consciousness and family-consciousness there arises a city-consciousness, that instinct which is willingness to struggle for the common weal, and suffer for the common woe— then, and not until then does the city spring into life."[7] Others also object to the ordinary distinction in terms of number. Dwight Sanderson, in *The Rural Community*,[8] suggests that to be of sociological value it must be qualitative rather than quantitative since "a mining or industrial village is more urban than rural." This remark obviously uses "rural" and "urban" in a different sense, but it is not made precisely clear what sense. The reason is, perhaps, that Professor Sanderson is more concerned with the meaning of "community," which is the genus within which the distinction takes place. His mode of treatment, a survey of varieties of communities (e.g. hunting, agricultural, types of village both primitive and modern), implicitly suggests that there need be no single universal basis of distinction. It may be best, in each country, to select that definition of rurality which most appropriately described the concrete distinctions therein existing.

Let us look, as a final example, at Sorokin and Zimmerman's full treatment in *Principles of Rural-Urban Sociology*.[9] They suggest that a definition in terms of several traits is required, not any traits but causally-connected ones. The truth is, however, that if they are causally related, there is no need to put them all in the definition, since the remaining marks can be found present when one is present. The authors are, however, under the influence of Weber's "typological method," and say "we need to construct a type of urban and rural community," and turn to "a description of the differential characteristics of the urban and rural community whose totality gives the type of each of these social aggregates." They find these differences in occupation, predominance of and directness of relationship to nature, size of community, density and homogeneity of population, social differentiation and stratification, mobility, and varieties and character of social contacts. Yet though this is supposed to be distinguishing "rurality" and "urbanity" we find such remarks as "urbanity and size of community are positively correlated," "urbanity and heterogeneity are positively correlated," and so forth, as if urbanity already had an independent meaning. Their conception is made clear when they say after their summary: "The fundamental characteristics, as has been shown, are all causally connected, or interrelated. As soon as one takes the agricultural occupation and the people engaged in it, he finds the other differences enumerated. The first 'variable,' so to speak, carries the rest with it." Thus they are really using occupation as the basis of division, and cluster or type is only a name for the field of investigation.

Logically the point is a very simple one. Whichever basis of division the social scientist may be using, he must first make clear and very determinate what he is talking about, by what characteristics he is defining. Then he may look for other traits that are found conjointly with these. He may accordingly begin with any definition he likes, for the definition is only the beginning, and no special sanctity attaches to it. If, however, after his inquiry he comes to think the division which he defines to be fundamental, he must then explain what he means by fundamental.

3. The most important candidate for a basis of class division is Marx's distinction of men in society by the objective role they play in the processes of production. In present society, the distinction is phrased as one between the proletariat and the bourgeoisie, that is, between the men who, having no property, support themselves by offering for hire their labor power, and those who, owning the instruments of production, hire the labor power of others. The question becomes more involved because Marx asserts that the worker who sells his labor does not get full value in

return, but produces surplus value for which he is unpaid. If, therefore, we take the distinction in this form, it is between those who receive the full value of their labor, those who receive more, and those who receive less. The implication would be that the first class is almost an empty one, for example, the producer who produces for his own consumption with his own tools. It is encumbent upon a man affirming this distinction to offer a standard of value and to show how it could be determined for any individual, whether he receives the full value of his labor power, less, or more. Even then the usual subtleties arise. What of the workingman who has shares in some other company? May not his resulting income equal the value of his labor power? What of the businessman who suffers a loss for some years? Or again, what of the unemployed who having no jobs do not labor and so, if there is a "dole," get more than what they have labored for during that time? Such objections make it clear that the basis of division may perhaps best be expressed as we did first, as between those who own the instruments of production and those who can support themselves only by selling their labor power. Let us call these capitalists and proletarians, respectively. The further propositions of which we spoke would then have to be proved empirically for any society: viz, that the capitalists on the whole get more than the value of their labor, the proletarians less. There would still, however, be the class of people who both labored and had shares in companies owning the instruments of production. It is not necessary for the Marxist division to apportion this class by some revised principle of division. It may recognize it and then go on, as it in fact does, to describe its role.

Further complications have been introduced, according to some, by the separation in the development of the modern corporation of management and ownership, so that the owners dispersed have little control over their property. This might perhaps affect some of the assertions the Marxists make about classes; for example, it might involve interpreting the theory of the concentration of capital as one of the concentration of power. The precise locus of power would have to be determined empirically in each society. It need not be associated universally with any one form; for example, it may go with land in one community, money in another, practical control of quasi-public corporations in a third, and so on. The basis of the division into classes would not, however, be altered. The question which faces the Marxist, as it faces all others who hold an importance-selection theory, is to explain the sense in which he thinks his division fundamental.

II

Having illustrated some of the types of "fundamental" divisions into classes (though only a few of those suggested), we may now proceed to the examination of the various senses in which one basis of division is called more important, basic, or fundamental than any other. We shall distinguish four senses and in illustration pay more special attention to the economic theory.

1. The first is a psychological sense which refers the judgment of importance to the strength of motives. Thus the division into the elect and the damned would be called most important or fundamental in this sense, if most men's desires to be saved or to behave morally were stronger than any of their other desires. For mankind at large, it would be the fundamental division if men's motives of this sort were stronger than any of their other motives. The urban-rural division might follow this sense of fundamental by attributing different sets of desires to each class, for example, desire for change in the one and stability in the other, and arguing that these desires in each were stronger than any others. Or again it may not mean this sense of fundamental. In the literature on the materialist conception of history, Marxism has frequently been taken to be a doctrine asserting that an economic motive is stronger than any other, and though one finds scant justification in Marx, it has no doubt been asserted by some and is a widely prevalent popular interpretation of what historical materialism means. To take one illustration, Professor A. J. Todd, in his well-known book *Theories of Social Progress*, argues as follows:

> Why does the savage spend months decorating his spear or shield or pottery? Why does the college professor or pure scientist work year after year at a far lower wage than he could command in other work? Why does the preacher or the social worker or the Salvation Army undergo deprivations and insult for the sake of men's souls and a cleaner, better world? Why does a vigorous, independent, prosperous woman leave her economic independence to marry and suffer the pangs of maternity and the pinch of limited income? What prompted that famous group of young doctors to

submit themselves to mosquito fever tests? ... Is progress in medicine due to the economic motive, to a desire for higher fees, to a desire to conserve human life because of a reverence for life or because of a sense of the economic value of life and labor power? Granting the presence of a dose of the economic in these cases, it is perfectly obvious to an open mind that it is completely out-weighed by devotion to science, passion for life, love of men.[10]

Obviously, Todd is here taking the materialist conception of history to be that the economic motive is either sole cause or chief cause of human action, that whenever a man does some self-sacrificing deed, or is devoted to art, or is in love, a further analysis would reveal an underlying motivation for personal economic interest.

We need not dwell too long on this first sense of the term "fundamental." As presented in all these cases it is quite meaningless, simply because no operations are indicated by which we can compare the strength of motives and judge the sole efficacy or superpotency of one. We have no means of determining the strength of the desire to be saved, to achieve stability, to gain economically, and so forth. With regard to an individual's single act, we may pose alternative courses of behavior. We can say, for instance, that when he is offered two jobs, one giving opportunity for research at a low salary, the other merely time-consuming but at a high salary, that if he chooses the former, the economic motive is less strong in him than his love of science. But even for an individual over a long span, we have little means of judging or weighing his acts. How much more difficult is it for a general comparison of two motives in a society? How impossible to speak for all mankind at one time? How meaningless for all mankind for all time?

Perhaps it is easiest in the case of a single institution such as a bank or a stock exchange, where the motives in question are standardized, but even here it is precarious if we take a complicated institution such as a college. Again, judgment might be passed on the relative frequency of the occurrence of certain pursuits in certain cultures and (by inference) on the prevalence of some very specific motives, for example, the desire to be president, to raise wages, to promote a certain church or belief. But it does not hold of such very general motives as economic, religious, moral, and others. Broadly speaking, greater precision in the defining operations is achieved to the extent that a "mentalistic" interpretation of motive yields to one in terms of modes of behavior and discoverable order in conduct. Differences such as that between aiming at material gain and aiming at gain to further other ends become expressed as a different patterns in conduct. Explanation of some such patterns in terms of others is then offered. This approximates what we shall examine as the fourth sense of fundamental, or, more accurately, a special case of it.

2. A second sense of *fundamental* is suggested by Professor Sidney Hook in the chapter on the "Class Struggle and Social Psychology" in his book *Towards the Understanding of Karl Marx*. It is not the only sense that he employs throughout, but it is emphasized in the formal part of this chapter. He approaches the matter gradually, phrasing the problem as why economic classes are fundamental, as distinguished from differences of interest among capitalists, or religious or racial differences. Antagonisms among groups of capitalists are not class antagonisms: firstly, because they can be ironed out by mergers, and so forth, whereas the worker-capitalist antagonism is constant; secondly, because all employers have a common interest against all workers, in that lower wages mean higher profits; thirdly, because oppositions among different vocational groups in capitalist society are not exploitation of one group by another. That last is an ambiguous point depending upon the precise meaning of exploitation. But his general argument is made clear when he says, "For class oppositions cannot be resolved without changing the structure of society, whereas the other social oppositions are continually being resolved within the unaffected framework of the capitalist mode of production."[11] That is, the test of a *fundamental* social division is the difficulty of eradicating it; that is, the eradication of its consequences requires a change in the structure of society. In this case, unfortunately, there lurks an ambiguity in the term "social structure." If it means the mode of production, the very aim of socialism is to retain it and yet get rid of class antagonism. If it means the mode of control and distribution, it leads to tautology, since this was the basis on which the economic division into classes was made, so that the assertion would be, in effect, that class oppositions cannot be resolved without getting rid of class opposition. Or, finally, if it means that the empirically discoverable consequences of the economic division cannot be eradicated without eliminating the economic division, this does not justify asserting that a change in the structure of society is involved,

without identifying social structure and the economic division, which if merely assumed would beg the question at issue.

The proof of this claim would lie in showing the economic division to be more fundamental than the political, religious, and so forth, thus entitling it to be deemed social structure. "Fundamental" might again be taken as *most difficult of eradication.* This, if it could be roughly estimated, would constitute a possible meaning of the term. I do not believe, however, that it would be an ultimate sense. For, on the one hand, the division may be merely the most difficult of the ones that you want to eradicate, and this would involve reference to your values, thus giving an ethical interpretation of the concept, which we shall discuss as its third sense. On the other hand, if the ethical reference would be eliminated, we would be left in the following situation. All proposed social divisions would have to be examined in an attempt to see which is most difficult of eradication. Standards of difficulty would have to be elaborated and then the contenders for the proposed *fundamental* character would have to be empirically tested—racial differences, religious differences, age differences, sex differences, and so on. It must be remembered that we are not necessarily referring to age and sex, but to any *social* differentiation which may have been standardized on the basis of the age or sex distinction. Thus we might not be estimating the difficulty of eliminating the difference between city and country in the sense of evening out population, but of getting rid of the attitudes and social traits which had become differentially attached to this distinction. Or again we might actually be concerned with the first. In either case, the special concern will be with the breadth of social behavior attached as consequence of the division in question. We shall elaborate this as a fourth sense of "fundamental." The interpretation in terms of difficulty of eradication, we must conclude, resolves itself into either our third or our fourth sense, or both.

3. The third meaning of "fundamental" has, as we have suggested, an ethical preference in its character. It amounts to this: that division is fundamental which is pivotal for securing what you really want or value. This may best be illustrated in the kind of argument which Marxists sometimes use to convince intellectuals and members of the lower-middle class that they belong in the working class whether they realize it or not. Marx and Engels expressed it in the *Communist Manifesto* when they said:

The lower middle class, the small manufacturer, the shop-
keeper, the artisan, the peasant, all these fight against the
bourgeoisie, to save from extinction their existence as frac-
tions of the middle class. They are therefore not revolutionary but conservative. Nay, more; they are reactionary, for
they try to roll back the wheel of history. If by chance they
are revolutionary, they are so only in view of their impend-
ing transfer into the proletariat; they thus defend not their
present, but their future interests; they desert their own
standpoint to place themselves at that of the proletariat.[12]

More simply it is this: the Marxist asks X, "What do you want
of your society?" and receives as an answer a general set of
values such as a secure job and certain types of rights and
opportunities. Then he argues that, given the present system of
control and distribution and the class division on this as basis,
there will be progressively less achievement by X of his values,
that the instrumentalities on which he relies (e.g., a small savings
account, a stable job, a few investments) will in the development
of now existent forces be swept away, and that by stressing all
other divisions (e.g., national, racial, religious, skilled-unskilled,
sexual), no stable solution will be discovered. Only by stressing
the economic division so as to override all the others in securing
a class unity will he be able to achieve abidingly his own values.
The analysis of the proposition, "The economic division is the
most fundamental," therefore becomes: (1) most men have certain
values, v_1 v_2, v_3 (either uniformly or with diversity) and in respect
to those it is true that (2) the present arrangement of forces is
such that these values are not likely to be abidingly achieved, (3)
the attempt to achieve them by stressing other bases of division is
not likely to succeed, and (4) the attempt to achieve them by
stressing the economic basis of division into classes is likely to
succeed.

These four objective conditions constitute a meaning of the
notion "fundamental." Whether in this sense the economic division turns out to be fundamental is now a matter of empirical
investigation for social scientists. There can be no a priori answer.
Thus with regard to (1), if most men in a society do actually want
security, and certain opportunities of education, self-expression,
and so on, then we must go on to examine the truth of the
remaining proposition with respect to these values. Likewise if, to

take a hypothetical example, most men were to say in any society that what they valued above all, even above life or security, was to obey explictly the representatives of their religion, then we would have to ask again whether for this value of v_1, v_2, and v_3, (2), (3), and (4) remained true; (2) involves assumptions about the present-day economic system, the habits of men in our society; (3) is about, for example, international politics and economics, that exploitation of fresh markets cannot continue for very long, that international rivalry will have certain consequences; (4), that men will be able to break habits which have kept them apart, for example, religious, racial, or sex oppositions. All these assumptions, the evidence for which lies in the fields of economics, psychology, history, anthropology, physiology, politics, and others, must be examined independently for their truth-value. Upon them depends the assessment of the probability that the economic division is the fundamental one. But what is meant by calling it fundamental, that is, the conditions satisfying which the proposition will be true and failing to satisfy which it will be false, is discovered by its philosophic analysis. These conditions constitute its meaning.

4. The fourth sense of "fundamental" is a scientific one. To call one division more fundamental is to suggest that it is a more fruitful hypothesis for explanation in diverse fields of social behavior. The meaning of a more fruitful hypothesis is not at issue; it is identical with what logicians call a systematically simpler hypothesis, one which unifies a great many facts which are then seen to be special cases of it under special circumstances. Thus those who stress the importance of the urban-rural distinction in this sense mean that family cohesion or dissolution, strong or weak control of parents over children, stability or instability of moral standards and a varying ability in performance tests in the factors of speed and accuracy may all be seen as special consequences under special conditions of compact or scattered population or of diversity of occupation. In this sense, Sorokin and Zimmerman, after defining a social class as "the totality of individuals whose occupational, economic and socio-political status (rights and privileges, duties and disfranchisements) are closely similar," go on to say: "Man's economic, occupational, and socio-political positions practically are responsible for the most of the traits of his 'acquired' personality. Directly and indirectly three-quarters of such traits as education, manners, customs, beliefs,

tastes, convictions, ideas, traditions and so on, are decisively determined by these three statuses."[13] We are not concerned with the truth of this hypothesis, but with the way in which it would be tested. This is:

1. It would have to show that the facts to be explained are really deducible as necessary or probable consequences of it—in this deduction there might be added assumptions which would have to be established if questioned.
2. It would have to show that its hypothesis explains these results more simply than any proposed alternatives—it should try if possible to predict, in which it must again show that the prediction follows from it and is not attached in an arbitrary fashion, as I might predict from the fact that the sun was shining when I wrote this paper that you are enjoying reading it.

The economic division into classes is frequently called by its propounders more fundamental in this sense, and the attempt is made to show both in the past and at present that particular stresses in particular situations are explicable as special cases of this type of class opposition. In its more extreme forms, it is sometimes said to *explain* the character of any social behavior at any time, and it is phrased as the cultural character reflecting its economic substructure. Its more careful advocates urge it as an explanation of why at particular times certain ideas, attitudes, inventions, and religions, spread widely or fail to advance. Thus Dutt, in his work on *Fascism and Social Revolution,* [14] points to present widespread social phenomena: the depression in the economic realm; the revolt against the machine in discussions of technology, and even in many edicts putting men to work with hand labor; the destruction of productive forces; in politics, a revolt against democracy; in the international field, a stress on national self-sufficiency; in intellectual matters, a growing mysticism and an attack on the basis of science as the most reliable means of securing knowledge; and so forth. Hypotheses might be advanced to explain these independently: for example, diplomatic relations as personality questions in the international field; a weariness with disputation in politics; a periodic swing from rationalism to mysticism; and so on. Dutt suggests instead that all these phenomena are special instances of the opposition between capitalists and workers, under the special conditions of an economic system that is breaking down and a working class that is developing a consciousness of unity. He does not maintain that these conditions are a cause of national feeling, mysticism, and so on. These are in some fashion or other always to be found. What he attempts to show is that under present conditions they are utilized as instruments in a struggle, and consciously or unconsciously fostered and spread in the struggle.

A priori, there is no reason to bar any trait from acquiring any social function. Even false biological theories may, as in Germany now, be the ostensible bases of different treatment. The presence or absence of an Oxford or Harvard accent may likewise act as evidence to open or shut certain paths of social opportunity. The interrelationships of social traits is in any particular age an empirical question. The sense of fundamental we are now considering is, therefore, the suggestion that a certain division into classes will be found to be a fruitful hypothesis explaining a great variety of the interrelationships of social traits in any, or many cultures. That is its meaning; the truth or falsity of any particular hypothesis can be verified only empirically by showing that it does or does not satisfy the conditions indicated.

Of course, the task of actually performing this kind of investigation in the domain of social behavior is no easy one. For example, the explicandum is not always clear, and two theories which may conflict when stated abstractly may become complementary when it is seen that they are referring to different realms. One may turn out to be dealing with a more pervasive aspect, the other with a special field. Fruitfulness in the hypothesis will have to be interpreted (less strictly than in physics) as suggesting a mode of analysis probably applicable over a wide range. It might also be possible to work out a hierarchy of such leading principles for more general and more limited domains, and likewise for the connection of domains. And finally, the historical and temporal nature of the material must be kept firmly in mind, to avoid such confusions as the assertion that a certain class division denies its fundamental character by offering the means of predicting accurately the conditions under which it subsequently ceases to apply. For this would be part proof, not refutation of its fundamentalness in the period in which it was most important.

We may summarize roughly the results of our inquiry. A great deal of confusion arises because the notion of classes in society is ambiguously employed. Apparently contradictory propositions may really be talking about different things. When, therefore, we meet any assertion about classes, we must ask for its precise meaning and for the precise sense in which the classes are opposed to one another. Very frequently, the discussion turns out to be one about the relative *importance* or *fundamentalness* of some basis of division in society. In such cases, it may be conducive to clarity to translate the discussion into these terms. Then the precise sense of *importance* must be indicated. We have listed four, but there may be others. When this is done, and the proposition is found meaningful, the philosophic analysis is finished, but the investigation is only begun. The verification is then an empirical matter, since a priori there is no reason why under all conditions there should be classes or not be classes, why one division should be more fundamental than others or should not be. Hence, when the meaning is clear and is stated as a set of material propositions, the latter must then be tested by the special sciences. What the philosopher accomplishes is the analysis of the problem. Purely as a philosopher, he cannot give the answer to the problem, unless it be conceived to be the task of the philosopher also to synthesize the material results of the special sciences. The very least he can do is to prevent people from arguing about meaningless questions or making meaningless assertions and quarreling about them. That there is room for such a role, difficulties about such concepts as class, state, property and so on, adequately demonstrate. To the philosopher this clarity is a value. Whether at any one time it is actually valued or not, and why, is itself a matter for cultural analysis and investigation.

NOTES

1. A.F. Bentley, *The Process of Government: A Study of Social Pressures* (Chicago: University of Chicago Press, 1908), p. 304.

2. Ibid., p. 440.

3. Karl Marx, *The Eighteenth Brumaire of Louis Bonaparte,* trans. Eden and Cedar Paul (New York: International Publishers, 1926), p. 133.

4. James M. Williams, *Our Rural Heritage: The Social Psychology of Rural Development* (New York: Knopf, 1925).

5. Scott E. W. Bedford, *Readings in Urban Sociology* (New York: Appleton, 1927), p. viii.

6. Adna F. Weber, *The Growth of Cities in the 19th Century: A Study in Statistics* (New York: Macmillan, 1899).

7. Frederic C. Howe, *The City, The Hope of Democracy* (New York: Scribner's, 1913), p. 45.

8. Ezra Dwight Sanderson, *The Rural Community: The Natural History of a Sociological Group* (Boston: Ginn, 1932).

9. Pitirim Sorokin and Carle C. Zimmerman, *Principles of Rural-Urban Sociology* (New York: Holt, 1929), p. 14.

10. Arthur J. Todd, *Theories of Social Progress: A Critical Study of the Attempts to Formulate the Conditions of Human Advance* (New York: Macmillan, 1918), p. 227.

11. Sidney Hook, *Towards the Understanding of Karl Marx: A Revolutionary Interpretation* (New York: Day, 1933), p. 234.

12. Karl Marx and Friedrich Engels, *Manifesto of the Communist Party*, Authorized English Translation, edited and annotated by Friedrich Engels (New York: International Publishers, 1948), p. 19.

13. Sorokin and Zimmerman, p. 61.

14. R. Palme Dutt, *Fascism and Social Revolution* (London: Martin Lawrence, 1934).

2. The Concept of the Unconscious: Some Analytic Preliminaries

This paper emerged from work in the late 1950s and early 1960s. I had been giving a course in a doctoral program in a medical school, directed to psychiatric research ("Logical Backgrounds for Psychological and Psychiatric Research"). Contact with professionals in the field revealed how intense was the conflict of schools, especially in psychoanalytic thought, and how tangled their argument. By this time, ordinary language analysis and phenomenological analysis had taken their place alongside the positivistic logical reconstruction. From every direction there were Parthian shots at the unconscious, that is (in the style of the ancient Parthian bowmen who rode up, discharged their arrows at the enemy and dashed away), each approach offered a criticism or a counterinstance that had force chiefly on the presuppositions of that approach, but did not stay to have those presuppositions confronted. In such a complex situation, there was no getting together unless somehow the issues could be unraveled, and the presuppositions of the different criticisms of the idea of the unconscious made explicit. On the whole, I felt that when this was fully done, further research would likely bring fresh constructs and reformulate the basic questions entirely.

Methodologically, the paper thus illustrates the importance of the search for presuppositions on a very broad canvas in the case of ideas that are highly theory-laden or system-laden.

Some part of the growing attention which philosophers are today giving to psychoanalytic concepts stems from a desire to be helpful, rather than simply critical, in the present stages of psychoanalytic theorizing. One of the tasks for which philosophical analysis is especially fitted is the disentangling of issues in areas of complex controversy. I should like here to undertake this type of analysis with respect to the basic psychoanalytic concept of the unconscious.

In the usual controversies about the unconscious, there are almost a dozen issues thoroughly entangled. Whenever a controversy begins on this topic—especially on a cross-disciplinary level—you may never be sure what the issues will be, but you can be sure that they will involve so many different assumptions that never come to the surface, that no one will convince anyone else. And yet you get the sense of recognized gambits in the argument. Perhaps they ought to be standardized, as in chess, so that you will know what move to expect, and can go ahead enjoying the game. What I should like to say about the theory of the unconscious may be regarded as a prolegomenon to the ordering of controversy in the area with a view to scientific advance, rather than simply the enjoyment of style in controversy. Let me list the issues I find.

1. Is the concept of unconscious ideas and desires self-contradictory?

2. Is there an inconsistency among the properties by which the unconscious is characterized?

3. Does the theory use the concept of the unconscious in a way continuous with ordinary usage, or is it a technical term?

4. Can everything one might say in terms of the unconscious equally well be said in terms of the causes, consequences, and relations, of conscious elements, aided by finer phenomenological discriminations within consciousness itself? Or is the concept a construct carrying some further meaning?

5. If the unconscious be regarded as a scientific construct, are we methodologically justified in postulating unobservables? Are there limiting conditions for such a procedure, and how literally can we interpret the construct?

6. Does the notion of the unconscious embody a special metaphysics?

7. Does the concept of the unconscious obscure or spuriously supplant explanation on other levels?

8. Does the concept of the unconscious embody an unscientific concept of causality, appealing to unscientific forces?

9. What model of explanation is embodied in the idea of the unconscious—finalistic, mechanistic, or some hybrid of the two?

10. Does the concept of the unconscious embrace a single type of phenomenon, or a multitude of different phenomena, and in the latter case, does it denote a continuum or a gradation with sharp qualitative changes?

11. Has the stress on the unconscious unduly diminished the human significance of the concept of consciousness?

1. IS THE CONCEPT OF UNCONSCIOUS IDEAS AND DESIRES SELF-CONTRADICTORY?

Have we a right to use such a concept at all, or is it comparable to speaking of a round square? This oldest of the critiques persists in modern dress. For example, Arthur Pap writes: "I venture to assert that it is logically impossible for a pain or a desire to occur without the subject's being conscious of it, because pains and desires are just the sort of 'private' states that are meant by the old-fashioned expression 'state of consciousness.' " [1]

Now no sophisticated person today should be overwhelmed by such a claim of logical impossibility; it covers merely the fact that the terms "pain" and "desire" are being used according to certain rules. What we have to do in such a case, as Freud long ago recognized in his 1915 paper on "The Unconscious," [2] is to ask what prompts adherence to these rules and evaluate these considerations. Pap is, in effect, proposing a translation program. For example, if we say that a person's contempt for a colleague is really unconscious jealousy, what we ought to limit ourselves to saying is that while the person himself thinks the colleague's flaunting behavior caused the contempt, it is instead the colleague's higher abilities which were the cause. Again, if a jealous wife says to her husband that he is not pitying a poor widow but being sexually attracted to her, she is predicting the consequence that he would still pursue her even "if she turned into the happiest, most lavishly supported widow in the world." What Pap is thus doing is saying that anything interesting or informative expressed by judgments of unconscious mental states could more clearly be translated into judgments about the causes or consequences of conscious states.

Now, surprisingly enough, Freud himself talks like this with regard to affects, though not for ideas. He says: "It is surely of the essence of an emotion that we should feel it, i.e. that it should enter consciousness. So for emotions, feelings and affects to be unconscious would be quite out of the question."[3] But what then is to happen, he asks, to such psychoanalytic usages as "unconscious love, hate, anger, etc." or "unconscious consciousness of guilt" or "unconscious anxiety"? In some cases, he goes on to explain, the affect is perceived, but connected with another idea. "If we restore the true connection, we call the original affect 'unconscious,' although the affect was never unconscious but its ideational presentation had undergone repression." What we are concerned with, it turns out, is the fate of the quantitative factor in the instinctual impulse. I need not go into Freud's mapping of the diverse path of this fate; what is important here is that he rejects the parallelism in interpretation for idea and affect: ". . . the unconscious idea continues, after repression, as an actual formation in the system Ucs, whilst to the unconscious affect there corresponds in the same system only a potential disposition which is prevented from developing further. So that, strictly speaking, although no fault be found with the mode of expression in question, there are no unconscious affects in the sense in which there are unconscious ideas."[4] What seems to determine the difference is Freud's theory at that time of the nature of ideas and affects: the former are cathexes ultimately of memory-traces, the latter correspond with processes of discharge.

I have made no study of the subsequent fate of these distinctions in the development of Freud's own thought. But even as late as *Inhibitions, Symptoms and Anxiety,* Freud says carefully, speaking of distraction of interest, "Even the most intense physical pains fail to arise (I must not say 'remain unconscious' in this case)."[5] What I find significant in the earlier essay is the clear indication that the answer to the question of desirable usage is a function of the scientific answer to the question, "What is an idea?" Contemporary objections of Pap's type are then, in effect, saying that what Freud argued about affect equally well applies to idea. Our conclusion is, then, that we should stop arguing about the alleged self-contradictory character of the concept and get directly to issues which such an argument only disguises. These are: (a) whether the same phenomena can be described adequately without the concept (issue 4), or (b) whether there are specific scientific grounds warranting the construct (cf. issue 5).

2. IS THERE AN INCONSISTENCY AMONG THE PROPERTIES IN TERMS OF WHICH THE UNCONSCIOUS IS ANALYZED?

Sartre, for example, argues that the notion of the unconscious requires the notion of repression, and yet that if we analyze the process of repression and the repressed, we get results which are inconsistent with there being an unconscious. This criticism is to be found in his discussion of "bad faith" in *Being and Nothingness*. His criticism of psychoanalysis amounts to this:

> The one to whom the lie is told and the one who lies are one and the same person, which means that I must know in my capacity as deceiver the truth which is hidden from me in my capacity as the one deceived. Better yet I must know the truth very exactly *in order* to conceal it more carefully— and this not at two different moments, which at a pinch would allow us to reestablish a semblance of duality—but in the unitary structure of a single project. How then can the lie subsist if the duality which conditions it is suppressed?[6]

Sartre adds that I must be conscious of my bad faith and so be in good faith, at least to the extent of being conscious of my bad faith. Rejecting the "materialistic mythology of psychoanalysis" and distinction of id, ego, and superego, Sartre insists that the censor must know what it is repressing.

> How can the repressed drive "disguise itself" if it does not include (1) the consciousness of being repressed, (2) the consciousness of having been pushed back because it is what it is, (3) a project of disguise? No mechanistic theory of condensation or of transference can explain these modifications by which the drive itself is affected, for the description of the process of disguise implies a veiled appeal to finality.[7]

For Sartre, all knowing is consciousness of knowing, and Freud is going astray in rejecting the conscious unity of the psyche. Instead, Sartre looks for explanations in consciousness in the form of patterns of bad faith. He cites the case (following Stekel) of frigid women who, during the sexual act, think of their household accounts and asks, "Will anyone speak of an unconscious here?" [8] Such a woman does it, he says, to prove to herself that she is frigid. And so he moves toward the question, "What must be the being of man if he is to be capable of bad faith?" And I am not sure that it is wholly unfair to say that, having made this shift, Sartre is lost thereafter in the marshes of this question.

We must distinguish, however, three points in Sartre's criticism:

1. The very correct recognition that a theory of the unconscious has to furnish a fuller theory of the self. In the case of psychoanalysis, this means the demand for a fuller structural approach, that is, a more far-reaching development of the theory of id, ego, and superego, or its revision.

2. Insistence on finality or purpose in the phenomena that Freud assigns to the unconscious. Here Freud would be likely to agree to some extent, since the Freudian theory is often interpreted as involving the extension of finality from consciousness to the unconscious.

3. The quite arbitrary philosophical view that the unity of the psyche lies in consciousness. Here the subjectivism of the existentialist approach emerges clearly, and its rejection of a materialist account. Freud's view, on the contrary, shares with materialism the belief that consciousness reflects biological processes, and that the unity of consciousness is to be explained in terms outside of itself. Once again, then, the issues raised are not of consistency, but a demand for more knowledge, a call for clarifying models of explanation (see issue 9), and a philosophical disagreement either outside the specific domain, or else methodological or pragmatic (respectively, issues 4, 11).

3. IS THE USE OF THE TERM "UNCONSCIOUS" CONTINUOUS WITH ORDINARY USAGE?

The significance of this issue is that if there is the continuity, then there is no need for a fuss or a special justification. Of course, ordinary usage may be faulty, so that continuity would not be a special virtue. But in today's philosophical atmosphere, where there is often found the reverent assumption that ordinary usage has stowed away the wisdom of past experience, to be continuous with ordinary usage serves as a kind of *imprimatur*. For example, we find R. S. Peters in his rather insightful book, *The Concept of Motivation*, saying: "Ordinary language enshrines all sorts of distinctions, the fine shades of which often elude the clumsiness of a highly general theory." And again, "We know *so much* about human beings, and our knowledge is incorporated implicitly in our language. Making it explicit could be a more fruitful preliminary to developing a theory than gaping at rats or grey geese." [9]

In an interesting article, Herbert Fingarette argues that psychoanalytical use of the term "unconscious" is both continuous with ordinary usage and a technical term which grows out of ordinary usage by means of a fruitful convention. He itemizes several conditions for correctness of such a judgment as, "*A* looks as if he is calm. He even thinks he is, but it would be a mistake to suppose this to be true. He is now really, but unconsciously, intensely angry." [10] The first condition for correctness is that one know that under specific usual standard conditions anger would appear in consciousness. Second, we adopt a linguistic convention which throws emphasis on the conditions in which the anger would appear, rather than a convention in terms of the consciousness itself.[11] Third, additional complications would then be discerned which prevent the response from taking place, "although, in the technical sense, it is still *really* taking place." Fingarette justifies the technical usage by the fact that it would enable us to predict future behavior much more effectively.

On this view, the decision to create the technical term, "unconscious anger," is a frank policy decision in the use of terms. Before deciding, we must, of course, note that opposing policies are to be found. "Angry" might be used as a success-word, such as "breaking" in, "He's breaking down the door," which we would not want to say unless some cracking were going on. Unconscious responses might be analogous to, "He's trying to break down the door." Now Fingarette's justification for his alternative seems insufficient in two respects. First, the same predictions it makes possible could be made from a knowledge of the standard conditions and the preventing forces, so that more is required to warrant adding the technical use to the vocabulary of the field—at least the hope that it will point to areas of fresh research. Second, the actual analysis is insufficiently refined, since it might lead us to blur distinctions we already make in ordinary usage. For example, we would not want to speak of unconscious anger where the conditions which prevent the response from taking place are the kind that make the anger "vanish" or "dissipate"—say, some overwhelmingly happy surprise or discovery of a mistaken relevant fact.

What really tempts us to go on into a technical term is the gradation of successive intermediate forms. Certainly, "He's really angry though he's not showing it" would be relevant where the man was consciously holding back his anger so successfully that the typical observer did not notice it. The test would lie in the man's admission if asked. But what about, "He's really angry though he's hiding it from himself"? A.C. MacIntyre, in his book *The Unconscious,*[12] combines the criterion of avowal with that of behavioral differences, in analyzing human dispositions: the case of a disposition of which a man is unconscious would, therefore, be analyzed as one in which there were behavioral consequences, and in addition, the agent would avow his purpose *if* certain more complicated conditions were fulfilled (e.g., if he were successfully analyzed in a Freudian fashion). Fingarette seems to be treating unconscious anger like an "invisible cold" for which the evidence would lie in showing that a cycle of intrabodily events was gone through, but some obvious events usually associated with them, and particularly overt, were skipped; the taking of antihistamine after the appearance of the first symptoms constituted the interfering factor. MacIntyre adds the more stringent conditions that some kind of conscious experience be capable of eventuating. Both would probably agree that the term "an invisible cold" was a justified extension of the term "a cold."

Such analyses serve a useful, though preliminary function. They show that some of our terms referring to consciousness carry along with them a reference to some other level than that of consciousness itself. There is no reason why a technical term should be a one-level term rather than a term referring to a structured block of levels. To say, "Mr. X is now angry" would in the typical clear or standard case embrace the following:

1. Phenomenological level—X has such-and-such feelings.
2. Physiological level—blood pressure, release of sugar, etc., which I shall sum up by the vivid expression, "X's blood is boiling."
3. Behavioral level—X tenses his hand or clenches his fist.

4. Significance level—X is responding to an insult, or he is warding off criticism, etc. Some theorists would put all this under the phenomenological level, since a description of feelings would include a description of objects in the field; some would have it as sociocultural, involving symbols; some would make this a purely psychological level, as in psychoanalytic interpretation of the aggressive component.

Now if this depicts the clear case, what of the case in which there are variations and departures from the full picture? Certainly, on the behavioral level, we would allow a substitution of a spear-throwing gesture for a pugilistic response of our culture. We would even find this condition satisfied if the behavior were unusual stillness—provided we had satisfactory evidence of the holding-back going on within the organism. Similarly, in the absence of the subject's conscious feeling of anger, evidence of distorting or repressing forces would be the crux. As a technical term, "unconscious anger" would be laden with considerable theory, to be justified by scientific evidence on level-relations, not by purely linguistic considerations. It is worth recalling that the earliest Freudian formulation in terms of the so-called "economic" standpoint did concentrate on the fate of the energies that were moving to consciousness. And even today, the concept of psychosomatic illness in some sense involves energies that would in our example of anger have produced the consciousness of anger, but for the fact that they were diverted; moreover, repetition of such diversion might issue eventually in bodily damage. But the question remains: do such considerations justify a doctrine of unconscious anger in some literal sense, or simply one of specific unconscious bodily processes, that is, a physiological, not a psychological account? The linguistic procedures show we can fashion a construct, but not how literally we can take it or what kind it should be. A prior question, in fact, is whether we can dispense with it altogether rather than consider how to set it up.

4. CAN EVERYTHING THAT IS SAID IN TERMS OF THE UNCONSCIOUS BE EQUALLY WELL SAID WITHOUT IT?

Can a translation program be carried out so that we may dispense with the concept of the unconscious? There need be no quarrel with such an *attempt* as attempt. A reduction *program* is always permissible. Anyone may *try* to use Ockham's razor; whether the attempt will succeed is a purely scientific matter. Along these lines, we find the following translation modes offered for expression in which the term "unconscious" occurs:

1. Translation in terms of *causes* of consciousness. I referred above to one of Pap's illustrations—instead of saying that a man's contempt for a colleague was unconscious jealousy, we should say that he was wrong in thinking the colleague's flaunting behavior, rather than his higher abilities, caused the feeling. Now some cases surely can be treated in this fashion. But we have to be sure that it is the same state of consciousness whose cause we are disputing; Pap explicitly doubts whether contempt feels differently from jealousy. I think he is quite wrong, since in contempt I exalt myself, whereas in jealousy I feel myself cut out or downgraded. But this need not affect the translation program. It means simply that we have to add another mode, namely:

2. Translation into *finer phenomenological distinctions* within consciousness. Thus corresponding to different causes, we may look for and often find different qualities within consciousness. For example, the same industrious behavior may in one involve a consciousness that is an anxious drivenness, in another a feeling of realistic coping in difficult circumstances.

3. Translation into *different consequences* in behavior. This is expected by all points of view, except extreme phenomenologists. Here "unconscious desires" would be translated into more indirect, devious, less rational behavior.

4. Translation into *conscious efforts at distraction*. Sartre's patterns of bad faith illustrate this. So, for that matter, does Freud's discussion of how repression of painful experience begins on the overt level.

5. Translation into *modes of unawareness* which explain why some behavior does not take place. For example, Albert Starr offering a critique from a Marxian perspective lists: being unaware that certain ideas held are inaccurate; being unaware of the consequences in action of the ideas held; being unaware of the significance of

one's activity (e.g., that it is against one's best interests); being unaware of the significance of other's behavior and so misinterpreting their motives; being unaware of the full significance of an idea.[13] It may not be very easy always to carry out this translation program. For example, Starr himself says that a man may be unaware that a given idea "leads him to belittle himself to others as a helpless, incompetent individual in order to gain this sympathy and support." While such a reinterpretation may avoid the words "unconscious masochistic ideas," it seems to have quite as much of the content of unconscious idea-forces. But, of course, it may be the case that some other mode of translation could take care of this particular instance.

I have no doubt that this list of translation modes I have culled can be added to. My very serious recommendation to the psychoanalytic theorist who believes literally in the unconscious would be that he encourage the systematic development of this program. For unless this is done and it is found unsuccessful, how can he be sure that it is not because some translation modes were undiscovered?

However, since it is largely a program, one cannot at this point rule out the use of a construct of the unconscious on its account. We go on, therefore, to issues that arise about such a construct.

5. ARE WE JUSTIFIED IN POSTULATING UNOBSERVABLES?

Philosophy of science today is liberal enough in its permission to develop theoretical entities. "So far as unobservableness goes," Arthur Danto says in a charitable outburst, "there is little to choose as between castration complexes and psi-functions." [14] It is only fair to add that he goes on to qualify it. For he points out that beyond the use of theoretical terms lie two questions. Do they denote anything? Are there semantic rules which allow them to be significantly employed? With respect to the second question, there is no doubt for psi-functions; they fit into a tight mathematical system which is associated at definite points with specific procedures, so that one can know what is deducible and what is not deducible from the theory. With respect to castration complexes, the theory is much looser, the modes of application and evidence much more studded with gaps and vagueness. We ought, in fact, to distinguish sharply between having a theory strictly formulated with its logical structure showing, and having a mere theory-schema, or theory-sketch, which may be little more than a belief that the factors relevant to an eventual theory can be found in a given area, or even sometimes, relying on some metaphor to serve as a theory-surrogate. But such considerations would lead us into evidence problems which at the moment are not our concern. It is the clarity of the concept of the unconscious and what it denotes that we are investigating. And the point of our general methodological comment here is to recognize that a theoretical concept need not actually denote an existent entity. The psi-function in quantum mechanics, Ernest Nagel points out,[15] is not interpreted by some visualizable physical model, but serves a definite intermediary role in the construction and calculation of other terms, leading eventually to states that are directly interpreted and measurable. So that if he wanted to, the psychoanalytic theorist could confess and admit that by unconscious entities he does not point to anything actually existent, but to devices that help him reckon how people will react. Would Freud have agreed to this? In *The Interpretation of Dreams* he reports Lipps's view as follows, with apparent approval: "The physician and the philosopher can meet only when both acknowledge that 'unconscious psychic processes' is the 'appropriate and justified expression for an established fact.' " [16] However, in his very late work, *An Outline of Psychoanalysis,* we find: "And if, for instance we say: 'At this point an unconscious memory intervened,' what this means is: 'At this point something occurred of which we are totally unable to form a conception, but which, if it had entered our consciousness, could only have been described in such and such a way.' " [17] But the question is not one of interpreting Freud. It is the importance for the present-day psychoanalytic theorist of being quite clear what kind of a construct he is taking the unconscious to be.

Let me illustrate two possible types from a familiar field. Take the term "aging" as a biological term for a process in the individual organism and ask whether there is anything to which it literally applies. Compare the account given of the concept in, say, Hans Selye's *The Stress of Life* and P. W. Medawar's *The Uniqueness of the Individual.* Selye postulates a fund of "adaptation-energy" in each individual at birth, which he draws on to meet stresses as they occur during his lifetime. If we could measure the level of this fund at any point, we would have direct access to the extent of depletion. This is a literal interpretation of the theoretical term "aging." Medawar does not believe any of the measures usually given—decline of vitality, rate of wounds healing, acuity of senses, multiplicative power of tissues—is in fact measuring some independent process that the others are also measuring. Instead, he reinterprets aging as the increase of vulnerability to the mortal hazards of life coming from all sorts of sources, measured by the likelihood of dying within any chosen interval. In both cases, we have constructs. But the one is taken in a literal way—the philosopher would say that it is given a "realistic" interpretation. The other is a useful device within a theory—the philosopher would say that it is serving an "instrumental" role.

Various issues arise whichever direction we take. If the interpretation is literal, what kind of reality is designated—metaphysical, physical, or in some unique sense, psychological? If the interpretation is instrumental, what purposes, methodological or pragmatic, are to be served? What conceptions of causation or explanation are embodied?

6. DOES THE NOTION OF THE UNCONSCIOUS EMBODY A SPECIAL METAPHYSICS?

Dialectical materialist criticism frequently looks in the unconscious for romantic philosophical conceptions of the Will in its Schopenhauerian-Nietzschean obscurantism. Certainly it is a salutary warning to beware of ideological misuses of Freudian concepts. It is worth noting that there have been attempts to identify the Unconscious with the Kantian metaphysical thing-in-itself, or to regard the psychoanalytical process of penetrating the unconscious as a kind of direct Bergsonian intuiting of reality. Some of Freud's expressions could easily encourage a Kantian; for example, when he says in The Interpretation of Dreams: "The unconscious is the true psychic reality: in its inner nature it is just as much unknown to us as the reality of the external world and it is just as imperfectly communicated to us by the data of consciousness as is the external world by the reports of our sense-organs." [18]

Nevertheless, it is possible to shed these special accretions. An excellent critique of such conceptions is carried out in Fenichel's paper on "Psychoanalysis and Metaphysics." [19] He points out, for example, that "timelessness" in Freud's characterization of the unconscious need not mean some mysterious property of a reality beyond time; it means no more than "durability." Nevertheless, it may be that philosophical idealism touches not only external interpretations, but some of the content of the theory. If so, however, it seems to me that the idealistic influence is to be sought not in the theory of the unconscious narrowly construed, but in the theory of the instincts. For it is here that one may find the finalistic or teleological casting of libido, eros, thanatos, rather than a causal scrutiny of the typical career of more or less determinate energies. But this is a different issue. However, since Freud regards the theory of the unconscious as mapping, in part, the fate of instinctual energies, any unscientific treatment of the latter would be likely to affect the former. A thoroughgoing attempt to treat the unconscious as a purely scientific concept, therefore, requires some scientific recasting of the rest of the conceptual apparatus with which this concept is enmeshed.

Criticism of a quite opposite sort is found in the frequent charge that Freud is a physical materialist. That he cherished at the outset the hope of an ultimate physical reduction is clear enough. But equally clearly, he came to think of a uniquely psychological reality as the outcome of the modes of analysis and explanation he found fruitful. The charge of philosophical idealism and the charge of philosophical materialism are not, however, strictly parallel. For physical materialism as a metaphysical outlook was associated in its development with the growth and dominance of the physical sciences. The choice between a physical materialism and a psychological emergence conception is thus a scientific issue of methods and results in the development of psychology. In the work of the scientist, it takes the form of methodological, not metaphysical, issues. Criticism of the theory of the unconcious then charges either undue reduction or undue failure to carry out reduction. Or, in general, it provokes our next query.

7. DOES THE CONCEPT OF THE UNCONSCIOUS ERRONEOUSLY SUPPLANT EXPLANATIONS ON OTHER LEVELS?

The logic of reduction and emergence, or the relation of levels of phenomena in description and explanation, is a central topic of analysis well-explored in the philosophy of science.[20] I cannot enter into it here. Let me simply say that nothing in principle prevents one from looking for physical causes of any phenomenon, from reducing terms in psychology to terms in physiology or in physics, or deducing laws of the former from laws of the latter. Nothing in principle, if you can carry it out! Reasonable scientists differ in hopes and directions of inquiry. Surely one ought to work along all available lines. A good example is the renewed work on dreams, in which physical and physiological knowledge can interlock with psychological data and ideas. There need be no "supplanting" here.

Similarly, nothing in principle prevents one from searching for scientific results on a level far removed from the physical, and raising the question whether operating on a specific lower level may obscure fruitful results and hinder successful explanations. There is, for example, the criticism advanced by both Marxists and neo-Freudians that properties assigned to the unconscious are more properly to be understood in terms of the impact of sociohistorical processes on the macroscopic scene; for example, that passive behavior is to be understood not in terms of infantile fears and identifications but in terms of character developed in an authoritarian and obedience-demanding society; or again, that the grasping acquisitive aggressive characterization of the id is less native endowment than an internalized reflection of a predatory capitalism. These criticisms, directed against the assumption of certain specific properties of unconscious entities, constitute ultimately empirical issues. What is methodologically central, however, is that they be analyzed and refined to be capable of empirical resolution, and not simply constitute a program of verbal substitution, nor again simply a difference of preference in interpretation. For after all, the recognition of sociohistorical causes on the macroscopic level need not be incompatible with a supplementary theory of individual mechanisms on the individual-psychology level through which the macroscopic processes are mediated. But, once again, this theoretical possibility does not settle in advance the question raised above, whether the mediating mechanism may best be understood as physiological or uniquely psychological.

If the logic of reduction and emergence cannot prejudge this question, is there anything in the use of other methodological concepts, such as causality, which should incline us in one or another direction?

8. DOES THE CONCEPT OF THE UNCONSCIOUS EMBODY AN UNSCIENTIFIC CONCEPT OF CAUSALITY?

The very use of the unconscious as a causal explanation has often been subject to criticism. For example, Ernest Nagel raises difficulties about the whole notion of a "mental apparatus" with unconscious wishes, drives, urges, and intentions of a purposive sort, which are regarded "not simply as latent somatic dispositions possessing no *specific goals*," but "endowed with all the customary attributes of substantiality and causal agency." [21] Of course, Nagel points out, if all this were just metaphorical language for as yet unknown bodily mechanisms, and if the teleological language were in principle analyzable into statements about feedback mechanisms, it would be understandable. But if it is taken with any literalness, it is confronted with genuine difficulties. If causal efficacy is ascribed to these theoretical entities in a figurative sense, how can it provide a "dynamic" account of human personality and conduct? [22] If there is a literal reading, then how can such theoretical constructs be causal? (Nagel says, how can "*modes of organization* of human activities" be "causes of those activities"?) He concludes that the notion of "unconscious causally operative motives and wishes that are not somatic dispositions and activities" is unintelligible.

The dilemma about providing a dynamic account is the less serious one. For we must remember that the term "dynamic" is used in psychoanalytic theory in a very specific sense; it refers to the thesis that ultimate determination of behavior is by drives. The specific theory of drives and their nature may vary, and it has been qualified in the growth of ego psychology and concepts of ego autonomy. But insofar as the explanation of human behavior will involve "formulae" in which among the theoretical terms will be drive-terms or parameters indicating states of drives as a function of their past vicissitudes, the theory will be dynamic in the special sense intended. Even in a more generalized sense, I see no reason why the characterization of a theory as dynamic should not depend on the kind of variables employed in the theory, its use of energy-variables and state-descriptions involving time-reference and changes correlated with time and energy-states, rather than on whether a literal interpretation is taken by reference to "forces."

As for thinking about causal efficacy on other than a physical level, no doubt problems of logical analysis will always arise. But this does not show that psychoanalytic theory is uniquely at fault. The very concept of causality is a difficult one, as the history of its philosophical analysis amply confirms. But why should psychoanalytic theory bear the philosophic burden of analyzing it clearly, just because it may want its theoretical terms describing the unconscious to have a literal interpretation? After all, we find judgments of causality made on a social level; for example, we understand what is meant by saying that the threat of international conflict causes a contraction of civil liberties within a given country, without being able to carry through a precise analysis of energy transfers among individual organisms. We may even include among causal factors in a specific social analysis, "the passive attitude of the average man," though clearly "average man" is a theoretical construct. In short, although a naturalistic philosophy may believe that causal efficacy in a proper sense characterizes the relation and transmission of physical energies— that the physical level is the executive level, so to speak—it cannot refuse to allow the use of causal concepts on a variety of levels, leaving it empirically open what kind of levels they will turn out to be. After all, the same objection could be raised to ascribing causal efficacy to a conscious wish as to an unconscious wish!

Such a permissive attitude to the use of the concept of causality on a variety of levels, however, carries with it corresponding obligations. The use of the concept must be responsible, not reckless. At least two suggestions for criteria of responsible use may be offered, beyond the usual methodological insistence on verifiability and fruitfulness. One would be a greater refinement of elements or factors in a causal judgment, rather than simple resort to the unconscious en bloc. For example, Rapaport analyzes the slip of a man who says, "Now things are becoming queer," when he meant to say and believed he had said "clear." [23] He separates the subject's conscious intention, his failure to carry it out, his unawareness of the failure, his unawareness of the actual verbal expression used, his embarrassment on discovery. Each is referred to a structural element such as the id or ego and analyzed as a specific conflict or compromise; beyond these, there is probing for the specific character of the man's feelings toward the other participants in the scene. Whether the evidence would prove sufficient for the judgments is a separate question, but the refinement shows that causality is not ascribed to the unconscious wish as such. It is ascribed to analyzed factors in the wish and to the specific distorting forces that act against the wish. The second criterion would be the readiness to seek out the implications of other fields of reliable knowledge as they grow and develop, rather than encapsulating the constructs of psychoanalytic theory behind their own Maginot Line. For example, Lawrence Kubie reflects on the implications of Wilder Penfield's discovery of the electrical stimulation of "recollective hallucinations" and raises the research problem whether fully repressed experiences, as envisaged in psychoanalytic theory, can be evoked electrically and relived with somatic participation.[24] Methodological cautions are, of course, always required. In the discussion, when Mortimer Ostow points out that Penfield's published protocols show no instance of naked genital or pregenital fantasy evoked, and concludes that apparently electrical stimulation does not overcome infantile repression, should he not also have raised the possibility that some part of the theory of infantile repression might be affected? [25]

9. WHAT MODEL OF EXPLANATION IS EMBODIED IN THE IDEA OF THE UNCONSCIOUS?

The two chief models often referred to are the purposive or finalistic, and the causal (physical, physiological, mechanical). Strangely enough, in accounts of Freud's theory we find appeal to both as primary. How can this be?

A carefully worked out criticism charging an undue fusing of the two models in Freudian theory is offered by R. S. Peters.[26] Peters objects to the very attempt to work out an all-inclusive theory of motivation. There are different sorts of questions, and so different sorts of theories for different purposes. Ordinary explanation of human actions is by reference to conscious wishes, logical and ordinary causal connections, and the typically human phenomenon of rule-following behavior. If I write last year's date on a check early in January, that needs a special explanation, but not if I write the correct date. Peters cites a dispute in which philosophers explained this lapse by persistence of habit, while psychoanalysts invoked our fear of growing old and losing our virility. Freud's initial contribution, Peters argues, was to show that acts can be unconsciously as well as consciously *directed;* [27] that is the extension of the purposive model to the unconscious.

But Freud superimposed on this initial contribution a general theory of a physical-causal type of explanation. He never abandoned the Hobbesian view "that psychical states were reflections of material elements subject to the laws of motion," [28] and his account of the pleasure principle and primary process embodies this model. Accordingly, the account of unconscious wishes veers away from its being an extension of ordinary conscious explanation to being an extension of the causal picture; it is implied "that if a man's doings are to be explained in terms of an unconscious wish he is behaving more like a moth veering towards a light than a helmsman steering a ship to port." [29]

Peters contrasts extremes—the intelligent learning of a skill in training at one end, and securing a result by drugs, brain surgery, or reward and punishment conditioning at the other end. He recognizes that the kinds of materials Freud deals with fall somewhere in between. He poses the possibility of some sorting out of which is which, especially in considering different interpretations of mechanisms of defense, and suggests finally that perhaps neither the rule-following purposive model nor the physical-causal model are adequate for Freud's contributions.

It does not appear that Freud's theory can dispense with either the finalistic or the causal model. Both play a large part in the development of the system. Freud's original contribution, we are often told, was to assign to the unconscious a purposive or finalistic structure. He refused to regard unconscious processes as a falling apart of the purposive because of stress.[30] Emphasis on the causal character of the unconscious has several aspects:

1. It calls attention to the general fact that the construct of the unconscious was elaborated as a causal explanation. For example, Leopold Bellak says of Freud, in a recent symposium on "The Unconscious": "He observed neurotic symptoms, dreams, and parapraxes; he bridged the apparent discontinuity between rational behavior and symptom, between dreaming and waking life, between intention and parapraxes by one systematic inference; namely, that all of these seemingly discontinuous forms of behavior were part of a continuous, causally related series of events, a part of which, however, were not represented in the subject's consciousness and therefore must be considered 'unconscious.' "[31]

2. An unavoidably causal element is introduced even in the

idea of the *conflict* of purposes, if the outcome is seen as some kind of preponderance or weight. Since the unconscious in Freud's picture gives a central place to repression, the place of such conflict is primary. Rapaport distinguishes the two sides with conceptual sharpness: "The evidence for unconscious psychological processes did not, in the beginning, necessitate the assumption of unconscious psychological forces or conflicts." [32]

3. He goes on to show how specific phenomena suggested to Freud what we may regard as a more specific aspect of the causality stress, that is, the assumption of drives as providing directed energy and the conflict of different types of drives.

Can the purpose and the causal elements in the theory of the unconscious be reconciled? One way of attempting it is found in current efforts to fashion concepts of teleological mechanisms and to legitimize purposive description as one type of description within a causal framework. But there is a further possibility in the specific context of our inquiry. If the theory of the unconscious is dealing with materials that are intermediate between the comfortably causal and the comfortably purposive, and if sorting out the clearer specimens of each in this domain leaves a great part undistributed, can it not be that we are dealing with a *transitional* domain, not merely in the sense of sharing some characteristics of each of the extremes, but in the quite literal sense of a domain in which there is the repeated birth of consciousness and in which physical and physiological causes are transmuted into purposes? Whatever the state of his specific theories, Freud at least saw this problem in its fullest range—a domain of phenomena lying between what is going on in our organisms of which we never become conscious, and what eventually appears in consciousness. A theory of forces and their interplay and development might try to tell us not only the conditions under which consciousness arises, but the selection of materials within it, and also how purposive goal-seeking patterns (or rule following, if that language be preferred) arise out of causal-physical or physiological patterns. In this sense, his materialist assumptions paid off. They left him with the firm understanding that it is consciousness as an event in nature which needs the explaining—why I am the kind of person who puts the right date on the check as well as why I am the kind who puts the wrong date—and not that we have to reduce everything else to consciousness and its modes. Further questions—for example, whether purposiveness characterizes all consciousness or only some; whether it can be used in a descriptive sense for unconscious phenomena or for some of them; whether there are different laws for the unconscious and the conscious, as Freud distinguished primary and secondary process—these all require separate and distinct answers on the basis of evidence.

What we are led to expect, then, as a consequence of the conflict of explanatory models itself, is a rich domain of quite variegated phenomena. This, in turn, gives rise to issues of continuity and qualitative difference.

10. DOES THE CONCEPT EMBRACE A SINGLE SET OF PHENOMENA OR A MULTIPLE SET, AND HAVE WE A CONTINUUM OR A GRADATION WITH QUALITATIVE CHANGES?

This is, of course, primarily a factual, not an analytic issue, but it is worth noting that there is a growing search for variety, both with respect to the unconscious and the conscious.

Freud, of course, distinguished not only preconscious and unconscious, but also the unconscious that never becomes conscious and the unconscious that was once conscious, was repressed, and can be recovered. Bellak, in the symposium referred to above, tries to work out the idea of a continuum from unawareness of vegetative and neurological processes at one end, through unconscious automatization in the learning process, forgetting, unconsciousness of expressive movement, on through gradations of what Margaret Brenman calls "the embellished reminiscence, the static pictorial image, and the quasi-dream." [33] Bellak points out that, "Often one can show the relationship between real perception, fantasy, daydream, preconscious fantasy, hypnagogue phenomena, and dream, and it is a gradual transition not a sudden change." [34] Other participants in the symposium, however, want a sharper qualitative distinction within any proposed continuum. Brenman distinguishes the quality of the unconscious in conflict-free reality mastery, such as learning to walk and in such phenomena as the circuitous aggression of the masochistic character.[35] Nevitt Sanford finds the continuum idea applicable to the relation of preconscious and conscious, in terms of degrees of accessibility, availability, necessity, and appropriateness, but thinks that "the unconscious, in the sense of that which is forcibly prevented from becoming conscious, is of a rather different order of things," [36] characterized by its being out of communication. Lawrence Kubie proposes an attractive scheme in which preconscious processing has the central place, and both becoming conscious and becoming unconscious have to be explained.[37] I suspect, however, that many of the questions we raised about the unconscious would reappear as questions about the preconscious.

A comparable questioning of the notion of the conscious is also evident today. Here too there proves to be an extended range from full consciousness of one's awareness through central awareness, peripheral and accidental awareness recapturable in memory or image production, to registration outside of awareness, as in the popularized notion of subliminal sensitivity. At the borderlines, some of the issues we considered are bound to arise again. What is the embodied model in an idea of "registration outside of awareness"? Is it simply determinate physical effect which will play some causal role in the subsequent manufacture of consciousness? Or is the registration to be regarded in some sense, as George S. Klein describes it, as "registration of meanings"? [38] Klein cites experimental evidence that words as subliminal stimuli in virtue of their meanings affected perceptual awareness.[39] Is this to be interpreted as the having of unconscious or preconscious *ideas*? Such use of a concept of registration without awareness has a present advantage in that it pinpoints descriptively an intermediate area which fuses some properties of physical-trace notions and some properties of conscious-meaning notions. It shelves temporarily the more general theoretical conflicts and concentrates on widening the range of phenomena. It may indeed be the case that the growth of data and availability of new methods of research have reopened the whole area of the conscious and the unconscious to fresh development.

This appeal to the extension of the range of phenomena would provide a fitting scientific conclusion to our refinement of the issues concerning the unconscious, were it not that one set of controversies still remains. These are the issues concerning the pragmatic and moral effects of the theory of the unconscious.

11. HAS THE STRESS ON THE UNCONSCIOUS UNDULY DIMINISHED THE HUMAN SIGNIFICANCE OF THE CONCEPT OF CONSCIOUSNESS?

There was, no doubt, a note of triumph in Freud when he asked what role was left to the phenomena of consciousness "once so all-powerful and overshadowing all else." [40] And there are still today frequent charges that psychoanalytic theory stresses the irrationality of man over his rationality, or, as Marxian theory has sometimes formulated the criticism, that man is seen as helpless against his own inner forces. In principle, whatever be the effect of some of Freud's specific hypotheses, these criticisms are not tied to a theory of the unconscious as such. The discovery of causes of irrational behavior opens the path to its reconstruction. There is, in fact, a marked parallelism between the Freudian and the Marxian treatment of consciousness. In neither is it the primary reality, but rather the reflection of processes on a lower level. Both theories regard consciousness as an evolutionary emergent, and both seek to map the relations of the qualities of what emerges to the properties of the processes out of which it emerges. Both also recognize that consciousness, once it appears, plays a definite role and can play an active role when it is fully developed and has accurate insight. The Marxian concept of freedom is not very different in type from the Freudian concept of strengthening the ego in the acquisition of insight into oneself. But, of course, there are marked specific differences in the two theories, especially in their analysis of causality of these processes.

What is the outcome of the eleven issues we have discussed? Clearly, they do not settle the correctness of any specific theory of the unconscious. They have not touched on the factual issue of the content of the unconscious, the properties of constituents in familiar pictures of the unconscious, the relation between the theory of the unconscious and the theory of instincts, and so on. I have attempted simply to disentangle the logical, linguistic, methodological, metaphysical, empirical, and pragmatic components that enter into controversy. This can be regarded as a preliminary job of clearing the ground so that there can be concentration without distraction on the specifically factual issues. But it is also an attempt to see what is involved in the theoretical interpretations that are unavoidably associated with factual research, and that guide that research. Whether you look on the psychological or the physical level, how far you go into social or cultural components in analyzing mental phenomena, is not something that can be decided on philosophical grounds alone. But philosophical analysis can help clarify the kinds of policies that enter into the theoretical formulation as it operates in research.

NOTES

1. Arthur Pap, "On the Empirical Interpretation of Psychoanalytic Concepts," in *Psychoanalysis, Scientific Method and Philosophy, A Symposium,* ed. Sidney Hook (New York: New York University Press, 1959), p. 290 (hereafter referred to as NYU Symposium).

2. Sigmund Freud, "The Unconscious" (1915), in his *Collected Papers* (London: Hogarth Press and the Institute of Psycho-Analysis, 1934), vol. 4, p. 100.

3. Ibid., p. 110.

4. Ibid., p. 111.

5. Sigmund Freud, *Inhibitions, Symptoms and Anxiety,* trans. Alix Strachey (London: Hogarth Press and the Institute of Psycho-Analysis, 1936), p. 170.

6. Jean-Paul Sartre, *Being and Nothingness,* trans. Hazel Barnes (New York: Philosophical Library, 1956), p. 49.

7. Ibid., p. 53.

8. Ibid., p. 54.

9. R.S. Peters, *The Concept of Motivation* (London: Routledge and Kegan Paul; New York: Humanities Press, 1958), pp. 49-50.

10. Herbert Fingarette, " 'Unconscious Behavior' and Allied Concepts: A New Approach to their Empirical Interpretation," *Journal of Philosophy* 47 (1950): 515.

11. Ibid., p. 517.

12. A. C. MacIntyre, *The Unconscious* (London: Routledge and Kegan Paul; New York: Humanities Press, 1958), p. 57 ff.

13. Albert Starr, "Psychoanalysis and the Fiction of the Unconscious," *Science and Society* 15 (1951): 141-42.

14. Arthur Danto, "Meaning and Theoretical Terms in Psychoanalysis," in NYU Symposium, p. 315.

15. Ernest Nagel, "Methodological Issues in Psychoanalytic Theory," in NYU Symposium, p. 306 ff.

16. Sigmund Freud, *The Interpretation of Dreams,* in *The Basic Writings of Sigmund Freud* (New York: Modern Library, 1938), pp. 541-42.

17. Sigmund Freud, *An Outline of Psychoanalysis* (New York: Norton, 1949), p. 106.

18. Freud, *Dreams,* p. 542.

19. Otto Fenichel, "Psychoanalysis and Metaphysics," in *The Collected Papers of Otto Fenichel,* 1st ser. (New York: Norton, 1953).

20. Ernest Nagel, *The Structure of Science* (New York: Harcourt, Brace & World, 1961), ch. 11. Cf. Abraham Edel, ch. 8 in this book.

21. Nagel, "Methodological Isues," p. 45.

22. Ibid., p. 47.

23. David Rapaport, *The Structure of Psychoanalytic Theory* (New York: International Universities Press, 1960), pp. 80-82.

24. Lawrence S. Kubie, "Some Implications for Psychoanalysis of Modern Concepts of the Organization of the Brain," *Psychoanalytic Quarterly* 22 (1953): 46.

25. Ibid., p. 60.

26. Peters, *Motivation,* ch. 3.

27. Ibid., p. 70.

28. Ibid., p. 65.

29. Ibid., p. 70.

30. Cf. Janet, who assumed "that the 'subconscious' was created by dissociation caused by degeneration and precipitated by trauma." (Rapaport, *Psychoanalytic Theory,* p. 24).

31. Leopold Bellak, "The Unconscious," *Annals of the New York Academy of Sciences* 76 (1959): 1066-97.

32. Rapaport, *Psychoanalytic Theory,* p. 76.

33. Margaret Brenman, in Bellak, p. 1087.

34. Bellak, p. 1096.

35. Margaret Brenman, in Bellak, p. 1084.

36. Nevitt Sanford, in Bellak, p. 1094.

37. Lawrence Kubie, in Bellak, pp. 1089-1091.

38. George S. Klein, "Consciousness in Psychoanalytic Theory: Some Implications for Current Research in Perception," *Journal of the American Psychoanalytic Association* 7 (1959): 7.

39. Ibid., p. 13.

40. Freud, *Dreams,* p. 544.

3. The Citadel and the Supermarket: Reflections on the Logic of the Urban Concept

This paper was prepared for a meeting of the University Seminar on Contents and Methods of the Social Sciences at Columbia University on May 17, 1965. It was the last in a series of studies the seminar heard that year on "Methods and Philosophy of Research in Urban Life," which included papers on such topics as "Participant Observation in the Suburbs," "New Strategies for Research," "Social Class in Metropolis," as well as the ways of studying the impact of urban renewal and communication in the suburban setting.

The paper attempts to apply the new freedom in the theory of definition (as described in the Overview of the Introduction). It is quite explicit in this experimentation as a desirable way to face a complex definitional situation in a field where so much is going on, in so many different directions, from so many different points of view. Of course, definition in the case of such a concept as the city has to be attuned to what is going on in the research inquiry. Even more importantly, the search for a definition is itself a way of finding what is really going on!

I

The first thing that strikes a philosopher touring through the literature on the city—especially if he thinks he is taking a holiday from metaphysics to reckon with concrete realities—is the pervasive yearning for a definition of the city. It is cast in different ways. For example, Martindale, in his introduction to Weber's *The*

City, complains: "One may find anything or everything in the city texts except the informing principle that creates the city itself. One is reminded of Pirandello's *Six Characters in Search of An Author.* Everything is present except the one precise essential that gives life to the whole. When all is said and done the question remains, what is the city?" [1] As he goes on, he calls for "a genuine theory of the city," [2] criticizes Davie for devoting 119 pages to housing, 182 pages to health, 170 pages to education, and 149 pages to recreation, but "what did Davie contribute to the theory of the City? Nothing." [3] Or again, another writer is little concerned with "the basic theoretical meaning of the city." [4] He quotes Louis Wirth's estimate that, "In the rich literature on the city we look in vain for a theory of urbanism presenting in systematic fashion the available knowledge concerning the city as a social entity" as against theories on special problems of the city.[5]

Mumford, in *The City in History,* starts off with "What is the city? How did it come into existence? What processes does it further; what functions does it perform; what purposes does it fulfill?" [6] But as he tells us immediately, "No single definition will apply to all its manifestations and no single description will cover all its transformations"; [7] the "it" must refer to a series of successive forms, with some nonmonistic unity, whether of family type or continuity through successions or the like, so that history not definition is the aim.

Victor Gruen, in *The Heart of Our Cities,* asks, "What is a city?," [8] engages in some significant questioning I shall look at in a moment, but shifts to, "What makes a city a city?" He settles on compactness, intensity of public life, and "a small-grained pattern in which all types of human activities are inter-mingled in close proximity." [9] But immediately after, he is off to the picture of a "sound city," thereby slipping into the normative question.

I need not multiply examples. Either the question is raised as a fundamentally important one, or else we have thrown at us a whole host of features that are said to come in a bundle, with some suggestion of causality among them.

I should not like to judge in advance how important this search for a definition really is to the advance of scientific work. But it is worth noting that the phenomenon of definitional insecurity is a familiar one. Compare Kroeber and Kluckhohn's compendious inventory of the term "culture" in their book *Culture: A Critical Review of Concepts and Definitions,*[10] or Gordon Allport's fifty definitions of "personality" in his book *Personality*.[11] I have no quarrel with such studies; I ask only greater explicitness concerning the *grounds* on which selection is finally made. We need a logical reconstruction of the enterprise of finding a definition. And this is what I should like to probe for in the case of the city concept.

But why can we not be satisfied that we know what the city is? Why not start with what the logic books call an extensional or a denotational definition that simply lists London, Paris, Berlin, etc., etc. Gruen skirmishes pleasantly with this, but quite enough to show it raises too many problems: "What is a city? Is it a place like Manhattan, Paris, Rome, or Vienna, where there is still recognizable a concentrated, teeming, dynamic expression of urbanism? Or is it a place like Los Angeles, which has been called 'seventeen suburbs in search of a city'? Is it a place like Oakland, California, of which Gertrude Stein once said when asked how she liked it there: 'There? There is no there there'?"[12] Instead Gruen offers a host of incidents, which we may term "definition by kaleidoscopic impression," or if you wish a single interpretation I should define it as, "A city is what a city-lover loves." But the central point stands—the phenomena are now too varied on the historical scene, and we have to pinpoint what is significant in the denotation we offer, and for each significant item some alleged city will be offered to be an instance without it.

What is the purpose in demanding a definition? The traditional positivist philosopher will dismiss it as a metaphysical search for an essence, especially if he finds sociologists saying that the city of Los Angeles is not a real city! The question of definition, he would say, is purely arbitrary. But in fact even Aristotle—who, by the way, is very subtle in his treatment of definition, in spite of his belief in "essential" ones, said you could have all the arbitrary definitions you wanted, if that was what you wanted. (His example is: just give a name to a collection of words, such as the "Iliad" to Homer's poem, and the poem defines the term.) But what scientific help is this, he adds? He wants a definition from which the acknowledged properties will follow. Do we have some acknowledged properties in mind? Clearly we do. Take, for example, the list Dr. Ruth Bunzel presented to us:

The general characteristics of cities are as follows: (1) large concentration of population resulting in changes in patterns of social relationships, (2) diversity of ethnic and human types, (3) diversification of roles and division of labor, (4) qualitative differences in occupational structure, (5) movement from kin-based to territorially-based units, (6) personal anonymity, (7) personal relationships based on segmental roles, (8) tolerance of different value systems, (9) proliferation of specialized types (deviants), (10) close physical contact but distant social contact. [13]

Is the term "city" to be used for any society in which all these are found? Or a great many? Is it a descriptive term with a finite number of marks so that we can check whether X is or is not a city? Or is it more like a theoretical term, which we would like to have embedded in a theory that will explain these features when they occur and may in research lead to further as yet unrecognized features? Or is it something in between?

But what guarantee is there that it will be a useful theoretical term? Maybe it is only a tag word for a miscellaneous mass of features, and it will not appear in the laws or scientific generalizations. Recall that at our first meeting, Dr. Gans reported that many of the differences between the city and the suburb reported by others were not found by him in his study. He found no need to use a city variable in his exploratory account, but rather class variables, religious variables, and so on.[14] Perhaps the desired theory of the city will itself be just a lesser "theorem" in a more systematic theory of classes or economic development, or divided into several historical types whose explanation will be integrated within military history and economic history, and so forth.

Of course, another quite different possibility is that the heart of the city concept is normative rather than theoretical-explanatory—that the values which enter into the traditional concept of "civilization" are central, and that the search for a definition of the city is a search for the main functions whose successful performance yields the desired "civilized" life, whatever its precise contents.

Our analysis thus has two forms. We take first the theoretical, then the normative, and in concluding reflections, let them jockey for primacy or work out a philosophical *modus vivendi*.

II

Let us start the theoretical inquiry with Max Weber. In *The City*, he uses a logical technique of expanding the concept from an initial starting point, justifying each step by exhibition of historical material and appealing to uses of the term. The familiar idea of the city as a large locality is found insufficient. He starts instead by defining the city economically as "a settlement the inhabitants of which live primarily off trade and commerce rather than agriculture." [15] But soon it is seen that this "does not exhaust the concept" and that we speak in such uses of trade and commercial localities rather than cities. And so he expands the concept of the city to include extra-economic factors.[16] The expansion brings in political concepts, which are traced from the fortified city dependent on a castle to the "full urban community." [17] This is a settlement displaying a relative predominance of trade-commercial relations and the following features: "1. a fortification; 2. a market; 3. a court of its own and at least partially autonomous law; 4. a related form of association; and 5. at least partial autonomy and autocephaly, thus also an administration by authorities in the election of whom the burghers participated." [18] This sounds like history, but it becomes also a basis for judgments of what I can only see as incomplete fulfillment of citizenhood—for example, that Asiatic and Oriental settlements of an urban economic character lacked some of these properties,[19] that sixteenth century Constantinople had no city representation, that in the ancient world the citizen was a citizen only as a member of a clan, rather than as an individual participant on a local basis,[20] and so on. What seems to emerge then is a kind of ideal type of an urban community mapped along a few dimensions. Interesting as its historical insights are, I find it difficult to see the grounds on which this particular outcome is selected. If it is historical, then why not let history go on? If it is selective, why not select further dimensions? For example, Aristotle long before insisted that a *polis* had to have a moral dimension, that people had to be organized for a common good, not on a purely contractual-associational basis of individual agreement; the latter is merely an alliance which differs from alliances in which members live at a distance only by the fact that they live alone together.[21] We could map the emergence of common purposes and treat all alleged cities not manifesting these as not fully urban communities. Perhaps we've never yet had a real city! My point is simply that without an explicit formulation of the enterprise of defining, we have the liberty of multiplying dimensions or selecting among them. History is complex and usage is varied.

   How then shall we go about defining such a term as "city"? In fact, the contemporary logical theory of definition is extraordinarily liberal. The older formal definition is seen as rather stringent in its insistence on providing the necessary and sufficient conditions for application of the term to be defined. The current tendency is to see such definitions as simply a limiting case of a wider category of specification of meaning, in which the attempt is made to clarify terms in the light of the process of inquiry rather than only by the outcome of inquiry. For example, Max Black, in "Definition, Presupposition, and Assertion," in his *Problems of Analysis*, formulated what he called a "range definition," which starts with typical "clear" cases and maps variation in constitutive factors.[22] There is no bar to the attempt to formulate new modes of defining, or rather, clarifying concepts—provided they clarify.

Suppose we gave ourselves free scope to gather all the dimensions that have been suggested or that occur to us as possibly relevant to the analysis of the city concept. We could then go ahead and play with the resultant readings in much the same fashion that the results of diverse intelligence tests have been dealt with to produce general intelligence, correlated patterns of intelligence, primary senses of intelligence, and so on. The methodology this points to is everything from impressionistic clusters to factor analysis of masses of data. We could then be as definite or indefinite about what a city is—dependent on the outcome—as we are about what intelligence is. Consider a more simplified metaphor to illustrate this type of methodology. Let us think of a wheel on which the spokes represent the dimensions; a line like the hub which marks a reading on each dimension and connects them represents the city concept. In some of the dimensions, the city-mark is associated with a middle reading—for example, population size, since there is a too great as well as a too small. On other dimensions, the city concept is associated with an extreme reading—for example, occupational variety as against occupational uniformity. Now the utility of the definition depends on the kind of hub-line we get. If it is neat and disc-like, then we have a systematic, relatively clear concept. If it is jagged with some points pushing way out, it does not look very helpful. Of course, we can trim it by removing some of the disturbing dimensions—if we do not have to remove too many—or else by pulling back some of the jagged points and accepting the consequences (e.g., denying the title of "city" to Los Angeles). As we shall see, the degree of hub-line consolidation determines the scientific utility of the concept. For it embodies the question of the empirical relation between readings on the different dimensions. We can consider this best after looking at some of the various dimensions.

First, however, there is the question of pinpointing the material to be examined. In the older Aristotelian language, one would have asked what the primary substances are whose properties constitute the dimensions. Nowadays, one is more likely to ask what kind of subject is permitted by the formation-rules for the predicate "is urban," or what kind of nouns for the modifier "urban." Are we dealing with spatial regions or groups of people? Thucydides answered our question in principle when he had the defeated general, Nicias, cheer up the Athenians as they were retreating from Syracuse: the city consists not of land or walls, but of the people. In fact, they ended up as prisoners in the quarries in a concentration camp where most died, so that it showed a high population density insufficient to constitute a city. But let us not dwell on the obvious—our story is about people and what they do. A ghost town is a place where a town was, not a kind of town. Speculation on linguistic usage can be of considerable help in finding more and more spokes. For example, we find "urban" used in the phrase "urban life" as well as in "urban society," "urban problems," and so on, so we can begin to line up different adjectives modifying "life"—"castle life," "camp life," "garrison life." Such contrast suggests a dimension of part-whole in which terms like "urban life" and "rural life" characterize whole modes rather than partial modes. In any case, we might decide to have "urban" modify "society." We would then translate such terms as "urban group" into a group from an urban society; "urban culture" into the kind of culture that an urban society has. Some writers are inclined to reverse this—fasten first on urban culture as initial meaning and define society as a high density agglomeration having an urban culture. But if we keep an eye on historical development, or on causal relations as usually analyzed, this seems to be putting the cart before the horse. In any case, we should not preclude a priori a nonurban society having the kind of culture that an urban society has, though lacking some of other conditions of an urban society. The further question whether a nonurban society with an urban culture always has to have derived it from an urban society is a historical-causal one. We shall note a suggested case later.

Our spoke-wheel methodology of definition rests on providing ample dimensions to work with. Here there seems no lack, if we simply take all comers from the literature. Start with size. There is obviously a too-small-to-be-a-city size, perhaps a too-large, and an in-between. One feels tempted to quote what Jane Jacobs says about proper densities for city dwellings—that it is like the answer Lincoln gave to the question, "How long should a man's legs be?" Long enough to reach the ground, he said.[23] But this concerns the normative question, not the definitional one. Still, Aristotle objected to reckoning Babylon as a city on the ground of its size. Depending on what other factors shall we say, "This is not one city, but a batch of cities with no sharp lines"? Kingsley Davis points out that the demographic distinction between rural and urban must take account not only of density, but of absolute population and absolute area.[24] But one wonders whether a purely demographic distinction will suffice? Here it is only one dimension.

Take the economic range next: at one end is agriculture, in between are the historical forms of commerce and manufacture, at the far end are the projected national economies largely automated. Is a Brasilia, full of national management offices for the latter, a city? Move to the political dimension along Weber's lines. At one extreme is complete external control; at the other extreme is complete autonomy. Letting go such questions as whether Washington is a city on this ground, or whether a conquered city ceases to be a city, there is some sense in which the middle range falls into our hub—a completely autonomous unit is a state, not just a city. But what of the fragmentation of controls on different matters, for example, in New York, with state control of education, federal control of numerous functions, independent authority of some, and so on?

Social structural bases of distinction provide another dimension. Are the units entering into the city organization families or clans or individuals? We can arrange our gamut from clan to individual along a radial spoke from circumference to center. Of course, Rome, the ancestral city, is moved out from the hub on this dimension. Other social organizational dimensions can no doubt be developed. For example, there are regional ones from home, to neighborhood, section of a city, whole city, country, and so on, except that we must find some other word for "city" in this description!

Then there are the qualitative dimensions that can be suggested by the concept of community. When we ask of a given population in one place whether they constitute a community, it may be that we ask about their modes of interaction. You will recall that Dr.

Bennett raised the question of Dr. Gans's account whether he had some implicit concept of community in mind.[25] Would the answer, she asked, be some criterion of a descriptive sort, for example, a certain degree of mutual pressure on a residential street to mow the lawn? Or was it a normative concept—some goals of the good life? To work out a dimension of community is not easy, but there are various sources. For example, there are the older sociological treatments of the crowd versus the structured group. Or there are Redfield's probing analyses of the small community or the quality of life in the folk-society; for example, his criteria of the small community as having distinctiveness (apparent where it begins and ends), being small, homogeneous and slow-changing, and self-sufficient in providing for all or most of the activities and needs of its people.[26] And there are ample studies of the isolated individual in the large metropolis. The only question here might be on the reading to be placed in our hub. Is community in some degree or lack of it to be the mark attached to the city?

Sometimes the community criterion suggests instead a moral dimension. Redfield's distinction of the moral order and the technical order suggests this.[27] In this case, the contractual relation as the basis of morality, with its emphasis on the individual's will-act, becomes the pertinent feature in the city—quite contrary to the Aristotelian notion mentioned above. In our present methodology, of course, such decisions are not arbitrary. We are analyzing the actual incidence of traits in masses of alleged cities.

We need not elaborate further dimensions by way of illustration. Most lists of what characterizes the city will furnish additional starting points. For example, Dr. Bunzel's list adds at least another half-dozen, some dealing with degrees of differentiation in composition or role, some with attitudes, some with the psychological quality of interpersonal relations.

What kind of research would such mapping encourage? I have already mentioned statistical search for correlatives and clusters. For example, does anonymity always go with size or only with size plus special kinds of opportunities of moving about—that is, a freedom of motion? Does a sense of alienation go with an emphasis on individual versus community, or only in conjunction with a certain set of goals such as success goals? Is a "Protestant Ethic" distinctively urban? There might also be more conscious search for deviant cases. For example, Ruben E. Reina presents an instance of "The Urban World View of a Tropical Forest Community in the Absence of a City, Peten, Guatemala." The attitudes relied on for the study are individualization, emotional atomization, secularization, blasé attitudes, rationalism, cosmopolitanism, differentiation, and self-criticism,[28] and the writer shows the urban self-image to be consciously maintained in dominant groups of the society. Such a study, from our present point of inquiry, might furnish ground for distinguishing the concepts of urban culture and urban society. On the other hand, they might lead instead—if all such cases were in fact cases of the *influence* of a fully urban society on the nonurban environment— to sharpening the concept of city domination or city influence, rather than creating an independent concept of urban culture. A third type of research would be for specific profiles—the clustering of characteristics along different dimensions. These would probably suggest, or else emerge from, correlations or causal hypotheses—for example, the importance of different stages in the development of the economy for different profiles of the city.

We have moved far from the initial spoke-wheel definition. The further we go, the more we may be led to doubt whether a definition will in fact be the outcome, rather than a more or less systematic theory of man's development. In the first place, we may not get clear enough dimensions, or they may be too miscellaneous, or the results may be too complex, or the outcome may simply be to reveal a greater confusion than we even now think there is. But of course the answer to "there may be" is that there may *not* be, and such questions cannot be prejudged. I offer only the suspicion that progress in such inquiries will involve a selective element guided by some explanatory model. So perhaps we ought to look at these models explicitly, as varieties of approaches.

III

The models I have in mind chiefly involve ways of asking initial questions. Philosophers have become more and more conscious of the importance of initial questions in determining the path that inquiry will take. Even so general a remark as is sometimes made these days—don't ask what it is, ask what is going on—illustrates this point. Instead of looking for forms or essences or types, one looks to processes going on; it suggests an empiricist rather than an a priorist inclination. But perhaps this example is deceptive— there can be just as much eternalization or formalization of process as there can be of substance!

One way of looking at the city is from the point of view of the individual. It is assumed he has certain needs, and the city is one kind of way in which those needs are satisfied. The dimensions one looks for on such a perspective are partly need dimensions—greater dependability of food supply, kind of shelter, and so on, and partly phenomenological—sense of individuality, privacy, and so on. I am not sure that I am on a fruitful track here, but it does seem to me that setting the stage with the individual as central focus makes considerable difference in the kind of inquiry and so the type of definition or theory.

A second model is more group-oriented. It sees a society going on, maintaining a certain form of life. This is the structural-functional model. Its definitory concepts are in terms of the social functions served, the basic requirements of need satisfaction and social coherence required for the ongoing society. The concept of the city that such an approach would encourage is a social-structural one or social-organizational one, with physical-ecological background and psychological-cultural consequences or concomitants. It is thus not surprising to see the sociologists choosing economic-political-social group organizational dimensions, in the Weber style. Most of our consideration of dimensions and correlations above could fit quite readily in this framework.

A third type of approach gives a greater centrality to historical sweep. I mentioned Mumford's rejection of a single definition for the city at the outset.[29] His mode of approach—apart from any specific theory about history—can serve as an illustration of the historical model. The actors here are not men as having definite social needs to be serviced along the lines of definite functions, although they have such needs, to be sure. They are rather masses of men trying to survive under particular historical conditions, taking specific historical shape, and issuing in varied historical form. Every question one might ask about the city, every trait or feature one might fasten on to characterize the city, turns into a historical inquiry. One is struck by the penetration of the historicity—even where the history is speculative. For example, at the outset on the question of origins, Mumford says: "We beg the whole question of the nature of the city if we look only for permanent structures huddled together behind a wall." [30] Human life swings between movement and settlement—first there had to be settling down. What conditions made settlement possible? What forms did it take? What functions did it serve? And Mumford points both to "practical needs that drew family groups and tribes together seasonally in a common habitat, a series of camp sites, even in a collecting or a hunting economy," [31] and the early point of burial places for the dead.[32] The actual rise of cities is seen as the bringing together within a limited area of many functions hitherto scattered and unorganized—shrine, spring, village, market, stronghold, and so on.[33] The citadel is explored in the relations of chief versus the villagers, not only the villagers versus outside enemies.[34] For that matter, Aristotle had already pointed out in his *Politics* that heights were convenient sites for oligarchies, plains for democracies.[35]

Central to the historical model is the conception of the remaking of man that goes on in history. Cities remake the kind of person, and the consequences of one period becomes the starting point of the next. Hence there is an inclination in the historical model to reject a general account or definition, to stress the complex and local-historical over the generic, to come back always to the concrete and dynamic goings-on in a total situation. Of course, to stress the concrete and dynamic in a total situation is a necessary but not sufficient condition for the historical model. Nevertheless, it is in itself a definite methodological virtue. Take, for example, Jane Jacobs's approach in *The Death and Life of Great American Cities*. Its aim is normative—it is passing judgment on what cities should be like. But when it is describing the city, it has an eye on actual goings-on. The ballet of Hudson Street [36] tells who does what, how, when, where on the given setting; the analysis of its economic grounding [37] is equally specific. Somehow, this dynamic concreteness yields a perspective which is able to correct many a theoretical statement. The historical model stretches this through time and recognizes change.

A fourth model is a variant of the historical. The variation consists in having a more or less determinate theory of history. This type of model will have no objection to a theoretical account of the city, but it will be not the independent variable of the high sociological hopes we saw at the outset, so much as the integration of specific phenomena over a given historical period within a wider scheme of development. The city is a useful enough concept for certain historical periods, when the sharp contrast of urban and rural was of major significance. But other distinctions may be more relevant today, or fairly soon. In a cyclical historical scheme like Spengler's,[38] the city has a recurrent historical role and a distinctive structure and character as the metropolitan desiccation of life in the given culture. In the Marxian, it is the expression of economic processes at a given stage of their development. To overcome the great dichotomy of urban and rural (and so eliminate "rural idiocy," if I recall Engels's phrase aright), just as to overcome the dichotomy of brain versus brawn, is part of the task of ending class exploitation.

IV

We turn next to possible normative elements in the city concept—the second fork of our inquiry. Here we might profitably start with the frankly normative, the attempt not to define the city, but to distinguish the good city from the city as such. Then we can work back to see whether normative elements are incorporated into the usual city concept.

Take a quite early example—the section on city-planning in Aristotle's *Politics*.[39] The goals are, of course, explicitly presented, there is consideration of means in the light of given conditions, and some glance at alternative goals men have aimed at; there is also some consideration of the impact on human character. Site for the city is selected so as to be central, and the slope in terms of a theory of which winds are most healthful. Water supply is cared for, and drinking water specially separated. The use of citadels is found to depend on the constitution—as mentioned above, it is suited to oligarchies and monarchies. A level plain is suited to democracies. Shall the streets be regular or the housing arrangement irregular? This is considered in relation to military impact in case of foreign invasion; he confines regularity to some parts of the town. He defends city walls on security grounds and is careful to argue that they do not strengthen cowardice in the inhabitants. Common eating quarters, temples, market arrangements, are made to reflect the values in the already determined institutions. For example, the public square intended for leisure and recreation is kept quite separate from the market square with its buying and selling, and the public square is to be on higher ground! And so on.

The logical relation of goal, means, and possibilities has not changed in contemporary city planning. The problems are more complex, and the traps, especially with respect to scope of alternatives and likelihood of change, and controllable versus unforeseen factors, are more numerous. Weighting of economic and aesthetic factors is more sharply crucial. Shall shops be distributed throughout neighborhoods or gathered into shopping districts? Jane Jacobs argues for distribution on ground of keeping the sidewalks busy, which adds to both safety and exuberant diversity; [40] Mumford condemns the extension of commerce from marketplace to everywhere.[41] Similarly, Jacobs's arguments for small blocks, as against big blocks, is that people follow different paths and get to live in a neighborhood rather than a street. Her general goal seems to be exuberant diversity as the major contribution of sound cities. The question in specific recommendations is, of course, how far they are being made within limitations of the existent situation when the existent situation may itself be changeable. It is not surprising that there appears to be sharp division among planners about possibilities of sweeping plans, about the merits of building on what there is versus clearing the ground, about the adequacy of knowledge in reconstruction projects—the kinds of questions raised in Mr. Samuel Ratevsky's paper to us on "Urban Renewal and its Impact on People." [42] But we cannot avoid even the extreme questions, such as whether to abandon the city for centerless regions—note Victor Gruen's chapter title "Death or Transfiguration." [43]

The only observation philosophically applicable to these staggering complexities is the rather platitudinous one that judgment should be carried always as deep as possible. Prior to the question where the supermarket should be placed is the evaluation of the supermarket itself as a kind of social institution, in terms of means, goals, alternative possibilities, and so on. We are more and more compelled to make systematic judgments, not partial ones.

Fortunately, this is not my task here. We began with city planning to see the normative element explicitly. Now suppose we did extricate from city planning a clear picture of goals, that is, functions to be served by the city. How would these compare with the functions which a structural-functional approach would tend to incorporate in a definition of the city, or else a historical approach would underscore as basic at the given period? We can anticipate a convergence. For example, the sociologist has often stressed heterogeneity as one mark of urbanism. Jacobs wants exuberant diversity; Mumford criticizes More's *Utopia* in its city planning for uniformity.[44] Does this mean that the functions entering into theoretical definitions of the city themselves represent human purposes in the pursuit of the good life? Certainly the definitions do not tend to incorporate consequences of urban life that are contrary to human well-being. They do not define the city as a cockroach-intensifier or crime-breeder. But why not in terms of human historical purposes such as money making? It was once respectable to see the city as a place one went to make a fortune, but no doubt this effectively operated as a motive in human history in connection with cities.

We cannot neglect the possibility suggested earlier that the basic unity in the concept of the city is, after all, a normative one, rather than an expectation of a theoretical term in state descriptions for scientific generalization. In that case, it is possible that the confusion within the theory of the city is the confusion of human aims in the modern world, that the desperate yearning for the definition of the city is the search for meaningful living in the modern world, tied to the locus of traditional values—knowledge, culture, independence, material growth, individuality, and so on—in the notion of civilization.

If this were so, how would it affect social science research?

One possibility would be a recasting of the research into the city in a problems approach—very much along the lines Robert Lynd, in *Knowledge for What?*, proposed for social science generally.[45] The several problems of the urban world would then be the primary focus with the results of research aiming at reliable means-ends relations.

A second possibility, however, would be to maintain the theoretical outlook, but integrate the picture of men's values into a historical model. This would also remove primacy from the concept of the city. Not a theory of the city, but a systematic theory of man would be the central focus—the human population in its fullest physical, psychological, social, cultural, and historical development. The city would be part of the changing picture to be explained—and evaluated—and there would be room within it for change in the conceptualization of the city as well. Or even at certain points that the concept ceases to have application.

The logical reconstruction of the whole enterprise probably then is something like this. The liberating effect in human history of the growth of cities at an earlier period impressed man with the values involved in this "civilization." The study of the city is primarily a study of how men can advance these values. The theoretical problems in defining the city stem from incomplete causal and historical pictures. The inquiries into the concept represent attempts to develop a fuller theory of men and society, not of cities. The search for a definition of the city is thus no mere metaphysical yearning. But it will be transcended on both theoretical and practical grounds.

NOTES

1. Max Weber, *The City*, trans. and ed. Don Martindale and Gertrud Neuwirth, (New York: Free Press, 1958), p. 11.

2. Ibid., p. 16.

3. Ibid., p. 27.

4. Ibid., p. 28.

5. Ibid., p. 28.

6. Lewis Mumford, *The City in History: Its Origins, Its Transformations, and Its Prospects* (New York: Harcourt, Brace, Jovanovich, 1961), p. 3.

7. Ibid., p. 3.

8. Victor Gruen, *The Heart of Our Cities; The Urban Crisis: Diagnosis and Cure* (New York: Simon & Schuster, 1964), p. 22.

9. Ibid., p. 28.

10. Alfred L. Kroeber and Clyde Kluckhohn, *Culture: A Critical Review of Concepts and Definitions* (Cambridge, Mass.: Peabody Museum of American Archaeology and Ethnology, Harvard University, vol. 47, no. 1.).

11. Gordon Allport, *Personality: A Psychological Interpretation* (New York: Holt, 1937).

12. Gruen, p. 22.

13. These characteristics were suggested by Dr. Ruth Bunzel in a paper entitled "New Strategies for Urban Studies." It was presented in the series of studies on urban research during the academic year 1964-65 before the Columbia University Seminar on Contents and Methods in the Social Sciences.

14. Dr. Herbert J. Gans had reported this conclusion in an account entitled "Participant Observation in the Suburbs," the first in the seminar series of studies of urban research (see note 13). His report concerned a study of one of the Levittown communities, then recently completed. See his subsequently published *The Levittowners: Ways of Life and Politics in a New Suburban Community* (New York: Pantheon, 1967).

15. Weber, p. 66.

16. Ibid., p. 72.

17. Ibid., pp. 72-81.

18. Ibid., p. 81.

19. Ibid., pp. 88-89.

20. Ibid., pp. 98-99.

21. Aristotle, *Politics*, Book III, chapter 9. The exact reference is 1280b10 to the end of the chapter.

22. Max Black, *Problems of Analysis* (Ithaca, N.Y.: Cornell University Press, 1954).

23. Jane Jacobs, *The Death and Life of Great American Cities* (New York: Random House, 1961), p. 208.

24. Kingsley Davis, *Human Society* (New York: Macmillan, 1948, 1949), p. 316.

25. In the discussion of Dr. Gans's paper. See note 14.

26. Robert Redfield, *The Little Community*, and *Peasant Society and Culture* (Chicago: Phoenix Books, University of Chicago Press, 1960).

27. Robert Redfield, *The Primitive World and Its Transformations* (Ithaca, N.Y.: Cornell University Press, 1953).

28. Ruben E. Reina, "The Urban World View of a Tropical Forest Community in the Absence of a City, Peten, Guatemala," *Human Organization* 24, 1964, 265-278.

29. Mumford, *The City in History*, p. 3.

30. Mumford, p. 5.

31. Ibid., p. 9.

32. Ibid., p. 7.

33. Ibid., p. 31.

34. Ibid., p. 36, cf. p. 65.

35. Aristotle, *Politics*, Book VI, chapter 7. Cf. Book VII, chapter 11 (1330b19ff.).

36. Jacobs, pp. 50 ff.

37. Ibid., p. 153.

38. Oswald Spengler, *The Decline of the West* (New York: Knopf, 1929).

39. Aristotle, *Politics*, Book VII, chapters 11-12.

40. Jacobs, ch. 7. See her four conditions for generating exuberant diversity, pp. 150-51.

41. Mumford, p. 318.

42. Mr. Samuel Ratevsky's paper to the seminar, "Urban Renewal and Its Impact on People" studied both the evolution in public policies and the then current explorations of problems and effects in different neighborhoods in New York. It led into normative issues.

43. Gruen, *The Heart of Our Cities*, ch. 4.

44. Mumford, p. 327

45. Robert S. Lynd, *Knowledge For What?* (Princeton, N.J.: Princeton University Press, 1939).

4. Some Reflections on the Concept of Human Rights

This paper was written at the end of the 1960s for a conference on human rights. One of the striking intellectual phenomena in the philosophical milieu of the period was the resurgence of the concept of right in morals and rights in legal and social theory. Philosophers were reassessing the relation of these to the hitherto fairly dominant utilitarianisms, in which moral judgment was determined ultimately by reference to the greatest good or well-being of the greatest number. It had seemed settled that such an approach was the only intellectually tenable one, that right and rights expressed generalizations about the rules that brought the greatest good and that they could be revised as experience taught us better. Attempts to treat right and rights as primary concepts, independent of the good, were regarded as simply vehicles for individual dogmatisms, or habits of the Establishment carrying on in individual consciousness.

In the resurgence, coteries of philosophers appealed once again to their intuitions. They neglected goods and ideals to muster ordinary language uses of "right" and "rights," going back to the intuitionist moralists of an earlier Oxford era such as W.D. Ross and H.A. Prichard. John Rawls's articles, which were working toward the individualistic contractarian position he later expressed in his A Theory of Justice, attracted enormous attention. All this seemed an extraordinary exhibition of the phoenix phenomenon—dead theories springing to life from their ashes!

When one takes a functional approach in sociohistorical terms, the surprise evaporates. It was not simply an intellectual phenomenon. The UN had been busy turning out tables of human rights. The civil rights movement in the United States led off with a demand for full rights for blacks. It was followed by other liberation movements. Welfare aid was construed as a right, not as charity. Liberation movements—in turn of women, students, aged, homosexuals—were demanding or were shortly to demand a recognition of their rights, not tolerance. It was not to be justified by the general welfare. Indeed, the general (established order) welfare might be badly upset. And properly it should be, for the greatest happiness of the greatest number often rested on the backs of the remainder. Why not then a belligerent conceptual scheme of rights rather than a weary and smug utilitarianism?

Were we repeating on the intellectual scene the scenario of the late eighteenth century when the French Revolution proclaimed its version of the Rights of Man, echoed in British moral philosophy by intuitionists such as Richard Price, while the utilitarianism of an Archdeacon Paley preached contentment and resignation in the well-designed social order? The reactions of philosophers in the 1960s—for all their ostensible pursuit of clarity and truth by analytic and phenomenological methods—suggested strongly that, whereas in the 1930s natural rights theories had been the voice of the Establishment in resisting change and utilitarianism the voice of reconstruction, in the 1960s the "greatest good" was in the hands of the Establishment—it was not enough for the dispossessed and the disadvantaged. Rights betokened the hard intransigent demands of the oppressed.

It was to such a realization that I was coming slowly in working through the paper. But the way it went is interesting. Beginning in a kind of Aristotelian-analytic way—burrowing among the uses, theories, arguments—I used, wherever necessary, different modes of analysis (a bit of logical reconstruction, a touch of ordinary language analysis, an infusion of pragmatic analysis to show that theories facing each other as enemies could have the same consequences), but I gradually worked up in Part 2 to a functional-genetic analysis. Here I faced an array of whole conceptual systems. What role did and could they play? And finally the normative issue—how far is it desirable to employ a needs framework, an opportunity framework, a rights framework? A full answer would get us into the social context of the times and into a reconstructive attitude toward systems of ideas themselves.

A phenomenological mode was missing. I think this is because I felt it would just reveal our present field of consciousness rather

than point directions for conceptual reconstruction. But it might
be worth depicting the phenomenology of outraged rights with its
burning sense of injustice. Since then, we have come to realize the
importance of seeing things from the perspective of the outraged.

Human rights fall into the family of rights. It is a large family.
There are legal rights, moral rights, and many believe there are
also natural rights. There is considerable overlapping. A right that
is legal may also be a moral right, though not all are. A right that
is moral is often not legal, though some also are. A right that is
taken to be natural is, so far as I can see, invariably considered
moral as well; some of them are legal, though some are thought to
be beyond the scope of the law.

Each branch of the family of rights, moreover, is felt to have
something distinctive about it. The legal has the element of human
enactment, bringing in much that is conventional, and adding the
typical sanctions of the law. The distinctive character of the moral
has been subject to philosophical controversy in the history of
ethics, in which sometimes the good and sometimes obligation are
given central position. Natural rights, in the theory of that subject,
whenever they have faced the charge that they are merely moral
rights, have added some metaphysical conception, whether cast in
the metaphysics of deity or of original nature or of essence.

Where in this family do those rights called human belong? The
conception of human rights is a relative newcomer on the scene.
Its emergence in the eighteenth century French declaration of the
rights of man seems to involve a basic philosophical humanism, in
which man-as-such becomes the touchstone, or often reason-as-
such if reason is taken to be the essence of man. Many would no
doubt regard the concept of human rights as simply a modern
version of natural rights that sheds some of its older philosophical
entanglements. In any case, the attempt to analyze what is distinctive of human rights is not only of theoretical importance, but also
increasingly of practical social importance. For the concept is
being employed with growing frequency in the arena of claims
advanced to both morality and law. This is evident in general, and
in particular in the practice of formulating codes and bills and
declarations of human rights, most notably in the work of the
United Nations.

My reflections on the concept of human rights fall into two
parts. In the first, and larger part, I pose the problem as if we

have before us the whole pool of rights of whatsoever description, and I ask how we can pick out among them which are the human rights. The proposed answers come from traditional theoretical speculation on natural law and natural rights, and from the data on human rights from the lists and declarations of recent centuries. Once the idea of human rights is approached in this way, I shall go on in the second part to compare the conceptual framework in which it has a central place with possible alternatives, in order to see whether it is indispensable or what is gained by its employment. In both parts, there is the ulterior aim of determining the direction in which human rights theory is to be developed and advanced.

I

Suppose that, in a Benthamite passion for clarity and precision, we wanted every human right in books on law and morals and political theory printed in red ink (symbolic, no doubt, of running in the blood as distinct from mere convention) to set it off from the rest. Could we identify the set of red-ink sentences in time for the next edition of the books?

The candidates that rush forward to answer our question are of several different formal types. There are *properties* that are claimed to mark off the difference. There is a special *status* which is invoked. There is some special *job* or *office* or *role* or *function* that furnishes the key to human rights as against the rest of the rights pool.

Among the properties alleged, a few have been perennial. They are inherited from the older natural rights theory. One is greater *generality*. A second is *importance;* human rights are frequently subtitled fundamental rights. A third is seen in the claim that human rights are *essential and eternal,* not simply historical or transient. A fourth is that they are the *individual's inalienable* rights. Of the status claims, perhaps the most common is that human rights are those *grounded in reality and not existing only by convention.* The job claims may take a narrower or a wider form: we may look to the *way human rights function with respect to the rest of the pool of rights* (for example, in organizing them into a system), or we may look to *the way they function also in relation to the broader field of values,* that is, human interests, purposes, aspirations (for example, organizing and advancing their achievement).

All these candidates merit some consideration. Even when inadequacy is apparent, we may find a necessary, if not a sufficient condition for being a human right, or we may find some clue to the character of the problem or the context of the inquiry itself.

GENERALITY AND HUMAN RIGHTS

Human rights are said to be general, not particular; we are led to expect acts described in broad terms, not in the detail of circumstance. They are also generic, not specific; they characterize men as such, not a subcategory of men. And as a special case of the latter, they are global in scope, not local and cultural.

We do find some degree of universality in human rights. The particular age set for voting or marriage without parental consent or the particular rules of inheritance hardly seem to have human rights status. On the other hand, the UN Universal Declaration of Human Rights does include quite particular items, such as periodic holidays with pay (Art. 24) and security in event of disability or widowhood (Art. 25), while the general right of contract nowhere appears in general form and might have to be routed through liberty or property.

Again, human rights are primarily rights of human beings, not of specific subcategories of human beings. But we do find further declarations of the rights of women, or of children, and there seems nothing anomalous if we should get declarations of rights of the aged or the sick, or of intellectuals.

In the case of the global and the local, it would seem strange to speak of the human rights of Indian or Chinese culture or of the Roman world, except in the sense of those all-human rights they happened to recognize. There is no inconsistency, however, in the idea that some parts of the globe developed earlier the social and cultural patterns which support, for example, the individualistic orientation of human rights, while other parts of the globe developed more intensively the social and cultural patterns that support familial or other group orientations whose rights (for example, the right of the family to arrange the children's marriage) may not jibe as readily with the human rights concept. Such localism is thus only the localism of development or discovery, it does not regionalize the concept of human rights.

One way to avoid human rights being particular and characterizing specific subcategories would be to insist that all such alleged instances are really derivable from, or subsumable under, or serve as an implementation of the general human rights that pertain to any human being. Human rights would thus be expressed only in the form, "For any human being, he has the right to ..."; they would not be extended into the form, "For any human being, if he has these special properties or belongs in this special category, then he has the right to. . . ." The UN Declaration on Women's Rights seems to go in this direction in deriving consequences for women from the general fact of human dignity and from the need to remove special discriminations against women. And a provision such as that for paid maternity leave (Art. 10), concerning exclusively women, could be derived from the general right to security in event of disability, mentioned above. For that matter, the reference to widowhood in Article 25 of the general declaration could equally well have been moved to the declaration on women's rights.

Logically, it would always be possible to work out a more general right from which the subcategory right would be derivable. But it is not inconceivable that the specific right might be felt as a human right while men were unwilling to acknowledge the generic formulation as a human right. Thus a right to prenatal medical care might be accepted, whether construed as a right of the pregnant woman or of the embryo, even while a general right to medical preventive care (as against care when actually ill) might be felt as too broad. It is the old methodological point that the alleged "theorem" may be commonly accepted while the "axioms" offered to demonstrate it are debated, and alternative sets of axioms compete for acknowledgement. The theoretical proposal is worth entertaining that some rights or subcategories of humans be recognized as human rights *when the defining properties of the subcategory have a requisite significance for all men.* The chief problem would be to spell out the criteria of such significance. (This question will be touched on below in considering the possibility of groups having human rights.) This proposal need not be construed as substituting for derivability from more general human rights, but as supplementary in cases where such derivation was not readily accessible. It has its own way of broadening the area of human rights. For while the insistence on derivation might force the recognition of a generic human right broader than hitherto allowed, the criteria of significance would open the way to empirical inquiry where changing conditions brought new subcategories into the range of significance.

On the whole, then, there seems to be a strong inclination to include generality in its various forms as a necessary condition of a right being a human right. It is not a sufficient condition for at least two reasons. One is that there may be universal moral rights which are not, at least on the face of it, the kinds of things one would call human rights; for example, the moral right to help from a stranger in an emergency might not qualify as more than a strong moral claim. This reason is not decisive since, if the proposed right is important enough to concern men and be brought into the language of human rights, a hunt is at once instituted to relate it to human rights already in the arena. There is no stopping human ingenuity in these searches. The more decisive reason is thus that all ways of relating that are used to argue for generality as a characteristic mark of human rights and to urge its sufficiency themselves involve some use of a further criterion of *importance.*

HUMAN RIGHTS AS IMPORTANT RIGHTS

In what senses may it be true that the human rights are those general rights in the whole pool of rights that are more important, more basic, more fundamental, than the rest of the rights?

Two major senses are found. One refers to importance in theoretical processes of explanation and justification, the other to practical weighing in some value balance.

In the theoretical sense, we have already suggested the claim that human rights would be the general "axioms" from which all other rights would be derived as special applications under special conditions, for special classes of people engaging in special activities requiring special material and institutional arrangements. This view stems, in the history of the subject, from the attraction of the rationalist deductive model, which saw all law as a deductive system. The glamour of this model is now gone, but the analysis of "important" or "basic" in terms of some theoretical construction in which the concepts of other rights are fashioned out of the concepts involved in human rights remains a theoretically possible path. So does an expanded and refined notion of derivability of some rights from others. Such theoretical relationships are complex and would require very detailed analysis.

In the practical sense, the reference is to comparative value measurement or ordering. "More important" means simply outweighing in some balance. (It does not matter for this abstract formulation what the mode of value measurement may be.) Thus the right to express one's opinions with impunity is for most people more important than the right to smoke, though for some the right to take drugs might outweigh both of them. It may be the case that human rights are simply those general rights that are most important in this sense. But there are many contingencies in life which might make specific run-of-the-mill rights more important than many human rights—for example, the rights of birth to an aristocracy, or of trade to a plutocracy, or of importing arms to a revolutionary movement. Perhaps the presumed greater weight of human rights rests on more complex or more inherent relations.

Importance in the area of value ordering can be divided into weighing of intrinsic value and assessing instrumental value. (Such a distinction cannot always be neatly carried through, though in some fields it is quite clear.) Thus the right to communicate freely with one's fellows may have greater intrinsic value than the right to work, and the right to work greater instrumental value than the right to travel. Again, in the weighing of instrumental importance, we are looking for the extent to which the right weighed is a necessary condition or its exercise an effective way of securing or preserving either other rights in the general pool of rights or also values (aims, interests, purposes) in the broader field of values. Importance in the domain of rights seems to furnish a narrower scope for human rights than does the reference to the whole arena of life and the human good. This may be deceptive, insofar as all rights in the general pool of rights may have their place as rights because of their service to values outside the pool. In any case, the importance which elevates rights to the position of human rights may lie in their constituting structural supports for the system of the good life. The human rights to life, liberty, security of person, or access to law are all important in this sense. They make all the difference in the kind of life that is possible and, when respected in law or custom, constitute the key to multitudes of opportunities. The instrumental and structural sense of importance is clear in the usual occasions on which bills of rights have been constructed. The American and French lists were directed against tyranny. The UN declaration in 1948 emerged from the whole context of World War II, when men had faced Nazi racist brutality and genocide, when there was the breakup of colonialism, and when there was a mass upsurge throughout the globe for industrialization and material progress. The rights enunciated have their special force in the barriers they would break down and the discriminations they would remove and the opportunities they would open.

Whatever additional features go into the concept of human rights, some notion of their basic character either in the theoretical sense or in the value-ordering sense, with respect to the general pool of rights or to furnishing structural conditions for the good life, definitely seems to be required.

ARE HUMAN RIGHTS ETERNAL AND ESSENTIAL OR CHANGING AND HISTORICALLY GROUNDED?

Traditional views of natural law and natural rights, cast in a theological and metaphysical vein, had them eternal and expressive of the essence of man, rather than changing and expressive of historical conflicts in succeeding epochs of social development. Let us state first the temporal theses, using their own language of description.

Historically-minded views, taking as data the claims about human rights and precursor concepts, and the bills and codes and lists of the last few centuries, point to such facts as: (1) variations in the lists and controversy over items, and what historical study of the context of declarations finds; (2) the conflicts of interpretation about even the rights accepted; (3) the emergence in history of completely new human rights; and (4) the disappearance or replacement of older ones. Each of these is worth illustrating.

1. At each historical point in the formulation of a list of natural or human rights, some items are unquestioned, for they are central to the movement that is producing the list: property in the Lockean explication of natural rights when the revolution of 1688 is waged by the propertied middle class, the career open to talents in the French declaration when the privileges of the old order are being overthrown, marked social welfare provisions in the UN declaration issuing from the twentieth century experience of economic depression, unemployment, and mass starvation. But there are startling omissions, if we consider the matter from the contemporary perspective. For example, the UN declaration specifically includes universal suffrage (Art. 21), rules out slavery (Art. 4), and guarantees the right of association (Art. 20). There was no right to vote among the Lockean natural rights, no forbidding of slavery in the original ten amendments to the American constitution, and no

freedom of association in the French declaration of the rights of man. In none of these cases can we assume it was an oversight. The right to vote had been claimed by the Levellers almost half a century before Locke's treatise was published; their demand, which we see advanced in the Putney debates in Cromwell's army, was rejected with the argument that suffrage by the poor would be a threat to property, and votes belonged only to those who had a property interest in the kingdom. Slavery in the United States until the thirteenth amendment, after the Civil War, obviously reflected first the strength of the South and then the growing conflict of systems. The omission of freedom of association in France was also deliberate: association connoted the older guilds that had stood in the way of economic freedom, and it came later to mean trade unionism, itself first construed as a conspiracy in restraint of trade.

2. Controversy often centers about interpretation of the human right even when it is being accepted. Let us take two examples from the touchiest of rights in modern times, those about free enterprise and property. In the growing atmosphere of postwar planning toward the end of World War II, the National Resources Planning Board in a report for 1943 proposed a New Bill of Rights to go with the Four Freedoms (freedom of speech and expression, freedom to worship, freedom from want, and freedom from fear) that had been enunciated earlier. In his message to Congress in January 1944, President Roosevelt proposed an Economic Bill of Rights to supplement our traditional political bill of rights. Now compare what the Planning Board and the President said about free enterprise. The Board includes in the list: "The right to live in a system of free enterprise, free from compulsory labor, irresponsible private power, arbitrary public authority, and unregulated monopolies." The president says: "The right of every business man, large and small, to trade in an atmosphere of freedom from unfair competition and domination by monopolies at home and abroad." Again, compare the formulation on property in the UN declaration with what is said by a UNESCO committee on the theoretical bases of human rights. The UN declaration says: "Every one has the right to own property alone as well as in association with others. No one shall be arbitrarily deprived of his property" (Art. 17). The UNESCO committee says: "Every man has the right to private property in so far as it is necessary for his personal use and the use of his family; no other form of property is in itself a fundamental right." [1]

The contrasts are instructive. The Planning Board apparently broadens the concept of free enterprise so that it will mean a quality of the individual's life, directed against various types of coercion. Contrastingly, in the same period, Herbert Hoover was writing about free enterprise as the fifth and most fundamental freedom, in the sense of the freedom of business enterprise, and claiming that the war was being fought to restore it throughout the world. Roosevelt's formulation keeps the term in its restricted characterization of business, but directs it against monopolies. The UN declaration states the traditional rights to property for individuals and associations (including corporations). The UNESCO committee explicitly removes large-scale property in business activity from the protection of a fundamental right. In all such conceptual skirmishing, we see that the social conflicts of the age are finding intellectual expression.

3. The emergence of completely new human rights need not be traced laboriously in past history, though the succession of declarations readily shows them. Today, with the rapidity of change, both technical and social, we can see hosts of rights lining up in the wings, ready to step on the historical scene. The universal right to education in its general form is quite modern, and in its inclusion of higher education quite new. In fields of sex and the family, there seems to be emerging a unified right of private decision, but its form and scope is not yet clear. With respect to the natural environment, we shall soon, no doubt, have human rights to clean water and clean air. Significantly, demands in this direction are finding expression as the right of a growing generation to inherit an unspoiled physical environment from the older generation; a recent pressure demand in Cleveland for the cleaning up of Lake Erie was formulated in some such way. Inspired generalization in the area of human rights is one of the ways in which basic principles spring into being. The UNESCO committee cited above in relation to the UN declaration includes in its list "the right to share in progress." The novel significance of this general right lies in its assumption of a social claim to the results of technical, material, and cultural progress in a social system in which individual appropriation for profit of new techniques and processes has been the rule, and in which every step away from this has been seen first as private charity, then as a government dole, then as a preventive necessity to avoid revolution. The current movements for organization of the poor and the disadvantaged, where they go beyond the interwoven issues of removing

racial discrimination, have begun to work in the new conceptual framework.

4. That rights regarded as part of the natural order can disappear or be replaced is clear from the way in which the divine right of kings was overthrown and the aristocratic prerogatives of birth followed. But human rights also seem to undergo change. The right of revolution that Locke asserted as last resort when one can but appeal to heaven has tended to become domesticated in recent times. The democratic tradition prefers to rely on the rights of active participation for citizens, of free expression, of political asylum—all of these are to be found in the UN declaration. Perhaps civil disobedience as a right of conscience, including even the right to refuse to fight in a war which one's conscience finds immoral, will enter future lists. One of the rights that may lose its human rights status in the global upsurge of population is that of having children at will—beyond a reasonable number. A recent newspaper item speaks of "disincentives" established in one Indian state for having more than three children,[2] including higher rents in public housing, no free medical service, no maternity leave with pay, school fees, and so on. It is too early to predict whether such measures will be conceptualized as forced compromises under drastic conditions, analogous perhaps to income limits in war-time which are not felt as denying the right of property, or as clearly denying that the right to have children beyond a certain number is an unqualified human right. The latter would be comparable to the claim noted above concerning property, that property beyond personal and familial use is not a human right.

Such is the picture of human rights given by the historically-oriented interpretation. Let us now turn to the claims of an eternal and essential character for human rights, insofar as they grapple with such data. A number of countermoves to the historical approach are to be found.

1. For some changing or new human rights, the simplest claim would be that they constituted a correction. The old view was wrong, or held to on partial or biased grounds. Thus the right to share in progress is recognized when we realize that progress in all its forms rests on social contributions of a collective past, not just the immediate participants in invention or development; sole individual appropriation was always wrong. Or again, the right of universal suffrage was not properly appreciated by a self-regarding propertied class taking over power for itself. Certainly such a

move would take care of some cases, though for the partisan of a Platonic type of theory in which the human rights are eternally what they are, it might raise serious epistemological questions as to the mode of cognition which admits of such mistakes.

2. The second move is to pare down novelty in the alleged emergence of human rights by hypothesizing that a continuity with older human rights will always be found. This is like the traditional rationalistic attitude to the American constitution, which insists that it contains the justification for all apparent turns that the Supreme Court may take, including reversals. In effect, this is like the effort we saw above to diminish particularity and specificity by insisting on derivation from the universal and the generic. Certainly it would cover many cases. For example, if Article 12 of the UN declaration guarantees against arbitrary interference with a man's correspondence, we are tempted to say that this right could not have existed before the discovery of writing. Nor could the right to vote exist before there was some form of representative government, nor the right to a job before the development of free labor relations, nor the right to education before there were schools of some sort. Yet such a piling up of new techniques and new social forms is not conclusive. The search for continuities might argue, for example, that the guarantee against interference with correspondence is simply a later form of the right to privacy, and that, of course, this basic right is today increasingly important in even newer forms occasioned by the development of micro-electric auditing devices. But even preliterate societies sometimes recognize privacy by some such convention as that if a man turn his face to the wall in a crowded dwelling he is to be treated as if he were absent. And privacy itself may be interpreted as deriving from human dignity. The same might be worked out for the other examples.

Such a search for continuity is no doubt often successful. There is not much difficulty, for example, in seeing the right to travel as an extension of the right to movement, even though the social crux may lie in the distant arena of passport regulation. And it is not possible to deny antecedently that some connection may be thought out for any right, however novel, as we saw above in the relation of particular to universal. But once again, it is important to point out that in the more difficult cases the deduction of new consequences from old premises would show, if it were formalized, that the meaning of the premises was itself changed. Thus if we can derive the right to a job from the right to life, rather than a right to be fed and clothed if one cannot get a job by one's own efforts, we have construed the right to life as the right to acquire food and the rest in the dominant way in which the members of the given society acquire it; or else, if we have coupled the right to life with the idea of human dignity to get this result, we have extended the scope of dignity. It is as if in Locke's day we had deduced from his natural rights that one had the right to plant on land that was not being used (or else the right to be assigned land for this purpose). Locke would have been much surprised to have the principles of the Diggers deduced from his premises.

The degree and extent of continuity is thus a historical matter, and insistence that it will always be found or contrived is not readily disprovable. But it does look as if sometimes the novelty is not being dispensed with so much as shifted from a more obvious to a more hidden position in the construction of the system. And in any case, there is often enough change even with continuity to allow a comparison of the emergence of new rights to the appearance of a *critical point,* in the sense in which physical science uses that notion.

3. A third move is to accept novelty and regard it not as the emergence of a new human right, but rather as the new discovery of a truth hitherto unknown. This might be applied to cases in which the novel right did not contradict previously formulated human rights, but entered into a fresh domain—for example, whatever human rights might be asserted for a crowded globe or concerning organ transplants. Basically, this move consists in using the category of discovery where the historically-minded use the category of becoming or emergence. Such categorial controversy is familiar in the legal field in the old question whether the judges find or make law. If it is sharpened into an empirical question with clear enough marks for the application of each category, it becomes possible to see what parts of the law are found and what parts are made; similarly, in our present problem, how much discovery of hitherto unrecognized human relations and how much construction goes into the emergence of a human right. But it looks as if the present move is usually a metaphysical counter dictated by the antecedent presupposition of the eternal character of human rights. It thus makes no specific or practical or discernible difference in the context of our present inquiry.

4. A fourth move, directed not so much to the eternalist's position as to the claim that human rights express the essence of

man, is to give free play to claims of change and novelty, but to regard the whole process as a continuing search. The real human rights will be those that emerge at the end of the human quest, just as truth emerges as the ideal limit of the process of inquiry (somewhat in Peirce's sense). The practical effect of this view is to predict a growing consolidation of an account of basic human rights in the long-run experience and reflection of mankind. However, the same outcome can be envisaged on a historically-oriented theory, which foresees unification of the globe and the development of at least a minimal common culture and common morality.

On the whole, I suggest that whatever metaphysical interpretation be taken about the eternal and essential character of human rights, the concrete work of formulating and developing lists and of justifying them or applying them to the modern world will have to go on with careful attention to historical context, historical changes, conflicts of social position, and social movements in which different rights and different interpretations of rights constitute different ideals and aspirations. Some suggestions as to how to deal with the metaphysical aspects within the arena of moral and legal consideration of human rights will be offered below in considering the contrast of "grounded in reality" and "existing by convention."

ARE HUMAN RIGHTS INALIENABLE INDIVIDUAL RIGHTS?

In spite of their close connection, we have here two asserted properties of human rights: one that they are rights of individuals, the other that they are rights that individuals cannot alienate or surrender. I shall deal chiefly with the first, and then add a few comments on the second.

A most striking illustration of the utterly individual character of human rights is to be found in Thomas Paine's treatment of religious tolerance. Government, he tells us, has no right to legislate, even in favor of religious tolerance; it is like passing a law that God is permitted to receive the prayers of infidels. In short, the whole matter of religious belief is the individual's right and can in no way be touched by government. (Government does come in where the individual cannot execute the natural rights on his own.)

And yet in this very same book, The Rights of Man, Paine tells us how Richard Price, in his sermon that so provoked Burke as in part to precipitate his *Reflections on the Revolution in France,* claimed for the people of England the fundamental rights to choose their own governors, to cashier them for misconduct, and to frame a government for themselves. And Paine points out that these rights are not claimed by Price for any single person or description of persons, but that we have in each a right "resident in the nation." There would seem then to be no problem, even in the individualistic natural rights tradition, to thinking of a group as having human rights. (And, of course, there is less trouble when corporations are declared to be persons.) This is a stronger departure from an extreme individualism than the suggestion offered above that subcategories of human beings could have human rights in their own description. For in the illustrations there given—women, children, the sick, the aged, intellectuals—the rights were the rights of each individual, of the group in a distributive sense, not of the group in a collective sense.

In this vein, there is no need to argue in general whether human rights are the rights of the lone individual—at least from the point of view of working out the formal types of human rights. One could, instead, distinguish the rights of individuals as such, rights of individuals in virtue of unavoidable conditions, rights of special subclasses of persons in local-historical but pervasive conditions, rights of individuals in groups they form, rights of groups individuals form, and so on. Religious belief and freedom of thought and expression would fall into the first; rights of children and the aged in the second; rights of the sick in the third; rights of illegitimate children to be treated on a par with legitimate children, or of slaves to be freed, in the fourth. All such rights have been found in human rights lists. One might well argue that, given the fourth class, there is no reason to oppose the idea of human rights of first-generation freed slaves to compensation, or the special opportunities to be afforded a social class emerging from discrimination, or the human rights to special assistance of Negroes emerging from centuries of discrimination, or the human rights to special treatment of people in countries released from colonialism. (Had philosophical attention gone into these problems, many a painful decision of the present period might have been easier.) As was noted earlier, the restraining condition on the specification of such subclasses is that the mark of the subclass be of significance to all men. But it was also noted that this made the legitimacy of the subclass as a subject for human rights in its own name in part an empirical question.

As for the rights of individuals in groups that they form, this is generally recognized as a human right under the rubric of voluntary association. In the case of group rights, we have already noted the political rights of a nation with respect to its rulers; quite parallel is a right like that of every family to a decent home, included in Roosevelt's Economic Bill of Rights. The spirit of the human rights conception is too individualistic to go too far into the construction of the human rights of groups, but it can deal with some basic groups in which all individuals unavoidably or probably find a place, or more specialized groups of clear all-human importance. But note that it is not so much the group that has the human rights as the individuals cooperating together in the group. I doubt whether we would feel comfortable with the idea of the human rights of groups made out of groups—for example, the human rights of a regional federation of nations, or of the UN itself.

As to the inalienable character of individual human rights, I doubt whether it could be strictly maintained for all human rights if the coverage of the concept is extended. What a man might not part with (such as his liberty by a voluntary enslavement) and what he might part with or forego (such as an eye or a kidney, or the right to practice a profession for which he is prepared) would be a judgment of basic policy which might tax to the utmost our criteria of refinement of human rights. I doubt whether we have any general antecedent criteria which could settle it in advance of specific moral inquiries. Nevertheless, there does seem to be an inalienable core in the character of human rights, in the sense that some rights would always have to be maintained to have a self that judges and decides. In this sense, the determination of the inalienable among the human rights is at the same time the determination of the kind of individuality men are minimally to possess.

ARE HUMAN RIGHTS "GROUNDED IN REALITY" OR DO THEY "EXIST BY CONVENTION"?

We move next from attempts to identify human rights by a list of properties to characterizing them by some special status. The view that they are the rights grounded in some metaphysical status was a familiar one. The natural law was conceived to be God-given. Natural rights had the status of being somehow inherent in the nature of things or in the original makeup of things. The rights of man were taken to express, as we have seen, the rational essence of the human being. The contrast of reality versus custom or convention has beset moral theory itself, from the time of the ancient sophists to the present day. These issues are too vast to be pursued here. But the question of whether and how they impinge on the working enterprise of dealing with human rights in morals and law is of central concern, and it is chiefly to this that the following comments are addressed.

1. The terms in which the metaphysical questions are asked tend themselves to be hardened or crystallized and have packed within them a great many presuppositions. Progress in answering the questions consists more often in reformulating them than in debating them in their original terms. Thus in this issue whether human rights are grounded in reality or exist by convention, it is this sharp cut between the real and the conventional which must first be investigated. How sharp a difference is it? May there not be many forms of reality and many forms of convention such that some in the one range are closer to some in the other range than either is to its own extreme kin? "To be grounded in reality" betokens some form of philosophical realism; the statement or the experience in question is taken to correspond to or to mirror or represent some reality. But there are many modes of representing. A mirror image represents by being a kind of copy; a map by isomorphism in corresponding relations; an arrow by pointing direction (if one knows enough to follow the line and not see the arrow-head as stopping one's movement and turning one back!); regular consequences, as in the case of smoke representing fire, by embodying causal knowledge; a symbol by all sorts of traditional connections. Even an "instrumental" relation, often opposed to a "realistic" relation, in some sense represents the reality; thus the shovel selected for a particular digging job tells an informed observer how hard the ground is expected to be.

In parallel fashion, existence only by convention is not a simple concept, but covers a whole range of varying quality, from arbitrary whim to deeply rooted development. If we regard convention as purely arbitrary and simply willed or stipulated, we may be oversimplifying the notion of will or stipulation and the extent of the controls that guide or operate in the particular contexts.

Conventions may represent habits which are stubborn enough realities; if commitments are regarded as conventions—and the language of commitment is often found in these ethical disputes—then some basic commitments have as much hard reality as rocks and are less easily smashed.

The fact is that the sharp contrast of reality and convention itself is a categorial cut representing a specific metaphysics, one which often involves a sharp separation of intellect and will. If this separation is questioned on scientific grounds, the terms of our problem about human rights and their reality become transformed and the question loses its sharpness. Apart from such presuppositions, there is no need to regard languages, cultural patterns, and other typical illustrations of the conventional as less real just because they allow of variant forms. Biological species are not less real for constituting families of variant forms.

We cannot pursue this metaphysical issue further here, but these brief considerations point to the usefulness of a pragmatic approach which looks primarily for the properties of human rights that the metaphysical contrasts aim at discovering or supporting.

2. Presumably, the practical differences sought in grounding human rights in reality are dependability, security or strong support, a position beyond the reach of tampering, and a lack of arbitrariness. Those sought in looking through the spectacles of convention are flexibility and possibilities of human control. There is no genuine conflict between these aims. In either formulation there is room for the opposite's properties, although the properties may shift location. And above all, neither can secure what it wants by postulation; the degree of order or stability, or possibility of change or control, reflect the empirical character of human life, not the antecedent value-inclinations or the metaphysical framework.

Dependability of a human right is already presupposed by its status, for no very transient content is thus elevated. Even candidacy for human rights status means that the principle corresponds to strong human desires, needs, or interests that are not likely to shift easily. There are thus real forces at work, even where the right is given an instrumental interpretation. Dependability in human affairs does not rest on finding something to correspond to literally, as in the case of human dignity one might look for a Stoic bit of divine fire in the organism or a Cartesian soul at work in the pineal gland. Again, in the case of security or strong support, something outside of the human scene has to be summoned only if a theory of human needs, interests, and desires sees them as volatile and evanescent, or sees the human appetites through Platonic eyes as a voracious and capricious dragon. In short, beliefs in the security or insecurity of human rights themselves presuppose theories of psychology and sociology and history. It is interesting to note that in the thought of Burke it is tradition (itself a weight of custom) which provides the property of dependability; natural rights are accused, as they were by Bentham too, of being the vehicle of caprice and arbitrariness. The battle of such basic categories itself is set in particular historical problem-contexts.

The properties sought in a grounding in reality have thus a certain independence from the specific metaphysical underpinning and can be provided in different ways. For example, a theory of human rights as certified by God or Reason or Nature is clearly an attempt to put the rights beyond tampering by man or government—as in Paine's treatment of religious tolerance referred to above. But the very command, "Thou shalt not tamper" can itself be justified on other grounds, as J. S. Mill, for example, did in arguing for liberty of thought and expression as a kind of pragmatic absolute or necessary condition of long-range human welfare. (In his system, many human rights would appear in the language of principles of justice, determined by general utility.) And in a different vein, it is possible to regard thought, when freely exercised, as the creative growing point of a human being, and so give it a status of an intrinsic value, rather than merely a constant policy or a metaphysical natural right. In all these groundings, the human right has stability and dependability—in one case on a metaphysical basis, in a second on the basis of policy reckoned on the assumption of stable human purpose and stable features of human conditions, in the third on a simple value basis.

On the other hand, but in the same fashion, all these differing views need not exclude the variability and controllability that conventionalism focuses on. In human rights theory, the differences emerge in the competition of rights and their weighing, in minor premises or operative values that play a crucial role in deriving the human right and in applying it. Thus religious premises as grounding can yield an authoritarian or a democratic turn in human rights. Utilitarianism can be steered to laissez-faire or to socialism by appropriate minor premises. Human dignity can be turned in many different directions, and even the minimal sense of respect for the life of a man is not incompatible with executing him as a rebel, after no doubt saluting him!

3. This pragmatic approach that looks for the properties in rights sought through different modes of justification need not be simply side-stepping the metaphysical issues. For it may itself embody a theory of the character of these justification modes. For example, with respect to the religious justification of human rights, it may find that the aims and commands ascribed to God at any period are, in fact, the projection of established or rising human rights, so that the religious justification symbolizes the desire for dependability, security, immunity to tampering, and the rest, rather than endows these properties. (It matters little in the present context whether this is presented as a humanistic naturalization of religion or a religious theory of man's way of knowing the divine.) Similarly, the metaphysical justification may be taken to reflect a conception of the human being that is already embodied in the established or rising rights—for example, an atomic individualism—and so at most be a philosophical forum in which comparable concepts in psychology or in religion may converge with that in the social theory. At worst, the metaphysical justification may be hardening what is an experimental category in human history. But that depends on what kind of a metaphysics it is.

HUMAN RIGHTS AS OFFICES OR FUNCTIONS

The understanding of human rights in this approach is that they constitute a conceptual framework for ordering and systematizing the area of rights in general, to make them more serviceable in the achievement of human values and the good life. An explicit comparison to the justification of political theory is enlightening. We may ask how to justify democracy as against aristocracy, or how to justify one kind of democracy as against another, or going back to the beginning, how to justify having government at all. So too, human rights, in their special fundamental sense, constitute a system of offices or functions within the domain of rights. We may ask for the roles and tasks pertaining to this office, for the conditions and modes of selection among rights to be elevated to the office (as we have been doing in previous sections). But we can also ask (as we shall in Part II) why we should have this type of office system at all.

How one goes about to campaign for or against a particular

human rights candidate has already been made clear at several points above. Privacy should not be elected because it can be deduced from dignity, or its very definition involves dignity. In any case, dignity would be a more powerful office-holder with a wider spread. One candidate is not general enough, another not universal enough, a third not important enough. In all such electioneering, the criteria for selection suggest the requirements for office. If a utilitarian said, "Let's elect the right to happiness as the sole human right and we won't need any others, and can forget about human rights as a theoretical problem," it is like saying, "Let's elect such-and-such a person president, because that kind of person would boss the whole show and we wouldn't have to have elections any more."

In describing this process, it should not be forgotten that the whole domain of rights, run-of-the-mill as well as elevated human rights, itself consists of officeholders. The ultimate constituency is that of human needs, interests, purposes—in a word, values. So it is not surprising that occasionally a member of this value set may himself aspire to the high office of a human right. He is, of course, an outsider to the rights arena and so very much like the occasional individual who goes out for the Senate or the presidency without having been even district attorney or local councilman. Sometimes this is the only thing to do. The right to vote would probably not have been urged as a human right if it had had free access to the position of a pedestrian legal right. Perhaps a more far-reaching phenomenon in the history of human rights is the way in which whole segments of human needs and values were excluded for a long while; for example, the lists of human rights were long political before economic items began to compete. And of late, psychological items have come into the fray; it is not too farfetched to expect, as knowledge grows, a campaign for emotional security as a human right.

Particular human rights are thus justified by being shown to be the best candidates for the position of organizing rights in general in the service of human values. The justifications are complex, containing logical, empirical, and valuational criteria, but presupposing some conception of the job requirements of the office.

Such concern with human rights as a system of offices raises questions about the internal organization of the system, a problem that has not been sufficiently explored in the history of the subject. Yet it is as complex as the internal organization of a form of government. Why should we have a set of human rights rather than a single pervasive one? How large can the list be? Can we get along with a finite set or should we allow an infinite set? Should we introduce the conception of a human right of a given age, or should every human right have unrestricted temporal reference? Should the relations of human rights and run-of-the-mill rights be cast in the deductive model, or in some instrumental model? These questions are very much like the issues in political theory of bicameralism or unicameralism, the division of powers, or whether to have a distinction between a head-of-state and a prime minister or combine them in a president. The justification will be in terms of the effectiveness and adequacy of the job done in the rights field, and in the values in general that are thereby advanced or hindered.

It is important to note, in the light of what was said earlier, that it does not matter whether such questions are raised in the language of serviceability of construction or in the language of truth and correctness. In both cases, there will be a convergence when the reasons or defenses of the structure are elaborated. The advantage of the constructional language is that it need not feel so strongly the opposition of the different positions. It can transform them from competing theories into possibly serviceable types, categories, and models, for possible use in different types of human rights and different fields of their application. There is no reason why a system of human rights should have less complexity than a political system. Thus, for example, instead of arguing whether human rights are absolute or relative, we should analyze those positions to see them as a controversy over the degree of definiteness and scope that rights should be assigned. The political analogue again proves helpful. A political system distinguishes: constitutional rules not to be violated at all, provisions changeable with a two-thirds vote, provisions changeable with a majority vote, provisions that can be invoked by a prescribed number of people, provisions that can be invoked by any one person, and so on. Thus there could be a category of human individual rights treated as absolute—for example, that of intellectual freedom, or of access to the law. There could be different degrees of qualified rights, with different degrees of specificity of the qualifications— for example, in rights of property and contract. And so on. In all cases, the justification for having such a category would be one thing, the justification for a particular right falling into that particular category or another.

If we are to have a human-rights framework, then its internal development involves perennial philosophical labor, since new categories may emerge and be desirable, and older less-refined categories may have to be replaced. Just as the development of logic showed that there is a tremendous complexity in the notion of a "universal" or a "law," with beneficial results to the analysis of generality in the philosophy of science, so the theory of moral law and of human rights cannot remain immune to the refinement that is necessary as human knowledge advances. Such advance helps the theory of human rights by increasing its scope and possibilities. It does not of itself compel that all its constructions turn out useful.

II

In Part I, I have examined distinctive features of human rights in the family of rights, taking as data largely the lists and declarations of modern times and drawing for suggestions of the distinctive features largely on traditional theoretical analyses and speculations. Some of the features emerged as satisfactory necessary conditions; some (as in the case of the individualist emphases) as a value-orientation so characteristic of the traditional notion as to be in part constitutive of it; some, especially the jobs or functions, as the particularly identifying features of the human rights concept. On the whole, there emerged the picture of a special conceptual framework operating in the field of law and morals. We have now to ask how we would go about justifying such a framework as a whole.

Like the comparable question of political theory—why have a government at all?—this inquiry helps us to probe to alternative possibilities and underlying purposes. Government is needed where social life achieves a certain degree of complexity so that simpler forms of regulation no longer can do the jobs men need to have done in order to achieve their aims and purposes. The same answer holds comparably for a system of human rights. But it is not equally clear what are the pervasive problems of complexity and what the possible alternatives, if any, in performing the basic jobs. It is late in this paper to begin such an inquiry, but a few leading comments will indicate the scope of the question and the proposed method of treatment.

1. Inquiry into the subject of human rights has not taken seriously enough the question whether a human-rights framework is indispensable or whether the systematization of the rights field

and the advancement of human values thereby can be done by some alternative conceptual system. The existence of utilitarianism as an ethical theory should have given warning that at least some alternatives were logically possible. To dispense with the concept of human rights is not to dispense with the general concept of rights. It is to work out some other system of organization for rights and the advancement of values than the selection or fashioning of a list of all-human general, important, historically-centered, individually-oriented rights to do the marshalling or organizing of men's claims.

A number of alternatives come to mind. There could be a human-needs framework instead of a human-rights framework. It could be argued that underlying every human right is some need on the part of men, and therefore the organization of rights and values might as well be directly in terms of a scheme of generalized desirable need-satisfactions. In the second place, there might be a simple obligation framework, stating the fundamental duties of men without necessarily pinning corresponding rights on individuals at that high level. A third possibility would be a framework of opportunities. The concept of opportunity is a fairly new one that falls in between liberty and security. It might well take over in the present controversies of liberty versus security and combine the demands for economic rights to supplement political rights into a new framework that sets forth the basic opportunities that organized society should provide for human beings in the world today. Let these three frameworks suffice as illustration of alternatives to the human rights concept. It is agreed that the ultimate notion of goods or the good life is not itself sufficient to guide law and morals. Some structural relationships are needed to set basic policy in regulation, including the organization of rights.

2. The first reaction to a presentation of alternatives may be to attempt absorption of such possibilities in the human-rights framework. It might, for example, be urged that any basic human needs could be incorporated by asserting the right of their satisfaction. But such jockeying can go in both directions. The basic-needs framework urges, as mentioned above, that since every right expresses some need, the organization of rights may be carried on directly and more explicitly in terms of the needs. Again, do human rights when acknowledged create opportunities, or are they themselves the expression of historical situations in which opportunities have come to exist?

A comparison of such attempts at mutual absorption makes clear that the absorption of one framework need not remove the empirical content of the others. For example, if we take a rights framework, needs may enter into the justification of particular rights, and opportunities may be the causal ground for certain rights being realistic at certain times. If, however, we wish a responsible comparative inquiry into these and other possible frameworks, then a great deal more analytic work will have to be done first to sharpen the conception of each one, to work out its inner structure and its external relations. Once this is done, we may anticipate that the competition of frameworks may be weakened. We could treat them in turn as the pragmatic approach suggested above for theories of natural rights. We could ask what kind of jobs could best be done by each, under which conditions it could function better than its rivals, what dominant values it would impart. And it would be quite possible that some areas of human life might best be treated within one of them and other areas under another, or again that some synthesis could be accomplished to yield a comprehensive framework. For example, the human-rights framework clearly is oriented to the ideal of a responsible human individual; it has historically reflected, at times, an excessive atomic individualism, but even when this diminished in the modern world, it remained basically interested in the individual and his individuality. An opportunity framework would share this concern, though focusing more on the conditions of possible activity. A needs framework is oriented more to the conditions of need-satisfaction that are required in the modern world. Its orientation is to providing the need objects, such as food; the impact of mode of provision on individuality would enter only insofar as active participation was found to be one of the needs. But since some need-satisfaction turns out to be a necessary condition of the development of the human individual and of his functioning with some hope of success, the needs framework may suit some segment of human problems better, while the human-rights framework suits other segments. Or alternately, the human-rights framework might take care of the structure of human relations, and the needs framework might be relegated to content or to justification. We need not pursue this inquiry further here. In principle, there is no reason why lists in the modern world should not be lists of "human rights, human needs, and human opportunities," rather than simply human rights. There is some room within a declaration that furnishes a list for shifting around as to what should occupy the position of preamble, what should be found in the numbered sections, and what should go into the general statement in each section and what should take its place in the implementation. The UN declaration deserves careful study in this respect for sorting out its diverse elements. (For example, why only a general preamble? Why not a preamble for each section?) My general point here is simply that, even on this highest level of formal inquiry, there is room for genuine philosophical experimentation about categories.

3. Whatever the outcome in the reckoning of alternatives— whether judicious selection or synthesis—it is obvious that to reach a conclusion will require a more intensive analysis of the human rights framework itself. We need to know better how rights get into the list and what kind of items are kept out; also how human rights grow and, so to speak, reach maturity.

Why, for example, has so much attention gone to the rights that are included in lists and not to logically possible rights that are not even considered as candidates, nor enter themselves in the contest? Beauty is a high value that rarely gets into the act, though roadside billboards and automotive junk heaps and urban dinginess may eventually force it into the running. Also, surprisingly for a concept that has had a long legal history, freedom of contract has not been prominent in human rights lists. Perhaps that is because it is taken so much for granted under life, liberty, security of person, and so on as to need no special mention. Or perhaps it is sufficiently entrenched in modern times in the legal system and is so central to economic enterprise, that it needs no listing as a human right to promote its security. Perhaps, then, rights that get into lists of human rights are not just those that do important jobs as such, or are themselves important, but they also have to be rights about which there have been problems, tensions, struggles. It is the same as in moral codes; it has been pointed out that the Decalogue includes the injunction to honor parents, but not the equally important job of taking care of children. In short, part of the understanding of human rights includes the historical understanding of human problems and struggles and tension points. Every human right would do well to carry with it a preamble setting forth its historical context.

As to the growth and maturation of human rights, historical study often shows a surprisingly tortuous way in which they inch their path on to full recognition. In twentieth century legal struggles over workmen's compensation and unemployment insurance, in social struggles over old-age pensions and medical assistance, it almost seems as if men had first to be treated as things in order to get the rights they would have had directly if treated as men. Perhaps the most decisive theoretical arguments for making employers pay a share of the cost of workers' accidents and slack periods was that the workers were factors in the process of production, like machines and raw materials, that the employers who stood to gain from production bore the costs of the wear and tear of machines, and ought equally to bear the costs of the human wear and tear. Roscoe Pound, in his later writings, was afraid that such reasoning might indefinitely extend the burdens of social responsibility, but so far as I recall, he did not raise the question whether an enterprise that could not stand the costs or pass them on to consumers who were serviced by the enterprise should be allowed to continue. By the time that the welfare state became generally entrenched, the rights to social security and medical care and the rest became human rights in their own name. I note in a recent press item that Professor Louis B. Schwartz, of the University of Pennsylvania Law School, has proposed allocating the unemployed to the major industries. "Unemployment," he argues, "is an externalized cost of industry, just as air and water pollution are beginning to be recognized as externalized costs of mining, refining and manufacturing operations. These costs must be reimposed on the industries that give rise to them." [3] Such a theory of obligations cast in economic terms and resting upon tracing economic and social processes throughout the totality of the society is obviously working up to a theory of human rights. If the right to a job is accepted initially, then the proposed allocation has the status of a possible means to be considered in comparison with other possibilities.

4. I suspect that, in the long run, a human-rights framework will become increasingly stabilized, partly because of its structural character, and partly because of its orientation to individuality. But I also suspect that it will be integrated into a wider framework of morality in which there has been a comparable age-old controversy about the relation of the right and the good, of obligation and value. And finally, I suspect it will become increasingly clear that there is a continuous interplay between the human rights and the totality of human needs and purposes; that when the purposes are particularly overwhelming, it is the conception of the human rights that has to be reshaped, though they in turn play a part in fashioning and transforming purposes. Thus

justification will never be wholly a one-way process. Still, there will be themes in justification that will have peculiar and often poignant force, when they touch on basic aspirations of men and struggles for human dignity; for example, the utter simplicity with which in the Putney debates in Cromwell's army, the Leveller, Colonel Rainborough, argues for the universal right to vote by saying, "For really I think that the poorest he that is in England has a life to live, as the greatest he." Of such stuff is the reality for which one is looking when one seeks to ground human rights in reality.

NOTES

1. *Human Rights, Comments and Interpretations, A Symposium,* ed. UNESCO (New York: Columbia University Press, 1949), pp. 286 ff.

2. *New York Times,* September 12, 1968.

3. *The Sunday Times,* New York, February 16, 1969, p. 55.

5. The Meaning of Human Dignity

This paper was written in the late 1960s in response to a request for an expression of attitude on humanistic ethics and a case study of the humanist approach to a particular moral problem. In the first part of the paper (not here included), I argued that humanism should not regard itself as a full-scale philosophy, that it fell within the materialist-naturalist tradition. Humanist ethics seemed to me essentially "a corrective endeavor within a naturalist ethics under the specific distortions that produce a neglect of creativity and responsibility"—in short, when naturalism overdid the determinist interpretation of man and minimized individual responsibility and effort.

The grounds for choosing dignity as a case study were clearly the widespread alienation of spirit and the way in which contemporary institutions seem unavoidably to run roughshod over the individual. The concept invited analysis because it has been analytically fuzzy while phenomenologically strong. The question that particularly interested me was whether it could be given a clear and distinct meaning. The use of different modes of analysis was quite self-conscious. First, there was the genetic-functional mode in initiating the inquiry. Second came the phenomenological mode in describing the basic field of experience to which the analysis is related. Third, there was a treatment in logical empiricist fashion of the way in which the concept could operate as a construct. In developing this, the analysis merged finally with a pragmatic-functional mode in considering dignity as an instrumental construct.

On the whole, this paper illustrates well, though briefly, how an inquiry may move at need from mode to mode, with no sense of changing imposing school commitments in so doing.

The concept of human dignity is increasingly invoked, especially as a protest when men are abused, herded in concentration camps, and in general treated in mass. Sometimes it is spoken of, in the context of interpersonal relations, as "respect for a person." An individual is said to "have dignity" and so to "deserve respect." Because dignity oftentimes is coupled with other concepts (e.g., freedom and dignity, justice and dignity), it is important to see what distinctive content it has, if any. Moreover, the problem of its analysis is complicated by the fact that it is often built into another concept, such as "person" or "man," so that "to be a person" immediately connotes "to have dignity," and "to treat him as a man" connotes "to treat him with respect."

Such complexities compel a methodological aside. There are various ways in which different analytic approaches would attempt to clarify the concept. At one extreme is the classical method which holds up the concept by itself and seeks a Platonic type of essence. It seems to assume that "dignity" is a quality-term and that the mind can grasp the quality by a comparison of instances. Modern philosophers inclining toward such a method are prone to look for a phenomenological quality in the situation in which one "observes" dignity. At the other extreme are the linguistic analysts who would refuse to discuss the term directly or by itself, claiming that it has meaning only in contexts of use, and even perhaps that each contextual use could be explicated separately without yielding an "essence" common to all contexts. For example, if you treat a man as having dignity in a conversation, you listen seriously to what he has to say, not just let your mind wander until you can break in; if legal officers treat a prisoner with dignity, there is no torture or bullying, no forced confessions, and so on.

I should like to try out something in between these extremes—the kind of approach well-developed in dealing with concepts in the philosophy of science, rather than metaphysics or ordinary life. It is more contextual than the first method, more systematic than the second. A term as complicated as "dignity" is more likely to be a *construct* than a simple quality-term, more likely to be a *theoretical term* than an observational one. Compare it to a term such as "intelligence." One does not think "intelligently" in the same sense as one thinks "quickly," nor does the former submit to so simple a mode of measurement as the latter. If we wish to clarify the term and do not have an articulated meaning or an explicit criterion for its application, we have first to locate phenomena in connection with which it is used, even though we may not be able as yet to trace the precise connection. Just as we point to an intelligent performance, so we can point to a respectful treatment. Now a construct can be interpreted in two ways. It is given a *realistic* interpretation if there is some distinct descriptive property with which it is identified or (more often in complex cases) if there is some discoverable structure with which it is identified. It is given an *instrumentalist* interpretation if it serves some theoretical purposes in organizing data or facilitating inferences. Thus early positivism (Ernst Mach), taking the view that concepts were instruments for organizing the flux of sensations, held that the scientific idea of an atom is a convenient fiction; for that matter the idea of a table or a chair is also a convenient fiction. Yet many who believed there were literally chairs and tables in existence did not believe there was an existing entity corresponding to "atom." Others took a realistic interpretation of "atom," especially after the discovery of Brownian movements, which were thought to be the consequence of individual particles in motion. Obviously, the economic concept of "gross national product" is an instrumental construct; it cannot be put before you in the same way as "the total amount of gold in the country" could in principle be gathered. Interesting issues arise concerning those concepts whose status is uncertain: for example, is "aging" to be taken realistically as the literal diminution of some fund of chemical energies related causally to the various phenomena that are the symptoms of aging, or is it a useful way of referring (as P. B. Medawar has argued) to the increase in the probability of dying?

One final methodological caution: instrumental does not necessarily connote fictitious, nor does it lack criteria for evaluation. There are always purposes of some sort in mind, and some constructs advance those better than others. Whatever the range of conventionalism, there thus remains a hard core of control by the actual processes going on in the world. Hence, while realistic interpretations incline one to ask for truth, instrumental interpretations quite properly allow us to ask for adequacy or fruitfulness. How ultimate the distinction may be is a further matter we need not explore here. Those who argue on metaphysical grounds that all ideas are constructions might say that the difference in the two types of interpretation is only one of degree. Some, like Reichenbach, have treated th₂ concepts of "realistic" and "instrumental," as referring to different modes of speech, between which one can decide only on grounds of convenience.

It is time to return to the concept of dignity. I propose that we treat it as an ethical construct and inquire about its interpretation along both lines suggested.

Certainly one would not expect a simple realistic interpretation. One does not find a man's dignity by locating a substantial fire within him, burning with a hard gemlike flame, as an ancient stoic might have thought, nor a soul precipitating distinctive movements in a pineal gland. Where then would a realistic component be sought?

One may look first for the phenomena of the inquiry. While some ethical concepts may start with behavioral phenomena (e.g., helping a man in distress), questions of dignity are more likely to offer a foothold in phenomenal qualities and in the discernible qualities of human feeling in interpersonal relations. A phenomenological psychology could well undertake the task of locating and analyzing the gestalt we find in those undoubted cases where we experience human dignity as present. In the case of interpersonal relations, the approach is perhaps easiest from the point of view of the "recipient" who senses whether he is being treated with respect "as a person." But it is often clear also to a third party observing the "transaction."

There is no dearth of illustration. Step into any classroom, and after a few moments' observation, you will be able to tell whether the teacher is treating the students with respect or as raw materials to be stamped or manipulated. Listen to any conversation, and you can sense whether it is a mere formality or a genuine meeting of mutually-respecting parties treating one another with dignity; even worse—for the lack of respect there is perhaps easiest to detect—it may be an aggressive pushing of verbal counters, or concurrent monologues with intersecting moments. The central theme of Martin Buber's analysis of authentic human relations may be seen as the identification of dignity, the difference between being related to you as a Thou, and being related to you as an It. It is not a simple question of sensitive differentiation of feeling: I can have all sorts of variegated responses to you, but if my focus is on my own sensations you have receded into a cause of my sensations, not a participant in a genuine meeting. Buber rightly contrasts authentic interrelation both with sensationism and with the use of the other as a means to social-institutional ends. (We have to separate in Buber the particular small-group social philosophy from the very insightful delineation of the phenomena of human dignity.)

We need scarcely go on. The reader will think immediately of all he has suffered in bureaucratic action—not through inefficiency, for the action may sometimes be fully efficient, but through feeling himself treated as an item or a case. Or perhaps even worse, he may sense the falsity of a brittle interest which itself so often becomes a counter in commercial relations. In addition, it is important to note that not all examples come from face-to-face interpersonal reactions. There is dignity and lack of it in individual action, even in physical isolation. Observe a man through a one-way screen, or catch him in an unguarded moment. You will see that there is a way of bearing pain which has dignity and a way which lacks it, and similarly with the reception of joy. So too, fear is not incompatible with dignity, though fright or panic is. A man engaged in rational decision may have dignity, though pompous ratiocination lacks it.

In general, I am suggesting that there is a large mass of phenomena to be identified for the study of human dignity. There may be mistakes in particular identification, localisms in which the standards of a particular culture or class are imposed as the criteria of dignity—as Aristotle insists that the proud man walks only with a slow step and never raises his voice or talks quickly, or traditional aristocracies could not recognize dignity unless it were dressed in the right clothes. But certainly the phenomena of human dignity and respect for man are as identifiable as the phenomena of intelligence were in the early days before the initiation of psychological study and intelligence testing. In fact, we might do well to keep in mind the history of the study of intelligence—the diversity of measures, the disputes over the unity of the quality, the correlation of results, the debates over inherent intelligence, the revision of the concept—as a paradigm for a comparable study of dignity.

So far, we have looked at the realistic interpretation of the construct in terms of the mass of phenomena denoted. But is there a structure also to be discovered, either within the phenomena or underlying them? This is the claim so often found in the conviction elevated into a metaphysics—that respect and dignity are somehow deeply rooted in the nature of man, that they betoken inherent properties of the human being as such, that no man wholly lacks the quality, at least in the sense of an ability to respond to respect, though much in the way of distortion and mishap, as well as systematic conditioning, can obstruct its view. Such hypotheses purport to be about what men "essentially" are like, not initially proposals about how they should be treated, although the logical jump is often too quickly made. How can hypotheses of such broad scope be submitted to verification?

It is well to admit at the outset that we do not presently know enough about man to settle such questions. Nor are the terms in which the hypotheses are usually posed very clear. Man's dignity is said to lie in the fact of his rational powers, or in the fact that he is able to entertain a morality, sometimes that he can bind himself by law or operate with rules, sometimes that he has the capacity for outgoing sympathy and mutuality, sometimes merely that he is a conscious being capable of self-consciousness. Some of these need trimming down; certainly rationality cannot win respect if it is just scheming cleverness, and yet the schemer has self-consciousness. Although we cannot be sure what it is that is to be verified, we do have the feeling that some lines of verification point to a hypothesis that is to be built up. For example, the minimal meaning might be that every man, while he is alive, remains a potential source of good or evil—no man is to be "written off." Evidence would lie in the remarkable cases of men who have pulled themselves up from near-despair and have shown a never-die character in their effort; an extensive field for such investigation unfortunately is the psychology of people in prisons and concentration camps. Such investigation can help describe the phenomena; it is premature to expect it to determine how widespread dignity in fact is, or to preclude the view that dignity can be not merely covered, but wholly eradicated. Like a great many other disputes about inherent powers and properties of man, the one about inherent dignity allows of several antecedent alternatives: it may be a property that always remains active, no matter what the degree of distortion; it may be a mere general potentiality which requires cultivation to mature and can be permanently shut off quite early in the development of the person; it may be wholly an outcome, where it occurs, of certain types of social relations, having no determinate base of its own in the human makeup; it may be a characteristic in one or another of these respects in some men and not in others. Whatever the convictions of an ethical theory, it is well to remember the wide range of interpretation still possible with the kind of evidence that is usually offered today.

There may, however, be attempts in one or another form to show the universality of certain types of responses in human beings that would fall within the hypothesis that man, as such, has dignity. Much of the older dispute, as in the attempt of British moral sentiment ethics of the eighteenth century to show that Hobbes' egoistic predatory conception of human nature was wrong—for example, Adam Smith's view of inherent sympathy—heads in this direction. The form of such hypotheses may be stated thus: in some form not wholly clear as yet, man calls to man and man responds to man. Consequently, there are many directions in which inquiry may go, and different emotions and feelings of the interpersonal situation which it may explore. A fascinating study of this type, dealing with the reactions of wounded war veterans to sympathy on the part of others and the forms that sympathy could take, was carried out by Professor Tamara Dembo and her coworkers in the years after World War II. Professor Dembo worked on the assumption that sympathy from the recipient's point of view would always be felt as a value, and attempted a careful phenomenological and situational delineation of the relation, as well as pointing to explanatory concepts from the psychology of personality.[1]

Another fertile field for study is the social and historical experience of mass movements, especially where human exploitation and indignity have been central. Slavery and slave revolts, peasant movements and peasant revolts, the rise of trade unionism, and passive resistance all constitute areas in which data for hypotheses about human dignity might be found by the analytic historian. In our own day, the revolts against colonialism, the prevalence of resistance and guerrilla movements in occupied countries, and the emergence of passive resistance in civil rights struggles furnish a widespread field in which understanding of human dignity becomes a very practical problem.

So far, we have treated the belief in the dignity of man purely on its descriptive side: it indicates that there exists a field of phenomena, and that the clarifications of meaning and the principles of interpretation are difficult but by no means impossible to achieve. The entire question of human dignity is so deeply enmeshed in theories of personality of individual and social psychology, in the complexities of political and social phenomena now at the center of controversies in the social sciences, and in philosophical disputes about the nature of man, that we cannot expect a definitive solution short of tremendous advances in the psychological and social sciences. But we cannot reject the search, assert the irrelevance of inquiry, or even ignore the evidence that has been gathered up to the present.

If we turn from the search for a realistic interpretation of the construct of human dignity to an instrumentalist interpretation, the nature of our inquiry is considerably altered. Dignity is now regarded as an ideal, like justice or well-being, and it is evaluated by the type of life it makes possible, the human purposes it helps achieve, and the human problems to whose solution it contributes. These purposes and problems constitute its psychological and social base; its function is the articulation of principles and the mobilization of multiple human energies and feelings, furnishing a direction for the achievement of purposes and the solution of problems, both perennial and contemporary. As an ideal, human dignity obviously is an ideal of interpersonal relations and social organization. Whether it is a distinctive ideal or merged in a contributory or ancillary way with others depends on how distinctive is its psychological and social base, whether it simply makes its contribution to solving general problems—as it clearly would to helping achieve peaceful human relations, a desideratum on numerous grounds. The ideal of dignity may acquire on its way a human devotion of high intensity, but this could be a mark of great efficacy rather than of a distinctive base.

The ideal of human dignity as a normative program requires, today especially, that it be woven into concrete areas of human life. As a dynamic ideal, it is united in a powerful way with the ideals of well-being, justice, liberty, equality, and in the efforts to remove the major discriminations and exploitations that have beset mankind. If the appeal to human dignity can play a large part in such enterprises, it earns its keep quite easily. Yet for this large-scale task, it is not important what is assigned to justice and what to dignity. For we are dealing here with the opportunities for the good life, not the detailed form of the good life. But there are increasing areas in which dignity will have to stand on its own feet, and make demands in its own name, and become a ground for decision itself—areas in which to say "It's an indignity" will mean something beyond "It's unjust" or "It deprives one of liberty." This is not a simple issue. We are so accustomed to using the concept of human dignity in the processes of justification—for example, as equivalent to individuality in the justification of lists of human rights—that it has not occurred to us that it may have a place of its own in processes of decision and among the lower-level phenomena themselves. There are many ordinary expressions that seem to embody such a recognition; for example, "You can't treat a human being that way," or "I wouldn't do it to a dog." And there are the well-known moral crises in which a man feels that he simply could not live with himself if he behaved in a certain way—for example, if he were an informer. What seem to be intuitions without justification in terms of external reasons may turn out to be instances of the ideal of dignity.

Increasing areas now raise this problem explicitly. For example, in law, rights of privacy raise questions of dignity, and so do issues of wiretapping and spying. Increased control over men makes the problem more pressing. It is suggested that in the administration of justice, men may have to choose between dignity and truth, when instead of a jury reckoning, the truth can be discovered by hypnotic or drug-induced revelations.[2] For example, in the treatment of helpless patients and the dying, the *impersonal* element has come increasingly under psychological as well as moral criticism. Florence Nightingale long ago remarked, I have heard it said, that it was a sin to whisper in the room of a dying man. Whispering is a form of shutting out, and her sensitive remark hits directly at the crux, that the psychological basis of dignity may lie in the phenomena of acceptance and rejection— simple acceptance, not qualified or conditional acceptance. Again, not only medicine, but education, now so vast an enterprise, has the problem of treating the student with dignity.

I am well aware that I have been making but probing suggestions, and the work of analysis and investigation is still to be done. Human dignity is an ethical construct. It may have some realistic interpretation, but there are serious difficulties in the complexity of the scientific inquiry. It does have suffcient indices to identify phenomena, and to adhere to something when other, better-identified aspects are stripped away. It has already a clear meaning in the normative program of removing major discriminations and exploitations. It is increasingly becoming pertinent to problems of individual as against impersonal treatment in a large-scale and highly-organized society with growing powers of controlling—and crushing—the individual. Dignity is tied to individualism, but it is not equated with it. It is tied to securing well-being, but is not equivalent with it. Its psychological base is perhaps unconditional acceptance and self-acceptance, its phenomenological quality is respect for a person. Its emotional expression is sympathy, its practical expression is care and concern. In the long run, it may turn out to be a bundle that can have its strands untied. But in its potential importance in the present state of human problems, it seems to be a clue to a vital element in human ethics, an element that may well characterize the humanist emphasis in any philosophical framework.

NOTES

1. "Adjustment to Misfortune—A Problem of Social-Psychological Re-habilitation," in Tamara Dembo, Gloria Ladieu Leviton, and Beatrice A. Wright, *Artificial Limbs*, Prosthetics Research Board, National Academy of Sciences (Washington, D.C., 1956).

2. Cf. Bernard Botein and Murray A. Gordon, *The Trial of the Future* (New York: Simon & Schuster, 1963), ch. 2.

6. The Place of Respect for Persons in Moral Philosophy

This paper was written for a conference on the concept of respect for persons at Cleveland State University in 1974. It is a natural extension of the preceding paper on dignity, since respect is generally taken to be the attitudinal correlate to dignity. Nevertheless, there is a marked contrast in the tone of the papers, only five years apart. The first tried to extricate the concept of dignity from confusion with other concepts. The second focuses on the inner complexity of respect for persons, and raises the strong possibility that it has an inner ambiguity and expresses varied phenomena and different practical aims. The paper concludes by suggesting several distinct roles the concept plays in an ethical theory and by rejecting the view that respect for persons can serve as an ultimate supreme moral principle.

The methods of analysis employed are no different from the ones used in the paper on dignity. But the changed perspective is directly related to the career of the concept in the intervening period. It is no longer a question of helping it to independence, but rather of sobering it in its rapid expansion; indeed, views were becoming more frequent on the ethical horizon which would make it the monarchical moral principle. The transition between papers well illustrates the historical character of the mind's confrontation with its own concepts.

Respect for persons is increasingly invoked in moral philosophy today, and it appears about to be cast in a major theoretical role. It is indeed a promising candidate with powerful support. It can, in the first place, always make a broad allusion to the Hebraic-Christian tradition and so swing the weight of religious aspiration behind it. In moral theory, it can hitch on to militant equalitarian sentiment and appear to be justifying the equality of human beings and the universal scope of justice. Perhaps strongest of all is the practical motivation: since today's world is one of violence, conflict, and alienation, respect for persons appeals to us as the very antithesis of brutality in human relations and meaninglessness in individual life. It is not surprising, therefore, that we are increasingly called upon to rally around respect for persons as a fundamental value, a first principle in ethics superior to and above all other moral principles, as an absolute in a flux of changing moral rules.

A few words of caution obviously are required:

1. The phenomenon of respect is too unclear to bear the weight of a full moral theory. Something is definitely there, but just what remains to be spelled out. Respect for persons may very well take different shapes, and the moral significance may lie in the shape rather than in any core phenomenon.

2. The philosophical accounts that attempt to explicate respect for persons are too diverse and yield moral and social consequences that are too different to provide a common morality. "Respect for persons" may be furnishing just a new language within which all the old battles of ethics have to be fought out over again, without advancing theory very far. This is a perennial danger in moral philosophy.

3. Explanatory theory for the phenomena is not sufficiently developed to yield a unified theoretical basis for a respect for persons ethics.

It would seem, on the contrary, that respect for persons involves a diversity of fairly independent factors that are brought together by their importance today—perhaps much like an alliance against a common enemy on different grounds and for different goals. My argument is not, however, intended to be disrespectful of respect for persons. I argue, rather, that the phenomena are too rich and too significant to be contained in the theoretical role into which they are being forced, that the package should be unwrapped rather than made into a tighter bundle. What worries me most is that present tendencies will yield a pseudo-ethical theory which serves us an intellectual pie dominated by an unexplicated principle. Like little Jack Horner we can put a finger in such a pie and pull out plums of equality, justice, democracy, rationality, and all the other goodies that we cherish.[1] The result will be a moral ideology rather than a critical moral instrument for facing contemporary vital problems.

We shall next consider, in turn, the three cautions that have been raised.

AMBIGUITIES OF "RESPECT"

The ambiguities of "respect" appear readily in ordinary discourse. "Respect for the law" may mean simply to obey it. But in other contexts, obeying the law need not entail respecting it. And respect may be directed behind the law to underlying purposes, to its place in supporting a form of human life, or to the human wills that are expressed in it.

If respect be regarded as a sentiment, it often is difficult to distinguish from other sentiments, such as admiration or love. This refers not to the ordinary vintage of these feelings but to their exalted occurrence—for example, in hero worship or in the character ideals of various cultures (admiration of the bully, the wealthy man, the modest man, the man of guileful resources, and so on). Similarly, though ordinary love of fellow mortals may not resemble respect, the love of God is often hard to distinguish from awe, and the love of honor from self-respect.

If, following some philsophical analyses of the sentiments, we do not worry about distinguishing the feeling side of the sentiment—whether it is admiration, love, or awe—and attend exclusively to the object, we are scarcely better off. At first sight, it might seem that respect is attuned to persons or to the moral law (between which Kant wavered), but in fact, we find no such limitation. In the Senate Watergate hearings, Senator Lowell Weicker at one point asked John Mitchell whether he respected the office of attorney general, and what other things he stood in awe of. Indeed, we speak so often of respect for persons these days that it becomes salutory to be reminded that we can also respect institutions, laws, offices, groups, ideals. Even Kant found himself in awe of the starry heavens above, as well as the moral law within. Clearly then, whether we are concerned with the phenomenology of the sentiment or the nature of its object, we need a full-scale scientific study of the sentiments and their operations.

Interestingly enough, Kant, who developed the distinctively moral character of respect in modern moral philosophy, laid the analytic foundations for the scientific study of sentiments in his pre-Critical period. In the collection of his earlier lectures *(Lectures on Ethics)* [2], we find careful differentiation of self-love, self-esteem, and respect, in the best analytic tradition of Joseph Butler. But in the *Critique of Practical Reason* [3] respect is turned into a rational a priori sentiment resting solely on the apprehension of the ideal object, the moral law. It is thus rescued from any natural relations to natural feelings. The moral law, in turn, reflects the universal autonomous legislation of the self for the whole community of selves. Respect thus becomes the thread which leads the person from the phenomenal to the real moral community.

If Kant moved away from the naturalistic study of the sentiment of respect, there is a just retribution in the fact that twentieth-century psychologists such as Freud and Piaget take his theory as a point of departure and naturalize it. Freud, in his *New Introductory Lectures on Psychoanalysis,* [4] sees Kant as having distinctively identified the phenomenon of conscience, but to have overexalted it. He translates conscience into the superego, formed by the internalization of parental standards in the resolution of the oedipal stage of development. The awe of the Kantian notion of respect is thus tied to the qualitatively different sense of guilt that has emerged from the earlier fear and anxiety. Later on, psychologists like Erich Fromm (in *Man for Himself)* [5] took the Freudian analysis to apply only to the authoritarian conscience, fashioned under specific cultural-familial situations, and called for the cultivation of a more humanistic, democratic conscience—that is, an altered quality for respect and an altered direction for its objects.

Piaget, in *The Moral Judgment of the Child,* [6] takes Kant's treatment of respect as his explicit point of departure and attempts to put it to experimental test. He understands Kant to be offering the moral law as the object of respect, and lines up two different hypotheses with it. One is Durkheim's view that the ultimate object of respect is the social group; the other, which he assigns to Bovet, is that the individual is the unique object of respect. Studying the unstructured situation of children playing games and their attitudes to rules and to one another, he concludes that there are two different kinds of respect. One is unilateral and directed toward rules; it arises in the relations of old and young. The other is interpersonal and arises in the relations of the peer group. Clearly, this is only a beginning in the scientific study. For example, subsequent sociology would suggest that the kind of respect arising in either case may differ according to the social structure of the group. There can, for instance, be a tyranny of the peer group as well as democratic mutual relations, and a loving relation of old and young as well as an authoritarian one. Again, one would have to study the relation between respecting others and self-respect, the quality of human association necessary to engender both, and how far and in what way each is learned.

We have here then one of the necessary areas for research in the question of respect. Its philosophical impact is seen in its analytic consequence—that there are different meanings for the apparently single term "respect"; and in its descriptive consequences—that there are more varying phenomena than we think, which can be discovered by subtle phenomenological analysis and careful observational description of the working of the sentiments. At present, one would be inclined to the hypothesis that, insofar as it is an identifiable sentiment, respect is subject to diverse object-direction under varying psychological and cultural conditions, and that, therefore, its philosophical consideration would lead to the normative question of what place is *desirable* for the sentiment in human life.

QUALIFIED VERSUS UNQUALIFIED RESPECT

If we turn, secondly, to the theses that explicate respect for persons, they can be seen on the whole to go in different directions. One calls for what we may term *qualified respect,* the other for *unqualified respect.* Perhaps an analogy from parental love which has been popular in psychological consideration of the family may prove helpful in making this distinction. The mother may say to the child, "I won't love you if you don't do this or that." The child learns that love is conditional on a certain type of performance, and his learning problem is to identify the rules of parental conferring of love. Or the mother may simply love the child, so that even in disobedience and punishment it is only the line of action that is rejected, not the child who maintains throughout the secure feeling of being loved for himself without conditions. The distinction of qualified and unqualified respect is roughly of the same type as qualified and unqualified love.

The chief theoretical problem arising in qualified respect is to determine the marks or properties that warrant respect. They may be sought in actual behavior and feeling, though caution is required in interpreting the evidence. To take a simplified example, if people say they respect wealth, we may find on interrogation that they say it is because the wealthy can do a great many things; thus the ground for respect is more likely to be the power or capacity for achievement.

Caution is also required in dealing with sophisticated explications that call for respect for persons as such, since this seems to be a move toward unqualified respect. But in many cases, this move is halted by a limiting account of what it is to be a person, which by its limiting character shows that the respect is directed to whatever demarcating quality is selected. The marks sometimes come from a metaphysical theory of the "essence" of man (e.g., his rationality) or from more recent philosophical anthropology (e.g., man as a toolmaker, as a symbolizer, as capable of deliberate decision, as one who makes himself, and so on).

In the case of qualified respect, the problem of extent or scope is quite central. If respect is directed toward the presence of a mark or quality, then where the mark is absent (a human being behaves irrationally, or is not functioning autonomously but follows blindly, and so forth), it would seem that respect is not due, or in strong cases, that there is even a place for disrespect or contempt. On the whole, respect for persons theorists are usually unwilling, even when it is qualified respect, to follow this argument to the conclusion that not only do we not respect all our fellow men (which may be be *our* shortcoming), but that not all our fellow men are *worthy* of respect. Sometimes this consequence is avoided by choosing marks that are assumed to hold for all human beings. Thus we may say we respect a man who is blatantly irrational for the rationality he was endowed with, and attribute his irrationality to distorting circumstances (psychological or cultural) with the accompanying feeling that there, but for the grace of God, go I. Or we assume that there is hidden rationality in all apparent irrationality. Some of the saving hypotheses are worthy of serious examination; some are quite trivial. But at least their very multiplication suggests that there is a strong drive toward the unqualified even in qualified respect.

Unqualified respect does not have this theoretical problem,

though it has others. From the outset, it is directed to *all* human beings, irrespective of their behavior and their actual sentiments. Perhaps the best illustrations historically are to be found in religious and metaphysical doctrines. Jesus' injunction in the Sermon on the Mount that we forgive our enemies and turn the other cheek, and nonviolence as practiced by Gandhi and in the civil rights movement in the United States during the early 1960s, postulate a universal potential for response in all human beings. This inclusiveness is reflected in the marks or properties assigned to a person as such. Every human being is taken to be a person by virtue of sheer existence. Or else, if some other mark of personhood is offered, it is insisted that there is a fundamental distinction between being a person and having some specialized property. For instance, Kant made the distinction in value terms when he differentiated between the finite worth of particular properties and the infinite worth of persons. Or there may be some tendency to see a person as the *source* of all abilities and values. Downie, in a recent work,[7] argues that to be a person is not to play one role among others; one does not assume personhood as one assumes a particular office. The reason he gives is a rather restricted one—that we do not choose whether or not to be persons. In any case, the chief theoretical problem for unqualified respect lies in the determination of what is a person, and even before that, how to decide on criteria.

Although the qualified and unqualified types of respect are species of a common genus, the kind of morality they yield would seem to be quite different, as far apart as any two fundamentally opposed ethical theories one may take in the history of ethics. Unqualified respect would apply to all mankind, and would even lead to some moral regard for all life, animal as well as human. Qualified respect would be compatible with some forms of elitism. The unqualified allows less room for struggle and competition among human beings; the qualified could make room for it, if not enjoin it. Perhaps the two types also yield differences in the role of feeling and intellect in moral decision, although the precise role would depend on the underlying conception of man and the world associated with qualified and unqualified respect.

THE ROLE OF THEORIES

Behind *all* these attempts to explicate the nature of respect for persons lie different theoretical conceptions of man and his world.

In brief, the different explications are highly theory-laden and make little sense without reference to their presupposed philosophical outlooks. The chief difficulty then is, of course, that there are many theories, on different levels—theological, psychological, sociohistorical—so that the appeal to theory leaves us in a fairly indeterminate position. But this is a familiar dilemma in moral philosophy. If the theoretical aspect is indispensable, to pay no attention to it will mean not a firmer account of respect, but simply the use of either the ancient hidden theories that have been built into linguistic usage or the traditions that have captured "common sense." If we have appropriate intellectual humility and are truth-oriented, we do the best we can with the insights available at the time and recognize the tentative character of our conclusions.

Obviously, we cannot here scan the scientific and humanistic horizon for all theory relevant to understanding respect. References to Freud and Piaget above suggested some research areas. Let me simply add a few comments about others.

1. I suspect that there is not much to lean on in any definition of "personality" for the clarification of "person." For example, if we look at Gordon Allport's classic book, *Personality*,[8] we find fifty definitions gathered and classified, and even the one he approves is a clear vehicle for values of individuality. One might as well be directly normative in one's appeal to a kind of character.

2. The kinds of properties selected as the ground for qualified respect fit readily into different psychological or sociocultural accounts of man and his development. It is not surprising that different cultures develop and transmit different social models of human distinctiveness. Different models are of practical importance in dealing with new problems generated by the growth of medical technology—for example, in arguments about the precise point at which embryos are to be regarded as persons and as such render abortion as disrespect of personal rights, or at what point a human being might cease to be a person under the disintegrating effects of accident or senility.

3. The theoretical basis for unqualified respect, as of unqualified love (with which at times it tends to be merged), is more difficult and has not taken definite shape as yet. The religious hypothesis of man made in God's image with a total destined orientation to God, as well as Gandhi's conception of love-force, would tend in the contemporary intellectual atmosphere to be given psychologi-

cal interpretations. Some, especially in biographical analyses of central figures in such movements, turn to explaining by psychological aversion reactions to violence. Others, confident that some deep stratum of human nature is here being tapped, look to the kinds of ideas of mutual aid and mutual interpersonal affiliation that first the anarchist social philosophies and then some contemporary psychological schools have made widespread. These are cast in interpersonal terms, but similar accounts are given of long-standing phenomena of devotion to causes. This used to be an acceptable form of respect phenomenon until Nazism showed how it could be conjoined with the most inhuman causes.

4. In the historical explanatory area, there is often comment on the growth of the in-group in the gradual integration of the globe. In ancient times, Christian universalism gave expression to the outcast in all societies, and Stoic universalism expressed the breakdown of the ancient city-state which left the lone individual facing the totality of the world. The eighteenth-century universalism of reason reflects the growing connections of travel and discovery, exploration and commerce, and the liberation of the individual from older traditional bonds. Nineteenth-century Marxian universalism reflects the growing integration of the globe and the growing hope of human control over environment and social organization. Twentieth-century universalism reflects the intensification of many of these strands—both the sweeping away of old bonds, the economic integration, the more powerful technology with its prospects of man remaking himself and his life, the accentuated individualism, and the reaction against its strong component of isolation and alienation.

With the diversity of theoretical directions added to the vagueness of the phenomena, it is surely premature to fashion a moral philosophy which pins all its hopes on respect for persons as an absolute foundation. It is not, however, too early to project the roles that respect for persons may have in moral philosophy in the light of the kind of researches we have indicated—keeping in mind, of course, that progress in the philosophical use of the concept of respect for persons depends on the progress of scientific research into the phenomena themselves.

ROLES PLAYED BY RESPECT FOR PERSONS

In line with the complex multiple roots outlined above, we can only conclude that, at present, the demand for a significant place for respect for persons in moral philosophy calls for a separation of meanings, functions, and roles rather than a consolidation into one foundational principle. Respect for persons is not the basis of moral philosophy, but probably a hard-won set of moral demands. It is like the victory sought in a war waged by disparate allies, for one of whom it will mean safeguarding its land, for another the acquisition of raw materials, for a third the removal of a commercial rival, for a fourth covering up internal dissensions, though for all the preservation of the nation. To treat respect for persons as the unitary underlying principle is likely to repeat the story of earlier attempts in the history of ethics to treat survival or pleasure or self-preservation or self-realization as the systematic unifying concept: the wider the concept became, the more jobs it was assigned, the less it meant.

Separating, therefore, rather than bunching the roles that respect for persons covers in moral philosophy, I find at least the following:

As presupposition about the extent of the moral community.

Every morality is some group's morality, just as every religion has its congregation. Before we ask what the morality is, we have to know what people it includes and governs. The history of mankind has shown familial moralities, kin moralities, national moralities, race moralities, class moralities. In the contemporary world, there is growing up a global morality. Visions of brotherhood of man apart, whatever supports the phenomenon of globalization supports (at least as instrumental) a morality for mankind as such. In this, everyone *counts*, though the criteria of responsible participation may be narrower. Respect for persons thus serves as one way of saying that we want a global morality today.

In formulae of justice.

Within any particular morality today, given the history of slavery and exploitation, it is not surprising that formulae of justice should demand equality of treatment. Thus there is an element of respect for persons conveyed in most contemporary formulae for justice, although it is a mistake to try to derive equalitarian formulae from the accounts of the extent of the moral community. Respect for persons thus serves as one way of demanding equality within the formulae of justice.

In the concept of human rights.

Beyond equality of treatment lies the substance of treatment—

what actually is demanded for all human beings. The growing lists of human rights constitute a remarkable ideational phenomenon (whatever their theoretical merit). They say, in effect, that to be a person (in special lists, a woman, child, practitioner in a given role) entitles one to these benefits. The call for respect for persons often serves thus as the call for substantial specific treatment.

In virtues of interpersonal relations.

Within many moralities today, there is a strong stress on affiliative as against aggressive-competitive interpersonal relations. Hence, attitudes of mutual sympathy and mutual aid loom increasingly larger. They are supported by the evils, learned in experience, of excessive aggression, of alienation and loneliness, of the isolation and dislocation of the individual under sharp social changes. Respect for persons thus serves often as the call for broader human sympathies and mutual aid.

In moral decision.

The complexity of problems, added to the dominant individualism, throws increasing weight of decision on the individual. Therefore, ideals of autonomy are promulgated. Respect for persons often serves to protect autonomy by insisting on the prima facie legitimacy of autonomous decision, whatever might be one's judgment of the content of the decision. And self-respect involves the satisfying sentiment of the agent in the fact that he is deciding.

In anticorporate reaction.

The growth of organization that overshadows the individual intensifies demands for privacy and for individualization. Similarly, the standardization of roles throw emphasis on the individual's demand for freedom in choosing among roles. Whereas in aligning itself with mutual aid, respect for persons was curbing an aggressive individualism, and in promoting autonomy, it was stabilizing a basic individualism, here it is protecting both mutual aid and autonomy by crying out where the threats are seen as structured rather than as individual.

In practical problems of the limits of personhood.

There are whole areas in which the criteria of personhood have suddenly become very urgent practical issues. As noted above, they concern abortion, euthanasia, and other problems of thanatology, such as whether to prolong life after most vital and intellectual functions are permanently gone. In these cases, respect for persons serves as a conceptual way in which values may operate to set limits in such practical decisions.

There are, no doubt, many other factors in contemporary morality that contribute to a central position for respect for persons, but perhaps these seven are sufficient to show the drift of the argument. Demands for a global morality, equality of treatment, specific substantial treatment, broadening human sympathies and mutual aid, autonomy in decision, defense against ruthless organization, and determining practical limits—these are different demands which, for the most part, do not entail one another. It follows that the moral recommendation of respect for persons as a high-order general principle is not an antecedent principle, but an attempt to unify a vast number of answers to a large variety of distinct problems, supported by multiple instrumentalities and varied human aspirations. If this is so, then the current analytic tendencies to settle at one blow the status of the respect for persons principle—both as regards the meaning of the concept and the validity of the principle—are barking up the wrong tree. What is needed is wider and more intensive research into the phenomena, the development of explanatory theory, and the consequent possibilities of more systematic evaluation.

NOTES

1. Look what happens, for example, if respect for persons is tied to the contemporary analytic effort to enshrine universalization in moral theory. It takes off from the frequent argument that to say, "I ought to do this" entails, "Anyone in this situation ought to do this." A more moderate attempt to build in universal reference argues that "ought" presupposes having reasons and, because reason operates by universals, the universal component emerges for every ought-judgment. What is this, a respect for persons theory might claim, but the recognition that respect is addressed to everyone, or else that respect is tied to rationality?

I do not believe that such attempts to settle the question of respect for persons on analytic grounds are internally successful, but I cannot argue it here. In any case, there is a gap between universal rules and respect; as Richard Peters somewhere points out, the bureaucrat acts by strict general rules, but often with contempt for the person whose case he is deciding! This need not, however, stop the respect for persons theorist:

universality and rationality may be only necessary, not sufficient, conditions for respect; if the sentiment of respect is lacking, it can be added to the behavior as a further requirement.

2. Immanuel Kant, *Lectures on Ethics,* trans. Louis Infield (London: Methuen, 1930), pp. 129-38.

3. Immanuel Kant, *Critique of Practical Reason,* trans. Lewis White Beck (Indianapolis, Ind.: Bobbs-Merrill, Liberal Arts Press Books, 1956), pp. 71-92, section on "The Incentives of Pure Practical Reason."

4. Sigmund Freud, *New Introductory Lectures on Psychoanalysis,* trans. W. J. H. Sprott (New York: Norton, 1933), ch. 3.

5. Erich Fromm, *Man for Himself* (New York: Rinehart, 1947), pp. 141-72.

6. Jean Piaget, *The Moral Judgment of the Child* (New York: Collier, 1962), ch. 4.

7. Robert S. Downie, *Roles and Values* (London: Methuen, 1971), p. 132. See also Robert S. Downie and Elizabeth Telfer, *Respect for Persons* (New York: Schocken, 1970). The latter is a comprehensive treatment of respect for persons, attempting also to construct a respect for persons ethics.

8. G. W. Allport, *Personality, A Psychological Interpretation* (New York: Holt, 1937), ch. 2.

7. Power as an Organizing Concept in Social Theory

The concept of power had a quite lustrous career in political science and political theory in a great part of our century. With wars, class struggle, revolutionary overturnings of governments, there was a rich social background for its prominence; with the growth of technical means for war and the exercise of control, it stood out in practice as well. The latent mixture of realism and bravado that is to be found in the tradition, from one wing of the ancient sophists (for example, Thrasymachus in Plato's *Republic* and Callicles in the *Gorgias*), to Machiavelli and Nietzsche, and to the twentieth century "Machiavellians," now attempted to take over the intellectual field. In book after book it was proclaimed (from the 1930s to the 1950s) that the central concept of political science is power, that political phenomena are, at bottom, power conflicts, that human motivation is the pursuit of power, that everything else—and especially morality—serves as merely a counter in the conflict.

The tough realism was attractive in a let's-see-what-is-really-going-on sort of way, especially in a world of propaganda and deception. But from the first, it seemed to me to vulgarize everything it touched. It could sound Marxist but without economics or the growth of freedom, it impoverished the psychology of motivation, it made a mockery of human aspirations in morality.

This review of Lasswell and Kaplan's *Power and Society* evaluates their attempts to give the concept ideational respectability and dominant status. I had always suspected that the basic value content of a movement is most clearly reflected in its abstract ideas. At least in this inquiry, I came to the suggestion *that the dominance of the power idea in political theory had as much of the ideological in it as the realistic—perhaps more. But most importantly, I came to see how far (in its theoretical perspective) it represented the standpoint of the manipulator of power, not that of the would-be subjects of manipulation. Power phenomena would have a quite different character viewed from the "underdog's" perspective. This realization of the general importance of standpoint in theoretical or conceptual analysis proves a useful weapon in tracking down values (especially ideological ones) in political and social theory. (It is continued below in chapter 13.)*

Power and Society [1] is the collaborative effort of a psychologically-oriented political scientist and a methodologically-oriented philosopher. It offers a framework within which the authors believe that political inquiry can best be cast. A long introduction sets forth central principles of approach. The great body of the work consists of a network of definitions and their explication, building up complex conceptions on the basis of commonly intelligible undefined terms. In addition, there are propositions scattered throughout the work constituting leading hypotheses for inquiry.

The principles of approach embody methodological lessons of contemporary social science; for example, that the generalizations of social theory are not absolute laws but refer to specified social conditions, or that power phenomena constitute a process in time and are, therefore, subject to both equilibrium and developmental analysis. The principles are not refined to show how they would themselves be certified, nor what central differences might arise within them. For example, the "principle of indetermination," emphasizing a multiplicity of factors in any given political event, does not consider the logic of judgments of "primacy" among the factors—a central issue between liberal and Marxian social theory.

The undefined terms employed are familiar concepts, such as "actor," "act," "value," "welfare values," "deference values." No difficulties arise, so far as I can see, from any ambiguities in these notions. The term "value," whose range might have caused some trouble, is used as a tag for a desired event. Nothing is begged, thereby, from an ethical point of view; when the authors define "valid interests" later on, they refer to "component expectations" which are "warranted by evidence available to inquiry" (p. 23).

The defined terms build up concepts for dealing with persons, groups, their interrelation through influence and power, the role of symbols, political practices, political functions, structures, processes. Standard topics of political inquiry—classes, ideologies, elites, authority, sovereignty, democracy—all find their appropriate niche. The logical strength of the book is to be found in its definitions, in the careful distinctions made, in the richness of classification suggested—for example, in mapping the variety of bases on which influence and power may rest. In general, great care is exercised to distinguish factual from value issues, so as to avoid the besetting sin of political inquiry—smuggling value assumptions through definition or factual assumption.

The various propositions throughout the book are intended to be, according to the introduction, not laws or hypotheses, but "*hypotheses-schema*: statements which formulate hypotheses when specific indices relate them to the conditions of a given problem" (p. xxii). The logical character of such schema is not, however, explored in detail. For example, to what extent, if the indices employed come from several domains (psychology, history, etc.) does the formulation of a schema presuppose a correlation of *results* in the different domains? Many of the propositions, when analyzed, suggest that the schema functions simply by extending or generalizing the results from one field as a model for another. It might have been better then to indicate instead the narrower empirical basis, the proposed extension, and also, if possible, the problems of underlying mechanism involved. As it stands, many of the propositions give the impression of loose laws without specification of conditions or limits.

Along these lines, for example, instead of saying, "The positions of a person or group in different value patterns tend to approximate to one another" (p. 57), I should be tempted to quote from the authors' explication: "The rich tend to be the healthy, respected, informed, and so on, and the poor to be the sickly, despised, ignorant," and add the question: How widely scattered do we find such concentrations in various historical contexts, and in how many does wealth carry the rest along with it, so that someone acquiring wealth tends to acquire more of the rest? Or again, take this very important proposition: "The amount of power tends to increase till limited by other power holders" (p. 94). This suggests a sort of inherent expansiveness in power itself. Why not an alternative: for example, that power tends to increase as long as it is insecure? The familiar quotation from Hobbes about the "restless desire of power after power" (given on p. 95) states explicitly the insecurity basis of the encroaching nature of power. Instead of setting up a schema that is worded like a law, it would be better to pose the problem of the expansive character of power-seeking in limited areas of certain cultures and raise questions of the conditions—psychological, social and historical—under which this quality arises. To take one more proposition as an example: "The rulers alter the regime whenever conformity to it is expected by them to constitute a significant deprivation" (p. 190). This simply indicates the psychological aspects of the struggle of a ruling class to maintain its benefits under attack. Would it not be better to pose the problem of the conditions under which ruling classes make political concessions, those under which they buy off segments of their attackers, and those under which they go under with a blindness and bitterness that subsequent historians often find hard to understand? Some of the propositions throughout the book may deserve the status of laws, but many are probably best translated into problems.

The more searching appraisal of the enterprise contained in this book must go to its foundations. I should like, therefore, to consider a few fundamental logical issues and conclude with a few historical ones.

One is a problem of definition, which may perhaps best be focused by example. The authors define a *class* as "a major aggregate of persons engaging in practices giving them a similar relation to the shaping and distribution (and enjoyment) of one or more specified values" (p. 62), and a *social class* as "one defined with respect to all the values important in the society" (p. 64). They add: "More confusing, however, is the use of the term class, not as a classificatory term alone, nor even as a normatively ambiguous expression, but as an over-condensed way of stating hypotheses about the social process" (p. 64). (The Marxian definition is offered as an example of this process.) Now why should they object to formulating definitions so as to embody the results of a scientific study of social processes? After all, have not physical concepts of matter and time been redefined in the history of physics to embody the results of the sciences? One reason is no doubt to avoid the presentation of empirical issues under the guise of definition. This is all to the good, but it can be achieved by recognizing that definitions in some sense "rest" on established results. A second reason is also, no doubt, the conflict of views in social theory. But here one can expect different definitions on the basis of different theories of social dynamics. The authors are then, in effect, trying to work out neutral definitions to correspond to nominal definition in mathematics and physical science. One wonders how possible this is in social theory. In the example of classes, the authors' definition would suggest that every society has classes, or at least one class. The Marxian definition allows one to speak of a classless society. May there not be real issues of fact and value and method in these differences? Even the most neutral definition orients inquiry in one way rather than another. I am tempted to suggest a radical alteration in the whole definitional procedure of the authors. The definitions should be construed not as definitions within the field of social theory, but as a kind of definition-schema embodying on a higher level a study of conflicting definitions in various social theories. It might then be stated as a set of problems to which the varying definitions are directed and distinguish empirical, valuational, and methodological issues. But this would tie the inquiry to the historical-developmental picture of political concepts and would require a major reorientation in type of inquiry.

The same outcome follows, I think, from a second logical problem. The authors say: "That we begin with the concepts of an act and a single person acting is not to be taken as minimizing the importance of groups rather than individuals in the political process. The significance of this starting point is purely logical: the group act is construed as a pattern of individual acts" (p. 3). But if this is purely logical and embodies no factual thesis or individualistic valuation, then why is this *one* construction to be preferred? The only answer I can find is a later statement: "We are interested in neither groups nor individuals as 'social atoms', but in interpersonal relations, which under specified conditions exhibit organization of varying kinds and degrees" (p. 33). But this is no longer a logical issue. Another possibility is that the authors are relying on a narrow interpretation of meaning according to which the meaning of a proposition is equated to the mode of verifying it, and clearly verification of statements about group action is in terms of the behavior of individuals. But this conception of meaning has always been opposed by materialists, and the equation has recently been abandoned by most positivists themselves. It is, therefore, quite possible to formulate the logic by which qualities of group behavior can be *verified* by observing individual behavior, but not logically *reduced* to the latter. Logically then, one might use group categories, interpersonal relation categories, or atomic individualistic categories. The issue is thus more than logical. It may be that, at bottom, the authors are here taking a stand on the view that the psychology of interpersonal relations is more fruitful for formulating political inquiry than the results of history about group relations and conflicts. If they are saying this, I think they are wrong. But, in any case, the issues are more far-reaching than indicated by treating the problem as purely a logical one.

The same mode of analysis can be extended to their fundamental belief that power is the central category for political inquiry. This is so often taken for granted today that it should be challenged directly even for the purposes of intellectual provocation. Just because conflicts of power take place in the modern world on a large scale, does it follow that fruitful unification of theory must be centered around the concept of power? The recurrence of world wars does not necessitate the theoretical structuring of the social sciences around a concept of war. Again, power may be too highly generalized a concept for theoretical purposes. To draw a broad analogy, a general theory of *skill* might be constructed covering every type of skill, from digging a ditch to brain surgery and mathematical analysis. (Incidentally, power could be regarded as a subspecies of skill.) Yet it would probably prove too broad to be fruitful. Thus a treatment of the foundations of political inquiry might profitably inquire into alternative central formulations, especially, for example, those that treat power always in more intimate relation to the goals to which it is directed. It may very well be the case that the unification of political inquiry in power theory has historically reflected the character of a culture in which control over other lives played a central role.

Such a mode of inquiry leads finally to historical reflection on power theory in political philosophy. This type of approach began its modern forms with Machiavelli teaching the arts of control to rulers and Hobbes urging obedience on the ruled (cf. p. ix, note). Its progressive cast came from its secular aspect, divorcing the state from religious formulations tied to feudal society. On the whole, it expressed the predatory and acquisitive values of the emerging society, leaving equalitarian aspirations to take various dissident religious garbs. In recent times, divorced from cohesive social aims, power theory in political inquiry, under the guise of neutral science, painted a picture of society in terms of power conflicts and framed its "laws" of the rise and flux of elites. Often, power as a goal replaced the underlying practical aims for which state power has been historically sought. Pursuit of power was sometimes turned into a psychological category, so that no human aim or value could enter political theory without being exchanged into the currency of power. Ideals and symbols were assessed as instruments of power maintenance and control from above, not in terms of the concrete aims and aspirations of the mass of the people below. In all these respects, power theory emerged clearly as upper-class ideology.

The authors are conscious of the degree to which power theory has been associated with glorification of power as a value, the disparagement of democracy, and the commitment to "power politics." They accordingly stress their own democratic commitments as explicit valuation. But in their whole discussion of structures and processes, there seems to me to be a conflict between these broader values and the framework within which they are confining them. For example, they recognize the role of modes of production and exchange in the power process, as well as the pivotal role of the extent to which values are realized for the mass (pp. 263-64). But power has been so construed that the *mass* is defined as those with least power (p. 201). Again, there is a marked discrepancy between the treatment of equality and liberty. The latter is far-reaching. It is not enough to exercise power with the consent of the governed. We must look to "what is consented to and how consent is obtained. Slavery is not limited to the coercive deprivation of liberty; enslavement is even more profound when it is internalized, and not only consented to but even demanded by the self" (p. 228). And "there is liberty in a state only when each individual has sufficient self-respect to respect others" (p. 229). On the other hand, equality is severely restricted. It must not even be defined as an ideal to exclude an elite: "If political equality were defined so as to exclude the existence of an elite, the concept would be vacuous" (p. 226). Stress falls instead on equal access to the values used as a basis for recruiting an elite. It is even conceivable that in an oligarchy "the autocrat might be chosen by lot" (p. 227)! In short, the authors are ready to use the best lessons of psychology to give content to a concept of liberty, but are not ready to use the best lessons of history to give content in terms of men's aspirations to the concept of equality. This disparate treatment is very reminiscent of the nineteenth century middle-class slogan of liberty against equality, and it rests on the general assumption of traditional power theory that the mass of men are unable to govern themselves. The Jeffersonian antithesis to this assumption is not explored in this book.

I should conclude therefore that the authors have strained the framework of power theory to the limit, that a further pursuit of democratic commitments will break the framework. Certainly, at least, it would be worth looking to see how political inquiry would be shaped if it were viewed not from above but from below—not in terms of power and the maintenance of power, but in terms of the expectations, hopes, fears, demands of the people who, in the power framework, are reckoned merely as obeying or rebelling.

NOTE

1. Harold D. Lasswell and Abraham Kaplan, *Power and Society. A Framework for Political Inquiry* (New Haven, Conn.: Yale University Press, 1950).

8. The Concept of Levels in Social Theory

The social sciences have a great stake in the philosophical concept of levels for it has played a large part in the intellectual fortifications of their right to exist as independent sciences. Whatever their internal quarrels—for example, whether political science is independent of economics or whether sociology is better seen as an extension of history—all have a common interest in not being conceived as just a halfway house to a future physics. They want a "reality-base of their own" with the right to use their own concepts, build up their own laws or patterns to try out and not be limited to physical models. If future physics relates them to its concepts, it is to be a bridging of at least kindred sciences, not a "reduction" of one to another.

This attitude developed in the struggles, early in the twentieth century, to build up the social sciences. It had hard going. Even after it grew to some maturity, there were still many scientists who would begin with a pious invocation to the protons and electrons before moving on to their own business. The philosophical concept of levels helped out because it tried to expound how qualitative levels could "emerge" in the evolutionary development of matter without requiring reduction to the physical laws of matter. In its philosophical bearings it served many functions. It was modern and progress-oriented; such an idea of emergence would be anathema to the medievals who held that nothing greater could be found in the effect than had existed in the cause (and a perfect God was the first cause). Levels theory, tied to an idea of emergence, allowed for novelty in the development of the world.

Of course, all sorts of mystical elements attached to the idea. It *could be turned to a vitalism in biology (but need not be), to a superorganicism in sociology and anthropology (but again need not be). It could even be put to theological use with God as the highest level of developmental outcome of evolution. When the logical positivists got around to its analysis there was considerable obscurity to clear away, and they went at it boldly by discussing the comparison of systems (as relations of concepts and of laws). But clarifying as this was, it left out the distinctively historical component in which emergence described a temporal or evolutionary process; this had really prompted the development of the modern levels concept.*

In this paper, which was written specifically for Symposium on Sociological Theory in the late 1950s—a volume largely devoted to methodological issues—I tried to retain the nonreductionist and historical emphases in the concept, but at the same time to free it from traditional doctrines, to liberalize and concretize it, and trim it for action in different problems of sociological theory. It was thus a bold experiment in the relations of metaphysics, epistemology, and analysis. Three kinds of tier-like problems are drawn on in the paper. One is the traditional metaphysical attempt in different philosophical schools (idealist and materialist alike) to establish rising rungs on the ladder of being—physical, biological, psychological, social, and so on upwards. The second is the epistemological struggle in the sciences of man to give a preferred status to certain units of description, to characterize the ultimate subject of the sciences as either acts of consciousness or individual behaviors or group properties or actual historical stretches. (Each candidate here was in effect proposing a reductive program, but when all are lined up they constitute quite a clear levels scale.) The third tier-like problem, quite distinct from the others, is the analytical use of metalevels in ordering the terminology of a field. My guiding idea was that a similar process was going on in all three cases. If we could extricate the concept of levels and level formation and free it from the special forms, we would have an extraordinarily valuable methodological idea for applying to fresh fields, as well as in reconstructing the problems from which we had derived it. But the value of the levels concept lay not in its being purely methodological, but in reflecting accurately the historical character of processes of development, with intellectual development itself seen as part of natural history. Thus the refinement of the apparatus of theorizing about a field is itself dependent on actual differentiations emerging in the field itself. Precisely how this works out in social theory is the subject of the paper.

The mode of analysis employed combines the search for presuppositions with logical reconstruction, but all in a background of genetic analysis. Its aim is to transform the question so as to yield a conceptual retooling. In this sense it has a pragmatist component. Perhaps the most important lesson—whether this experiment succeeded or not—is that methodological concepts need the same type of analysis as substantive concepts.

I

The concept of levels, which was sharpened primarily in evolutionary philosophies, refers initially to the emergence of qualities in the process of historical development. In this familiar sense, the appearance of life in the world constituted a new integrative level; the appearance of consciousness another; and again, in human affairs, new steps (fire, farming, machine technology, etc.) brought in new stages by altering profoundly and pervasively the qualities of human life. Philosophically, the concept of levels involves the ideas of some continuity of the new with the old, a maturing causal process which constitutes the emerging, a field of novel or distinctive qualities with some order of its own (hence an element of discontinuity with the past), some degree of alteration in the total scene and its modes of operation because of the presence of the new. Methodologically, a new level requires new descriptive concepts and, many believe, new empirical laws, independent of those of the old level.

I should like to comment briefly on each of these several strands in the levels concept because it seems important in the work of the social scientist to distinguish them and to realize that they constitute, to some degree, independently applicable theses for a field of investigation. There has, of course, been considerable philosophical discussion of these ideas in recent decades, in attempts to get the "mystery" out of the emergence concept, in refining the notion of causality and determinism involved, in seeking to remove the "epiphenomenalist" character of the new (its supervening or helpless floating above, as it were, while the real "executive" work is being done on the lower order).[1] Much of this seems to me to have been successful in breaking older philosophical stereotypes. But it would carry us too far afield to discuss even the general philosophical issues that have been raised. Many of them, while interesting and important as problems in the logic of science, do not directly affect the actual work of the social scientist, at least in the present stages of the social sciences. I shall, therefore, limit myself to the points indicated.

The concept of emergent levels involves a historical or developmental perspective, not merely a concern with the relations of qualitatively distinct bands of coexistent phenomena in a static field. A quality is novel not because it is distinctively different, but because nothing like it existed at an earlier period, and it does exist and recur at a later period. However, the mere occurrence of a particular novel quality is not usually greeted as a fresh "level." A new art style may be unique without affecting a revolution in art, let alone in human history. The concept of emergent levels thus contains additional ideas which may be of rather different orders of strength or scope. The minimal sense is probably simply that the novel quality (or a family of them) reappears with sufficient frequency so that it should be regarded as a regular inhabitant of the world, worthy of separate systematic study. But most actual use of the levels concept in biology and in the sciences of man involves also the element of continuity, the additional thesis that there are causal conditions under which the novel phenomena came into existence and conditions which support their continued occurrence. These are statable as historical descriptions and translevel laws. Thus, sensory color experiences came into existence with a certain development of animal eyes and are supported under definite optical-retinal-brain conditions. Similarly, that the political state came into existence at a definite point is generally agreed by social scientists, although it is not wholly established what were the critical factors involved.

Wider concern with transitional periods prior to the definite emergence of the new phenomena increasingly calls attention to the variety of intermediate forms, the piling up of variations, and the processes of consolidation and crystallization of the new levels. This is found, for example, in contemporary genetic studies of the borderline of the living and nonliving, and in discoveries of the probable transition in the animal world from the prehuman to the human type. Comparable study in the social sciences provides clues for generalizing about the conditions of the historical origin of specific social institutions. There has not always been a careful enough distinction, however, between conditions of historical origin and conditions supporting continuation. These need not always coincide, but when they do not, one should always be sensitive to the possibility that there has been a qualitative transformation in the character of the phenomena themselves.

Most conceptions of integrative levels add to the discontinuity in the appearance of the novel qualities the further assertion that there are discoverable laws on the higher level in terms of that level—for example, biological, psychological, and social laws. There may, of course, be a parting of the ways in future prospects of reduction. Although there is general agreement that we have at present a set of sciences, each of which is, so to speak, on its own, a reductive view sees this as a halfway house to a future unified science in which all the sciences are integrated. For example, chemistry is integrated within the framework of physics. A non-reductive view expects all sorts of intermediate fields (biochemistry, physiological psychology, etc.), but interprets these as literally relations of separate fields, not abolition of some on behalf of others. The levels concept is usually nonreductive in type; this involves at least the insistence that all translevel laws are genuine *empirical* laws, with terms descriptive of higher-level novel qualities as part of their statement.

A further addition is sometimes found in the assertion that the behavior of lower-level elements after the emergence of the higher-level phenomena may follow different laws from what it did when the higher-level phenomena had not yet existed, or from what it does in areas where they are not present. This may be loosely described as the interference of the higher-level entities in the lower level, or the assertion of higher-level causality, or the denial that the higher-level phenomena are epiphenomenal. Precisely how it is to be described depends on the analysis of these terms. Descriptively, in ordinary language, the point is familiar enough in the view that once man is on the globe, part of the explanation of what happens in the domain of the physical is in terms of what men want to do and actually do, whether it be in denuding or planting surface areas or creating new elements. Nor need this refer to man alone. For example, if the oxygen in our atmosphere is the result of photosynthesis, then important phenomena in our physical environment can only be explained by reference to the interaction of the higher-level phenomena of life.[2] And the same thing can be said concerning the effects of water once it has emerged from earlier gases. How far the interference of higher-level phenomena may go in the lower level is of course a separate empirical question. A great part of the physical world goes on its way, even on our globe, impervious to the existence of life. But in the case of man, even as compared to the other animals, the cultural level permeates the individual fairly completely, so that man is often described as "biosocial." If there are distinguishable levels in society itself, one may completely replace another in which it grew up, as something like urban life may conceivably wholly replace rural life.

What can the methodology of social theory hope to gain from these distinctions, or the use of the concept of emergent levels as a whole? The past gains from the general concept have been clear enough. It has helped the social sciences resist the reductive tendencies to impose upon them the concepts and methods of the physical and biological sciences in a priori fashion. It has also, in the reverse direction, helped them oppose the attempts to isolate the study of man from the sciences, in the interests of non-naturalistic conceptions of man. Again, it has helped them avoid falling into the seductive metaphysical trap of seeing whatever order they discover in a partial segment of human history as the permanent nature or essence of man and society. For the levels concept brings, methodologically, a constant historical perspective to social description and explanation. It can become a sensitive alertness to the possible emergence of stable new forms, to their interaction, both in their rise and their maturity, with the milieu in which they emerge, to the conditions that make for continued stability or change, and to the way in which interaction at any given point may produce further incipient transitions.

It is also clear what, as a methodological concept, the levels concept cannot do. It cannot supply out of itself the specific hypotheses—in this case, what are to be marked out as the major stages in the development of mankind, how varied and how globally interactive this development has been. It cannot specify in advance even which of the components within itself—the various possible theses we have seen as constituting the idea of levels—will be found applicable in the various domains of human phenomena. For example, when fresh areas of phenomena are staked out for systematic study, such as linguistic phenomena and value phenomena, it may be possible that one turns out to have a considerable internal "autonomy" on its own level and in its own terms (as language apparently does), while the other may not, and its phenomena may require constant explanation "from below." (We need not prejudge this question at the present stage of development of the value field.) Nor again, in applying each methodological strand, does the levels concept itself prejudge the specific content of that strand. For example, it insists on the search for continuity, for causal conditions under which novel phenomena come into existence. But whether such determination will come from a single preponderant source or a shifting source is not settled antecedently. To take a simplified illustration, Comte emphasizes mode of thought in explaining successive stages of human development, Marx emphasizes changing mode of production, and Buckle appeals to geographic factors as crucial in earlier stages and intellectual factors in later stages. All these and many other important questions not here raised have to be settled as theses or hypotheses or investigatory principles in a *specific* levels theory in the social sciences. Such are the tasks involved in the growing current attempts to work out a social evolutionary understanding which will avoid the mistakes and simplifications of nineteenth-century evolutionism, and will see the outlines of economic institutions, social structure, political institutions, and intellectual and emotional forms of expression in relation to the whole mode of life of the given stage of human development.

The distinction of the several strands, and the recognition that some may apply where others do not, liberalizes the levels concept considerably. It suggests that we have within the major integrative levels all sorts of processes going on which are not in character different from the "level-producing" processes on the broad evolutionary scene. The common generalized use of the term "levels" itself suggests as much. In physics, we find distinctions between macroscopic and microscopic levels, and there are levels of complexity or organization. There are qualitative changes of "state," as when a gas turns into a liquid form or a liquid into solid form. Biological evolution is constantly going on, issuing in new forms, if not constant consolidation of new species. When we pass from contrasting the inorganic level with the level of life, or the animal level with that of the human being capable of symbolic representation and wide purposive-planning activity, to the delineation of level stages in the historical development of mankind, we have already liberalized the use of the term. In social life, we see new levels frequently emerging in behavior, organization, and thought. Nations emerge, and some day we expect mankind to achieve an international level, not as mere organization but as altered quality of life. Social classes congeal to present a ladder-level structure. Thinking rises to a new level when systematic science emerges. We are so used to the historical comment that moral consciousness reached a new level that we may forget to take it literally. For there was a time, for example, when men in parts of the globe looked on men of other bands or tribes as food rather than as fellow men! Now much of this use of the term "level" may be metaphorical, but there is enough in common to suggest a general type of process. To cease to think of levels en bloc is, in effect, to try to apply to everyday processes and their description the same broad attitude and methodological approach that proves enlightening on the wider evolutionary scope. We shall suggest that it is possible to develop more specific senses of the levels concept, set within the basic *qualitative-emergence* sense, that prove useful for clearer social description and for the sharper formulation of research problems; and that the general methodological approach itself helps break up and restructure issues that have proved stumbling blocks in social theory.

II

Within contemporary social theory, we find that many of the fundamental controversies about the nature of the field itself are cast in terms reminiscent of levels disputes. There are accusations of reduction of the social to the psychological, occasional insistence on the autonomy of the cultural and the reality of the superorganic, assertions about the distinctness of subject matter of group phenomena and social structure, and so on. These questions—usually precipitated in sociological works by the innocent preliminary inquiry, "What is society?"—are a tempting field for a philosophical investigation sharpened in terms of the levels concept. We shall first consider this question as a whole, then break it into several parts, attempting to show that its central sociological relevance is clarified by restructuring it as a special type of levels problem.

The question, *"What is society?"*, raises what we may call the *locus problem*—the selection of basic unit or object in terms of which social and cultural traits or properties are to be analyzed, or subjects to which they are to be referred. If we gather the answers in a comparative fashion and range the elements out of which theorists have attempted to "construct" society, or into which they have sought to "break it down," in an order from the smallest to the largest, we get a most impressive array. At one end are the states of consciousness, out of which the nineteenth-century introspectionists wished to compound bodies, selves, economic processes, and social relations. The modern analogue is more behavioristic, consisting of behavioral acts, or compounds of attitudes as dispositions to acts. Next in line come individuals, for in some sense, society "really and truly" consists of individuals. Some prefer this locus because only the individual has consciousness, others because the individual does the physical behaving, still others because the forces of cohesion which hold the group together are spotted within the individual's needs and psychological economy, as for example in Freud's view that love relationships or, more neutrally, emotional ties constitute the essence of group mind.[3]

One step beyond and the central focus becomes interpersonal relations. Social science is here called on to think in terms of bundles of relations, or interactions, or transactions with individuals as parties, but the individual himself is either denied meaning or shipped off to individual psychology.

Next come groups. As Logan Wilson says in a review article, "Regardless of the analytical framework used, the group factor is an important one." [4] And indeed it is. From Aristotle's definition of the polis as the union of families to achieve the good life, to contemporary studies of all sorts of groups in society, all sorts of extensions have been invoked as basic—from the local community and the country to the whole of mankind.[5]

From the description of groups, especially in structural terms, one can slip quite readily into a view of social science as concerned with traits and patterns. This has been found especially in anthropological controversy. Individuals and even whole peoples can be seen as merely vehicles for the patterns whose career is being traced. People do not have social forms so much as "it is the cultures which possess the people who have been born into them." [6]

If the locus problem is pursued through different analyses of culture, the array of locus candidates is further increased. Many writers treat culture as a going concern so that we have a kind of interactive whole of multifarious activity as the subject. Lowie takes the view that, "There is only one natural unit for the ethnologist—the culture of all humanity at all periods and in all places." [7] On such a view, the subject of the whole story is mankind. If we go to the idealist philosophers of history, we can round out this end of the spectrum. At the extreme, there will be the Hegelian conception of the whole of history as exhibiting the growth in the self-consciousness of the Absolute; in such a sense, the ultimate subject is the Totality.

Our appreciation of the locus problem is enhanced by comparison of various specialized fields of social inquiry. The same range, for example, appears in ethical theory as the problem of the ultimate subject or locus of value. Is the subject to which the predicate "good" is to be attached ultimately the present momentary feeling or state of consciousness of a human being? Is it the total life of an individual self? Is it states of mutual relations or interaction, whether cast as meaningful shared experience or joint activity? Is the good really a property of a community living a kind of organized life, and the notion meaningless when referred to any fragment or abstraction? Or is the fit subject of good ultimately some ideal pattern to which striving is really directed, to be distinguished from its existential embodiment? Or again, is the ultimate good nothing less than the totality, so often cast in religious ethics as God?

In political theory, there is the familiar problem of loyalty or allegiance. Where is loyalty ultimately to be conceived as directed? To myself, in a Hobbesian vein, to my family ("my own"), my friends, to those beyond with whom I have "contracted," to my country? To the group Will, in Rousseauesque style? To ideals ultimately? To all mankind? To the historical totality, as in Burke's famous description of the state as a partnership between the living, the dead, and those who are to be born? To the religious object as overall totality?

Recent psychological-anthropological study reveals a similar set of problems in the picture of the self. What is the actual feeling or picture that an individual has of himself, viewed as a phenomenological problem? Does he see himself as an isolated individual? As a continuous being over many lives, as in Hindu transmigration theory? As a multiplicity or bundle of roles? (Gabriel Marcel complains that modern man feels himself as a set of functions and is left with a hollow center.) As a cog in a machine or a branch of a social organism? As a fragment of a wider totality, whether in the ancient Stoic sense of a spark from the central fire or in the religious sense as part of God? As an instrument for an external or transcendent purpose? Hallowell's pioneering paper in which he examines such problems on a transcultural basis has brought this subject within the scope of scientific treatment,[8] extremely difficult though it be to penetrate to the phenomenal self picture of different cultures. (The recent rise of the self concept to a more central role in psychology can help this development immensely.) By examining the basic orientations provided by the culture and the ways in which the functioning of societies depends on the kind of self-awareness in its members, Hallowell seems to me to have shown, in effect, that theories about what the subject matter "really is" are not to be regarded merely as theories, but as describing patterns of effective or functioning "social reality," in short as qualitative emergents in the individual person. This is the sense, I take it, in which Kroeber and Kluckhohn in one of their formulations speak of culture as "the topmost phenomenal level yet recognized—or for that matter, now imaginable—in the realm of nature." [9]

The most abstract formulation of the locus problem is to be found in metaphysical theory. Is reality to be regarded as a flux of sense elements, a set of events, qualities, and relations? As substance? As pattern of universal? As process or goings-on? As absolute totality? And so on. These controversies provide the sharpest formulation of the general alternatives. Those who regard metaphysics as providing basic truth will be tempted to seek there a wholesale solution to the locus problem and derive from it an application to social theory. Those who, like the present writer,[10] tend to regard metaphysics rather as the domain in which basic categories are compared, analyzed, and evaluated as alternative possible modes of organizing linguistic instruments, long-range factual lessons, and basic purposes will look to a solution of the locus problem in a specific field like social theory by probing for the variety of underlying interests, hypotheses, and purposes which are to be found there.

In the locus problem in social theory, there are after all two separate questions involved. One is the claim for some type of "reality" for the preferred candidate; the second is the claim that it has some basic character or role which qualifies it as the ultimate subject matter of the social sciences. (Let us refer to these as the reality claim and the ultimacy claim, respectively.) We may restructure the first question as a levels problem, in the liberalized sense of the term indicated above. This means that in the arena of human social life there are all sorts of forms crystallized, with qualities of their own appearing in behavior, organization, and consciousness—emerging, stabilized, breaking down, reemerging, almost comparable, if we allow an oversimplified analogy, to the way in which some matter passes from liquid to solid, or liquid to gas, and back again. In social theory, we may assume that such locus candidates as individuals, interactions, interpersonal relations, and various subgroup and group levels in their claim for reality correspond to definite qualitative levels in the living activity of a definite span or spread of human beings. Let us call this type of level *group-generalization level*. The different locus candidates may then be construed as different types of possible group-generalization levels. We do not here raise the question whether all actually occur among men, for example, whether the sheer individual or the sheer superorganic is more than a speculative possibility. Our interest is rather in the methodological question of what they would have to show in order to establish their reality.

Methodologically, the point may be made rather simply if we take our cue from sociological practice rather than sociological speculation. For in practice, terms specifying some qualitative organization over a given span have always some explicit or implicit *empirical* interpretation. When it is asked whether a particular assembly is a crowd, or a mob, or a meeting, more or less identifiable criteria are involved, so that one gathering can be identified as a mob, another as a meeting, another in flux from one state to the other, and so on.[11] Or again, when detailed investigation is carried out in a rural area of the form of the household group, the dooryard group, the neighborhood group, the village group, the country group, or the regional group,[12] each is identified in particular terms. Then it is possible to ask under what conditions such groups can exist, under what conditions they tend to break down, and what role the existence of the several groups in this order plays in processes of transformation. Or again, when it is asked whether a particular getting together of definite people who proceed to inquire into and give their views of a controversy is an informal gathering, a structured group having opinion-forming influence but no coercive power, or a formal court, there is no difficulty in establishing the answer in a particular case.

Similarly, in conceptual development oriented to actual descriptive study of the span or spread of groups and the comparative incidence of types of behavior among them, the mode of identifying levels is thoroughly empirical. For example, A. M. Lee [13] develops Sumner's concepts to distinguish the *individual* level with "a continuum of patterns that ranges from practices to habits," the *group* level, with a continuum "that extends from folkways to mores," the *societal* level with a continuum "running from conventions to morals or moral principles." He is thus able to diagram the divergence in levels and the deviations thus found, and to employ such concepts as "immoretic morals" and "immoral mores." His primary interest is in the relation of society-wide cultural elements and subsocietal group elements. Similarly, concepts of institutional variation and deviance might be analyzed by reference to group levels; for example, when R. M. Williams says, "Many of the so-called contradictions in a large, complex, heterogeneous society reflect *diverse levels of sociocultural regulation*," [14] these regulation levels may themselves admit of analysis in terms of specific group interactions. (An obvious example would be the problem of legal rules on divorce versus actual practice.) Again, concepts of the local, national, and global level provide a ready empirically identifiable framework for mapping certain types of attitudes—for example, how far in America assistance to other areas of the world is seen as participation in a global community, how far as means beyond national boundaries for national aims. And similar conceptual approaches are readily discernible in studies of the impact of technical change on cultural patterns.

All this is commonplace enough both in sociological practice and in the fashioning of middle-sized concepts. Extended to locus candidates asserting a reality claim, it would mean that, even though they may have been advanced as categories for an analytical framework structuring the whole field of study, they still must exhibit some empirical content and maintain a material status. Thus, instead of asking whether our subject matter pertains to individuals, interpersonal relations, or groups, once we have the empirical criteria, we will be able to ask of a given population or part of a population, "How far are they operating on an individual level and in what respect, how far on an interpersonal relations level, how far on a (more or less structured) group basis?" For, in effect, if these terms indicate qualitatively different levels, then to describe a situation in one way is to assert that it is, in fact, qualitatively different from what it would be like if described in the other way. It should then be possible, speculatively at least, to think of a society operating wholly on an individual basis (a Hobbesian state of nature with each on his own), or wholly in terms of ties between individuals, or in terms of various sorts of groups. The question of *whether* particular societies can so operate or do so operate would then be an *empirical* matter. Other important scientific questions, some requiring extensive research involving sociopsychological collaboration, might be: Does the existence of the higher level always presuppose the existence of each lower level? Is higher-level behavior always instrumental (for example, as in groups over a wide area with unacquainted participants)? Does the individualistic pattern emerging from a group pattern always involve a sense of disintegration? (cf. Merton on anomie; or compare Redfield's view of the shift from folk society to urban society as a kind of loss of firm scope in the moral order with Tawney seeing the shift from one morality to another.) [15] Are certain types of qualitative levels grounded in psychological needs so that if they lose their character in one context they will reemerge in another, as has been suggested by the way in which the breakdown of familial primary groups sometimes is followed by the assumption of primary-group quality by other types of association?

If we generalize this procedure, we would have to ask whether a given population does in fact have a culture, or whether people there do have roles, or whether they constitute a social system. This may seem strange, but perhaps the strangeness may come from the fact that these are always to be found where populations have managed to survive. Certainly, there is nothing strange in asking whether a population uses language (even though we can predict the answer invariably), or whether it constitutes a nation or just a tribe or a village. Similarly, it may seem strange to ask whether a man has a self; but I doubt whether the concept will really be clear until we can answer such a question and show under what conditions a human being would be without one and why, if it is the case, he would not survive. A further advantage of such an empirical interpretation of structural categories is that it makes possible a clear evaluative approach thereafter. We can ask whether it is desirable for a population to fall under a certain category, what are the advantages and disadvantages, and so forth.

Methodologically, therefore, the proposed reinterpretation involves treating locus candidates seriously as empirical or material categories structuring the inquiry prior to beginning it. Two objections will occur at once. Some of the candidates, such as sensations, obviously cannot fit too comfortably into such a reinterpretation—for only in a dream, or perhaps under the influence of drugs, could social reality take the phenomenal form of isolated states of consciousness in associated bundles! The other objection is that an inquiry must be structured somehow, or else how can it get started? That is, it must be either a psychological or a culturological inquiry, or within a framework of some theory of action. Both these objections can be analyzed if we turn to the second question raised above, the ultimacy claim of the locus candidates.

At the more atomistic end of the range, which thinks in terms of states of consciousness and units of behavior, the reality claim is usually in the background, whereas the ultimacy claim is prominent. Here we find a dominant epistemological interest. This locus has appealed to investigators because verification of statements about social configurations does lie in observing items of behavior, though not perhaps going all the way to sensations as general verification termini. This trend was encouraged by the earlier positivist view that equated meaning with mode of verification. But a pendular swing has come in philosophy. The distinction between what the statement asserts and how it is verified is coming into its own again. Hence, the locus candidates at this end of the spectrum are robbed of their philosophic support and must stand on their own feet. Once they do this, it becomes clear that their ultimacy claim is relative to a concentraton on what they regard as the most available units of observation. For example, Nadel says that "no legitimate isolate can be discovered more basic than that of a standardized pattern of behavior rendered unitary and relatively self-contained by its tasklike nature and its direction upon a single aim." [16] He gives as examples of such a "behavior cycle" a mother tending her child, farmers working on the land, and the performances of a sacrifice. But obviously this is geared to a particular state of anthropological observation. Why not, instead, a mother feeding her child, holding her child, washing her child, in the one direction, or in terms of the meaning of the act, a mother building up the family, or providing supports for her old age, or rearing a defender of the state, in the other direction? Instead of a conception of basic isolate, we have really the proposed level on which observation may start, or the area of verifying observations, or something of that sort.

The objection that some categories are required for initial structuring of investigation need not mean that these have to have other than the empirical or material status we have described. The ultimacy claim can be taken here as equivalent to the confident prediction that inquiry guided by these material categories—for example, exploration of this particular level of phenomena—will prove scientifically fruitful in terms of readier conceptualization and greater facility in the discovery of laws. For example, the culturological thesis says, in effect, that we should forget about the culture-bearers as other than—in extreme cases—space-time positions, just as in describing individual behavior we ignore the particular molecules in the body. And indeed this is not impossible in many fields. We could map the appearance, distribution, and extent pulsations of a disease or a language on the face of the globe without asking how it spread or who were the carriers. The central question of scientific significance is whether such a perspective will, in fact, put us in a position to advance systematic theoretical knowledge in the terms that it provides. This cannot be settled a priori. But it is this, and not the desire that one's own scientific garden have a separate identity, which constitutes the legitimate core of the ultimacy claim.

I am not suggesting that all social categories have to be taken as descriptive. But I am suggesting that most of the locus candidates, other than those expressing a purely epistemological interest, can most fruitfully be treated as types of group-generalization levels. I do not underestimate the difficulties in making such wide sociological concepts subject to such limitations. For example, it may be that considerably more work will have to be done from a phenomenal or phenomenological type of approach to understand how people see themselves and their relations. But there will be a tremendous gain in clarity and perhaps also a vast increase in theoretical power.

III

Once the concept of levels has been liberalized beyond the original sense of *quality-emergence* levels to cover also *group-generalization* levels, it becomes possible to suggest further senses of a more specialized sort. The basic setting is, of course, still the process or social change in which group differentiation takes place. But as there occurs an increasingly complex division of labor among groups, areas of activity are sifted out which may be compared on a means-ends basis in some type of ascendance order within a total interactive organization. Let us speak of these as *instrumental-functional* levels. For example, in the economic life of a country, one may distinguish the levels of consumption, production of consumption articles, and production of instruments of production (tools, factories, etc.). In such a mapping, the higher levels constitute a kind of functional generalization. For example, a factory is set up to process a metal which will be used in a variety of ways in many other factories. Similarly, schools may teach skills of wide applicability instead of letting children learn particular applications at work, as in much of primitive learning. Or in another area, basic scientific research may become a specialized occupation, with results widely applicable in technology, and these again applicable in actual production. In this sense, many of our institutions—schools, banks and money, scientific research—may be thought of when they become socially established separately as on a higher generalization level. On the other hand, it must never be forgotten that all these elements in a society function interactively on the primary level. Material processes and tool factories, as well as schools and banks and laboratories, all involve buildings on terra firma, with a corps of men and women who often have specialized interests. Thus to speak of higher generality in this sense is to point to an ordered variety of functioning relationships, but all in concrete contexts of human interaction.

Historically, economics has probably dealt with the relation of such levels and their interaction most concretely. Certainly, traditional economic theory is a storehouse of controversies concerning the relations of consumption, production, exchange, and all the various processes that enter into the economy and the functional groups that become separated out. Valuable general lessons might be learned from seeing economic questions in the light of a levels mapping in the present sense. For example, the way in which a particular material such as gold became a commodity and then a standard for exchange seems to be precisely an account of concrete generalization in social activity through instrumental-functional relationships. In this process, money became almost the universal social symbol of the means. (On the other hand, it may be that it has reached its limit, and that in the present stage of productive development some category more directly concerned with production—even physical energy itself—may come to play the role of generalized means.)

There are areas of human activity far removed from the economic in which instrumental-functional levels may fruitfully be mapped. Many areas exhibit a socially-differentiated structure in which there is a basic ground floor of social activity of some sort, a second story in which some *regulative* process occurs directed toward the ground floor, and a third story in which some kind of ordering takes place and is directed toward the second story. Technology in production, technological research, and basic scientific research constitute one example. Teaching, teaching teachers, and developing the theory of education are another. Law-abiding and law-violating activity, positive law, political and legal theorizing make up a third. And so on, in many distinct fields.

Whether or not a general theory of means-ends relations can stem from a levels differentiation along these lines, I do not know. General theories have to be approached with caution. But certainly there can be a discernment of common types of problems and perhaps the development of some general criteria for the evaluation of means. For example, there are obvious analogous problems of the overweighting of the ground-floor level by the higher levels. When does the regulative mechanism use up so much of the resources as to begin to drain the basic activity area? Under what condition does the burden of heavy industry become so great as to bring consumption to the danger minimum? Or the activity of literary criticism so heavy as to threaten literary enjoyment? Or the weight of morality so great as to take the joy out of life? Obviously, there will be no uniform answer. The desirable level for courts and political controls is to have a minimum use; for scientific levels, the increase of the highest theoretical level has its own intrinsic values, and a desirable ground-floor situation might be one of a development in which less work on that level was required. Other general problems that have in one way or another been raised include: problems of distance among levels and difficulties of communication; problems of control and tendencies to iron law of oligarchies and hierarchies; problems of standardization at higher levels and the degree to which they produce liberating or constricting effects at lower levels; and so on. Since many of these issues arise in different particular fields, they may perhaps most fruitfully be discussed there rather than in general terms. But the comparison of areas is likely to be highly suggestive.

In order to examine the utility of such levels analysis concretely, I shall take an extended example from a field in which such mapping is, on the whole, rather untried. Let us see how far such formulations would help clarify concepts and facilitate empirical research in ethics. We may begin by distinguishing a basic or ground-floor level of conduct, with its associated feelings and desires; a second story of moral codes or patterns, which involves some sort of regulative-selective function in relation to conduct;

and a third story of ethical justification which involves reflective support for or criticism directed upon the second level. All three function interactively in the arena of human behavior. For moral reprimand of a violator is as much human behavior as the goal seeking in the violation of the code, and the justification is, like any other discourse, a part of human symbolic-manipulative behavior. The use of particular functional relations for initial identification does not, however, preclude the discovery of various other empirical relations between the levels. In fact, it helps open up numerous such problems for research.

For example, a clear distinction between the levels makes us sensitive to the different functions that the same content may have in different cultural patterns—how a particular goal or character trait or feeling or sanction may be nonmoral in one society, be profoundly moral in another, and be on a still higher level in a third. Happiness, for example, may be on the ground floor in an ascetic morality—it is simply something not to be overdone. In another, it may be one of the goods to be sought. In still another, it may be the ultimate justification of all goods. We also have to keep an eye out for change, or for the circulation of elements among the levels. Perhaps the best example on a large scale in Western civilization is the rise of egoism. Egoistic behavior or "selfishness" was for a long time regarded as conduct inimical to morality, therefore ground floor or perhaps subbasement! In the breakup of the medieval world outlook, it moved up the ladder to the moral rung and became acceptable partly as a means to the good life, and partly as the content of the "self-regarding" duties. In Hobbesian and later Benthamite ethics, it blossomed on the justification level as the inevitable principle of justification of all conduct.

One might feel tempted to look for "laws of motion" among the levels. Do high values in the second level tend to become ethical justification principles? Are they forced up by the "pressure" of values below? Love, for example, seems to have come from the moral pattern into the third level by a process of generalization and extension? Plato's *Symposium* is a good illustration of a moment of transition, in which its meaning is moving from a valued feeling into the idea of a unified quest of the self embodying all aspiration. On the other hand, reason seems to have followed the opposite path. If unreasonableness as a vice is to any extent now approximating a position in the moral level, it is only because the efficacy of reason as a mode of ethical justification has gradually become established. However, the attempt to find laws of such types is premature. A more careful study of crystallization processes and critical points on a wide comparative basis is first required, and then some integration of these studies within a theory relating our three levels to other phases of civilization or culture in action.[17]

A consequence of progress in such a study would be the possibility of wider historical and functional investigations of the relation of levels. What are the further relations that a moral pattern may have to the conduct pattern, apart from guidance and control? How may it be "geared" to serve varieties of social, economic, political, and cultural needs? Does a justification level merely provide "major premises" for a morality? Actually, a considerable variety of relations is possible. There may be justification that supports, as for example, a hierarchical view of each soul aspiring only so far as its nature permits served to support a hierarchically-ordered feudal morality of duties according to rank. Or again, the justification level may have a critical impact, as an individualistic conscience ethic challenged the feudal moral order. But if the third level can have opposite relations in this way, then it is to some extent an independently variable order. And so we find ourselves dealing not merely with logical relations, but with problems of historical interaction between all three levels.

Again, there can be no a priori assumptions about the comparative order and rates of change on the three levels. It is very likely that changes on the ground-floor level come first, but these may sometimes be advanced only far enough to raise problems, not to alter patterns of conduct. We cannot assume, however, that given social changes, the moral pattern must change first and the justification pattern change as a causal consequence. Sometimes, the justification pattern cracks first and serves as a lever for shifting the moral pattern. In our present world, for example, a globally-oriented ethical justification system is increasingly taking hold following the practical interconnections of the globe. Many elements in existing moralities require alteration as a consequence. In general, just as in the relations of ideas and practice, shifts in justification often reflect changing forces and prefigure changes that are to come in existing institutions and beliefs. That is why institutions of great scope and practical importance in human affairs have, in their maturity, tended to pay great attention to the principles upon which they are justified, and why theoretical disputes in religion, politics, and social theory have had such immense practical significance.

Another levels problem in the relation of the three stories takes us back to questions of emergence. Selective-discriminative behavior is clear in the prehuman animal world. But at what point does such behavior pass into organized aspiration? And where does the sense of obligation appear? Darwin thought it highly likely that any people having familial or close group relations would have a moral sense, and Freud speculated about a specific origin of guilt feeling. Julian Huxley illustrates a fuller type of historical approach when he offers the thesis that, in preagricultural society, moralities are largely concerned with propitiation and group solidarity. He suggests that, in postagricultural early civilization, moralities relate to class domination and group rivalry.[18] Huxley looks also for the psychological functions of morality and for its changing forms in contemporary life, then ends up with proposals for its orientation in the modern world. Similar detailed inquiry is possible for justification patterns. Some may have been implicit in the particular forms the morality took. But conscious ethical theorizing was a later product whose origins we can trace, to some extent, as part of the growth of what we call civilization. The answers to these questions are scientific-historical matters, not to be settled by postulation or sheer speculation, or even by present introspection into the state of consciousness at a particular stage in the development of mankind. Even where we do not have the answers, the recognition of the questions will keep us from uncritical approaches.

IV

The various senses of the levels concept we have so far considered together point to a way of looking at the work of the social sciences. Ongoing human activity is seen as crystallizing into structured forms on various historical levels. It involves group and subgroup differentiation and integration in virtue of interactive processes which embody instrumental functions. But where in all this does conceptualization as the activity of the social scientist itself fit? In the preceding section, theoretical activity was itself treated as one type of level in connection with other human activities. In the first section, there was some suggestion that human consciousness was to be regarded as a level in the development of the natural world. Obviously, conceptualization is not to be construed as a purely contemplative outside-of-the-world act. This has far-reaching consequences.

The Cartesian notion of mind as a contemplator, a noninterfering spectator, has dominated the Western intellectual horizon. Its effect in social theory is still greater than we are likely to assume. Only such a conception—to take a current sociological example—can explain why such a theoretical fuss has been made over the "discovery" that predictions in the social field can affect the outcome of the subject matter they are purporting to predict. The self-fullfilling prophecy is simply the case in which the act of prophesying helps produce the result prophesied. A man bellows, "There is an avalanche coming any moment!" By the energy of his sound, he might produce the avalanche itself, if the physical balance was precarious and he was strategically located. In the usual social examples, the result is produced by effects on the understanding of others and their response in terms of their habits of reaction (to rush to sell shares if a noted economist predicts a depression, etc.). What does this show? Simply that the act of prophesying is part of the phenomena in some cases. Therefore, its effects have to be measured if it is public, or else the form of its expression entered into the description of initial-state conditions. In this respect, it is parallel to the use of energy in observation of minute physical phenomena, where the apparatus of observation as an act (e.g., use of light) may interfere in the phenomena to be observed. The problem is one of the careful formulation of the initial conditions so that we can tell what will have been proved by the results of the experiment. Or else it is one of ingenuity—as in the use of one-way transparent screens to observe what nursery children will do when the adults are absent! [19]

Yet, why should contemporary social science be surprised to find that mind or intellectual reflection is to be viewed as an event in nature, arising under determinate conditions, involving in itself an expenditure of energy, and having effects of varying range depending on conditions? In short, why be surprised that intellectual reflection itself, together with its products, constitutes a social phenomenon which may be rising to a new level or sublevel position? One might have thought that this point of the natural character and office of reflection, upon which Dewey spent his major philosophical energies, would have had effects in social science at least comparable to those that his analysis of human nature had in educational theory. (Why it did not is itself probably an interesting social-science research problem.) In any case, it follows from this point of view that the formulation of abstract concepts itself expresses the conditions and problems of men and, in varying degree, reformulates outlook, mode of thought, and mode of handling the processes of life.

This means that the growth of more and more general concepts in the social field is to be regarded as a complex process. We may speak of levels of abstraction, as the semanticists do—from the lowest "unspeakable" level of microscopic events to the highest rung of the abstraction ladder—but we must not regard it as a simple verbal matter, or even as a stripping-off process in which more and more of the initial mass of properties are stripped away to leave more widely applicable ideas. Nor, on the other hand, is it to be understood purely as free intellectual construction which in the hands of genius provides organizing relations so that, lo and behold, where there was a great deal of scattered information, now there is science. The emergence of a high-level concept or category is a real event in the natural world, and so what is really happening requires not merely logical examination, but a whole psychological, social, and historical picture. The descriptive inquiry maps the career of the concept. The causal-explanatory inquiry offers hypotheses about its rise and the reasons for its spread. The logical-evaluative inquiry is itself a creative development of the concept, in instances where it is not a mere orderly presentation of how the concept has been used; for such an inquiry shows what the meaning of the concept is. This inquiry can be in relation to different theoretical areas and possible applications.

All that goes into the development of an abstract concept is not always appreciated. Even on a rudimentary level, there is a selective-generalizing process. For example, to speak of one's "brother" already sets aside differences of age in the family, or the sex of the speaker; "sibling" is even more abstract. And the idea of "kinship" itself is a fairly high-level concept, inviting formal systematization, study of correlation with patterns of control, and modes of feeling and prescription. As a high-level concept, it is only one step removed from the abstract category of "social relation"; one may venture the speculative suspicion that, had it not been held back by the definite content of the biological relationship involved, it might have climbed to the heights and competed for the very definition of sociology. For, after all, Aristotle discusses various business and social relations in his *Nicomachean Ethics* under the rubric of "friendship," and all that was needed was to reinterpret friendship as a kind of social brotherhood or kinship of interests! In the social sciences, while high-level categories seem to get giddy in their rarefied atmosphere, middle-sized terms are more often conscious of their roots.

Perhaps the best analyzed examples of high-level categories are to be found in relation to the physical sciences, where the development of concepts of force, matter, space, and time constitutes a fascinating chapter in the history of thought. The evaluative determination of the conditions for their proper use in the light of contemporary scientific knowledge is a major occupation of the philosophy of science. It is not too much to say that it took Western man two millennia to develop adequate conceptions here, even though the pace of recent progress sometimes makes it seem a question of only three hundred years!

Let us compare two contemporary general concepts in social science, one of which has climbed to a position of categorial eminence on a high level, the other of which remains simply a tag for a variety of specific qualities. The two concepts are *power* and *skill*. Power has made a definite and not unsuccessful bid for domination in current political science. It is often cast for a fundamental role in social science comparable to that of *energy* in physics.[20] This implies that, in principle, laws of human social behavior would be stated in terms of power seeking as a basic variable. Meanwhile, other classifications are refashioned in terms of its demands. Men are divided not into workers and capitalists, or city folk and country folk, or occupational groupings, but into leaders and followers. Creeds, philosophies, and even social theories are examined as sources of power. Human desires and needs are reckoned chiefly as causal bases for maintaining or losing power. By contrast, there has seemed little temptation to make skill a general category with a general theory. Instead, the social scientist is impressed by the diversity of skills and their heterogeneous quality. A single abstract concept embracing the different skills of an orator, a scientist, and a baseball player would seem to be nothing more than a creation out of an artificial analogy. And yet are not the power of a priest in whom men have faith, the power of a gangster pointing his gun, the power of a doctor explaining the X-ray to a patient, and the power of a statesman resting on a democratic election quite different in type? Or for that matter, we might observe the diversity of forms in which physical energy appears—as heat, light, electricity, mechanical motion.

Why the power idea should have risen to a higher level and the skill idea not is a problem of social and intellectual history not perhaps as yet fully explored. Some points are suggestive. The central role of certain problems in modern life which involve force and power—war, economic conflicts, general insecurity—does tend to give a sharper focus on the power concept. The existence of states as political mechanisms and the possibilities of "taking over power" give an institutional basis for its conceptual unification. The existence of political theory as a single science gives it an intellectual head start in terms of a set of theoretical formulations which it may undertake to unify. On the other hand, for skill there are only a few recent tendencies. Among these few are the need for a great variety of skills involving special education, the need for encouraging youth to enter these fields, the development of testing to determine promise of skill, and the increased rapidity of social change in occupations calling for development of skills in such a way as to ensure transferability. As for theoretical fields in which skill might play a part, there is very little, except perhaps that branch of psychology which deals with the emotional conditions of effective functioning. The concept of *productivity*, as used by psychoanalytical writers like Erich Fromm, might fit into a science of skill. But, on the whole, the notion of skill does not stand a chance compared with power, at least for the present.

When we look to the evaluation of the concepts, power finds itself drawing considerably more on credit than it pays in cash value. Compare it with energy. Energy is defined clearly on a macroscopic level; power is vague and leans on its denotation or exemplification in the police, the courts, the government, and the army. The scientific use of the energy concept is enhanced when it is related to the microscopic level in terms of precise measurement of what goes on within the atom; the individual's love of power is a concept wavering between the general desire to get something in particular on given occasions, and the promise of an internal psychological mechanism that becomes visible when it goes astray in sadistic-masochistic phenomena. In the case of energy, the microscopic theory is complete enough to explain and control the large-scale release of energy. At its best, the psychological theory of power does little to explain large-scale social, even political, events. Our task here is not to evaluate fully the concept, but to illustrate the kind of promise that warrants extending credit to it. The gap between promise and payment seems so wide in the case of the power concept that I am tempted to look for its ideological role as a large component of its rise to prominence.

Forgoing any generalizations about causal conditions, we may note that our brief samples suggest at least three conditions that warrant the extension of credit to a general or abstract high-level category for structuring an area of social inquiry: (1) when there is a promise of the development of greater theoretical knowledge by its use, in reference to some specific set of theoretical problems already articulated; (2) when there are definite institutional forms or practices which it expresses, so that it has at least an anchored meaning whose extension is being proposed for a wider field; (3) when there is some set of unified purposes that the concept can help to articulate. These criteria add up to what may be called a contextual approach to categories.

This type of approach was involved in the evaluation of the locus problem in section II, and especially in the insistence that locus categories either be referred to specific epistemological problems or be treated themselves as embodying explicit descriptive content. I believe that the contextual approach should be extended to all top-level categories in social theory, that these categories have explicit or implicit relations in at least one of the three ways indicated to some context, and that they cannot be fully understood and evaluated without reference to the context. For example, the older conception of *superstructure*, as it appeared in historical materialism, was readily intelligible in terms of the theory that states that changes in the mode of production determine changes in a definite way in the realms of consciousness; the utility of the category stands or falls with the adequacy of the underlying theory. Or again, when MacIver drew a sharp distinction between *civilization* and *culture*—the former embracing material and social apparatus of living in man's endeavor to control the conditions of his life, the latter embracing ends (modes of living and thinking and expression)—it was evident that, in part, this rested on an underlying distinction between the material and the expression of spirit, and in part, it also involved the explicit belief that cumulative evolution could be traced for the material products and social techniques, but not for the ever-varying and spontaneously recurring spiritual life. Recent presentation of cate-gorial schemes does not always make clear the context from which they stem or to which they refer. For example, to set off culture as a separate symbolic system does make sense if we are thinking of the learning-in-growing-up context *from the point of view of the learner,* but not if we are thinking of the stable ongoing social situation in which almost every property of action or every habit of action can be seen as broadly "cultural." In the latter context, we would feel much more inclined to use the traditional Tylor category of culture. It would be worth multiply-ing categorial sets even speculatively, to throw open more widely this whole area of inquiry. Some categories would stem from considering the diffusion situation; others from inquiry into uni-formity of behavior and deviation, with an eye to controls that keep men in line; others from looking at a distance as a man may at an anthill; others perhaps from looking at society through the eyes of a particular occupational group (as Holmes in the nar-rower field of law tried to see how the law looked from the bad man's point of view); and others from approaching the field with a particular interest, such as looking for patterns in psychological-personality terms. Kroeber and Kluckhohn's valuable review of the culture concept should provide an excellent starting point for testng the merits of a contextual approach in making sense of the extreme diversity of definitions.[21] This would be a necessary preliminary, I believe, for an evaluation of the concept as it has emerged in recent scientific work. For it cannot be too often repeated that the mere use of a generic concept—as in our exam-ple of skill, if one were to write a "General Theory of Skill"—is no guarantee of a fruitful systematic unity, whether for theoretical or practical purposes. The decision to develop the general concept, or the realization that it has been done, represents an accomplish-ment in moving up to a high or abstract conceptual level only if it corresponds to something more than arbitrary stipulation.

The problems just raised and the approach worked out can be illustrated more fully from the current usage of the terms "value" and "norm," both of which have broadened out to cover an extraordinarily wide range of content. Although the term "value" has become well-entrenched in ethical, psychological, and so-ciological writing, there have been divergent trends in its use. There has been a wider use equating value with interest generally, and a narrower use insisting on some element of appraisal or preference in the idea itself.

The wider use has, on the whole, prevailed among philosophers. A man's "values" means the totality of his attitudes *for or against* anything. R. B. Perry, in his classic *General Theory of Value,* set the preponderant mood by defining a value as any object of any interest. This covers everything that a man wants, enjoys, is awed by, or responds to aesthetically, as well as what he feels he ought to do or pursue as the good. It is interesting to note that Laird went even further in developing a principle of natural election to cover physical "attraction" and chemical "affinity" in the material world.[22] Departure from the broader notion is to be found chiefly in writers who, like Dewey, stress the role of appraisal in value judgment and contrast it with the immediacy of affective quality or prizing.[23]

In psychological and social or cultural descriptions of men's values, the usage of the term varies. Sometimes value is equated with object of any desire (e.g., Ellis Freeman).[24] Sometimes the stress falls on preference among motives or goals (e.g., Kimball Young).[25] Sometimes the term is used to denote affective quality in attitudes (e.g., Sherif and Cantril).[26] Often it becomes simply a synonym for affective-motor attitude. Sometimes, however, the value is seen as an entity which affects thought and behavior, in part by generating attitudes. (Broom and Selznick speak in this way of personal identity as a deeply rooted value having such effects; to be a value is equated apparently with being prized.)[27] Recently, however, some writers have been explicit in limiting the term. Kluckhohn says: "A value is a conception, explicit or implicit, distinctive of an individual or characteristic of a group, of the desirable which influences the selection from available modes, means and ends of action."[28] He adds that it is not just a preference, but one felt or considered to be justified. Similarly, R. M. Williams, in formulating concepts for sociological description, says: "Values are not the concrete goals of action but rather the criteria by which goals are chosen."[29] Kingsley Davis says: "A value is that which is considered desirable, which is thought worthy of being pursued."[30] Parsons distinguishes sharply between the "cathectic" orientation and "evaluation" as a process of ordered selection.[31] In general, the somewhat narrower and critical conception of *value* is becoming predominant in scientific work.

The concept of *norm* provides an interesting contrast. Here the tendencies are reversed. Among philosophers, "normative" generally, perhaps even universally, connotes *oughts.* It therefore embodies the critical selective component which the broad use of the value concept lacks.[32] Among psychological and social scientists, however, the term has often been broadened in a way analogous to the extension of *value* among philosophers. Every social custom or cultural element comes to be seen as a *norm*. For example, Cantril calls standardized ways of a society "social norms." [33] (It is interesting to note that such broad use of "norms" forces a narrow use of "values"; Cantril calls prevailing evaluations of norms "social values.") [34] Williams uses an extremely broad concept of norms. He regards the concept of culture as a normative structure, pointing to "a continuous gradation from almost purely technical or cognitive norms (how to boil an egg, the most efficient way to manufacture TNT) to 'moral' norms (thou shall not kill). At the intermediate steps, one finds, among others, conventional norms ('custom,' 'etiquette,' etc.) and aesthetic norms (standards of taste, of beauty, etc.)." [35] Davis similarly sees the whole social system as normative: "Its integration rests upon the fact that its members carry in their heads, as part of the culture heritage, the notion that they *ought* or *ought not* to do certain things." [36] Although norms are said to represent "an imaginary construct" and to be "subjective," [37] they are central to understanding society. Bierstedt gives the concept of norms a central place, and uses it to refer "not to ways of thinking but to ways of doing"; [38] norms are the "grooves" in which conduct runs along, but they also function as rules or standards, as societal expectations.[39] By presenting a wide concept of norms which can accommodate all sorts of different types, Bierstedt is able to dispense entirely with the term "values." On the other hand, Broom and Selznick, who appeared to use a wider concept of values, appear to use a narrower concept of norms, regarding them as "blueprints for behavior, setting limits within which individuals may seek alternate ways to achieve their goals. Norms are based on cultural values." [40]

One may wonder why the concept of norms should be conceived so broadly that every social custom or cultural element should come to be seen as a norm. In line with our insistence that there has to be some basis for the higher-level abstract concept, unless it is merely a tag word for an area of possibly miscellaneous elements, we have to look for some theory promised, or some instituion or practice given expression, or some purpose furthered. So far at least, it is hard to see any theory advanced or promised; at most, there is an attempt to classify. And, from the point of view of theory, there is, in both the case of norm and value, a definite disadvantage which comes from the occasional tendency to reify, to regard the terms as designating existent forces or generative sources, as if to refer to the value or the norm were to explain the cause of an attitude or behavioral tendency. In this sense, the terms, intended as theoretical constructs by the methodologically self-conscious scientist, may function as a last refuge or surrogate for spirit, in the sense in which the older dualistic philosophies used it as a mode of explanation. On the other hand, if we look to general point of interest in the use of the norm concept, the context of use is overwhelmingly clear. It arises in a concentration on the process of socialization of the growing individual, in an interest in the mechanisms of transmission of existent forms and patterns to the next generation, also in the methods of control and regulation to maintain the pattern. From this perspective, the use of the general concept of norms makes sense at least at the beginning. I suspect that in the long run, it will prove as strong as, but no stronger than, the theory of a general social psychology which it expresses, or perhaps implicitly promises.

And what about the basis for the general value concept, whether taken in its wider or in its narrower appraisal sense? I have suggested elsewhere [41] that the mere use of a generic value concept cannot settle the question of its utility. Stipulation alone, or the existence of a generic mark, is not enough. The unity sought has to be found either in some quality that is central in experience; or else in some central tendency in human desire; or else in some unifying psychological, cultural, or social pattern; or in some set of practical needs or converging historical demands. Thus, to argue that all life is the expression of a single quest,[42] or that every culture must have a patterned unity, can possibly become a base for fashioning and justifying a general or abstract concept of value. It is interesting to note that Bentham, who reduced all disparate qualities to the uniform search for pleasure, nevertheless used the concrete term "pleasure," not the term "value" in this context. For him, value literally refers to measurement, to finding the value of a given lot of pleasure by reckoning its intensity, duration, and so on.[43] In this older, and in many respects, very appealing sense, one would not speak of a *value* in any other sense than one would speak of a *price* or a *weight*. Value was, so to speak, not a substantive, but a question to be answered by reference to comparative standards of measurement.

That there has been some distortion in generalizing what was essentially a process of comparative measurement seems fairly clear. But whether the distortion is in theory, or in the quality of the life which theory reflects—such as the measurement of aesthetic value by the price the work will bring—is another and very complicated social question.

I used to think sometimes that the psychological and social sciences would gain in concreteness and lose little theory if such terms as "value" and "norm" were demoted to a lower level! But apart from its being too late, the question is not a purely verbal one, even though words can cause confusion. We are embarked in contemporary social science on the large-scale study of value phenomena—for example, in the Harvard Value Studies, to cite only one of the numerous approaches in the behavioral sciences. It is up to results to show whether the general value concept has a unified structure, or whether it remains at best a tag. But methodologically, what is here proposed is simply that, in fashioning a high-level abstract concept, we firmly maintain the lines of relevance to the promise of theoretical advance, to the institutional or practical forms or historical tendencies, or to any unified purposes involved.

The trend of our argument in this paper may be summarized briefly. The traditional concept of emergent levels requires a logical overhauling which, at the very least, disentangles its several theses. When liberalized, however, it helps provide a historically-oriented methodological approach that can bear considerable fruit in social theory. Further senses of "levels," specialized with a view to mapping types and degrees of group-generalization and instrumental-functional relationships, can help clarify connections and formulate research problems within the framework provided by the basic sense of qualitative emergence. Intellectual production as participant in historical process admits of such treatment as well, and when this is done the development of categories acquires greater scope. Their evaluation is rooted in a fuller reference to their implicit operations and underlying tasks.

NOTES

1. For analysis of some of the problems in the concepts of emergence and novel qualities, see: A. O. Lovejoy, "The Meanings of 'Emergence' and Its Modes," *Proceedings of the Sixth International Congress of Philosophy* (1926): 20-33; Gustav Bergmann, "Holism, Historicism and

Emergence," *Philosophy of Science* 11 (1944): 209-21; Paul Henle, "The Status of Emergence," *Journal of Philosophy,* 39 (1942): 486-93; Abraham Edel, *The Theory and Practice of Philosophy* (New York: Harcourt, Brace, 1946), pp. 48-64; Maurice Mandlebaum, "A Note on Emergence," in *Freedom and Reason,* ed. Salo W. Baron, Ernest Nagel and Koppel S. Pinson (Glencoe, Ill.: Free Press, 1951), pp. 175-83; P. E. Meehl and Wilfrid Sellars, "The Concept of Emergence," in *The Foundations of Science and the Concepts of Psychology and Psychoanalysis,* ed. Herbert Feigl and Michael Scriven (Minnesota Studies in the Philosophy of Science, Minneapolis: University of Minnesota Press, 1956), pp. 239-52. For integrative levels, in relation to different fields, see: Alex B. Novikoff, "The Concept of Integrative Levels and Biology," *Science* 101 (1945): 209-15; R. W. Sellars, V. J. McGill, and Marvin Farber, eds., *Philosophy for the Future* (New York: Macmillan, 1949); essays by J. B. S. Haldane, T. C. Schneirla, and B. J. Stern. For related problems of whole and parts, see Ernest Nagel, "Wholes, Sums, and Organic Unities," *Philosophical Studies,* 3 (1952): 17-32.

2. J. B. S. Haldane, "Interaction of Physics, Chemistry, and Biology," in Sellars, McGill, Farber, eds., *Philosophy for the Future,* p. 215.

3. Sigmund Freud, *Group Psychology and the Analysis of the Ego,* trans. James Strachey (New York: Bantam Books, 1960).

4. Logan Wilson, "Sociography of Groups," in *Twentieth Century Sociology,* ed. Georges Gurvitch and Wilbert E. Moore (New York: Philosophical Library, 1945), p. 140. He is referring to Znaniecki's view that "the same basic facts about man in society can be subsumed under a systematic theory of social actions, of social relations, of social persons, and of social groups."

5. For a review of some of these aspects, see Florian Znaniecki, "Social Organization and Institutions," in Gurvitch and Moore, eds., *Twentieth Century Sociology,* pp. 172-217. See also S. F. Nadel, *The Foundations of Social Anthropology* (Glencoe, Ill.: Free Press, 1953), chs. 5, 7; and N. S. Timasheff, "The Basic Concepts of Sociology," *American Journal of Sociology* 58 (1952): 176-86.

6. Leslie A. White, *The Science of Culture* (New York: Farrar, Straus, 1949), p. 126. Compare his assertion: "Culture thus becomes a continuum of extrasomatic elements. It moves in accordance with its own principles, its own laws; it is a thing *sui generis.* Its elements interact with one another, forming new combinations and syntheses. New elements are introduced into the stream from time to time, and old elements drop out." ("Ethnological Theory," in Sellars, McGill, and Farber, eds., *Philosophy for the Future,* p. 374).

7. Quoted in A. L. Kroeber and Clyde Kluckhohn, *Culture, A Critical Review of Concepts and Definitions* (Cambridge: Papers of the Peabody Museum of American Archaeology and Ethnology, Harvard University, Vol. 47, No. 1, 1952), p. 87.

8. A. Irving Hallowell, "The Self and Its Behavioral Environment," in his *Culture and Experience* (Philadelphia: University of Pennsylvania Press, 1955).

9. Kroeber and Kluckhohn, *Culture*, p. 148.

10. Abraham Edel, "Interpretation and the Selection of Categories," in *Meaning and Interpretation*, University of California Publications in Philosophy, Vol. 25 (Berkeley: University of California Press, 1950), pp. 57-95.

11. Cf. Hadley Cantril, *The Psychology of Social Movements* (New York: Wiley, 1941), ch. 4.

12. Betty W. Starr, "Levels of Communal Relations," *American Journal of Sociology*, 60 (1954): 125-35.

13. A. M. Lee, "Levels of Culture as Levels of Social Generalization," *American Sociological Review*, 10 (1945): 485-95.

14. Robin M. Williams, Jr., *American Society* (New York: Knopf, 1955), p. 31; cf. ch. 10.

15. Robert K. Merton, "Social Structure and Anomie," in his *Social Theory and Social Structure* (Glencoe, Ill.: Free Press, 1949); Robert Redfield, *The Primitive World and Its Transformations* (Ithaca, N.Y.: Cornell University Press, 1953); R. H. Tawney, *Religion and the Rise of Capitalism* (New York: Mentor, 1947).

16. Nadel, *Social Anthropology*, p. 76.

17. Such investigation needs a clearer mapping of the constituents of a morality. For an attempt to do this on a comparative cultural basis, see May Edel and Abraham Edel, *Anthropology and Ethics: The Quest for Moral Understanding*, rev. ed. (Transaction, 1970). The question of methodology and the three levels is more fully discussed in Abraham Edel, *Method in Ethical Theory* (Indianapolis, Ind.: Bobbs-Merrill, 1963), ch. 9.

18. T. H. Huxley and Julian Huxley, *Touchstone for Ethics* (New York: Harper, 1947), p. 127.

19. For a careful formulation, including some physical parallels to the self-fulfilling prophecy, see Adolf Grünbaum, "Historical Determinism, Social Activism, and Predictions in the Social Sciences," *The British Journal for the Philosophy of Science*, 7 (1956): 236-40. Cf. also the treatment of this problem in Merton, "Social Structure and Anomie."

20. Bertrand Russell, *Power, A New Social Analysis* (New York: Norton, 1938); H. D. Lasswell and Abraham Kaplan, *Power and Society, A Framework for Political Inquiry* (New Haven: Yale University Press, 1950).

21. Kroeber and Kluckhohn, *Culture*. See my review of the book in *Journal of Philosophy*, 51 (1954): 559-63.

22. John Laird, *The Idea of Value* (Cambridge: Cambridge University Press, 1929), ch. 3.

23. John Dewey, "Theory of Valuation," *International Encyclopedia of Unified Science*, 2, 4 (Chicago: University of Chicago Press, 1939).

24. Ellis Freeman, *Social Psychology* (New York: Holt, 1937), p. 123.

25. Kimball Young, *Social Psychology* (New York: Crofts, 1945), p. 123.

26. Muzafer Sherif and Hadley Cantril, *The Psychology of Ego-Involvements* (New York: Wiley, 1947), p. 24.

27. Broom, Leonard, and Selznick, Philip, *Sociology* (Evanston, Ill.: Row, Peterson, 1958), p. 278.

28. Clyde Kluckhohn and others, "Values and Value-Orientations in the Theory of Action," in *Toward a General Theory of Action,* ed. Talcott Parsons and Edward A. Shils (Cambridge: Harvard University Press, 1951), p. 395.

29. Williams, *American Society,* p. 374.

30. Kingsley Davis, *Human Society* (New York: Macmillan, 1948, 1949), p. 124.

31. Talcott Parsons, *The Social System* (Glencoe, Ill.: Free Press, 1951), p. 7.

32. This does not mean that the theorists using the broad concept of value necessarily neglect the evaluative side. Perry couples his initial tolerance of any interest with elaboration of criteria for the integration of interests. Even his initial tolerance is given a justification explicitly in a general conception of love, which supports any interest whatever it may be, as a starting point in evaluation.

33. Hadley Cantril, *The Psychology of Social Movement* (New York: Wiley, 1941), p. 4.

34. Ibid., p. 7.

35. Williams, p. 25.

36. Davis, pp. 10-11.

37. Ibid., pp. 52-53.

38. Robert Bierstedt, *The Social Order* (New York: McGraw-Hill, 1957), p. 140.

39. Ibid., p. 175. Cf. also pp. 149-50 on "ideologies."

40. Broom and Selznick, p. 64.

41. Abraham Edel, "Concept of Values in Contemporary Philosophical Value Theory," *Philosophy of Science,* 20 (1953): 198-207.

42. As in Plato or Freud. Cf. Kingsley Davis: "All human behavior can be interpreted as motivated by the need for unity. Particular motives are simply expressions of this main motive." (Davis, *Human Society,* p. 239.)

43. Jeremy Bentham, *An Introduction to the Principles of Morals and Legislation* (Oxford: Clarendon Press, 1907), ch. 4.

Part 2

Values and Methods in the Analysis of Social Concepts

9. Context and Content in the Theory of Ideas

This paper was written in the late 1940s as a contribution to a volume presenting the contours of a modern materialism. The 1940s witnessed a number of bold attempts to modernize older philosophical traditions. Positivism on the American scene was fusing to a point with pragmatism. A naturalist manifesto had appeared in a volume, edited by Y.H. Krikorian, entitled Naturalism and the Human Spirit. It stressed largely the nonreductive character of a naturalism that used the method of science in understanding the works of the human spirit. The volume on Philosophy for the Future: The Quest of Modern Materialism stressed the primacy of materialism and its growth from the older physicalism to modern historical and dialectical materialism and beyond. My own view, expressed in a book on The Theory and Practice of Philosophy (1946) saw the "materialist-naturalist tradition" as a broad stream in the history of philosophy characterized by a belief in the primacy of matter and change, an emphasis on the method of science in advancing knowledge in all fields, and a this-worldly outlook on values. I could, therefore, see no reason why there should not be a drawing together of the several vital movements in a way that clarified their differences so as to be able to resolve them by future research. (Indeed, I wrote papers for both the naturalist and materialist volumes, and later on a monograph for the positivist-pragmatist Encyclopedia of Unified Science.) Actually, what happened in the 1950s was that professional philosophy lost interest in the strife of philosophical systems and stopped talking about metaphysical 'isms, shifting instead to a problem orientation and methodological 'isms. Perhaps some degree of unity had, in fact, been achieved, so that the older

205

issues lost their impulse. Or perhaps it was simply a change in fashion. But since methodological conflicts raged as vigorously as ever, even intensified by the struggle of positivism and phenomenology and existentialism, perhaps little had changed below the surface. I find the lessons of the present essay still very important for achieving a broader approach to the analysis of concepts.

The aim of the paper was to reconcile the genetic modes and the logical-analytic modes of dealing with concepts. A purely logical illustration will show the issue. Alfred Tarski, in his Introduction to Logic, points out that if a person tells us, "I am leaving town on Monday or Tuesday or Wednesday," and we find out he had already decided to leave on Tuesday (and bought a travel ticket), we would say he deceived us. But technically "or" has a firm meaning: it signifies only that at least one of the constituent propositions is true, which is the case in the person's statement. The older idealist logicians (F.H. Bradley, for example) would go into the element of hesitation in analyzing the use of "or." But the formal logicians had revolted against "psychologism." They found it irrelevant to ask whether the person enunciating a proposition held it in belief or hope or doubt or fear. Let the psychologist worry about that. The logical analysis dealt with the meaning of the assertion, not the psychology or sociology of its utterance.

Such differences, while they became passionate, were nothing compared to what happened when a Marxist branded democracy as a "bourgeois" concept and traced the growth of different strands in the democratic idea in relation to the rise of the bourgeoisie. The controversy became bitter. How we got the idea, argued the logical analyst, is one thing, how we assess its truth or value is quite another. To judge truth or intellectual adequacy on the basis of origins is a genetic fallacy. The history of an idea is scientifically interesting, but logically irrelevant to its meaning and its truth.

As a pendular reaction in the history of philosophy, liberation of logical analysis from genetic considerations was understandable, if logical considerations had indeed been previously swamped in historical ones. But it was possible that "genetic" covered a diversity of uses, some of which helped at one point, some at quite another. If historical study of ideas was to be of assistance in understanding and evaluating ideas, we would have *to see precisely where and in what respect it was useful, not settle the question in an all-or-none manner.*

Today the issue is perhaps less traumatic than in the late 1940s. The emphasis on context in ordinary language analysis has pushed beyond the formal meaning of an utterance to concern itself with the contextual implications in asserting it and the presuppositions it involves. Work in induction and probability has brought a fresh focus on the beliefs of the speaker in his act of utterance; the pragmatic element has loomed large in evaluating formal constructions with respect to their application. Work in the history of science has related historical considerations more intimately to the growth of scientific issues. And although sociohistorical aspects of meaning still remain on the edge of the professional philosopher's field of labor, cultural analysis of ideas has been advanced by studies in philosophical anthropology and in the theory of symbolism generally.

The central and unique contribution of a materialist theory in the analysis of ideas has been to relate ideas to the sociohistorical context in which they arise, take shape, and exert what influence they may. Other elements in the materialist treatment of ideas—an empirical stress in opposition to a Platonic intuitionism, a readiness to regard and explore thinking as a natural phenomenon—are shared in varying degrees by other philosophical outlooks such as pragmatism or positivism. For this reason, attention will be fastened in this paper primarily upon exploring the meaning, scope, and limits of the sociohistorical analysis of ideas.[1] Some corollaries will be drawn for the relation of theory and practice and the role of ideas in history.

The view that exploration of sociohistorical context yields a fuller understanding of ideas contains a number of distinct theses. One is the view that ideas have sociohistorical causes or are sociohistorical products. A second is the view that ideas have sociohistorical functions or roles. A third—and much more difficult notion—is the view that ideas have sociohistorical content. In discussing these different theses, illustration will be taken primarily from philosophical ideas.

1. *The causes of an idea.* It is commonly agreed that ideas must have causes. As parts of nature they have physical causes, and as qualities of organic bodies they have physiological causes. As growing out of human experience, they probably have determinate

psychological causes. In historical writing, there is usually very little reference to physical and physiological causes of ideas. Occasionally, there are references to the psychological properties of thinkers as causally relevant. Thus Kant's moral rigorism is sometimes associated with anecdotes about his methodical habits, with the suggestion that his categorical imperative was produced by a personal order obsession. Schopenhauer's pessimism is often treated in similar fashion.

Materialist theory in its earlier forms stressed the physical and physiological phases of thinking. In ancient times, Democritus identified ideas with the movement of special fine round atoms. Seventeenth-century Hobbesian mechanism reduced ideas ultimately, through sensation, to the meeting of external and internal (bodily) motions. Eighteenth-century French materialism, when it did not, with Cabanis, reduce thought to a secretion of the brain, fitted man's mental life into a world described in the language of mechanics and physiology, supplemented by the language of introspective psychology. Marxian dialectical materialism in the nineteenth century, treating ideas as reflections of the material world, both physical and social, first proposed a systematic theory of social causation of the development and career of ideas.

The general view that ideas do not grow merely out of previous ideas, but stem from, and change in response to, changing human needs, is so widely established in historical and social investigation today as to seem almost commonplace. Even where ideas develop simply as part of reflective inquiry by curious minds, there are causes to be sought for this comparatively rare phenomenon itself, the disinterested pursuit of truth. And whether these causes are best described in the psychological terms of a surplus allotment of wonder or curiosity in some temperaments, or the social terms of scientists caught up in the movement of a class whose material interests are closely bound to the discovery of truth in special areas, is entirely an empirical matter upon which a disinterested sociology is not without evidence today. While there is no unanimity on the social coordinates to be used for the analysis—whether economic, narrowly technological, political, or simply diffusion from other cultures—there does seem to be dominant agreement that there are social causes.

The dissenting opinion comes chiefly from those circles in liberal sociological theory that tend to deny all determinate causality in social affairs. Taking their inspiration from Max

Weber, they end up with parallels and loosely related multiple factors. Thus the growth of the Protestant ethic parallels the growth of the rationalizing spirit of capitalism, hierarchical philosophic conceptions parallel hierarchical social structures, mechanistic conceptions line up alongside of the spread of machine industry, individualistic morals keep pace with the growth of the open market. These are regarded as either parallels or as interwoven factors, but no judgment of primacy or causal direction is permitted. On a purely commonsense level, it would appear very difficult sometimes to avoid causal judgments. For example, during a great part of the nineteenth century, there was a shift in the southern states of the United States from regarding slavery as an unnecessary evil to justifying it as a positive good. This parallels the expansion of the cotton market, as the invention of machines for the textile industry and the tremendous growth of its trade created a veritable hunger for cotton. T.V. Smith, summarizing the process,[2] has no compunction in concluding: "Economic advantage begot cultural compensations. Cultural compensations conjured up humanitarian mitigations. Logical justification followed. And a certain spiritual sanctification crowned the whole." Can there really be much doubt that such arguments as "slavery is good for the slave," "it brings Africans to missionaries rather than missionaries to Africa," "the Negro really has no soul,"[3] had their social causes?

In such judgments of causality, there is no special problem for the theory of ideas. Whatever interpretation of causality be taken in speaking of the causes of war, or the emergence of an institution, can likewise be used in posing the problem of the causes of an idea, its emergence, and its development. This is not, of course, the place to enter into the overall problem of the legitimacy of causal judgments in social science. It should be noted, however, that the denial of such causality leaves the phenomena of parallelism we have noted unexplained. As a consequence, it almost invites such theories as "pre-established harmony" or "spirit of an age."

2. *The functions of an idea.* It is generally recognized today that ideas have not merely causes, but also functions or uses, that they are or can be weapons. The meaning of such an approach varies. Sometimes, it points to the emotional role of ideas. Ideas, over and above their ideational content, give expression to, or are associated with, emotions, so that the use of the idea gives satisfaction to, or is a way of controlling, the emotion in oneself

or others. William James, for example, classified philosophers as tender-minded—rationalistic, idealistic, free-willist, and so on—and tough-minded—empiricist, materialistic, fatalistic, and so on.[4] Carnap holds to a somewhat similar view: monism expresses an even and harmonious life, dualism expresses life felt as an eternal struggle, realism expresses the extroverted constitution, idealism expresses the introverted type.[5] Since, however, Carnap regards metaphysical propositions as having no factual content, this expressive function constitutes, so to speak, the whole of the idea.

Such a treatment, suggesting that certain ideas are only instruments for achieving emotional effects, has attained to some prominence in political theory. It is easy enough to point to Mussolini's letter to Bianchi demanding that a philosophy be produced for fascism in two months, for "Italian Fascism now requires, under pain of death, or worse, of suicide, to provide itself with a body of doctrine," or to Hitler's reassuring explanation to an industrial leader that he was using socialist slogans because nationalist slogans alone would no longer attract German workmen.[6] Karl Mannheim points out the way in which what he calls "the particular conception of ideology" operates with a psychology of interests and first finds itself by unmasking doctrines to reveal the private interests that they serve.[7] Thurman Arnold, in his *Folklore of Capitalism,* has popularized the view that abstract ideas operating in political and social life may serve ritual or emotional functions and hinder the satisfaction of concrete human needs. Writers such as Lasswell, James Marshall, and Burnham tend to regard abstract ideas and ideals largely as propaganda symbols.[8]

The Marxian view that the dominant ideas of an age express the interests of the dominant class may also be taken in this sense, that the ideas serve as weapons for the dominant class. But the theory also admits of other emphases as well. It may be a causal analysis pointing to class elements in the genesis of ideas. It may be a complicated thesis of social selection analogous to natural selection: all sorts of ideas arise, but those congenial to the dominant class achieve prominence. This analysis is most effective when it can predict the intellectual trend. An interesting example is Hilferding's prediction in 1910 on economic grounds of the role of racial ideologies.[9] Finance capital requires a powerful political state, the regimentation of independent individual capitalists at home, protection for the home market, and conquest of foreign markets. This expansive force revolutionizes the Weltanschauung of the bourgeoisie, condemns liberal humanitarian elements, free trade, and the ideal of peace, and substitutes the might of the state. It alters the national idea: "The economic advantage of monopoly is mirrored in the favored place which must be ascribed to one's own nation. The latter appears as chosen above all others. . . . Thus in racial ideology there emerges a scientifically-cloaked foundation for the power lust of finance capital, which in this way demonstrates the cause and necessity of its operations." 10

In addition to such combinations of causal and instrumental analysis of ideas, the Marxian theory may also, as we shall see, be a thesis concerning the content of ideas.

The pragmatist philosophies elaborate the instrumental function of ideas most systematically. In Charles Peirce's initial formulation, ideas were regarded as habits of action,11 which, in itself, might point to a content analysis (that is, what ideas *really are*) as well as an instrumental one. In Dewey, however, the latter phase is dominant; ideas are instruments functioning in the resolution of problem situations. Portions of experience assume an ideational character by the role that they play: "Ideas are anticipated consequences (forecasts) of what will happen when certain operations are executed under and with respect to observed conditions." 12 He attacks the traditional view of ideas as copies of perceptions for ignoring "the prospective and anticipatory character that defines *being* as an idea." The opposition to this broad operationalism comes largely, in the materialist-naturalist tradition, from a realism which insists on a correspondence in some sense or other between experience and existence, in short, an essentially representative role for experience rather than merely a prospective role.

3. *The content of an idea.* All treatments of ideas recognize, in one fashion or another, the existential aspect and the referential aspect of an idea. The latter—which is our present concern—has been referred to in many ways. Some use the omnibus term "meaning"; others more technically speak of the "referent" or the "designatum." Some narrow it to the "mode of verification" of the proposed statement in which the idea occurs; others prefer a more material treatment and speak of "the aspects of existence represented." Logicians commonly refer to the "connotation" of the term. We shall here, without further refinement, speak of the "content of an idea" as quite literally what it contains or what is rendered clear in its analysis.13 The central question, however, is what kind of analysis; the issues at stake in controversies on this

question are largely problems of how the analysis of ideas is to be carried out.

It is at this point especially that we find a marked difference within the materialist-naturalist tradition today. This is best seen, perhaps, in the contrast of the positivist logical analysis and the Marxian historical analysis of an idea.[14] In the former, the study of ideas is transformed into the study of language and its uses. Instead of analyzing ideas, it analyzes terms, the rules for their combination, their transformation into other terms, and their application. A logical analysis thus yields the factual or scientific content of an idea, which is often regarded as the sense perceptions with the prediction of which the analysis terminates.[15] Everything else is relegated either to an expressive or pragmatic function in the use of a symbol,[16] or else to a causal examination of the situation in which the symbol is used.

The common philosophic conception of an idea's content does, in fact, tend to draw sharply the distinction between content and context. The career of an idea or the existential conditions underlying its development tend to be regarded as external to the idea itself. This is the domain of causality or natural history—the story of how ideas are grasped, their influence over men when they are clearly understood. The studies of the social history of ideas are thus regarded as purely separable scientific ventures, irrelevant to the philosophical analysis of the ideas. History is thus intrinsically irrelevant to ideas, except where it is an inner history of their unfolding, or where the idea happens to be specifically about historical matters. There is even a standard fallacy—the "genetic fallacy"—to connote the confusion of the causal and ideational orders and the attempt to assess the content of an idea by the way it happened to come into existence. Hence, the search into the context of philosophical ideas is often dismissed as irrelevant "psychologizing" or "sociologizing."

In the Marxian analysis, on the other hand, the exploration of sociohistorical context is relevant to the exhibition of the idea's content. For example, Marx and Engels say of philosophic ideas, in *The German Ideology*: "All epoch-making systems have as their real content the needs of the time in which they arise. Each one of them is based on the whole of the antecedent development of a nation, on the historical growth of its class relations with their political, moral, philosophical and other consequences." [17]

On the face of it, such a thesis has innumerable difficulties to overcome. In what sense, when Kant is discussing the a priori, or

Bentham the meaning of pleasure, or Plato the immortality of the soul, or Aristotle the law of contradiction, can they be said to be talking *also, and in an important sense, about the needs of their time?* Is it possible to carry sociohistorical coordinates into the very inner sanctum of ideas? Does not the logical analysis of the ideas give us sufficient content to be able to proceed to judgments of truth or intellectual adequacy? Why should the analysis of content be expanded in new directions?

The general thesis that an examination of sociohistorical context tells us more fully what ideas "are about" was perhaps implicit in the idealist conception of objective mind. Marx and Engels gave it a materialist formulation and also offered a special theory of the kinds of sociohistorical factors pertinent. Since their time, the general thesis has become the property of much practicing sociology, anthropology, and history, insofar as ideas are regularly dealt with by these studies in a social matrix. Mannheim, in attempting to found a sociology of knowledge, gave the thesis a specialized and, at times, almost predominantly political form. Dewey, at times, employs such a thesis in generalized form, when he explain philosophical dualisms in terms of social cleavages and looks for the meaning of philosophical ideas in terms of the social practices in which they are embedded.

It is quite clear, however, that materialist philosophy cannot hold to this thesis in an unrestricted fashion. For materialism operates with an epistemology in which true ideas are regarded as accurate reflections of the world, and it must, therefore, allow of some purely physical assertions. Engels sometimes, in fact, speaks almost as if the sociohistorical content of ideas were that part, in virtue of which ideas deviate from truth: "Indeed the materialistic outlook on nature means no more than simply conceiving nature just as it exists without any foreign admixture." [18] This phase of the materialist writings leads Mannheim to regard the Marxian contribution as negative, merely directed to unmasking opponents and unconscious of its own similar character. Actually, however, once we distinguish, in using sociohistorical context, the three separate elements of causality, function, and content, then there is no inconsistency in holding that all ideas have sociohistorical causes, that most ideas have sociohistorical functions, that many more ideas than we think have sociohistorical content, that the truth or falsity of ideas is a thoroughly objective question not to be confused with the preceding propositions, and that the holding of true ideas has sociohistorical causes.

In order to come to grips with the problems thus raised, and especially to determine the scope and limits of the thesis concerning sociohistorical content of ideas, it is necessary to explore both the wider question of the extension of content as well as the specific one of extension to include sociohistorical content.

4. *The extension of content in the analysis of ideas.* The first identification of an idea is, at most, tentative. A statement about the content of an idea is a hypothesis for an inquiry whose terminus may very well be a stipulation. The inquiry is, in the first place, directed to the intentions of a man or group of men as expressed in action, speech, and writings. In this sense, the ideas we investigate for content are qualities of natural events over periods of time, which we call men thinking. The inquiry may be addressed to ourselves as well as to others. We may examine our own ideas in any field with the intention of exploring and articulating them. We may similarly examine other people's ideas or the ideas of another age. Evidence and analysis are required to determine where the content of the idea begins and ends. The examination of one's own ideas has this distinctive mark, that the person himself is examining them; therefore, the creative element is stronger, and examination may mean growth or alteration. If I discover discrepancies in my idea of "content," for example, I alter the idea. If I discover such elements in Aristotle's notion of "nature," I can only report that they are there and try to see them on a wider canvas in his writings.

This example itself suggests one way in which content may become broadened beyond the initial elements identified, that is, when one is led on in the analysis by gaps and discrepancies. It need not be this alone. One may simply note relationships that suggest a demand for further specification, or even try out some theory of interpretation to see what light it sheds.

In principle, the problem is the same in imagination, in perception, in art, in thought. It is that of drawing a line between data and interpretation, and what I am suggesting is that no sharp line can be drawn. Suppose a man reports a dream and comes to interpret it in the psychoanalytic process in a given way. Why should the particular form of his first report determine in privileged fashion the content of the dream, and everything else be regarded as *its* interpretation? In one sense, it is true he dreamed, let us say, about a certain friend. He comes to see that the friend in the dream represented his father. Is it purely a verbal matter to say that his father was part of the content of the dream, or even that it was "really" his father he was dreaming about? Actually seeing the friend as the father may give a systematic character to the happenings of the dream which otherwise they would not have. The case is even clearer if we deal not with a person but an emotion. Erich Fromm, for example, says of faith that: "Psychologically, faith has two entirely different meanings. It can be the expression of an inner relatedness to mankind and affirmation of life; or it can be a reaction formation against a fundamental feeling of doubt, rooted in the isolation of the individual and his negative attitude toward life." [19] Presumably there would be differential qualities of feeling involved which the individual, if sufficiently discriminating, might detect. But whether he did or not, if the psychological interpretation in a given case is correct, then the interpretation may be regarded as broadening the *content*, rather than as simply giving a causal explanation of it.

On the other hand, both in these cases and in ordinary perception, it is possible to pursue the opposite policy and insist on narrowing the content. The dream was not of the friend, but of certain color and shape patterns; similarly, what you now see is not a man running a race, nor even a man running, but certain successive color and shape patterns. The feeling is not faith, but something much narrower, hope or anxiety. The various entities are either constructs out of feeling and sensation, or, if you wish to be a realist, they are existing objects and attitudes which *cause* these feelings and sensations. The sole content of thought would turn out on analysis to be some type of sense-data, a view found in a number of the forms of positivism.[20]

Let us take a further example from the field of art theory. A painting before you shows certain color and shape patterns. Or it shows a mother and child. Or it shows Mary and the Christ child. What is the content of the picture—sense patterns, familial relations with their emotional implications, a particular religious complex? Even if we are concerned with esthetic content, any a priori limitation really presents a valuation: for example, defining the content as the one the artist intended is a stress on communication as central value. Even then, the question of what is expressed by the artist would allow a fresh range of selection, from motives and feelings to patterns of the age of whose broader contours the artist may have been personally unaware.

If the same analysis holds for the content of ideas, any attempt to limit the content to abstract or structural elements, to sensory elements or individual psychological elements, can only be regarded as valuational in character. The desire for a full elaboration of content as against partial analysis is likewise, of course, valuational, but the values it embodies are those of the fullest or most systematic description of the world. Hence, its intent is scientific understanding.

5. *The sociohistorical content of ideas.* So far, we have merely insisted on the right to look for sociohistorical content. It remains now to see whether and to what extent such content is really discoverable in philosophical ideas, and to what extent it is required in the analysis of an idea.

Perhaps the simplest way to make the point is briefly to examine a few ideas. Take, for example, ethical ideas of an abstract order such as justice or equality. Can we really understand them by such definitions as, "Justice is giving each man his due," or such distinctions as Aristotle makes between arithmetic equality (everyone the same) and proportionate equality (to each what he deserves)? Either the notions must be so refined as to be almost purely mathematical propositions, or else the meaning of "due," "same," and "desert" requires amplification. Aristotle pointed out that what a man deserves is reckoned differently in an aristocracy, an oligarchy, and a democracy.

Once the Platonic approach to pure ideas is abandoned, there is no reason to see the abstract formula as *the idea* and the interpretations as *applications* of the preexistent idea. Justice will mean simply the fundamental principles that systematize the operations of an existing legal system—for example, its particular assumptions about property structure, responsibility structure, and so on. Universal justice will mean any discoverable invariant elements in such systems, or else the fundamental elements of a projected ideal system—where "ideal" refers to existent patterns of striving, with the aims of man seen in sociohistorical terms. Similarly, if we look at Engels' treatment of equality as a moral ideal in his *Anti-Duhring,* we can see that he is not so much exploring causes or describing instruments as showing that the very idea of equality has had different meanings at different stages of man's history. Among the Greeks and Romans, it could not mean human equality, embracing slaves. In early Christianity, it meant that all were equally born in original sin, the ideational expression of the status of slavery and oppression. Among the bourgeoisie, it means the demand for removal of class privileges; while for the proletariat, it means the demand for the abolition of classes themselves. "The idea of equality, therefore, both in its bourgeois and in its proletarian form, is itself a historical product, the creation of which required definite historical conditions which in turn themselves presuppose a long previous historical development." [21]

The conclusion of such an analysis is not merely that without reference to sociohistorical content the idea is vague and confusing. This normative proposition is often asserted today in one or another fashion when a demand is made for specification of a term in observationally verifiable consequences, or in the semantic insistence that we speak of equality$_1$, equality$_2$, equality$_3$. The significance of the analysis lies in the hypothesis, over and above the assertions about good usage of terms, that the sociohistorical content is, in fact, present even where the terms are abstractly used. In short, it is the hypothesis that further analysis of text or context, in dealing with philosophical ideas, will reveal sociohistorical content to complete the idea, that without it the idea is fragmentary.

I should like to illustrate the thesis at this point from two philosophical ideas which seem to me to be immeasurably clearer when so regarded. Since they are well-worn ideas from the philosophical stock, often treated and the center of many interpretations, whatever success is attained with them may be indicative of what may be achieved with other philosophical ideas. One is the Aristotelian idea of the mean, the other the Benthamite idea of pleasure.

As is well known, Aristotle uses the idea of the mean to identify virtuous conduct and the states of character which are virtues. If we ask ourselves, however, what after all is the idea of the mean, and explore the Aristotelian texts and the Greek cultural contexts, many phases of content arise as candidates. Abstractly regarded, the mean appears sometimes as the exactly right, measured out to the correct point, with a rejection of too much and too little. This is the artist's or craftsman's concept of due proportion. It also appears as a synthesis of opposing forces which do not disappear, but are balanced in the resultant. It appears again as the cultural prohibition of "hybris," a specific type of arrogance or ambition which, by aiming at what is more than one's mortal lot, invites the envy of the gods. And in Aristotle's *Politics,* it appears quite definitely and explicitly as the compromise between oligarchy and democracy, a kind of middle-class rule to avoid the disorder attendant on the strife of rich and poor. The first temptation, from the point of view of traditional philosophical habits, is to call the abstract content *the* idea, and to speak of the others as applications. But such selection of the abstract elements for a central and identifying role appears arbitrary once the full range is exhibited. A second way out is to start with a plurality, and speak of mean$_1$, mean$_2$, mean$_3$, mean$_4$. But this may beg the question by stipulating that they are distinct and unrelated. Of course they may be, but this is a hypothesis about Aristotle's writings and ideas which requires testing. Perhaps the fairest approach is to recognize that identification of the idea may start with any phase, that many phases of content may be discovered, that whether they are to be regarded as phases or as the content of distinct ideas is itself to be decided by what degree of unity one actually discovers in the analysis. This implies that criteria of unity can themselves be worked out in the systematic study of ideas. One of these, in the case of a single writer such as Aristotle, would be, no doubt, the degree to which he intends his various treatments to be dealing with the "same" idea; others would be the degree to which they are bound together by common procedures or central purposes. Without entering at this point into the fuller investigation of relation of phases of content, it is clear at any rate that once a minimum of unity is established, we may speak of the one idea and its various phases of content. And if the analysis is correct, clearly the substantial political and cultural content in the idea of the mean cannot be ignored.

The case of pleasure in Bentham's ethics shows this even more clearly. The questions of the meaning of "pleasure" in Bentham's use, whether it has the additive properties he assigns to it, how one can speak of a whole of pleasure when it is a fleeting feeling, why every man should be regarded as the best judge of his own pleasures, and numerous other issues, are familiar enough in the controversies over the logic of hedonism. Now there is no doubt that one phase of the content of the idea of pleasure is the psychological one: it refers to a type of feeling with which we are introspectively familiar. But the feeling, as we so discover it, scarcely seems to have the properties Bentham assigns to pleasure either explicitly or implicitly in the way the idea appears in his ethical, legal, and political writings. The furthest we can get, if we limit our analysis to the psychological content, is to criticize factually Bentham's psychology and to wonder why he made such obvious blunders. Or we can try to save him by arguing that even if pleasure is not an extensive magnitude, a revised Benthamism can get along with it as an intensive magnitude. If, however, we pay attention to the sociohistorical phase of content, much becomes clear that before was puzzling. Bentham turns out to have his eye not on subjective feelings, not on behavioristic description of patterns of preference, but upon the acquisition of wealth as a typical and dominant goal of his time. The properties he assigns to pleasure are the properties of money, and the reduction of all specific value qualities to pleasure is, in effect, the reduction of all aspects of human activity to the test of yielding wealth. This is a strong thesis; a weaker one would be that he is using a pecuniary model in building his social philosophy. In either case, can one really understand the ethics of hedonism, both in the origin of modern Utilitarianism and in its various historical expressions, without embracing the sociohistorical elements—institutional, cultural, and specifically historical—as part of the very content of the idea of pleasure? [22]

At this point, let us state the view in its minimal terms: philosophical ideas have different phases of content, among which sociohistorical content may often be found. In the examples of the mean and pleasure we recognized abstract, psychological, general cultural, and specifically sociohistorical phases. There is, of course, no a priori limit to the types of phases there may be, just as we saw before that there was no a priori limit to the expansion of content.

6. *Relation of phases of content.* The next problem that naturally arises is whether the various phases are to be regarded as independent, a simple plurality, or whether their relations are to be construed in a special way. All sorts of metaphors are sometimes used to suggest a relationship. For example, one phase may be said to be the "garb" or "cloak" for a second, to "reflect" or "express" or "represent" it. Obviously, these problems reproduce with respect to ideas the problems of the relations between economic, political, religious, intellectual, and other phenomena. A full examination of the question would involve analysis of the reflection or expression relation in much greater detail and with greater specificity than the distinction of causality, instrumentality, and content made above. Although the metaphor in "reflection" is that of mirror image, involving correspondence of outline, this need not be the sole relationship involved. Just as the meaning of "representation" varies in each of the arts, even though in a general sense art may be representative, so the ways in which some phenomena reflect others may be quite diverse. The ways in which a charred scene reflects the fire that preceded it, an action

reflects a purpose, an ideal reflects a need, a dream reflects a wish, an instrument reflects a purpose, are quite different. There may also be secondary senses: A may reflect B because central parts of A reflect B, or because A is constructed by procedures that were developed in the construction of B, and so forth. A critical analysis of such relationships in the light of scientific results in the relation of phenomena would provide the conceptual tools for connecting the phases of content in an idea.

The relation of phases of content may be studied at a particular time or over a period of time. The relation of primacy in content, for example, may sometimes refer to stability; thus ritual may be primary in comparison to myth in the content of a single religious complex, in the sense that it remains the same while explanatory myths associated with it may shift. Or judgments of primacy may refer to causal relations. Or they may refer to purposes, as when one compares a political platform to the interests to which it "gives expression."

To examine more carefully the problem of relationship, let us look at another old philosophical illustration, the question raised by J.S. Mill whether there are qualities of pleasure. Bentham said that provided the amount of pleasure was the same, pushpin is as good as poetry to those who prefer it. Mill is unwilling to have the superiority of pleasures of the intellect over those of the body lie merely in "greater permanency, safety, uncostliness, etc." He claims an intrinsic qualitative difference. "If I am asked, what I mean by difference of qualities in pleasures, or what makes one pleasure more valuable than another, merely as a pleasure, except its being greater in amount, there is but one possible answer. Of two pleasures, if there be one to which all or almost all who have experience of both give a decided preference, irrespective of any feeling of moral obligation to prefer it, that is the more desirable pleasure." And his defense of the view concludes with: "It is better to be a human being dissatisfied than a pig satisfied; better to be Socrates dissatisfied than a fool satisfied. And if the fool, or the pig, are of a different opinion, it is because they only know their own side of the question. The other party to the comparison knows both sides." [23]

On its face, this argument (as we saw the original Benthamite hedonism appeared to) concerns what is to be found on introspection, namely qualitative distinctions in the feeling of pleasure. In fact, however, an important political potential readily appears on analysis. Bentham took every man to count as one and gave him permission to decide for himself about his own values. Mill not merely is appealing to discriminating persons and making their decision concerning what is good for the "fool" decisive, but is even risking the general equalitarian assumption, since a "wise man" might claim more recognition for his qualitatively higher desires than the "fool" for his.

What other phases of content can be discovered in this idea of differences of qualities in pleasure? One feels tempted to look for a personal psychological phase in an overintellectualized man of sensitive spirit. Perhaps this is so; certainly a marked preference for intellectual over bodily pleasures is part of the very content of the idea. But a careful study of Mill's other writings expands the content much further. One is struck by the formulation of the central problem in *Liberty*: the assumption that democratic government is as good as established and that, therefore, the chief theoretical task is to set a limit to what majorities may do to minorities. In his *Representative Government,* moreover, he indicates a mistrust of the people at large in a number of ways. Recognizing the major divergent directions of interest as laborers and employers, he thinks that both interests ought to be equally represented in influence in Parliament: "Since, assuming that the majority of each class, in any difference between them, would be mainly governed by their class interests, there would be a minority of each in whom that consideration would be subordinate to reason, justice, and the good of the whole; and this minority of either, joining with the whole of the other, would turn the scale against any demands of their own majority which were not such as ought to prevail." [24] He thinks that only those who pay taxes should elect those who vote the taxes, that those on relief should be disqualified from voting. He thinks that intelligence and virtue entitle a man to more weight in voting, but he adds that it is "entirely inadmissible, unless as a temporary makeshift, that the superiority of influence should be conferred in consideration of property." This is only because higher education is presumed in the wealthier; thus too, the liberal professions entitle a man to plural votes. The poorest man, however, should have a right to present himself for examination to prove his higher worth. [25]

It is clear from such materials—and they can be multiplied—that what separates Mill from Bentham is not an issue in introspective psychology, but the question whether a go-ahead signal should be given to the mass of men to proceed with complete freedom to determine public policy. Bentham is ready to do so because, like

Mill's father, James Mill, he has complete faith in the acceptance of middle-class leadership by the mass of men. It is the vista of endless growth from the middle-class point of view in the early stages of the industrial revolution. By the middle of the nineteenth century, the struggle has deepened; the socialist and communist movements have arisen. The revolutions of 1848 have shown the depth of the cleavage between middle class and workers. The development of industrialism has not spread the benefits to the degree promised, but has brought the misery that necessitated factory acts and subsequent social legislation. Mill, in the very act of fighting for the extension of the franchise, in struggling for the wider spread of benefits, finds within himself, in spite of his humanitarian outlook, a growing mistrust of the people, and wants them kept from full power. This is the sociohistorical content of the idea of qualitative differences in pleasures. One can find it by careful examination of Mill's texts. One can also see it in the fuller study of political theory of the nineteenth century. Mill tells us as much in his *Autobiography,* when he confesses that he began as a laissez-faire advocate and a democrat, and ended a kind of socialist but less a democrat.

If, in this example, we ask what is the relation of the phases of content, we can see that the sociohistorical aspect stands out prominently. It tells us what the idea is essentially about. The other phases do not disappear, but they fall in their place tied together and systematized by the sociohistorical content. Looking back at the examples given above, we can see that the very idea of equality is that of successively broadening demands for removal of discriminations, class privileges, and classes. The very idea of the mean in Aristotle is that of a Greek middle-class demand for political power and a middle-class ethic, cast in the categories of craftsmanship. The very idea of pleasure in Bentham is that of accumulating wealth in the typical amassing of profit in the period of the Industrial Revolution. Only in this way do the actual ideas, with all the properties they are assigned in the original texts and all the functions they serve in the contexts really "make sense."

The sociohistorical content, where it is found, thus rounds out the idea and brings fuller understanding. It does this not merely in the psychological or phenomenological sense of completing what stands out as incomplete and calls for completion, but in the logical sense in which a wider picture provides elements that systematize disparate fragments and reconcile apparent discrepancies. How far this proves to be generally the case, or in what areas of thought sociohistorical content, where present, may play a subsidiary rather than a unifying role, can only be discovered by careful specific historical and philosophical analysis. How conscious materialists have been of the immense labor required in such analysis may be seen from the remark of Engels that: "The development of the materialist conception even in regard to a single historical example was a scientific work which would have demanded years of tranquil study, for it is obvious that nothing can be done here with mere phrases, that only a mass of critically viewed, completely mastered historical material can enable one to solve such a task." [26] But the light shed by such an approach in the last century of philosophy would seem sufficient warrant for regarding the general hypothesis of sociohistorical content in philosophical ideas at least as a promising heuristic principle.

7. *Summary and formulation of the sociohistorical context hypothesis.* The general hypothesis that an analysis of socio-historical context is relevant to analysis of ideas may be summarized briefly at this point, putting together the various elements we separated for exploration. It constitutes, in the first place, a recommendation that, in beginning the investigation of ideas, one set up first the specific sociohistorical coordinates of the situation in which the ideas occur. It then predicts that causal elements, functional elements, and (with limitations to be discussed below) content elements—all sociohistorical in character—are discovera-ble, and where discovered will be found to play a central rather than a subsidiary role. The exact meaning of "central" varies, of course, according to the type of inquiry.

The three elements we have distinguished may themselves be related or independent. For example, in the case of Mill discussed above, it is probably true that the historical situation of the nineteenth century was a great part of the cause of his attitude to the people. But the sociohistorical content of his view would still be the same (provided that he had written the same books) even if his attitude had been caused by an earlier devotion to Plato, or even if it had been caused by an intense emotional attachment to someone who held that attitude. Again, the ideas, whether they have or have not a social content, may have social causes and serve social purposes. Thus Mill makes clear in chapter 3 of his *Autobiography* that his attempt to build an inductive logic was, in effect, a revolt against an autocratic or authoritarian mode of reasoning.

The hypothesis of the relevance of sociohistorical context to the analysis of ideas thus constitutes a composite picture whose various elements may be united in a general theory of the evolutionary development of human consciousness. As Marx and Engels put it in the *Communist Manifesto*: "Does it require deep intuition to comprehend that man's ideas, views, and conceptions, in one word, man's consciousness, changes with every change in the conditions of his material existence, in his social relations and in his social life? What else does the history of ideas prove than that intellectual production changes its character in proportion as material production is changed?" [27]

It follows also that we must distinguish between the general or minimum thesis that sociohistorical coordinates are integral to the analysis of ideas, and the specific thesis that these coordinates are of a definite sort. The general thesis seems already to be involved in much of the treatment of ideas in the social sciences. When an anthropologist, for example, investigates a myth, he may find it expressive of the history of the people, or the typical repressions associated with the familial pattern, or almost any phase of cultural life. The understanding of the myth or of a folk tale requires completion by the fuller picture. Even philosophical ideas, when studied by the social historian, are commonly seen as soaked in history, and changing in response to needs and circumstances.

A specific thesis that the sociohistorical coordinates are of a definite sort rests upon establishing a theory of social phenomena in general, therefore including ideas. Such theories of history have involved such specific coordinates as technology, struggle for power, mode of production, and so forth.

8. *Sociohistorical context and mathematical and logical ideas.* Controversies about the sociohistorical context of mathematical and logical ideas are considerably clarified by a distinction of the different phases of the context hypothesis. It is clear that the history of mathematics as part of human history is considerably enriched by causal and functional accounts—the land-measuring origins of geometry, the practical origins of counting, the rhetorical-political as well as the scientific origins of logic, the ethical and political use of mathematical eternity, and the relation of specific branches of mathematics to industrial and technical needs of their day. It is equally clear, however, that such historical analyses are not substitutes for content analyses nor assertions about the content of mathematical ideas. The question to what

degree mathematical and logical ideas may be developed independently of existential assertions and to what degree these existential assertions being scientific do or do not have sociohistorical phases of content can only be resolved by mathematical and scientific analysis and investigation.

Whatever the outcome, one need not, of course, assume a metaphysical domain of mathematical or logical ideas-as-such. The ideas are someone's idea (individual or group) and have to be investigated as such. Thus, if part of Plato's idea of mathematical ideas is that they are forms grasped by the soul as distinct from the body, then there is clearly some psychological and probably considerable social content in his mathematical ideas. On the other hand, modern logicians often claim to have purged $2+2=4$ and $a=a$ of all material, not merely ideological content. Their propositions are taken to be analytic truths, their definitions simply nominal equation of sets of marks, their postulates sentential functions constituting complex nominal definitions. No vestige of psychological content remains: not-p is neither vehement nor mild in its rejection of p. The purest mathematics becomes, as Russell is fond of pointing out, an idea of nothing in particular. If, in fact, a pure mathematics of such a character is an accomplished fact—and this is a mathematical and logical problem—and if no assumptions about our world are smuggled in in the process of its development,[28] then the sociohistorical-context hypothesis may be satisfied with expounding causes and functions.

If, however, logical ideas are regarded as metaphysical, or as ontologically grounded, as some have been prone to regard them in the history of philosophy, then they gain the widest content, and it is not surprising that part of this—purely as content, even apart from cause and function or role—should be sociohistorical in character. For example, the laws of contradiction and excluded middle, in Aristotle, are more than purely tautological assertions capable of exhibition by the truth tables. They express the concept of a fixed order of nature, and are therefore an integral part of his teleological world outlook. In their denial, as Aristotle explicitly says,[29] "those who talk like this do away with substance and essence, for they are compelled to assert that all things are accidents, and that there is no such thing as 'being essentially man' or 'animal.'" And to do away with substance means, in various fields, to deny natures or immanent designs in things. The laws of logic in Aristotle have many phases of content: instantaneous substantival change, for one thing, in physical theory, as well as fixed motions and places for physical elements, fixed species in biology, fixed human nature and fixed goals in ethical theory, fixed social places in political theory (natural slaves and natural subordination of women).[30]

It is not surprising, therefore, that when Engels, in his *Dialectics of Nature,* comes to attack the proposition that a = a, he deals with it as fundamentally the problem of permanence and change.[31] He allows, with reservations, its use in mathematics where he regards it as tautological, and, in application, its everyday use, where small-scale conditions or brief periods of time are in question. But he rejects it for nature, arguing that the individual changes, species change, laws change. He takes the old laws of logic, therefore, to be false. There is a real issue between Engels and Aristotle, but it is a question of science, not of tautologies.[32]

9. *Sociohistorical context and science.* There are, of course, many aspects of science as an enterprise or going concern which call for sociohistorical explanation that is causal or instrumental. And this is what is involved in many controversies about the sociohistorical character of science. A materialist sociohistorical approach often explains what aspects of scientific work are being stressed or neglected, and why. It shows what problems are set by dominant industries and social issues. It may also explain how by a kind of over-determination due to stimulation and direction of human inventive energy, discoveries of one kind or another are matured and hastened. And it likewise often explains why inventions once made are sometimes utilized, sometimes neglected or suppressed. These are problems primarily of the history of the growth of scientific knowledge and its utilization, not its content.

Again, there are aspects closely bound up with the way in which science is conceived which appear to have a sociohistorical character. The inner texture of scientific theory has often been cast in an ideological mold, for example when scientific laws are conceived of as inalterable expressions of God's will, or as conventions expressive of human subjectivity. And indeed the full sociohistorical context (probably including content elements) of traditional rationalist and empiricist approaches constitutes a still insufficiently explored segment of Western history and philosophy. But all such studies are clearly concerned with the sociohistorical content of specific philosophies of science, rather than with the results of science.

Even when ideological elements and specific or local sociohistorical aims are removed, there remain certain values in the basic aims of the scientific enterprise. Truth is not itself identical with reality or existence; it is a characteristic of some of men's beliefs, assertions, and opinions, in short, a property of the effort by men to see existence as clearly as they can. And this effort contains commitments which are clearly valuational in character. From the old determination to "save the appearances" (i.e., so to frame theories as to neglect none of the phenomena) to the formulation of experiments as questions to nature on which nature, not human wishes, shall give the answer, there is a deliberate harnessing of desire to what we may call a correspondence goal and the prediction and control that it entails. This is recognized by various philosophies in the common formulation that science seeks the dependable features of our world. The pragmatist may interpret this as turning truth into a value; the positivist may take it to be a conventional definition of science; the materialist may regard dependability as a criterion of correspondence. But all can agree on the presence of the value elements in the aims definitive of the scientific enterprise. The question then remains whether a sociohistorical content is to be found in these values themselves.

This problem presents a difficulty only if sociohistorical is taken in the narrow sense of class viewpoints or political perspectives. There are elements in a society which give expression to its mode of production more directly. For example, among the relations of production today, there are elements in the organization of work which express the necessities of large-scale technology, closely bound with elements expressing the capitalist control over technology. The whole of the history of practical activity—from the discovery of fire and agriculture through the development of handicrafts and then of machine industry, and so forth, enmeshed as it is by characteristics whose determination is more narrowly political—constitutes the growth of the struggle against nature. And this battle against nature, this growth of effective freedom, constitutes the sociohistorical basis of the widening of the area of prediction and collective control by the clearest presentation of nature's ways.[33] The removal of all ideological elements from science thus frees it of class purposes, but not of basic human aims.

There remains still the central question whether there are sociohistoric elements in the *results* of science, not merely its genesis, utilization, and basic aims. Certainly in dealing with the social sciences this may very well be the case. The hypothesis that the study of man is a sociohistorical study in some fundamental aspect is a plausible one which has considerable evidence on its behalf. Thus it would be contrasted with the view that the behavior of men can be scientifically explained in terms of biological factors alone, or in terms of an individualistic psychology, or of moral universals, and so forth. It is strengthened by the degree to which many human characteristics thought to be physiologically grounded turn out to be social products, by the extent to which economics has become infused with historical and institutional content, instead of being constituted by the deductive elaboration of the activity of an abstract "economic man," and so forth.

In some of the sciences of nature, there may be some sociohistorical content in an accidental sense—only to the degree to which the actual phenomena themselves may involve human participation. Thus the study of the development of animal forms in the last 5,000 years certainly involves reference to domestication; the future of many meteorological and geological phenomena will probably require some reference to control activities of men, the specific character of which will, no doubt, involve sociohistorical components. But there are obvious limits to these components, and in the past, certainly their role has been less. The question we are considering, therefore, stands out most clearly on its philosophical side if we ask whether there is any sociohistorical content to the results of the physical sciences, that is, the accumulating body of scientific laws or truths about the physical world—quite literally, the mathematical equations which together with specified operations yield predictable results.

At this point, certain philosophical approaches may be tempted to seek a persistent human element. For example, it may be said, the picture of the results of science at any time will include not merely laws and operations, but a full description of the equipment with which the operations are concerned, plus relevant elements of scientific techniques in construction and utilization of instruments. Can a sociohistorical phase of content be found in this area which bulks large in modern science? It might even seem that the operationalist element in scientific theory would make such techniques and instruments relevant to the full specification of operations and, therefore, to the content of the science, and not merely limit them to the conditioning effect of technology on the growth of the science. In this sense, a full account of scientific results at any given time, the argument runs, includes some reference to the state of technology of that time. And similar arguments are implicit in the pragmatic effort to see the results of physical science as in some sense an extension of "experience."

As was noted above, such a course of argument is not available to the materialist approach. For it is not ready to resolve science into statements about operations and their relation, and insists that the results of science be taken, in some sense, as telling us about the world. It accepts quite literally the scientific view that the world existed before man. Therefore, the sociohistorical character of scientific instruments will be taken quite literally to refer to the *instruments* of scientific inquiry rather than the results of scientific inquiry. And such sociohistorical elements could appear in the results of science only as explication of the relative or conditioned element in the result. In short, if the results of science at any time are regarded as "relative truth," the sociohistorical element enters only into the "relative," not the "truth." [34]

In general, it follows, the materialist approach to ideas is not limited to a sociohistorical approach. In the theory of physical science, the historical element may be relevant to the content of scientific results, since laws are interpreted, roughly speaking, as describing the regularities in the occurrence of material processes *at a particular stage in the development of matter.* But such attention to the change of laws, the emergence of new laws and new levels, and so forth involves no special reference to the human or the social, and the historical stress is equivalent to a stress on the primacy of change. In short, the sociohistorical represents only one phase of the material-historical.

10. *Sociohistorical context and truth.* In all these various ways in which sociohistorical context enters into science, no one can be interpreted as humanizing truth or rendering it other than "objective." This has, of course, been a central question in such discussions. For example, Mannheim, in his *Ideology and Utopia,* struggles with what appears to be the contradiction of maintaining a social point of view concerning ideas and holding to an objective theory of truth, and he abandons the latter, at least in historical and political science. He takes Marx to have discovered that there is a class or political view to knowledge and to have revealed the phenomenon of a false consciousness in historical classes.[35] But he takes Marx to have used this only against his enemies, insufficiently recognizing that the analysis could be used against his own side. Mannheim distinguishes clearly between treating the sociological analysis as an analysis of motives—a

narrowly genetic point of view—and discovering whole outlooks inherent in opposing political groups. In the social process, "every view should be equated with the social position of the observer. If possible, it should be investigated in every case why the relations appear as they do from every given standpoint." [36] He aims "to distinguish and isolate diverse styles of thinking and to relate them to the groups from which they spring." [37] In some sense or other, he takes these thought styles to be integral to the content of the group's thought, and when he comes to problems of validity of ideas, he takes a position in between the irrelevance of group perspective to the establishment of truth and its entire adequacy for determining truth. He believes that, in some way, epistemological concepts must be revised to take account of this view. But precisely how the nature of the genesis of an assertion becomes relevant to its truth is not entirely clear, even after much discussion.[38]

Perhaps the nearest approach to it is his statement that "in certain areas of historical-social knowledge it should be regarded as right and inevitable that a given finding should contain the traces of the position of the knower. ... The problem is not how we might arrive at a non-perspectivistic picture but how, by juxtaposing the various points of view, each perspective may be recognized as such and thereby a new level of objectivity attained." [39] It is to be noted in this connection that he has previously adopted the view that all historical knowledge is relative to the position of the observer,[40] that a dynamic synthesis is required, which must be reformulated from time to time.[41] Faced with the question how this can be done by perspective-bound groups, he takes refuge in the intellectuals. For they feel the impact of different classes; they alone are in a position to choose their affiliation; they are capable of carrying out their mission, which is "the discovery of the position from which a total perspective would be possible." [42] Mannheim's questioning here whether "it is desirable to throw overboard all of the opportunities which arise out of their peculiar situation," a situation in which a wider area of choice brings a need for total orientation and synthesis, shows pretty clearly the sociohistorical content of his own approach—the dilemma of the intellectual in our day. But this is the best he can offer in the way of objectivity in social knowledge.

By contrast, the Marxian theory is adamant on the objectivity of truth. No one in modern epistemology is more insistent than

Lenin, in his *Materialism and Empirio-Criticism,* on the absolute character of truth which science, with its relative truth, at any time is constantly approaching. And in the whole of the analysis above we have seen that the sociohistorical context hypothesis is concerned either with the cause and function of an idea—in which case it is not discussing its truth—or with expanding its content and relating elements of its content. In this latter case, the question of the truth of the idea arises only after its content is expanded, and the answer to the question is a matter of objective inquiry. Of course, in the process of expansion the form of the question may change. Instead of asking Mill's question whether there are qualities of pleasure, we should ask at the end whether, in the light of his own high evaluation of individuality, his fear of the masses is well-grounded. Whether the answer is yes or no— and I should say it is no—the resolution of his question is a scientific matter. Similarly, just as a question may be answered in a rough way prior to analysis, and after analysis, scarcely seem to need an answer, so many questions may tend to disappear on a fuller analysis, not that they are juggled away, but that they are answered on the road to clarification of content. In this respect, philosophical materialists tend to the view that questions about personal immortality are not well answered merely by showing that all perceptible consequences that could be deduced from the hypothesis that Mr. *A* is now a disembodied spirit are not verified, or that they are unverifiable. They are better answered by expanding the content of the idea until it appears as the demand for a richer quality of life, in the context of a collective insecurity engendered by lack of control over nature and the conflicts of man against man. Such a transformation has probably answered the question in its analysis of man along the way. Where desired, such steps may be rendered explicit.

It need scarcely be added that there is no inherent obstacle to the application of the general thesis to itself as an idea, and that there is a sociohistorical context to the very idea that ideas have sociohistorical content. It consists of the effort to ground the philosophical and scientific enterprise in the vanguard of the collective effort of mankind to achieve a greater measure of freedom, and in so doing, to give human reason a greater scope in the direction and organization of human affairs.

II

It is perhaps over-presumptuous, after attempting to deal in such small compass with so vast a problem, to try to dispose of two equally broad topics as corollaries of the above analysis. This is by way of apology for the programmatic formulation of what follows on the relation of theory and practice, and on the role of ideas in history.

The thesis of the unity of theory and practice summarizes results and attitudes in metaphysics, epistemology, methodology, and ethics. Its spread may be indicated briefly.

As a metaphysical theory, it is primarily anti-dualistic. If theory is taken as thinking and practice as doing, the unity of theory and practice is, in general form, supported by all the philosophies that struggled against the Cartesian dualism, in which thinking was the work of mind or soul and doing the work of body. The view that mind and all its works arose in an evolution of matter and development of the universe thus constitutes the broadest philosophical content of the thesis, and it rests for its support on the results of the sciences in many different fields.

As an epistemological thesis, the view of the unity of theory and practice is often expressed by materialists as a theory that ideas reflect the movement of matter or the properties of existence. In sociohistorical terms, this is the theory of causality, instrumentality, and content discussed above. In psychological, physiological, and physical terms, it is the familiar scientific attempt to trace the processes of perception, feeling, and thought as qualities of situations of organism and environment interaction. This is all that need be involved in a materialistic *representative* theory of knowledge. Clearly, it is a far cry from the traditional copy theory in the sense which a Lockean dualistic formulation employs.

As a methodological thesis, the unity of theory and practice summarizes a hard-won principle of the psychological and social sciences—a kind of functionalism which is the counterpart of the expansion of content of ideas examined above. Thus a Freudian postulate that there are no chance elements in the mental life becomes, in effect, a demand that some functional role be found in the personality development and expression of the given individual to which the mental element may be related. The historical and anthropological treatment of religion and philosophy as, in part, emotional security techniques of man in the face of an unknown world is also a demand for exhibition of the practical side of theory. And conversely, the whole growth of the psychology of personality and of the systematic study of societies lends its weight to the view that human practice is not best regarded as random movement of organic bodies, but involves determinable systematic relationships. Such methodological principles and the successes they bring add their weight to the general thesis of the unity of theory and practice.

Perhaps the most difficult aspect of the theory is to be found in the ethical domain. For here it has both descriptive and normative components. It tells a man that whatever he may say, his theory has a practical side, and at the same time, often urges him not to *divorce* theory from practice, which, if the descriptive component is correct, he cannot really do anyhow. The relationships involved obviously call for careful analysis.

The descriptive component represents a methodological principle in the description of a man's values which is as old as Socrates. Socrates contended that no man really knows the good and does evil. Aristotle's treatment of the problem centers about describing the way in which passion blinds a man at the moment of action so that, although in one sense he knows the good, in another he forgets it. The whole of the ethical literature about moral principles and their relation to choice grapples with the same problem. The results may be expressed as a resolution, widely held today, that a man's values are to be described as some function of his choices actually made or his directions of striving, rather than simply in terms of principles preached or even beliefs entertained. Theory is thus formulated initially as a systematic pattern of practice.

The fact that there is a normative element, therefore, does not deny the relation of theory and practice, but points to the added value of its *conscious* recognition. To tell a man not to divorce theory and practice is to warn him not to neglect the practical side of his theory or the theoretical side of his practice. It is also to recognize the way in which consciousness of their relation may modify the subsequent character of both. This raises the problem of the role of ideas in history which we shall look at below.

If the thesis of the unity of theory and practice has such wide implications and appears to be supported on so many fronts, two tasks are required in its explication. One is an extensive analysis of its meaning and the variety of specific relations in the various fields, and this obviously cannot be undertaken here. The other is some explanation of the appearance of separateness which has characterized theory and practice, and an estimate of what bases there may be for the relative separateness which makes it possible to speak of *their* unity in more than the historical sense of correcting a false dichotomy.

The answer to this latter question is not an a priori matter. Physiologically, the problem is that of the evolutionary development of the brain and its activity in relation to the motor activity of the rest of the body. Culturally, the problem is that of the growth of language and symbolic systems (from ritual to pure mathematics). Sociologically, the problem is essentially that of the division of labor; it includes the story of the historical separation of "brain" and "brawn," the development of intellectual classes,[43] and the separation and separate functioning of philosophers, scientists, and so forth. The separateness of theory thus reflects the physical and social separation processes, but the content, origin, and reference of theory is existence in all its qualities, on all its levels, and with all its conflicts.

III

If the role of ideas in history has at times seemed an insoluble problem, it is only because the question has been formulated in the premises of an implicit dualism, mechanism, or epiphenomenalism. Ideas taken in a mystical way are with difficulty related to the procession of material events. They either stand apart or are convicted of unreality, or else float helplessly over the flux. From the point of view of a modern materialism, the problem is a thoroughly empirical one, straightforward and without inherent mystery. As in the case of the unity of theory and practice, it has relatively distinct phases.

Physiologically, the question appears as the relation of brain responses to motor responses, and the degree to which—if we may put the matter so loosely—brain patterns at any time determine the form of motor responses, or instead are simply a clearinghouse for original stimuli to the brain itself. This is a thoroughly scientific problem, whose very formulation as well as solution rests with experimental physiology.

Psychologically, the problem is the role of thinking in the life of a man, and its relation to action and feeling. Here again, there are no obstacles to a thoroughly empirical study of the role of

deliberation in customary activity and in choice. The effectiveness
of ideas in this sense is sometimes great, sometimes small, depending on the external circumstances and the given individual.
Thus we can distinguish the thinking that is reasoning from the
thinking that is "rationalizing," and we can look for the determinants of both types.

Sociologically, the problem takes several different forms. It may
be a study of the role of planning in any field of social activity, its
scope and effect. Or it may be a study of the degree to which
science spreads and becomes the guiding method in human activity in all fields. Or it may be a study of the mode of functioning
of intellectuals as a social group.

In the first sense, it is clear that ideas are not only practical but
have come to have an increasing role in history. A modern war is
much more carefully planned than an ancient one; modern industry is, in its productive aspects, increasingly socialized and ra-
tionalized; and so forth.

In the second sense, ideas have, likewise, come to have a greater
role, subject to all sorts of limiting factors. It was Hobbes who
said: "For I doubt not, but if it had been a thing contrary to any
mans right of dominion, or to the interest of men that have
dominion, *That the three Angles of a Triangle, should be equall to
two Angles of a Square;* that doctrine should have been, if not
disputed, yet by the burning of all books of Geometry, suppressed,
as farre as he whom it concerned was able." [49] And Nazi racial
theory has shown clearly that even today the natural sciences are
not yet immune to external influences. Nevertheless, the physical
sciences are too intimately bound to modern industry to lose their
effectiveness. The psychological and social sciences are growing
apace, although their application lags and ideological elements are
frequent. But there is ample reason to believe that when interest-
bound obstructions to clarity are minimized or removed, the
social sciences may come to play as effective a role in social
organization as the physical sciences have in the organization of
production.

In the third sense, the role of intellectuals, has, of course, been
a variable one. For intellectuals have by no means constituted a
uniform group. The historical role of medical men is quite different in primitive tribes, in ancient Greece, in modern society; and
only at some points is it comparable to that of clergy in the
middle ages. Clergy, again, vary in the middle ages and in modern
times. Lawyers have, perhaps, had a more constant role. The role

of professors shares, to a large extent, the function of educational institutions at a given time. In general, the activity of intellectuals has reflected the state of knowledge and the conflict of social classes. Their lot has been assigned to them by the structure of the given society, and they have transcended it, at times, either by the content of their work (e.g., revolutionary scientific discoveries, whose effectiveness, however, was determined by other factors) or else by their alignment with a rising class (e.g., the French Encyclopedists, Lenin). Therefore there was, for the most part, no special problem of the effectiveness of their ideas. At any time, the ideas of the ruling class are effective enough, while the class is safely in power. The whole problem of the role of intellectuals is transcendend in a socialist society that educates the whole of its people and give full scope for intellectual activity in all phases of its life.

What then remains of the old problem whether ideas necessarily follow practice or lead it? Clearly this formulation is oversimplified, resting on the divorce of theory and practice. If ideas are visions of particular men and groups with differing degrees of clarity and opaqueness, and if, as a problem in the history of ideas, we wish to examine the occurrence of the ideas intellectually formulated, in relation to the social and historical activity of groups of men, then all sorts of relations can be discovered. Ideas can express the past, foreshadow the future, and guide what is coming into being. Ideas can play the part of hardeners, crystallizers, prognosticators, levers for breaking down vested forms, shadows of coming events, organizers. This is seen, for example, in the continual attempts men make to justify the social policies and beliefs which they advance. We cannot say that only actions count and reasons are unimportant. For the reasons given for action, when fully understood, may indicate the direction of further action; they will show where the paths of men now acting together may come to diverge. When the historian of ideas traces, for example, the arguments for the belief in God, with all their variety, or those seeking to justify absolutism, or private property, one can see through them the changing scene to which they respond, and their roles at particular times in crystallizing or sharpening men's attitudes, in covering or clarifying their motives, in comforting or rallying men. But all such functions are served by ideas at any time not as entities separate from practice, but as part of the whole ma rix of social life. On its active side, therefore, the theory of the role of ideas is the theory of how policies can and best may be formulated and become effective, in short, the theory of leadership as well as that of reflection.

In general, it is patently clear that wrong thinking has momentous results. It is, therefore, equally clear, that right thinking can have powerful effects. Once thought is seen in its manifold phases and in its intimate relations with practice, we can understand both its glorification in idealist theory and its crucial role in materialist theory. Aristotle conceived of God as pure thought thinking about itself. This continual rational energizing was the unmoved mover of all that went on in the cosmos. Hegel stretches the process out through time; the Absolute, instead of being self-consciousness is realizing self-consciousness in the processes of nature and of history. The materialist philosophy need give self-consciousness no less central a role, but it is a role cast for men, not gods. The evolution of man can be seen as the growth of effective freedom, of man's mastery over nature and over himself. It can thus be seen as the practical growth of a fuller self-consciousness. The active role of thinking in history, so far from being denied, becomes the measure of a society's approach to greater freedom.

NOTES

1. The ideas worked out in this part of the paper were suggested in much less developed form in two previous papers: "Levels of Meaning and the History of Ideas," in *Journal of the History of Ideas* (1946); and "Coordinates of Criticism in Ethical Theory," in *Philosophy and Phenomenological Research*, 7 (1947): 554-59.

2. T.V. Smith, *The American Philosophy of Equality* (Chicago: University of Chicago Press, 1928), p. 69.

3. Ibid., p. 178. This argument was used much later when the question of racial equality was seriously advanced.

4. William James, *Pragmatism* (New York: Longmans, Green, 1907), Lecture I.

5. Rudolf Carnap, *Philosophy and Logical Syntax* (Boston: Kegan Paul, Trench, Trubner, n.d.), pp. 29-30.

6. Quoted in Harold Laski, *Where Do We Go From Here?* (New York: Viking Press, 1940), pp. 126-27.

7. Karl Mannheim, *Ideology and Utopia* (London: Routledge & Kegan Paul, 1962), pp. 49-53.

8. H.D. Lasswell, *Politics: Who Gets What, When, How* (New York: McGraw-Hill, 1936); James Marshall, *Swords and Symbols* (New York: Oxford Press, 1939); James Burnham, *The Machiavellians* (New York: John

Day, 1943). Lasswell, for example, says: "From the 'divine right of kings' to the 'rights of man' to the 'proletarian dictatorship'; these have been the principal vocabulary changes in the political history of the modern world. In each case a language of protest, long a utopian hope, became the language of an established order, an ideology. The ruling elite elicited loyalty, blood, and taxes from the populace with new combinations of vowels and consonants" (p. 156).

9. Rudolf Hilferding, *Das Finanzkapital* (Vienna: Wiener Volks-buchhandlung, 1923), pp. 426-29; these pages are translated by Paul M. Sweezey, in his *The Theory of Capitalist Development* (New York: Oxford University Press, 1942), pp. 375-78, under the title "The Ideology of Imperialism."

10. Sweezey, p. 376.

11. In his famous essay, "How to Make Our Ideas Clear," in *Values in a Universe of Chance*, ed. Philip P. Wiener (Garden City, N.Y.: Double-day Anchor, 1958).

12. John Dewey, *Logic, the Theory of Inquiry* (New York: Holt, 1938), p. 109.

13. Metaphorically, what the idea contains is what we see when we hold it up to the light. If we are thinking of existence, we could speak of the content as what the idea stretches over or covers or mirrors. If we take the notion purely functionally, it is what the idea points to. There is no intention here to minimize the depth of analysis required in these epistemological problems. They are bypassed simply in the belief that the point of the present paper does not require any fuller treatment in this context.

14. These are, of course, extremes within the materialist-naturalist tradition. Both are united against an idealist or Platonic intuitionist theory of ideas.

15. Various current approaches derived from the positivist analysis or the instrumentalist analysis or both, show almost a phobia of abstract ideas and insist on translation to discover content in some form of particular experience, whether as with Bridgman (*The Logic of Modern Physics* [New York: Macmillan, 1927]) the concept becomes synonymous with the operations performed, or, as in the semanticists, the ultimate reference is to the "un-speakable" or "silent" level.

16. "Pragmatics" is the study of the relation of signs to interpreters, as distinguished from "syntactics," the relation of signs to one another, and "semantics," the relation of signs to objects. (See C.W. Morris, *Foundations of the Theory of Signs* [Chicago: University of Chicago Press, 1970], and his reformulation of the distinction in *Signs, Language and Behavior*, [New York: Prentice-Hall, 1946], pp. 317-20.)

17. Karl Marx and Friedrich Engels, *The German Ideology* (New York: International, 1970), p. 87.

18. Friedrich Engels, *Feuerbach* (New York: International, n.d.), Appendix, p. 79. Cf. Part IV of *Feuerbach*, especially p. 64 ff.

19. Erich Fromm, *Escape from Freedom* (New York: Rinehart, 1941), p. 78.

20. I do not pursue the question here whether there are in fact the kinds of sense-data spoken of, or whether elements of interpretation are not also here relevant.

21. Friedrich Engels, *Anti-Duhring*, ed. C.P. Dutt, trans. Emile Burns (New York: International, n.d.), p. 123.

22. For a presentation of this sociohistorical content in pleasure-theory, see my "Coordinates of Criticism in Ethical Theory," *Philosophy and Phenomenological Research* 7 (1947): 554-59. Of the two theses, I would now (1978) accept the weaker.

23. J.S. Mill, *Utilitarianism*, in Everyman's Library edition of his *Utilitarianism, Liberty and Representative Government* (New York: Dutton, 1910), pp. 8-9.

24. Mill, *Representative Government*, in Everyman's Library edition, ch. 6, p. 255.

25. Ibid., ch. 8, pp. 279-88.

26. Engels, in a review of Marx's *Critique of Political Economy*. Printed in the appendix to the International Publishers edition of his *Ludwig Feuerbach*, p. 94.

27. Emile Burns, ed., *A Handbook of Marxism*, (New York: International, 1935), p. 44.

28. See also, for example, the criticism that Russell assumes our world to have the character of simples in the sense required by his logical analysis, in M. Cornforth, *Science versus Idealism* (New York: International, 1947), ch. 8.

29. Aristotle, *Metaphysics*, vol. 1, trans. Hugh Tredennick (New York: Loeb Classical Library, Putnam, 1933), p. 171.

30. It is interesting to note that the atomists, who rejected the Aristotelian concept of nature, took slavery to be an accident; e.g., Lucretius, *On the Nature of Things* (Oates edition of *The Stoic and Epicurean Philosophers* [New York: Random House, 1940]), p. 77.

31. Friedrich Engels, *Dialectics of Nature* (New York: International, 1940), pp. 161-63, 182-83.

32. The propositions about permanence and change with which Engels is here dealing themselves constitute an abstract formulation or a boiled-down residue from the original Aristotelian position which is even richer in sociohistorical content than indicated above. For, in order to understand his whole teleological approach to which his laws of logic belong, we have to take seriously his basic assertion that nature works like the artist; and several of the fundamental discrepancies in his account will, I believe, become clear by reference to the actual character of the arts or crafts in his time. In this sense, the reference provides content, as well as possible cause or source.

33. The empirical thesis that scientific results actually grow up in the needs of the battle against nature, whatever specific form it takes in a

given society—as against the view that the results of science are gifts of the gods or products of disinterested wonder—is, of course, an essential part of the above view.

34. I owe this neat formulation to Dr. Stanley Moore.

35. Mannheim, *Ideology and Utopia*, pp. 110-11, 278.

36. Ibid., p. 153.

37. Ibid., p. 45.

38. Ibid., p. 258 ff.

39. Ibid., p. 266.

40. Ibid., p. 71.

41. Ibid., p. 135.

42. Ibid., p. 143.

43. See, for example, Farrington's suggestion in his *Greek Science* (New York: Penguin, 1944) that some intellectual fields developed from the administration of men, others from the crafts in their battle with nature.

44. Thomas Hobbes *Leviathan* (Oxford: Clarendon Press), ch. 11, pp. 79-80.

10. Education and the Concept of Ideology

Although this paper was written in the late 1960s, it is continuous with a long-standing interest in all forms of relativism, in ethics as well as the theory of knowledge. The ideological problem was touched in the discussion of Mannheim in the immediately previous chapter (dating from 1949). My book on Ethical Judgment: The Use of Science in Ethics (1955) was fundamentally a consideration of ethical relativism. It reckoned with the view that moral disagreement was ultimately a conflict of wills or a struggle of attitudes, and that no dependable cognitive judgments were available by looking to the impact of the theory of history, social science, and knowledge generally. This whole inquiry, in turn, had been prompted by the controversies in the 1930s and 1940s as to whether we could establish that Nazism was morally wrong or had only to admit that we would fight it to the death because we had been brought up with a sharply contrasting ethics. (Ralph Barton Perry, for example, wrote a little book at the time entitled Our Side is Right.)

The problem of the nature of ideology became particularly relevant again in the period of the Cold War. It seemed to me that both Russia and the United States were talking with a certain pride about "our ideology." Instead of prompting inquiry for prejudices that should be shed in the light of common knowledge and the recognition of common human aims, the concept of ideology was being thinned out. It was becoming a kind a private property in belief and attitude—each group was entitled to believe what it wanted and do with its beliefs what it wanted, without any responsibility to truth or common morality. Even if absolute *truth in science and morals is unattainable, enough could be done to establish a distinction between better and worse.*

The present paper was, therefore, a tract for the times, as well as a formulation of a basic theoretical direction. That is why, after having first published a general essay in an international journal (Praxis), I addressed a revised version particularly to educators.

The mode of analysis is both logically analytic and genetic in sharpening the antithesis of the two conceptions of ideology, and of course looks for presuppositions underlying the diversity of bases on which each one stands.

WHY THE PHILOSOPHY OF EDUCATION SHOULD BE CONCERNED WITH THE CONCEPT OF IDEOLOGY

Education is engaged in the transmission of knowledge and skills and the cultivation of general outlook in the younger generations. It therefore bears some responsibility for what it passes along. Invariably, some measure of ideology is included. In the older, disparaging sense, ideology was regarded as some type of deceit, conscious or unconscious, of other or of self. (There is within the ideological outlook so inextricable a fusion of values and beliefs that it is presumed even to shape the rules of evidence by which the outlook supports itself.) In that case, education would be at least accessory after the fact, and in higher education often the original perpetrator. The formulation of goals and policies for education should, therefore, involve an attempt to transcend ideologies. At least, it should set up a slogan of "science versus ideology" and welcome every sign that points to the end of ideology. If, on the other hand, a more neutral view is taken of the notion of ideology, and a more tolerant attitude toward its presence, then ideology is simply a fact of life, an unavoidable form of social thought; men live and think and act in terms of their values, and there is no cause for alarm in the permeating quality of value, only in the quality of a specific value. Education always belongs to a particular society with its particular culture, imbued with its traditions and facing its problems with inherited values. There is no general problem for education in the phenomenon of ideology. In a particular context, education need but clarify the conflict of ideologies and make its choice. If a slogan is wanted, it is not "science versus ideology," but always "which side are you on?"

Let me illustrate the conflict of approaches to the notion of ideology by taking a number of specific contexts where there is a clear difference to the educator according to which way he goes. I select one illustration from the content of teaching, one from determination of policy for the schools, and one from educational theory itself.

1. Take the case of a teacher of history teaching the period of the cold war. He is aware of recent books reinvestigating the end of World War II and the detail of American-Russian relations in the late 1940s. He asks himself how far the actual historical picture of this period taught in American schools represents authentic history, or the imposition of an anti-Communist ideology on historical writing. Is he to think of the reinvestigation as a possible corrective toward more authentic history, or is he to regard it simply as the expression of an opposing ideology, and his own choice in teaching to be a choice between ideologies? Perhaps the question puts the matter oversimply, but at least it throws the problem at us. Was the historical work on the rise of the great fortunes in nineteenth and twentieth-century America—the story of the "robber barons"—the historical expression of a socialist ideology and was the attempted reinterpretation in the 1950s a resurgent conservative ideology? For that matter, compare the treatment of the War of 1812 in American and Canadian high school texts.

What follows from the recognition of such phenomena? Should history teaching include a critical study of ideological influences in historical writing? What would be the general intellectual impact—that we have to be increasingly more scholarly, or that we have at bottom to make a choice of biases?

2. Take as an example of policy issue the crucial report on "American Education and International Tensions" by the Educational Policies Commission of the National Educational Association of the United States and the American Association of School Administrators published in 1949. The report assumed that we would have before us in the foreseeable future the cold war between East and West. It did not mean East and West in Kipling's sense, of course, but the implacable opposition of Soviet and non-Soviet worlds. It spoke of the "political system and ideology which we we call democracy" and the "political system and ideology which we call communism" (p. 4). Speaking of

American power and the need to use it responsibly, the report said, "Do teachers realize that what happens in their classroom may affect the fate of that world?" (p. 22). And though the report also said, "Changes in educational policy should not be made for trivial and transient reasons" (p. 25), it went on to state that, "the United States is engaged in a cold war because our people and their government believe that our political existence and ethical principles are threatened by possible external aggression. We are engaged in a cold war because that appears to be the surest and least costly way to provide for survival of the nation and its ideals. We must maintain our part in the cold war" (p. 30). The report even spoke of education as "an instrument of national policy;"and while it drew back immediately to say that the schools should not abandon their traditional purposes (pp. 35-36), the net effect of the recommendation was to gear American education to national policy in the cold war.

Suppose the report had said instead: "Within three generations the world will be basically different. Present alignments and ideologies will crack and become largely meaningless in the altered situation. Things are already—though we may not yet be conscious of it—moving much faster than our traditional over-stereotyped monolithic ideological intellectual-emotional patterns. To tie education to the present conflict of ideologies is to bind education to the past. Precisely because the conflict of apparently incompatible ideologies looms so large, education must undertake the task of taking them to pieces rather than consolidating them as intellectual weapons of war. Its business is critical reconstruction in the light of all-human ideals of peace and global development, not surrender to local and national transitional ideologies." Had members of the commission said this, would they have been applauded for transcending ideology? More likely they would have been accused of pursuing a subtle tactic in favor of the enemy ideology, and the NEA would have been investigated for subversion!

I shall not here go into the question of whether events have shown since publication of the report that the hypothetical statement would have been wiser than the actual one. Our present problem is the theoretical one: does it make sense to ask education to base its policy selections on transcending and overcoming ideologies, or is this simply the advocacy of a fresh ideology claiming greater adequacy? In the latter case, at any rate, the meta-problem of criteria of adequacy becomes philosophically central. Or is this again just a higher-level ideology? Whatever we may hold, the interpretation of the concept of ideology and the assumptions of what to do about it seem to have some bearing on how we go about forming policies to guide education.

3. Take as exemplifying a problem of educational theory the issue of the use of intelligence and aptitude tests in education. An interesting story in the *New York Times* of October 17, 1964, headed "U.S. and Soviet Educators Developing Similarly," points out that opposition to the tests is diminishing among Soviet educators just when American educators are toning down their reliance on intelligence scores. We are told that "the new educational technology and recent discoveries about the way children learn are pushing the two ideologically opposed systems on a number of technically parallel tracks." Such an interpretation seems to assume that facts and experience can push ideologies and partly correct them. This suggests the view that science, constantly increasing its grasp of truth, corrects ideologies. The opposing approach would look instead for determination of ideological shift by changing interests.

The Russians long interpreted American beliefs in fixed differences in ability and intelligence as an ideological justification for keeping the underprivileged in their place, but now the expanding American economy has greater need of skilled manpower and so must prune hampering ideologies. The Americans long interpreted Russian opposition to intelligence tests as their ideological utopian equalitarianism; perhaps the Russia shift expresses a growing need for efficiency, or even an increase in social stratification! But even if all these counterinterpretations were true, would they not concern only motivation? The question would remain whether the growing consensus represented the truth, with the new educational methods and the discoveries about the way children learn as evidence for the truth. The issue has, therefore, to be faced, how far objectivity or the transcendence of ideologies is possible in theoretical inquiry. The countermove, familiar enough, is to regard science and its ways as itself an ideology.

Perhaps it is admitted that for relatively fragmentary items coming within reach of firmly established sciences, it is possible to push back value biases, such as individual emotional projections, or class and national interests. But it is often denied that anything comparable can be done for the total ideologies found in the modern world—religious or conservative or Marxian or liberal. The fusion of beliefs and value-attitudes is such that no unraveling is possible to allow judgment in terms of truth for beliefs or adequacy for values, We remain irretrievably in the grip of bias. In asking whether the philosophical outcome is science versus ideology or one ideology versus another, we are thus brought to confront the basic problem of truth in social philosophies.

Because the problem has such direct bearing on educational practice, policy formation, and theory, although the links are complex and varied and certainly require much more analysis than the brief illustrations I have been giving, it seems appropriate to focus directly on the basic philosophical issue of the nature of ideology and the arguments for contrasting interpretations, and to attempt a philosophical reckoning.

THE TWO CONCEPTS OF IDEOLOGY

Corresponding to the opposing views that have been suggested, we may formulate two concepts of ideology. Let us call them ideology$_1$ and ideology$_2$. Ideology$_2$ is embedded in the slogan "science versus ideology," ideology$_2$ in the slogan "which side are you on?"

Ideology$_1$ developed first. It referred, as we have seen, to views that were somehow distorted to seem brighter and nobler than the reality they expressed. Science could unmask them to reveal the emotional or practical or exploitative purposes underlying them. Slaveholders, for example, were supported in ancient times by the doctrine that some men are slaves by nature; in American history, they argued, when driven into a corner, that Negroes did not really have souls. Whether the slave owners were trying to fool others, or simply screening from themselves the character of their own distorted relations to other human beings, is a point we may leave to psychologists and social theorists to argue—but there is room for both possibilities. In our own day, discrimination also decks itself with ideology, but politics is usually taken to be the area where ideology flourishes most luxuriantly.

To label an outlook as ideological in the sense of ideology$_1$ need not mean branding the outlook as a whole. It may contain parts or elements that are so labeled. When a natural rights liberalism is accused of being ideological in its shutting out of history or in its wishful attitude on the rationality of men, it is not necessarily condemned for its judgment that men ought to have some part in political processes. Nor need an ideological belief be necessarily always false. As Freud pointed out in the comparable case of illusion, the alchemists' illusion that metals can be turned into gold was not essentially false; the illusory character of the idea lay in the way the alchemist held it, in its derivation from his wishes, and in his disregard of relations to reality. In the case of a belief that is true, perhaps ideology$_1$ would do well to speak of the ideological use of the belief rather than to call it directly an ideology.

Whether, then, an outlook is called ideological, or said to contain ideological elements, or to be ideologically used, the employment of the term in the sense of ideology$_1$ is guided by the belief that there can be an increasing accumulation of common knowledge about human affairs which can act as the basis for an all-human social outlook. The existence of opposing ideologies is not fatal to this view, for ideologies are not final. They can be analyzed, their dross removed, and any actual opposing interests revealed among them can then be mediated, compromised, or else adjudicated in the clear light of day. The battle of science versus ideology will be won by the eventual growth of science and the increase of its domains in human affairs.

Ideology$_2$ developed by a ready transition out of ideology$_1$. For once the spotlight is focused on the motives and functions of a system of ideas, once there is a developed mode of unmasking, it is but a short step to recognize that the unmaskers too may be unmasked. Karl Mannheim, in his *Ideology and Utopia*, made this transition clearly in his critique of Marx. Marx unmasks the bourgeois character of resounding liberal ideas of liberty and democracy. But Marx's own outlook, says Mannheim, reflects, on his own doctrine, the perspective of the proletariat. The conclusion pointed to is the inevitability of social perspectives entering subtly into all social theory. Truth in social theory is not like truth in physics. Every social theory is relative to the social position of the theorist. The best we can hope for is that intellectuals with a foot in opposing camps may have a wider comparative perspective. To look for the disappearance of ideology in an eventual victory of science is a transparent use of the liberal ideology of rationality.

For ideology$_2$, then, ideology is not something to be rationally overcome, nor even just a system of ideas in a way of life. The term betokens a constellation of fused ideas, interests, and values, inevitably group-bound, unable to avoid bias. Ideologies are thus fundamentally not comparable; objective truth in social theory is unattainable, perhaps even altogether meaningless. When ideologies compete, there is essentially a battle for the minds and hearts of men.

IDEOLOGY$_2$ VERSUS IDEOLOGY$_1$—POINT AND COUNTERPOINT

I want to examine four arguments that have been offered for ideology$_2$ and present the rebuttal on behalf of ideology$_1$. They are:

> 1. The practical difficulties of resolution or even of a meeting of minds in the confrontation of opposing ideologies are so great as to render any kind of resolution hopeless. 2. The historical variety of ideological outlooks is extensive, and what usually happens is that there is replacement of one ideology by another rather than a refutation of the first by the second. 3. Analytically, we find that the human sciences which purport to resolve ideological conflict or dissolve ideology are themselves shot through with ideology. 4. The growing knowledge of and insight into man's ideational processes brings a realization of the full scope of irrationality at the roots of apparent rationality.

1. Anyone who has really tried to argue social questions with a person of utterly opposing social outlook experiences a feeling of intense intellectual frustration. Every point becomes disputable; there seems scarcely any common ground to stand on. The range of admitted fact becomes subject to such varied interpretation, the selection of evidence and the criteria of relevance go in such utterly different directions, the postulated premises in inquiry are so much at variance, the very rules of inquiry—what is credible and what is inadmissible—themselves become debatable. The only outcome is to adjourn the discussion. It matters little whether the debate is over an apparently factual issue (what happened in an important historical situation), or an apparently scientific proposition (such as when a conservative and a liberal debate whether men are capable of improvement), or an interpretation of causes in history (as when a conservative and a Marxian debate the comparative strength of moral and economic causes in human affairs). And while we may expect that political emissaries may

find themselves in such a stalemate, say the American and Chinese representatives in Poland, the same stalemate often characterizes the confrontation of intellectuals. It is as if the area of ascertainable fact is compatible with the broadest range of interpretive systems.

But what does the existence of such intense frustration in the confrontation of ideologies really prove? For one thing, the conflict is enmeshed in practical oppositions of interest; Hobbes long ago pointed out that, if property interests were involved, men would quarrel about whether the angle sum of a triangle was equal to two right angles. Again, lines of communication have either been cut, or not developed in the first place. If energy were expended on trying to understand one another first and on separating issues in a more logically coherent way, there might be a gradual elaboration of modes of solving particular questions and so the growth of a base of common meanings and agreed facts for further advance. The assumption that each ideology is monolithic and to be accepted or rejected as a whole is itself a source of practical difficulty of communication. In any case, practical difficulties of resolution are not to be equated with theoretical issues of solution; one concerns bringing men to agree (which may be on what is false, not true); the other with establishment of truth whether there is disagreement or not.

2. The historical variety of ideologies needs little documentation. What is significant for the argument of ideology$_2$ is that the vanishing of ideologies from the historical scene seems to be less a case of refutation than of replacement. Historical causes bring into existence new classes or new social groupings, modes of life change, new perspectives ensue, old perspectives either fade away or are overthrown when their proponents are cast from positions of power. This fact is clear where one religious ideology gives way to another, or where a religious ideology of a conservative type yields to a secular liberalism. But even within liberalism it is so when a democratic equality supervenes on a middle-class liberty—note the transitional point in the nineteenth-century controversy over liberty *versus* equality!

Such variety and such a mode of transition do not, however, rule out the possibility that the bias in each ideology can be understood and either rejected as false or distorted, or else integrated into a more comprehensive outlook. Neither practical explanations of victory nor replacement have the theoretical import supposed. In bitter social conflict, an ideology may be eradicated by the massacre of its adherents, but the destruction would prove nothing about its theoretical adequacy or inadequacy. And so generation changes in style or focus on issues, even in a theoretical field, may be due to looking for new worlds to conquer, rivalry with the scientific establishment, or even revolt against the father symbol!

3. The third argument represents the counterattack of ideology₂ upon those bodies of knowledge—psychology, social science, history—which may be invoked to resolve an ideological conflict in the spirit of ideology₁. The claim is that they are themselves thoroughly ideological and so give pictures of the world consonant with their own value orientation. Psychology and the social sciences are themselves the battleground of schools, and history is constantly being rewritten. It has been said that the different histories of the American Civil War represent successive increments of wisdom and experience less than they do the continuation of the same war by the pen instead of the sword! Bertrand Russell's jest about animal experiments may be taken as paradigmatic: in American maze psychology, mice scurry about and try one solution after another until they make it; in German animal psychology, apes sit and think until they get a solution in an "aha!" phenomenon. Ideologies thus confront one another in the sciences of men as well as in the social forum. Even claims for objectivity often turn out to issue from some special slant; thus Pieter Geyl in his *Debates With Historians* dissects Ranke, the great nineteenth-century German historian who aimed merely to describe "what had really happened." Geyl finds Ranke's objectivity to be really a passive reverence for the historical spectacle on a conservative assumption that God is discernible in the whole of history. Even in some contemporary studies in the history of physical science there is a tendency, as in Thomas Kuhn's *The Structure of Scientific Revolutions,* to disparage the view of continuity in the growth of scientific theory and to see revolutions in science as involving the replacement of one paradigm by another (a paradigm being some accepted scientific work which is rich in content and sets problems and modes of analysis for scientists in its time). The replacement itself is described in sociological terms, such as one theory's being disregarded rather than disproved, in a way at times more reminiscent of generation shifts in interest or styles.

The claim that there are numerous ideological elements in the psychological and social sciences and in the writing of history need not be contested in the name of ideology$_1$. The issue is one of interpretation: can they be spotted and removed, or else utilized to focus on a neglected area of phenomena? In the history of physics too, if we go back to ancient times, or in the history of physiology in Galen's day, we find plenty of the kind of school-conflict that is now offered as evidence of the permeation of ideology in the sciences of man. A growth and accumulation of knowledge on the level of observation and stabilization of laws ruled out eventually certain modes of theoretical interpretation, even though leaving room for alternatives in others. The kind of picture Kuhn gives of revolutions in science, in spite of its use of quasi-sociological characterizations, need not alter the verdict; for Kuhn himself does note a permanent residue in each of the succeeding paradigms. All that is needed to keep the way open for ideology$_1$ is an accumlating body of intellectually coercive fact and some degree of theoretical refinement and progress.

4. Paradoxically, the crowning argument of ideology$_2$ is itself one that relies on the growing impact of successive sciences— biology, social science, psychology, anthropology. Collectively, the impact may be described as the undermining of man's confidence in his rationality as a mode of grasping objective truth.

The theory of biological evolution struck the first blow by naturalizing the theory of man's thinking. It set the general theme: ideas are instruments for solving man's problems, helping him maintain some security in his struggle for existence; ideas are not cognitive apprehensions of objective antecedent reality. In the pragmatic philosophy of William James, which gave popular expression to such insights, truth itself is redefined as the expedient in the way of belief; rationality, instead of being contrasted with sentiment, is found to rest on a bed of sentiment, the will to believe is given a place in the mode of resolving vital questions for which decisive evidence is likely to remain indefinitely unavailable.

Marxian historical materialism carried out a similar job for social ideas, revealing their basis in the aims and interests of social classes, conditioned in their intellectual production by the mode of economic production and by the structure of economic relations. Marx stressed especially the way in which the relations of production in capitalism alienated the worker from his product, his fellowmen, his own self-expression, so that he felt himself governed instead by necessary laws of commodities. But Marx's concept of ideology went much further, it became a general method for exploring the meaning of abstract concepts, such as ideals of liberty and equality, and showing how, in reality, concepts differed in content when advanced by different social classes, and that content referred to the typical needs, aims, and interests of the class in question. After Marx, every ideal advanced by a social group became suspect, and with Mannheim's generalization of total ideology, described above, the ideological character of all social theory appeared manifest.

Freudian psychoanalytic theory unmasked the objective pretensions of reason in morals and in prescriptions about social institutions. The voice of reason is often the dictate of the supergo reflecting the repressions of childhood. The strength of the Freudian analysis of values and ideas lies in its penetration of diverse mechanisms which expose the inner meaning of the ideas. Sometimes, inner meaning proves to be the exact opposite of surface appearance, as when extreme kindliness in a particular individual is seen to be a reaction-formation to unusual aggressive tendencies. Though the frequent formulation that ideas are "rationalizations" for self-justification and mechanisms for allaying anxieties is no doubt oversimplified, the impact on the theory of thinking has, at times, been along these lines. Consciousness itself has been seen to arise under impulse frustration. Disinterested scientific curiosity has sometimes been assimilated to voyeurism, and philosophical ideas themselves have sometimes been interpreted as invoking anxiety-allaying mechanisms where realistic solutions were unattainable. Under the influence of psychoanalytic theory, men often became suspicious of their own motives, reasons, and formulations of ideas, and sought explanations in terms of inner functions.

Anthropological stress on the uniqueness of each culture has sometimes seemed to support the view that common understanding across cultural lines is dubious. And since each item in the culture is fully intelligible only in its relation to the total configuration in which it functions, there is no genuine comparison of institutions and values of different cultures. Each has to be understood from within. So is it too for ideas. Sometimes, the point is made in linguistic terms, as in B. L. Whorf's general thesis of the relativity of categories to linguistic processes and his view that markedly different grammars incline users to somewhat different views of the world.

In brief then, on ideology$_2$, systems of ideas in the human field are found to be expressions of inner demands, social groupings and conditions, cultural diversities. To a great extent, they serve functions rather than reveal truths. They cluster into opposing configurations corresponding to the diversity of needs and pressures. To attempt to establish a correct system of ideas or to validate a set of social values is to misread the practical function of the intellect. Ideologies are in conflict and some prevail.

I suspect that the fourth argument has been the most telling in our century, and that the attacks on rationality, showing its frequently irrational roots and its frequent ideological use, have given whatever plausibility the concept of ideology$_2$ has had. And it is precisely here that the ideological character of ideology$_2$ as a rational defense of irrationalism becomes most manifest. I do not wish to make a general paradox out of this. There would be an inconsistency in saying that reason shows that reason is untrustworthy. But this is not what is said—it is rather that reason shows in its application that its application is limited to the physical world. The inconsistency in the argument of ideology$_2$ lies in the fact that it actually transcends the limit of the physical world to show the irrational character of reason in the psychological and social and historical disciplines. In brief, ideology$_2$ misinterprets the significance of the vast body of actual scientific work on which it bases its own derogation of rationality.

The point may be more clearly seen if we focus on what actually goes on when you "unmask" a belief or attitude to show its ideological and nonrational character. You appeal to detailed and concrete knowledge that makes the unmasking possible. In the very appeal you are stabilizing or extending the specific empirical criteria for detecting ideology or distinguishing fantasy from realistic behavior. If you show that a hypochondriac is disguising certain anxieties as symptoms of a physical illness, you must have a way of showing that he does not have that physical illness and that he is having those anxieties. Similarly, if you call the Nazi outlook definitely ideological, it is because you have a way of knowing and showing that it asserts untruths on wishful or purposive grounds, that its avowed aims do not coincide with its practical strivings, and so on. You do not have to be able to convince the hypochondriac or the Nazi, as many moderns mistakenly suppose in throwing up their hands about the possibility of establishing anything; but you do have to offer evidence in the accepted scientific sense of the term. You have to show that Hitlerite racial biology is false. You have to bring out Hitler's own exposition of the Big Lie and show how he applied it. You can point out, for example, how he told an industrialist not to fear the Nazis' use of socialist slogans, since they were using them only because they found German workmen would not yield to nationalist slogans alone. And you will not stop with such evidence of deliberate falsification, for there were multitudes of adherents for whom the outlook meant both truth and salvation rolled into one. A generation of psychological study was required to unfold this aspect of the ideology—the functions served by the authoritarian mold in the inner life of people, the immaturity and lack of insight involved, the mechanism of scapegoating and the "escape from freedom." And a comparable job can be done for social functions—indeed, the Marxian theorist, Rudolf Hilferding (in his *Finance Capital*), had foreseen the social use of the racialist doctrine and traced the way it would fit into an imperialist age.

The basic mistake in interpreting the data furnished by the several genetic inquiries into the origin and function of ideas is to look for a wholesale criterion of rationality or irrationality, rather than to realize that what is being accumulated—piecemeal, not at one blow—is a growing set of indices for specific types of situations of the irrational. Thus indices of rationality are constantly growing in number and scope. This fact is clearest in the case of the Marxian and Freudian contributions. Marx, it should be noted, did not see any contradiction in applying his mode of analysis to his own social outlook. On the contrary, he claimed that his perspective would have the fewest elements of distortion in consciousness because it corresponded to the interests of the proletariat, and that in fact, the interests of the proletariat coincided with the historical interests of all mankind. The specific consideration of his claim does not concern us here, but the type of claim for validity—that one perspective may contain less distortion than another, that a clear reflection of reality also has its social causes which make it possible—is of the utmost significance. For the claim throws primary emphasis on the criteria for specific distortion and correspondingly for lack of specific distortion. Thus we can ask what kinds of distortion are produced by what kinds of classes and subclasses under what kinds of social conditions. The question could be applied to socialist and communist groups as well as to capitalist—for example what kinds of distortion are tied with being in minority parties, in stages of struggle for organization, in revolutionary and postrevolutionary situations, and so on. Much of this has become clear in the present day with the diversity of perspective in socialist countries under different conditions of economic development.

Similarly, Freudian theory, if taken concretely instead of in sweeping judgments of irrationality of man, provides hosts of indices for distinguishing the rational from the irrational in particular cases. Every delineation of a mechanism of defense helps one distinguish between the authentic and the unauthentic in qualities of action and character. The study of personality development and the conditions of ego strength provides tools for separating ideas and plans that are serving neurotic functions from those serving realistic functions. And so on.

Again, in the appeal to anthropological discovery of the uniqueness and integrated character of each culture, the general contradiction in the claims of ideology$_2$ and the gains in particular knowledge are both sharply revealed. The concrete evidence that establishes uniqueness consists in exhibiting the variety of meanings and configurations. It thus constitutes comparative knowledge of the allegedly not comparable, and at the same time furnishes indices for detecting oversimplified similarities and overisolated traits.

Finally, we may note that the general pragmatic approach which see ideas as plans for action need not dissolve objective truth into conflicting personal or group expediencies. Fairness to William James, whose theory of truth and the will to believe was cited above, requires us to recognize that he did not take a simple leap to ideology. Especially in his *Psychology* he was carrying on a scientific investigation into physiological determinants of the thinking process, and relating it to affective bases and to motor processes issuing in behavior. The will to believe need not mean enshrining arbitrary ideas; it can be recast as a model for decision where evidence is unavailable and action is necessary. The assertion of a basis for reason in sentiment need not make reason sentimental; it can point instead to a program of differentiating those sentiments which lead us to a common world and fortify inquiry, and those which lead us to private fancy. In this respect, the assertion parallels the comment made above on psychoanalytic theory.

If the rejection of the arguments presented to support ideology$_2$ is satisfactory, the rejection does not, of course, establish ideology$_1$. However, it does show that there is no inherent theoretical difficulty in the program of increasingly differentiating ideology from science. And it restores the meaningful claim to evaluate a social theory in terms of truth and valuational adequacy. How far such a possibility may be actually realized depends on how far there can emerge a *systematic* way of identifying and discounting distortions. This means, in effect, the development of a critique of ideological judgment.

CRITIQUE OF IDEOLOGICAL JUDGMENT

A critique of ideological judgment has the philosophical tasks of analyzing: (1) the categories on which ideological judgment rests, (2) the field or phenomena in which it occurs, (3) the methods by which ideological illusion may be dispelled, and (4) the epistemological and ontological conceptions that make the critique possible. These four tasks may be sketched briefly.

1. Ideological judgments are held to *reflect* or *express* underlying social aims or psychological needs. Conversely, these aims and needs are held to *determine* the idea. We have seen that difficulties arose from equating ideology with the fact of such reflection or expression rather than working out criteria for distortion in such processes. Hence, a critique of ideological judgment involves breaking up these telescoped categories and providing a more refined equipment for studying the relations of ideas to social life and to underlying psychological phenomena. Several distinct concepts may be separated out of the determination-reflection category.

One is a *causal* concept. The social or psychological phenomena may be the causal source of the ideational. The causality may be evidenced by invariable concomitance or suggested by the emergence or redirection of a belief in response to ascertainable pressures. Complex patterns are possible: for example, an ideational trait may persist into a later social state having been caused in an earlier, or it may react to the social shift. In reverse direction, a belief may act to tip the scales by triggering one rather than another of powerful social or psychological forces competing for determination.

A second concept in the unpacking of "expression" or "reflection" is ideational *servicing* or *functioning* on behalf of a certain need or process. Thus a religious belief may play a specific role in a social process—for example, ensuring cures or supporting irrigation or securing obedience to authorities or allaying anxieties.

The third concept involves the *qualitative* comparison of the social or psychological base and the ideational. Different types are possible. A simple one is almost mirrorlike reflection; for example, a celestial hierarchy mirrors a political hierarchy. Sometimes there is a more attenuated sense of representation, as when the idea symbolizes the underlying basis or process—it may even be by a complicated relation of opposites, as when a conception of the gods has them doing precisely what people are forbidden to do. The types of relations here are very numerous, since the diversity of symbolic relations may be mediated by various psychological mechanisms, as well as by purely historical connections.

To satisfy the first requirement of a critique of ideological judgment by providing a more refined conceptual equipment will also remove what has been a besetting fear in inquiring into ideologies—the fear of committing the genetic fallacy, that is, substituting a genetic account for an evaluation in terms of truth or adequacy. Ideology$_1$ is less open to such accusations precisely because it views ideology as distortion and uses explicit criteria for truth and adequacy. In any case, it is obvious that to discover the social and psychological causes of a belief is not to evaluate the belief; nor is the exposition of the function of a belief evaluative. However, the discovery of different causes or functions of an idea may lead to declaring the idea *unclear* or *insufficiently precise*. For example, the study of the idea of equality in social movements may lead to a division into political equality, social equality, or some other pattern of distinction, such as between the concept of equality in a slave revolt and in the rise of the middle classes. Such *clarification* of an idea out of the results of genetic inquiry may take many forms, some quite complicated; two ideas may even be split up and parts of each combined. But all this concerns the *meaning* of the idea and has to be settled prior to the raising of questions of truth or adequacy about judgments in which the idea occurs. Hence, it may be hoped that the refinement of the conceptual equipment for the study of ideology will, at the same time, determine the legitimate and illegitimate use of the genetic fallacy accusation.

2. A second requirement for a critique of ideological judgment is a range of rich phenomena for investigation. Here there is no dearth, not merely in the past, but even in the present, and all over the globe. And the phenomena are particularly significant for study where we find them in conditions of change, whether they be changes in Marxian ideology in the twentieth-century growth of socialism under different national conditions, or in capitalist ideology in the growth of corporations and the end of colonialism

and in capitalism's confrontation with communism. The same things can be said of liberalism in the diverse forms of its adjustment to communism; or again, the ideologies of developing nations in Africa and Asia, of struggle for modernization in Arab countries, or in Latin America; or struggle against discrimination in the United States; or the shape of modernization movements in traditional religions. In all these conditions of change, a scientific study can seek to correlate emerging social patterns and accompanying institutional and psychological stresses with ideational formations and reformations.

3. The third requirement is a methodology of inquiry. This is where the greatest care is needed. Conceptual analysis has an apparent neutrality before it is applied, and in the delineation of phenomena, the factual detail may be compelling, with opposing interests simply adding to the picture. But in fashioning a methodology, controversies may impede the development of the critique, while to limit study to what is agreed on may impoverish it. In part, the new observational and statistical techniques of the social sciences may widen the area of agreement. And in part, methodologies may be sharpened and evaluated in case studies on more "remote" ideologies. For example, an anthropological and psychological study of a "cargo cult," in which large numbers of people (whether in Pacific islands or in the Caribbean) have totally destroyed the physical possessions that tie them to the past and simply wait for the announced coming of a deity figure who will bring them the new goods of life or lead them to a promised land, is more likely to yield agreement than a comparable study of a shift in a major contemporary religion. Similarly for the study of nationalistic ideologies in remote lands as against cold war ideologies close at home; or of UN studies of specific democratic techniques as against general inquiries into democracy or totalitarianism. If, however, careful methods of inquiry are stabilized, there will be more force in their application eventually to the more controversial ideologies of contemporary struggle.

Therefore, I see no reason why it should be impossible to distinguish the case where a conservative outlook dishes up a doctrinal hodgepodge, salted with a sense of mystery and peppered with an appeal to Country and Religion, from the cases where there is a sober attempt to keep traditional values that have proved their worth, or where there is the explicit hypothesis that the disintegrating elements in sharp change will overpower the released creative elements.

Nor is it impossible to distinguish sharply between the cases where a Marxist begins an inquiry with pious invocation to dialectical materialism or substitutes a philosophical slogan for an empirical question, and the cases in which he offers historical hypotheses about the extent to which mode of production influences even intellectual and aesthetic categories.

Nor is it impossible to distinguish in liberalism the elements and uses that are ideological from those that express common human aims and clear lessons of experience—for example, what in the theory of freedom of speech represented an ideological glorification of an atomic individual, what a genuine insight into human dignity and the needs of any complex society that is to continue progressing.

It should not be thought a contradiction to look self-critically for ideological elements in one's own guiding ideas even while unmasking those of others, just as a psychoanalyst looks for any personal responses on his part that suggest he is reacting emotionally to aspects of his patient's case. In this sense, it may be possible to be wary of ideology without making a fresh ideology out of being antiideological, that is, without simply treating all theoretical systems about man and society as ideological and giving up attempts at a comprehensive theoretical view. The slogan, "let's be pragmatic" or "let's be realistic" will thus undergo careful scrutiny in each context of its use to see where it means "a plague on everybody's house" (in which case "down with all *isms*" may become itself opportun-ism) and where it involves a serious reckoning.

4. Perhaps these proposals for developing a systematic critique of ideology and applying it to contemporary ideologies sound utopian. But they do point in a direction worth trying. No other epistemological policy, calling on us to abandon the notion of objectivity, makes sense, though from a short-range standpoint certain ones may have a temporary appeal. To regard ideology as omnipresent sounds realistic. Indeed, it reflects the desperate intensity of human problems and conflicts in seemingly antagonistic knowledge-claims. But to abandon hope of objectivity so completely would simply transfer the search within the domain of ideology itself: we would have to work out ways of distinguishing between wild or fanciful ideologies and sober or realistic ones.

Similarly, if we look to the ontological concepts involved, the concept of objectivity is a notion hard won early in the history of philosophy that embodies the presupposition (whether cast in the language of reality or of fact or some other category) of a world that has definite characteristics which men are trying to discover, and by reference to which ideas are to be tested, tested for their consistency, tested for their clarity, for their predictive power, and the control they make possible. Because there can be partial systems of fancy that hang together is no reason for abandoning the concept of objectivity in the sciences of man, as a persistent effort to distinguish private or even shared dreams from public fact. To abandon the sense of objectivity. no matter how difficult the practical processes of the search for it may prove, is to open the way to nightmare logics.

From a long-range standpoint, some grounds are apparent for the hypothesis that the age of ideology may be coming to an end. Primary among these are the growth and extension of science and its recognition as something to be reckoned with—by the politician as well as the researcher, by the layman as well as the scholar. In short, the number of areas that are being withdrawn from the realm of possible subjectivity to the common world is increasing and seems likely to increase—just as ages ago magic disappeared from production and is receding from medicine. On a very broad view, I find some hope in the curve that can be traced through the history of philosophy. For example, there is probably more difference between ancient materialism and modern materialism, ancient idealism and modern idealism, ancient theologies and modern theologies, than between any opposing philosophical schools today. The area of unavoidable agreement, both in matters of fact and in intellectual refinement, has widened immeasurably. Until recently, one would have thought that this move was toward a broad unification, but the last two decades have produced a vigorous proliferation of differences. The divergence may, however, be a temporary phenomenon and more superficial than it seems. It is too early to tell, and different analyses of the divergence are still possible.

EDUCATIONAL CONSEQUENCES

I have tried to show that a critique of ideological judgment is theoretically possible, that we can work out a rich conceptual apparatus for transcending ideologies, and that growing knowledge in all its domains makes possible a systematic study of ideological distortions. Whether all this is practically possible depends on two major factors—one generally social, the other specifically educational.

The one is whether we can achieve a social framework which maintains independent thinking and puts an end to the terrific pressures for ideological conformity that have characterized our time. The coercive pressures are all too familiar. The experiences of repression in the early and mid-1950s in both communist and capitalist sectors of our world are too vivid and too recent to be easily forgotten; the question today is whether the trend of war will revive repression. To counter such pressures requires political and social action, in which, of course, educators have an important role and can play leading parts.

The second, and more specifically educational, factor concerns the intellectual mode of repression. We are sensitive enough to overt distortion of fact, but we have been less sensitive to oversimplification of issues, to the ideological determination of formulations and initial questions themselves. Any attempt to see things in other than pat alternatives has been regarded as excessive philosophical refinement, sometimes as near treason. In this sense, ideological pressures both from without, and still more from within, represent the cessation of education itself. For education involves primarily learning, and learning involves the reassessment of beliefs on the basis of experience, and the development of new criteria. The critique of ideology is thus an insistence on the reassessment of biases. In the United States, where education has been institutionalized in terms of a conservative ideology, the institutionalization of criticism becomes a central task in the reconstruction of education. This task is the practical import of our reflections on the concept of ideology.

11. Is the Concept of Human Nature Essentially Ideological?

This paper was written for the Zeno Symposium held in Nicosia, Cyprus, in September 1971. The topic of the symposium was "Human Nature and Ideology." It therefore seemed fitting to try out the Critique of Ideological Judgment (advanced in the preceding paper) not only on particular theories of human nature, such as Plato's or Hobbes's or Freud's (which is a familiar task), but to raise the question whether the concept of human nature itself is essentially ideological. In this inquiry, a few interesting points emerged about values in the deeper structure of intellectual questions.

The concept of human nature has a tremendous inner complexity, as its history and multiplicity of uses, both scientific and normative, are bound to suggest. When it is unpacked, how much of the constellation of ideas it contains will be found to be ideological? And do the ideological components touch only peripheral uses? Are they brought in only in particular theories of human nature whose construction has been affected by the problems of a given historical period? Or do they touch the core of the constellation of ideas so that the very quest for a nature of man is itself essentially ideological, not merely the particular answers that have turned up in the quest?

I should like to explore this question in three steps. Let us begin with particular conceptions of human nature, which are commonly recognized to have strong ideological components. From these, let us extricate some criteria for the ideological, or at least some range of meanings for ideology. Finally, let us turn to the general constellation of ideas that make up the concept of human nature and ask how much, in the light of our consideration of ideology, is to be regarded as essentially ideological.

I

There is little difficulty in discerning some ideological linkage between particular accounts of human nature and particular projects and attitudes to social and political structure. How else, when we witness the historical procession of great theories of man and society, are we to interpret the striking parallelism or happy congruence between the view of human nature and the proposed political structure? Let me remind you of the familiar roster, at least by reference to a few samples. Plato—the first really rich philosophical specimen—gives us a three-tier model of the human being. Each of us is a human, a lion, and at bottom a dragon, all tied in one, or getting beyond the metaphor, a rational part, a spirited part, and an appetitive part. The central motif is the blindly demanding character of appetite, unable to control its acquisitive and sexual and aggressive drives. And what is the social structure projected? Are we surprised that it is a repressive class structure in which the rational elite with the aid of the executive lion has the constant task of keeping the dragonian masses in check? Turn next to Hobbes. A less explicit picture of man nevertheless makes it clear that in untrammeled nature the life of man is "nasty, brutish and short"; to provide the rudiments of security, the political structure calls for a concentration of absolute power, complete obedience only being slightly hedged. Democratic theoreticians present us with a human being who is capable of initiative and rational decision; the mass of men are not, says Jefferson, a great beast already saddled and waiting for the spurs of the noble rider. Anarchist philosophers assume the natural cooperativeness of the human being issuing in affiliative mutual aid; political power has only to be smashed, whereupon its distorting effects will melt away and man become himself in cooperative social institutions. And so on. It is almost as if concepts of human nature were on display, ready to be adopted for the politics they would support—as the ancient satirist Lucian in one of his dialogues has philosophies on sale, with the auctioneer advertising their emotional propensities. Whatever "ideology" may turn out to be on refined analysis, this at least is transparent "ideological use."

But perhaps the transparency is not itself so clear. Surely, it will be said, the use of a theory of human nature is one thing, and the truth or adequacy of the theory is quite another. The Freudian concept of the death instinct, for example, has been used against the growth of a rationalistic atmosphere that sought deliberate social reconstruction, and concepts of inherent aggressiveness have been used over and over again to dampen the hope of overcoming war. But whether there is a death instinct of the kind that Freud described or whether the roots of aggression are social is quite a distinct theoretical question. Even with respect to social outlook, conceptions of human nature have a theoretical job to do which is distinctively theirs; they guide the domain of theoretical inquiry in the social and political disciplines by providing an indispensable *cognitive orientation.* They give us, so to speak, the actors on the stage, or the subtler units that underlie them, their dominant lines of action, the kinds of purposes or mechanisms that prompt them, and so forth. The theory of human nature is one part of the whole cognitive orientation of social theory, together with pictures of the world, of human knowledge and how it operates. It is true that philosophers have not sufficiently traced, yet, the precise relations of the cognitive orientations of theories to the various components of the theories themselves. But this furnishes no adequate reason for seeing the external use of theories of human nature as their inner essence. Anything can be ideologically used or misused.

This counterargument may be readily granted, but only up to the point where it distinguishes the external use of a theory of human nature from its inner constitution. It does not touch the question whether the elements of the inner constitution themselves, in taking the shape they do, may not embody values that reflect the external uses. The penetration of the ideological may be deep into the fine texture of the theory itself—in its selection of units, in its bunching of phenomena, in its search for types of laws, and so on. Instead of foreclosing the discovery and critique of ideological elements as merely the functioning use of the theory of human nature in politics, we have to track down the value components in the theoretical construction.

Let us continue the Platonic illustration in such an analysis. The ideological use of the way his theory of the human makeup is translated into a social theory was indicated above. But what about the units in the theory itself? What goes into the making of the ideas of reason, spirit, appetite? We have learned by this time, from the long history of thought about rationality, that it is itself a complex bundle in which ideas of unity, harmony, consistency, system, systematic effectiveness, universality, authority, and no doubt many others lie together not always in peace. The appeal to rationality is the beginning, not the end of philosophic inquiry. Take, secondly, the lion. Plato's own description of this second part of the soul ties together phenomena of ambition and desire for prestige and success, on the one hand, and the noble emotions of moral indignation, on the other. It is an insightful suggestion of possible connections in the psychology of shame, aspiration, and ego-ideals. But contemporary work on self-formation has gone far enough beyond this to suggest that we are dealing not with a particular psychological type, but a specific patterning of the self under very specific developmental conditions. It is, however, in the third part of the soul that we really see the depth of entrenched attitudes and the cultural clustering of the raw materials of human nature. The desires of Plato's dragon center around aggressiveness, sexuality, and acquisitiveness. Now these phenomena are certainly prominent as problems in most moralities, and major virtues and rules are concerned with their approved channels of expression. But what warrants tying them into a single bundle, as Plato does? Indeed, Thrasymachus, whose moral cynicism Plato is attacking, has the same presupposition, for he glorifies the tyrant's life as released from all restraint in his power to kill anyone he wants, take any woman he wants, and lay his hands on anybody's property. But if we try to justify the bundling of aggressiveness, sexuality, and acquisitiveness, the plausibility is strained. Does the unity of the three lie in their irresistible pressure, demanding immediately their objective? But all three may be calculating. Is it that they aim at pleasure or happiness? But all human desires may share this feature. Is it that they are egoistic? But it is doubtful that so complex a notion can be imposed upon them; in modern terms, we may rather compare the dragon to the Freudian Id, before the Ego arises, or below it, reaching out without brooking delay, and if there is concern with the other person, it is as a rival. Perhaps the unity of the three constituents is chiefly social—they are ones that cause trouble, and so are bracketed together as troublemakers. If so, then the human-nature status of the dragon seems to be surrendered for a unity that is historical and cultural, relative to institutions that have not successfully dealt with these powerful forces. It is not difficult to find in the "laboratory" of primitive societies examples in which sexuality, for instance, is treated in a less repressive manner, so that it enters into moral reckoning only on the rare occasions when it happens to be a source of violence.

Again, is acquisitiveness primary and coordinate with the others, or reducible to a means of satisfying them? And what of the interrelation of sexuality and aggressiveness? We have here a whole area in which not only is the basic psychology still insufficiently developed today, in spite of the work that has been done on sadism and masochism, but cultural attitudes and value attitudes are constantly playing a formative role. The twentieth century, for example, has seen the installation of sexual pleasure as legitimate, and to a high degree a revolt against acquisitiveness; aggressiveness, so far from being considered unitary, has been analyzed as a response to frustration with a variety of social meanings depending on the way the culture furnishes the means of satisfying other human needs. The Platonic bundle has been untied, and the strands are going in separate careers.

It is quite likely, therefore, that the Platonic insistence on a repressive authority did not simply employ an independent concept of human nature, but itself helped select, order, and organize the categorical unities that went into that concept. When centuries later Burke insisted that if men are to be assigned any natural rights at all, the most fundamental one is the right of a man to be protected against himself, we can really understand this only if we see how the whole raw materials of man's makeup have been intellectually patterned in a Platonic schema. The same is true for the neoconservative attacks in the contemporary world against the democratic conception of the will of the people as the irresponsible quest of thrills.

Let this serve as a brief paradigm of the tasks that are involved in depth probing for the scope of ideology in concepts of human nature. The same kind of analysis would have to be given for contrasting or anti-Platonic conceptions, such as the anarchistic and the democratic.

II

What is the conception of ideology implicit in this paradigm? Clearly, it is not the notion of the crude use of an intellectual instrument for partisan social purposes, although such phenomena are common enough. It is rather the far-reaching endeavor to see the way in which the particular problems, attitudes, and values of a given society and the embedded modes of thought and categorizations of its culture penetrate intellectual ideas. In most general terms, it is the search for the intellectual impact of the specifically historical. This inquiry replaces the rough intellectual instrument of branding a view as ideological and may be thought of as *critique of ideological judgment*. An analysis of the ideological side of a specific set of ideas would be an *ideological critique* of those ideas.

The critique of ideological judgment as so envisaged is thus a whole enterprise, with concepts and methods of its own. It generalizes the sense of "ideology" as traditionally employed. The fact is that the concept of ideology itself has undergone major transformations in the history of thought. At an earlier stage, it conveyed the sense of an idea-system employed for narrow (partisan) social purposes, so that the proper response to an ideology was to unmask it and show its value base. In the traditional original sense, as Mihailo Marković points out in his "Descriptive and Normative Conceptions of Human Nature," this value base lay in the interests and needs of particular *ruling* social groups. It was broadened to cover any particular social group, including the ruled and oppressed. The relation of Professor Marković's concept to the still more generalized one I am here presenting is that of species to genus. The more generalized concept allows the value base to be a more conglomerate assortment: it takes into one fold psychological needs and social purposes, and in each there can be marked differences. The former covers projective elements, neurotic drives with their illusions, as well as healthy demands for security in a turbulent world; the latter can speak for a particular class holding on to domination and arguing that some men are by nature marked for slavery or exploitation, or it can articulate the demands of a broadening sector of humanity. Moreover, the major philosophic issue of the relation of value and truth in the processes of inquiry has been far from settled. Thus in the social disciplines, we find occasional attempts to offer an instrumental rather than a cognitive account of theory. Most marked in this respect has been the effort, prominent for example in Mannheim's earlier work, to see the social sciences as inherently incapable of achieving objective truth, as requiring in some sense a social value-position, so that objectivity is merely the appearance engendered by value-consensus. In this sense, even the so-called "end of ideology," recently propounded as a kind of intellectual emancipation, would merely reflect achieved social consensus rather than the stripping away of bias. Where the conflicts remain, the greater objectivity betokens simply having a wider view because one has a foot in opposing interests—a prerogative usually claimed for the liberal-intellectual sector of the middle class, especially by itself.

Such developments in the concept of ideology have been thought to give it a philosophic respectability. No longer something to be unmasked, it is regarded as the inevitable value network in which an idea-system is enmeshed. It points to a vibrant Weltanschauung, not a aseptic theoretical system. In this sense, nations and classes today will speak of their particular ideology, as if it were a part of their private property, indeed a most precious heritage.

In the critique of ideological judgment here proposed, there is no conflict between probing for the ideological or for value components in intellectual ideas, and making judgments of their truth or intellectual adequacy. These separable tasks need involve no new sense for truth in the social sciences, nor abandon objectivity for consensus. One looks in the specific historical context of ideas and systems of ideas for causes of the emergence or transformation of the idea, for functions served by the idea or purposes to which it is geared, for qualitative changes in the idea or the way it is held corresponding to changes in the underlying conditions, for fissions and fusions in the ideas in relation to developing problems, and so on. But such a search for the ideological in the deeper sense here proposed is *prior* to evaluative judgments of truth or adequacy. It is concerned with exploring the meaning of the ideas, their inner structure, the presuppositions in the formulation of the questions to which the ideas are proposed answers. Thus an ideological critique is an indispensable part of the clarification both of what is to be judged and the criteria of judgment. It helps set up the judging process. It does not supplant or predetermine that process. In this sense, it shares the role of all genetic inquiry that is meant to be more than simply historical.

There are two further points about such a generalized concept of ideology which are worth noting. One is that *all* ideas might seem to be ideological, since there are purposive elements in all ideas as organizing and synthesizing experience in a particular way. And indeed, one might look for the cultural values and categorizations even in so simple a concept as that of a *chair*. It not merely builds in the general purpose of sitting, as against standing, but is no doubt relative to cultures that find the restful in sitting rather than squatting—even apart from times when chairs or types of chairs may have had a class character. The generalized concept of ideological critique points to the pervasive ways in which cultural values enter ideas and categorizations, but it rules out neither universal values nor fruitful differences of species in the social study of ideas. We can expect that a more refined terminology will be developed to indicate continuities and discontinuities between different contexts and types of values, and it may very well turn out that the term "ideological" itself will be reserved for the unacceptable range of value components of ideas and "nonideological" for the acceptable. There is much to be said for preserving this traditional tone of the pejorative. But the essential point is that the critique of ideological judgment as a broad enterprise replaces the narrow application of "ideological" by multiple distinctions. Such notions as "ideological use" of a theory, "a theory's being essentially ideological," as well as the use of the noun "ideology" to designate a set or system of ideas fused with emotion and purpose, would in a more extended systematic study, have to be differentiated and given precision by showing the kinds of roles played by specifically historical values in ideas and theories. It would probably yield a range rather than a few types, with differences lying in scope and strength of the values, or in specific point of entry of values into ideas and theories, or in modes of functioning, or in features determined by the kind of historical context.

Similarly—and this is the second point—the rough contrast of ideological and nonideological must not be assimilated to other distinctions such as that between the normative and the descriptive. For one would want to underscore the differences of value type in descriptions as well as in norms—for example, between "totalitarian societies" and "agricultural societies" as descriptions, in the first of which there are likely to be more embedded social valuations of the traditional ideological type than in the second, as well as between "power" and "glory" (or "success") as norms or prescribed values, the second of which is likely to have greater cultural specificity.

Let us take a broad illustration of such a critique as we are proposing, from the history of Stoicism. It is commonly said that the communal ideals of Plato and Aristotle gave way to the individualistic moral orientation of Stoic and Epicurean. So far, the evaluation poses simply the choice between community and individual. Note how the very question changes as the analysis of the context becomes richer, and how the meaning of Stoic ideas differs as we select different vantage points of the historian's perspective.

Suppose the historian concentrates on the shift from the Hellenic to the Hellenistic as the breakdown of the Greek city-state and the communal ideals it embodied. He may then evaluate the shift from communal to individualistic as a retreat. Such, for example, is Santayana's judgment: Stoicism and Epicureanism are the moral philosophy of these who tried the life of reason but failed to achieve it and settled into a compromise. If the historical probing of the ideas can tell us whether they were a crisis response to crisis conditions, it might help us learn what phases in the complex of individualism have a retreat and compromise character under what conditions. It might underline the constant tension in the Stoic ideal, the battle being waged to preserve one's peace of spirit.

Suppose, however, that the historian looks more comprehensively, but still in a broad sweep, at the shift the previous view characterized as the breakdown of the Greek city-state. It was also the conquest of the Persian empire by Alexander, the mixing of peoples and cultures, and the emergence of a large empire in the Greek world. The Stoics were the first to articulate philosophically the broadened vista of the post-Alexandrian world. The loss of the communal ideal was also the gain of the cosmopolitan, not merely individual ideal. Perhaps then, on its ideological side, Stoicism represents the aspiration, coming for the first time into view, to transcend the limits of the self-enclosed community. When we evaluate Stoicism, are we now to evaluate individual versus community or the independent world-individual versus the closed group?

Both the vantage points considered yield only a first approximation to Stoic ideas. They deal with general historical context, not with the richer specific historical material of the time of Zeno of Citium. Nor do they look at the five-hundred-year span in which Stoic ideas took different shape in ancient times alone. Stoicism is commonly divided into an early, middle, and late phase, but there have been controversies about the transformations. Was early Stoicism the incendiary revolutionary philosophy that Plutarch occasionaly hints at—for example in associating Sphaerus, one of the first students of Zeno of Citium, with the socialistic experiments of Cleomenes of Sparta, and later on the Stoic Blossius with the division of land by the Roman Tiberius Gracchus?

Certainly, there is enough on the condemnation of existent institutions, political and social and economic, in the early Stoics. The
very latest—Epictetus and Marcus Aurelius—are quite different;
the flux of the cosmos and the insecurity of life make no
externally directed purpose sufficiently abiding, and the inner
maintenance of the self and its serenity is all that is left to man.
The middle Stoics of the second century B.C. are sometimes seen
as hammering the earlier concepts of nature into line with existing
institutions.

The evaluation of the Stoic system of ideas is thus a quite
different matter according as those ideas are understood. And they
are seen in a different way—literally to have a different content—
as they are related to different historical contexts and analyses of
the social and historical situations. At the one end may be the
Stoic sage as revolutionary, bringing a cosmopolitan consciousness to basic reform. At the other end is a model of self-survival
under extreme conditions of permanent turbulence and insecurity.
The ideological critique would here furnish the analysis which
tells us, in fact, what we are talking about and what we are to
evaluate.

III

By our time, the concept of human nature is quite capable of
shedding intrusive values and social purposes that come through
the content of the conception. For example, it is long out of date
to furnish a list of "instincts" for human nature that simply
recapitulate the types of social institutions and practices whose
justification is sought—for example inherent acquisitive, parental,
and pugnacious instincts to support property, family, and war.
There are still occasional flurries that suggest such an outlook on
a subtler level; for example, there is the use of "territoriality" in
certain animal natures to suggest an inevitable source of aggressivity in man. But on the whole, the studies of human nature
tend to be either broadly developmental—such as the way in
which a self takes shape under environmental pressures and
sociocultural conditions—or more frequently a study of more and
more refined and elementary responses to stimuli at the earliest
stages of the child, for example whether a clinging response has
texture or voice as its cue, whether there is some set of higher
order aptitudes that show how a man is wired for linguistic
learning or interpersonal relation, and so on.

The possibility of ideological components in the very idea of human nature stands out more clearly in the philosophic history of the concept. For one thing, it shares the career of the concept of "the nature of a thing" itself. The notion that things have natures passed through many philosophies. It had its origin in the ancient teleologies where it served as the way of expressing both the search for the explanatory properties of a thing's regular behavior and, in the case of a human being, the norms to guide his actions. For example, in Aristotle's concept, the nature of a thing ties into a single bundle the ways in which it behaves universally or for the most part, what tendencies are inherent (in the sense of unlearned behavior), what modes of behavior are distinctive of it, and what lines of action are good for it. Aristotelian substances, in this sense, are very much like homeostatic systems, whose ground plan tells us how they are constituted, how they behave and what lines they pursue (find good) in the sense that when disturbed they try to restore these. We may, however, note two marked differences from the contemporary notion of such systems. One is that the idea of having a nature is ascribed to the *thing*—that is, all the lines of activity that constitute the phenomena of the system are focused upon or read back into the individual participant. Second, that the criteria of likeness which identify the class whose nature is being sought operate upon things and set up groups of a very definite kind. To take a bizarre example, we do not first decipher the phenomenon of rationality in small systems, some of which contain mice running a maze, others apes reaching for bananas with sticks, others computers going through their motions, others men planning, and treat them all as one class of objects having a common nature. We begin with humans. We operate thus with the sense of identity of the species. Of course in the long run, this may be justified in scientific terms, both general evolutionary and specific historical considerations.

The mechanistic philosphies of early modern times still look for ground plans written into the human constitution, although they see them in causal terms of the construction of a machine. Human nature is thus the specific raw material, and the extent of its malleability is seen as setting the broad possibilities of social and cultural reform in human life.

The dialectical philosphies, whether idealist or materialist, were probably the first to completely break through the isolationism of the concept of human nature we have discerned in the earlier views. For the regularities sought are systematic laws of the relevant whole, rather than of the isolated participants. The outcome is often, as we know, that man is conceived of as a wholly historical creature, and the nature of man is to be read either in objective mind (that is, social institutions) at that stage of the total development, or in the sociohistorical character of man's material development.

Alongside these dialectical conceptions, the theory of evolution also has the effect of breaking the older unity of the concept of human nature. At the very least, the idea of a changing nature comes to the fore. It is no surprise that Nietzsche can thereafter think of man transcending his nature and recognize an ideology of the status quo in human nature ethics.

An interesting case of the outright denial of human nature is involved in the appeal of a Sartrean existentialism to the full freedom of man. To see oneself as bound by one's nature is to see oneself as a thing, as finished or ready-made. It is, in effect, a kind of bad faith, an excusing of one's yielding in choice. But the distance from the older conceptions must not be overrated. Sartre speaks of man's predicament as furnishing the constants in his life. These share with the dialectical conceptions the situational character of the picture of man, rather than the search within for inherent properties or a wholly inner dynamics (the latter is well-typified in the standard Freudian approach). But while the general picture is the picture of man, the nature Sartre argues against is often the individual fixity of a man which may itself be the product of a special individual development. For important matters of human life, his treatment of nature is more individual-oriented than species-oriented.

The various types of theory that abandon an eternalist picture of human nature, or one fixed for all time, are faced with the conceptual problems of a *changing* human nature. These are not insoluble—no self-contradiction need arise—but they require considerably more analysis to produce considerably more refinement. The root idea of the *given* remains in any concept of human nature. But we need to distinguish categories of givens at least to the following extent:

What is irretrievably given and unavoidably expressed.

What is irretrievably given but expression can be checked.

What is irretrievably given but form of expression is changeable.

What is given, but not irretrievably, yet not hitherto changeable by means hitherto knowable or available.

Parallel to these would be an analysis of possibility of change,
according to types of factors that prevent change, the way difference of knowledge enters, the way in which conflicts of components allow changes to emerge for the first time, and so on.
Perhaps an era-variable might be associated with the concept of
human nature—for example, human nature under primitive conditions, human nature in industrial society, and so on. The adequacy of such conceptions would depend on having an adequate
typology of human development itself.

Perhaps the contemporary scientific way of thinking of many of
our questions is less in terms of human nature than in terms of
"models of man." Now here we find two different approaches.
One is to assume there is a correct model and seek it—whether it
be ultimately in physical-mechanistic terms or inner-psychologi-
cal, or sociohistorical, or an eventual unified model in which
these aspects find their proper home as appropriately delimited
variables. The second is a quite different tendency. It looks upon
a model itself as selecting an aspect for closer focus and perhaps
blurring the other phases. Accordingly, man is a creature who
cannot be encapsulated in a single model; the model for action
may differ from that for explanation, and the model for first-
person inquiry may differ from that for third-person inquiry.

Even these refinements, however, may be not without ideological components, Thus it is difficult to see how one could from the
idea of making models settle for all time that a general theory
accounting in a unified way for presently conflicting pictures, in
terms as yet undiscovered, will never be found. A great deal of
action theory in contemporary analytic philosophy was a revolt
against a deterministic view of man; it was a call to decisive
choice as against the security of deterministic accounts. I am not
sure that some of the positions expressed do not involve this
ideological strain.

We cannot, therefore, tell at this point how much of the
ideological remains in the concept of human nature. But we can
hope that the critique of ideological judgment systematically and
persistently carried on will turn up more and more of the
ideological components. And each one turned up becomes an
empirical test for the nonideological as well as the ideological. If a
concept of human nature is shown to be a quest for security in the

inner self, then the different modes of security are subject to scientific investigation, and the realistic can be differentiated from the neurotic. If some general desire for security is part and parcel of the effort to survive and imposes on us the need to look for order, then this can be incorporated into the pragmatic base of the whole enterprise of science, and by this conscious recognition and evaluation removed from the idiosyncratic ideological. Our conclusion is, therefore, not that the concept of human nature is inherently ideological, but that is a convenient residence for ideology; it has, as it were, a magnetic effect on wandering ideologies. Yet it serves, in its developed philosophical and scientific forms, an important role in the formulation of explanatory and directive accounts—both scientific and moral—and so cannot be discarded. There is no philosopher's stone by which the ideological can be discerned. It must be studied in its detailed contexts and criteria for its identification built up from the results of inquiries. Thus the corrective lies not in rejecting the concept of human nature, but in its constant association with the critique of ideological judgment.

12. Social Science and Value: A Study in Interrelations

This paper was written in the early 1960s for a volume on The New Sociology *in honor of C. Wright Mills. Mills had trenchantly explored the types and styles of doing sociology and shown their value content. This tied in with my interest in ideology, and I saw that it was no longer a question of arguing merely that there were value elements in social science, but of developing some systematic way—a framework—for locating them. This essay barely gets a start on the project. Chapters 13 and 14 outline it for political science and for judicial decision. The project could well be extended to such sciences as economics and sociology, and to applied fields such as social work, psychiatry, and so on. At the very least, it would show where values get smuggled into a science under the guise of neutral theory. More positively, it should show precisely where we are bound to specify our values to get our scientific work going or to advance it for solving human problems.*

In the long run, the program envisaged should be a normal part of the enterprise of every science. Education, for example, would profit from knowing where its policies and recommendations rest on an assumption of tendencies in the child (for which it needs a psychological certification) and where on assumed structures of the society (for which it needs a sociological certification) or on assumed social goals (for which it needs a moral justification). So too social science would gain clarity and self-consciousness if it saw where it makes value assumptions in its objectives, in its basic ideas, in its directions of work, in its carrying out of research, in its possible application, and in its assumption of responsibilities.

As indicated above, this program governed the explorations of the two following studies. And we shall meet it again in Volume 2, where the ways in which knowledge and value interplay will be one of the central themes.

When the intellectual history of contemporary social science comes to be written, one of its major themes will be the relation of social science to value. It will be a story of mutual isolation, affecting theory and practice alike, with losses to both the social sciences and the philosophy of value. C. Wright Mills was one of the powerful voices in American social theory of recent decades raised against this isolation. He focused clearly on the value potential of social science, and on the value consequences of its different styles of work. If he saw this as the politics of sociology, it was not in the debunking spirit of the older unmasking of ideologies. Rather, he tried to make social scientists self-conscious about the major ways in which their work did affect the solution of critical human problems, so that they could face responsibly the choices which they were often avoiding.

The practical understanding that Mills called for requires a more systematic cooperation of social science and philosophy on the very question of this relation of science and value. This is itself no simple problem, and an understanding of its complex structure is a necessary step in its systematic practical solution. Here, I should like to explore the interrelations of social science and value, and make a start on analyzing the entry-points, if we may so call them, where value issues enter into social science, and where social science assumptions enter into value theory.

Since three central concepts are involved in our inquiry—value, science, and entry—some initial refinement and consideration of present use is desirable.

Value is a high-powered concept, and in modern thought has shown a considerable tendency to become an imperialistic category. In philosophy, it was set up as a genus for a whole host of species, covering religious feeling as well as economic utility, and beauty as well as obligation. The guiding hope was that the study of generic problems of identification, measurement, and validation of "values" would yield important widely-applicable results. It is still an open question whether the whole development of general value theory in contemporary philosophy should not be regarded as a blind alley, in spite of some theoretically liberating effects it produced. In any case, it diluted the concept of value so completely that what remains is the general idea of a pro-or-con attitude. Recent social science, however, has not gone so far. It has tended to retain in the concept of value an element of judgment or discrimination, so that having a value often means in its studies not merely desiring something, but also thinking it or holding it in some way as desirable. Such conceptual history is not our present concern, but it conveys an important lesson for one who would study the entry of values into science. There is no existent discipline, philosophic or scientific, which validates the concept of value en bloc, or as more than a tag. There is no advance guarantee that as one type of value is relevant or irrelevant to science, so another type will be, or that any generalizations from one sample of value will hold for another sample from some other corner of the field. I would thus suggest that at the outset some formally distinct aspects be sorted out, that we differentiate at least a specific concept of purpose, a general concept of pro-attitude, a judgmental concept of worthwhile, and a prescriptive concept of obligation.

Science, in the present day, is likely to go in a number of different directions. Our concern with social science does not bind us too strictly, for boundary questions are themselves highly moot in the field. We can cross without passport into a large segment of psychology (even beyond what is labeled "social" psychology) and into a great deal of history, and we are not surprised—for example, when reading political science or sociology—to find ourselves occasionally in social philosophy. As to the meaning of "science," it sometimes is as broad as "systematic knowledge," sometimes it is limited to the "experimental"; sometimes it means invoking scientific method, sometimes scientific results, sometimes just the scientific temper. Discussions of value and science may have in mind pure science, applied science, or sometimes even the scientist operating on the social scene. All these distinctions are easy enough to make when required; it is only when we forget them that there is a tendency to overgeneralize from what is concluded in one sense of "science" to what holds for "science in general."

To speak of the entry of value assumptions into science, or conversely, of scientific assumptions into value theory, calls attention to the form of results we may anticipate, or rather the task of differentiating types of relations. Some values are smuggled into science, and the best thing to do when we uncover them is immediately to deport them. Others, however, may have been around a long time, and claim either prescriptive or native-born (not to speak of natural) rights. Here we may want to let them stay, but delimit carefully what influence they may or may not have: they may, for example, permissibly motivate budgetary support for science, but not dictate the questions of basic research. On the other hand, some value-attitudes—the virtue of impartiality, for example—are ushered into the inner sanctum of science and kept constantly at work. Certainly, then, two categories of entry will be external purpose and internal influence. But there is a third which may prove even more ingrained. Let us speak of it as a value parameter. What this kind of entry would be, if it actually exists, may be seen by analogy. The sense intended is the same in which a theory of society is seen to involve a specific picture of the nature of man. We would then say that a social theory has a human-nature parameter. The question would not be whether it can be eliminated, since some theory of human nature is unavoidable; rather, it would be a choice of which picture to accept, or at least the realization that unsettled questions of social theory are, in some definite part, a function of unsettled questions in the theory of human nature. Now whether there are value parameters in this sense in social science is a question for inquiry. If there are, the kinds of values that occupy such a position would be unavoidable or noneliminable. But whether or not there are, this type of concept is required. For there is not only the question of possible value parameters in social science, but also the comparable question of social science parameters in value theory.

No doubt, further conceptual refinements will be needed as research progresses. For a start, we should not be less refined than our four concepts of value (purpose, pro-attitude, worthwhile, obligation), our multiple meanings of science (at least the distinction of pure, applied, and social action), and our three modes of entry (external purpose, internal influence, and value parameter, and comparable converse concepts for entry of science into value) will allow us to be.

What kind of research questions can be raised about the entry of values into pure science? Unless we simply plunge blindly, we would first need a sketch of the scientific process as it takes place typically in social science, so that we can map the sensitive entry-points for values. Such a sketch would differentiate at least the following aspects: determination of the basic aim of the science, establishment of field boundaries, modes of identifying phenomena in the field, problem selection, problem formulation, concept formation, hypothesis selection, verification procedures, theory development, and concepts of adequacy in results. It would be too grim a task at this point to push on into each of these in the hunt for values to be assessed. Let us rather start from the different modes of entry and take illustrations, where relevant, from these many aspects.

First, then, as to the role of external purposes. This has been amply studied in theories of ideology. It is easier to spot a class distortion of economics or a racialist use of the IQ than to ferret out a subtle limitation of hypotheses through the use of a deeply hidden value-carrying model. But even in spotting ideology, there is considerable complexity. What exactly are we criticizing a thesis for, when we label it ideological in the derogatory sense of that term?

On the face of it, it seems simple enough. A view is enunciated as a scientific thesis—say, a doctrine of racial superiority in the early twentieth-century imperialistic era, or the wage-fund theory in nineteenth-century economics, or the identification of business success with evolutionary leadership in Spencerian or Sumnerian sociology. It is then found to operate in such a way as to enhance the economic interest and power position of a particular social group. What more is needed to warrant the attribute of an unmasked ideology, as intruding external purpose?

Actually, a whole host of differentiated requirements are called for. First, as to the view itself, what is its truth property? It may be classified as sheer nonsense, or as logically possible but actually false, as largely false though partly true, or finally even as wholly true. (Quite literally, in a given period, true theses in physics and chemistry may, by their discovery, enhance the economic interest and power position of a particular social group that controls productive resources.) Second, as to the way in which the view is held. It may be held on presumed (though incorrect) evidential grounds, or on "projective" grounds expressing unconscious demands, whether the thesis be true or false (Freud illustrates this by the belief of alchemists in the transmutability of metals), or for conscious advancement of the external purposes. Third, as to the locus of the ideological activity. The external purpose may operate directly in the act of discovery, or in the perpetuation of the thesis after discovery, or in influencing the direction of further scientific inquiry, or in the social application of the thesis. Fourth, as to the consequences of the ideological activity in the ongoing life of science and social activity. The external purpose may operate directly or indirectly (by limiting inquiry or by turning promising minds from a given path), deliberately or through unintended consequences, outside the science in applied areas or by standardizing presuppositions of the scientific pattern of inquiry (by affecting the philosophy of science so that certain models are given a privileged position). Fifth, as to the relation of the factors. Relations of truth-status of theses, purposes of holders, and consequences of action, may be logical or psychological or historical. They are hardly likely to be logical—in the three examples cited above, the truth would be logically compatible with an ethical demand for supreme sacrifice by the "superior" group rather than a demand for special privileges. But all sorts of combinations of psychological and sociohistorical relations may be found.

What combination of these, and no doubt of other factors, shall be dubbed with the title of ideology is not our present concern. It is more important to realize the vast program of conceptual refinement and social science research required to map the entry patterns of external purposes. But it would be a mistake to think of them wholly in malevolent terms. Dire needs may prompt scientific research, and hopes of practical solution stimulate hypotheses. Depressions have quickened theories of the role of consumer spending in maintaining economic stability. Desires to win elections have by no means been absent from the rise of political sociology. Studies of workers' morale grew to prominence in an atmosphere of apprehension about the rise of trade unions and a fear of their taking a class-struggle attitude. Institutional demands in education and in war developed intelligence testing; manpower demands and wide skill demands may militate against ideological theories of the fixed IQ. Large-scale organization has stimulated the study of bureaucratic structures; though sometimes prompted by the fear of socialism, it has also raised problems that socialist countries find it necessary to face as a result of their own experience.

At the present time, there has been a kind of consolidation of external purposes in relation to pure social science, a growing conviction that, on the whole, research in social life is practical. Thus external purposes are standardized in general support of *basic research*. Analytic caution is still required to a high degree to spot the operation of purposes within the scientific processes.

In fact, the general acceptance of basic research may tend to obscure these purposes by making all decisions of direction in inquiry seem intrascientific. But quite obviously today, to take the most glaring examples, there is incomparably more research on the social aspects of waging war than of advancing peace, and on the techniques of control and command rather than on the techniques of liberty and self-realization. Since the problems investigated tend to limit the kind of work done, the hypotheses suggested, questions asked, and models proposed, the impact of external purposes by this route is a strong one. There can, however, be no question of removing human purposes, of "neutralization" at this point. It is rather a question of agreeing on broad human purposes to guide interests in inquiry. This would help unify a variety of already recognized aims: greater facilities for freedom of research, conscious specification of guiding purposes rather than subterranean channels of their operation, and greater place to the goal of truth as against ignoring social sore spots or existing patterns of economy or power. And of course, there is also the question of facing realistically the human costs involved in moving from understanding to application. These are all familiar social issues.

We turn from external purposes operating on pure social science to internal influence. It is worth nothing initially that the very discovery of the operation of external purposes can itself have internal consequences—especially on verification procedures. The more one establishes a checklist of the kinds of purpose that have given a special turn to scientific work, the more one clarifies the operational concept of a "reliable observer"—just as the comparable discovery of color blindness, or different reaction speed, or influence of drugs or alcohol affects the concept of a reliable observer in other fields. Thus the realization that there are class attitudes has consequences for sampling techniques, for interview procedures, for assumptions about differential goal strivings, and so on. It is in the accumulation of a knowledge of specific biases, and thus of specific techniques for penetrating and avoiding them, rather than in some philosopher's stone to test for bias in general, that the contemporary theory of ideology can make its contribution to scientific rationality.

We may omit here the internal operation of general values, in the sense of obligations and pro-attitudes not peculiar to social science—regard for truth, objectivity and impartiality, clarity, systematic power, and so forth—in brief, the methodological virtues

of all scientific endeavor. On the whole, the internal value influences in social science seem most apparent in special pro-or-con
attitudes which affect such aspects as concept-formation and basic
theoretical schemata. Take the use of the central concept of power
in political sciences, often advanced to do the same kind of job
there as the concept of energy does in physics. Clearly, its
centrality comes from the existence of power structures in contemporary institutions, as well as the prevalence of power struggles in both individual and international relations. It would take a
long historical inquiry to see how and why older purpose-con-
cepts were driven out from a central role. We cannot assume it
was for scientific reasons alone. Since political science has not
flourished or made notable discoveries under the reign of the
power concept, its use can be seen rather as imposing or expressing a dominance-submission pattern than as exhibiting the fruitfulness of a meaningful scientific construct. Here the science
simply reflects the attitude rather than brings an understanding of
it. Consider, for example, what would happen if political science
were construed as the science of decision systems in all areas of
life—small-group decision, national decision, global decision. The
science would stretch out in different directions from those in
which it now moves, would focus on different additional phenomena, and would weave altered affiliations. This, too, would be
a very limited central category, no doubt reflecting the need of
decision and the growth of institutional mechanisms of decision in
modern times. But it would cast the science in a quite altered
pattern.

To illustrate internal influence in basic theoretical frameworks,
we may point to functionalist theory. By positing the existence of
a more or less stable system in relation to which the functions of
specific social forms are to be interpreted, a pro-attitude to stability is embedded in the scientific quest. Specific purposes of
adherence to or rejection of the status quo may be winnowed out
by warning against the conservative and the radical capture of
functionalist concepts. But the value tone may still remain. The
social scientist, who complains at this point that, after all, the
business of science is the discovery of order, is missing the deeper
philosophical issue. Is the order to be discovered within the social
system, or in the historical panorama within which social systems
rise and undergo basic transformation? How often is the very
expression "social system" used with the presupposition that there
must be equilibrium characteristics in all social organizations so

that history and evolution can be ignored? When Aristotle identified wisdom with the knowledge of causes, and thus with the contemplation of order—as he said, there is no science of the accidental—he assumed an eternal or fixed basic order. Perhaps today we should rather say with Robert Bridges, in his *The Testament of Beauty,* "Our stability is but balance, and wisdom lies in the masterful administration of the unforeseen." Whether the central stress falls on knowing what to expect, or having a large enough armory of expectations to deal with the unexpected, is a question of basic philosophical orientation to order and disorder. The value-tone in any specific use of the order concept seems quite clear in the history of social science.[1]

Whether such values as pro-attitudes in concept formation and in general schemata may be eliminated once they are tracked down is not an all-embracing question. Certainly some can, but others may turn out on deeper exploration to lead to value parameters in the sense defined above. Let us continue the political science illustration to trace the outcome. There is no reason why, having come to suspect that the power stress in contemporary political science is a value-structuring of social life in terms of an acceptance of dominance-submission relations, a political scientist may not try to correct for it by greater attention to interpreting governing from below—that is, from a wider view of the aims and purposes of men in terms of which they, on the whole, accept governmental structures. How far would he be removing embedded values? If he proposed the decision orientation suggested as an alternative for the field, he would probably be embodying a general democratic value attitude—human beings working out cultural devices to embody their decisions. If he began to study political phenomena in terms of the whole structure of a society, with its given cultural history, in the light of its patterning of human goals, he might very well be led to question the traditional boundaries of the field which is his science. Now in the physical sciences, it has already been established that the boundaries of a field are a function of the results already achieved in the sciences and may be shifted as new results emerge. Social science boundaries have frequently embodied value attitudes. How much of the traditional separation of political science from economics has reflected the separateness of governmental institutions from business institutions in the last few centuries of Western history? Insofar as the boundaries of the sciences are a function of the institutional structure, all "laws" discovered in each field as separate might hold only for limited given historical conditions. But what is more, the maintenance of these conditions in a given epoch may embody the policies of a given economic system, such as the state keeping its hands off business in traditional laissez-faire capitalism. Hence, the insistence on political science being developed separately from economics would embody a pro-attitude to such economic policies.

Critical consideration of the foundations of social science will have to decide whether selection of field boundaries and basic field concepts unavoidably embodies one or another basic value attitude to the continuation or alteration of basic institutional structures. If this is so, we would have at this point a value parameter in the inner structure of our science. Whether it is so in this particular example would require much more formal and factual analysis to determine. It might be suggested that the value parameter could be removed by treating all social sciences as one science and being attentive to changing structures, rather than by favoring or assuming a specific stability of structures. But it may be that such a change itself could be construed as a specific interpretation (or "value" in the neutral mathematical sense) for the parameter in question.

We cannot here pursue all the many general aspects of the scientific enterprise in which comparable studies would have to be made. Certainly the innumerable controversies in the history of social science methodology suggest sensitive spots where value parameters might be located. For example, the issue of whether social science is "ideographic" (painting portraits of individual wholes) or "nomothetic" (finding laws) has embodied a sizable component of value attitudes to the creativity of man as against his being "submerged" in a natural world. Issues of verification modes, such as behavioral versus phenomenological, or public observability versus private empathy, often rest on some interpretation of the self as social or as isolated, and an element of value-patterning of the self, rather than simply discovering its inherent nature. Similarly, whether to use a framework of individual behavior, some specially construed sense of "action," interpersonal transactions, or qualities of group relations as fundamental "units" contains, more often than not, a battle of a social against an individual perspective, with all the controversies about individualism that have accumulated in the past three centuries.

Now it is quite possible in principle to argue that these many questions, which tend to divide social scientists into theoretical "schools" and to send them off at times into quite different directions of inquiry, with different initial selection of phenomena analyzed in different ways (though perhaps all in the nature of scientific jobs), will in the long run admit of resolution in generally accepted scientific value terms of "fruitfulness." Just as teleological physical science gave way to a causal schema, so, for example, reductionist social formulations in terms of individual properties may run their course when it is found that they lead scientists to "psychologize" social phenomena and to be unable to explain or predict men's social reactions; formulations in terms of group properties and group structures may then prove scientifically unavoidable. Or again, present operationalist rigidity, which embodies a high pro-attitude to communicability and a fear of obscurantism, may find that to be fruitful it must relax and embrace some modicum of responsible phenomenological inspection, or risk remaining scientifically barren; phenomenological inspection, meanwhile, may shed its matrix of resistance to the scientific study of man as continuous with the order of nature.

Such theses of long-range convergence may themselves be seen as pro-attitudes toward the unity of science. At present, such methodological values are surrogates for long-range theories about how social science can most fruitfully develop. Whether their value character will diminish and their predictive character come to the front, it is probably too early to judge. In the physical sciences, this happened to some extent, but not wholly. In ancient times, differences of schools embodied not only value differences, but those of methodological direction. Ancient medical writings bear witness not only to the general conflict of functionalists and atomists, with their different feelings about the order of the universe, but also to their specifically different hypotheses in explaining the workings of individual organs in the body (e.g., how the heart works, or how urea gathers in the kidneys). Long-range solution of specific differences did not remove all value components; rather, they were standardized. The residual values were incorporated as built-in aims in the very meaning of "science"—systems for prediction rather than simple contemplation of eternal necessities; or again, into modes of verification—the sensory as yielding stable agreement, rather than emotional reaction as productive of divergence. The sciences of man today, resembling ancient physical science in their conflict of schools, may be destined to a similar outcome—that is, standardized "values" for basic value parameters rather than complete elimination of values. But more complex solutions are, of course, logically possible. Meanwhile, research can proceed in two directions. One is to render explicit the value parameters in existent theoretical structures; the other is the speculative reconstruction of theoretical structures with minimal, standardized value parameters, including possibly even conjectural attempts at their complete elimination.

Questions of value in applied social science, beyond those raised for pure social science, stem from the very notion of application. Does this notion involve a reference to additional values, and if so, what are they?

Some applied sciences, such as medicine, spell out specific values in their very definition—the science of curing or maintaining health. Others, like engineering, seem to embody a minimal idea of control in a given medium, whether that control be utilized for construction or destruction. Which path should a definition of an applied science follow? Or should it refer, in general terms, to satisfying human needs or solving practical problems?

This last straddling procedure will not bear up under analysis. Such concepts as needs or practical problems are by this time clearly seen to embody specific value considerations. To say that men need something is to say that the something is a necessary condition for their survival, growth, progress, satisfaction, or aim-fulfillment. To say something is a practical problem is similarly to point to specific hindrances or dangers and so to specific goals or values. After all, if to solve a practical problem meant simply to make the problem disappear, all human problems could be solved in a great thermonuclear bang.

To limit the additional value in the notion of an applied science to the aim of control has some advantage, but it is likely to prove misleading. The advantage is that it shows the double potential—for good or ill—in any body of knowledge that furnishes skills. It thus compels one to state explicitly and separately the values sought. Along these lines, medicine would have to be redefined as the applied science of body-state control; it would then be a separate value judgment to use medicine for healing rather than for mass-extermination and debilitation, as indeed the Nazis used it. However, this policy in defining an applied science is probably misleading in suggesting the value neutrality of an applied science as such, at least as an historical matter. The Nazi use of medical skill for extermination has seemed to most men an outrageous violation of the "nature" of medicine. And even the apparent neutrality of engineering stems not so much from any inherently value-free character of the discipline as from the fact that it has historically been associated with opposing values; its destructive use stems from its role in war. To be on one side or another in a conflict is not to be on neither side. (Even mercenaries do not belie this; they are neutral to sides, but not to their pay, their lives, their comforts.) To strip the notion of application, therefore, to the minimal idea of control does not conform to preponderant usage, nor to analytic necessities. In fact, it is a normative proposal for extending the presumed value-free character of science into the domain of application, and so to fashion a certain image of the scientist and limit his responsibilities as scientist. In the light of the confusion that reigns in this area at present, clarity can best be achieved by recognizing that any limited skill per se can be used in opposing ways, and by insisting that any actual applied science which has grown up as an enterprise of men in the pursuit of goals should specify the goals it has embodied, so that any controversy about their desirability will admit of an explicit sociomoral reckoning.

Once the value base of applied science has been made clear in this fashion, another feature emerges about the relation of applied to pure science, which may have special relevance to social science. There is not a one-to-one relation, so that every pure science has its unique applied science as correlate. Engineering draws on a whole range of sciences. Space engineering is the most recent and clearest illustration of the way in which biology, psychology, and social science tie in with the physical sciences in determining feasibility of accomplishment. The same holds for medicine, drawing on everything from physics to entymology and psychology. Is not the same thing true today for, say, developmental economics?

If the unity in an applied science is a problem-unity crystallized by human goals, the relation between the applied science and the pure sciences on which it draws becomes a closer one, to the extent to which these problems and their embedded goals in fact play a role in setting questions, encouraging theoretical development, offering guiding models, and so forth. It may even be that at the present stage of development of pure social science, it could prosper more with a goal or problem inner unity. For example, could not economics today advantageously be considered as the science of avoiding depressions and generating a high productive level throughout the globe, politics as the science of social control productive of the greatest human freedom, sociology as the analysis of society to find the points of control for removing obvious evils (crime, delinquency, discrimination, etc.) and advancing obvious goods, cultural anthropology as the science of achieving one world without a loss of all divergent cultural values, linguistics as the science of maximum effective and aesthetic communication, and so forth? Something like this, I take it, was at the root of Robert Lynd's approach in *Knowledge for What?* I am not sure about the answer. It may be that a goal reorientation of the social sciences might tend to disparage descriptive content and systematic relationship and risk a narrow pragmatism. But on the other hand, nothing could be narrower than the traditional disowning of values by the social sciences in modern times. The issue is not one to be settled in terms of external purposes. It is a question for the social scientists themselves to decide how to carry on their work to achieve the widest descriptive, historical, and theoretical results. That a value reorientation is a possible path, however, indicates that there is no inherent barrier to a constitutive role for values in the nature of a social science.

It is not unusual in the present social conflicts for a social scientist to engage in social action, in his own words, "as a citizen." That is, he draws a fine line between the neutrality of his discipline and the possession of certain values on his part as a citizen or a person. The analysis of this troubled question is helped by separating the different kinds of value judgments the social scientist may be called upon to make as a scientist.

The most obvious commitment he has as a scientist is, of course, to the dominant value of truth inherent in his enterprise. This means that if he speaks out on a question of his discipline, he is committed to stating what he knows as a scientist. Of course, the obligation to speak out is a separate strand, and occasionally, some philosophers have lauded a silent devotion to truth. But it is likely that the general obligation of the scientist to speak out where the truth is socially important stems from the wider obligation of the intellectual in modern society, which in its turn could be subject to a comparable analysis.

A second obligation is to maintain the conditions of his scientific enterprise. If he is committed to the pursuit and extension of truth, he is committed to maintaining and extending the conditions requisite for scientific work. Most social scientists would accept this obligation as scientists. But in doing so, they are not merely accepting a platitude, but opening an area for social science research. For the social conditions relevant to the scientific pursuit of truth are not discerned a priori, but are issues for social science evidence. Hence, quite correctly, a social scientist can oppose McCarthyite guilt by association and restrictive military secrecy in science, not just as a citizen, but as a scientist, if the evidence is clear enough that these are conditions which hinder scientific development.

A third sphere is making judgments about what is good for a man, or worthwhile, on the basis of the contributions of the scientist's area of inquiry. It is clear that many segments of social science furnish such judgments, or at least kindred judgments about human evils. Psychologists on the effects of repeated frustration and breakdown, sociologists on the existence and conditions of social disorganization and anomie, economists on the danger of unemployment and the destruction of economic resources, anthropologists on the loss of a sense of dignity in exploitative cultural contact, need no outside sanction—beyond perhaps a formal explication of the terms "good" and "evil"—to make such value judgments as scientists. Sometimes, they are hindered in such judgments by a failure to make conceptual distinctions in ethical terms. To judge something good if men could achieve it is one thing; to say that we ought at a given time to devote given resources to achieving it rather than some alternative realizable good, or that we ought to pursue it when it will involve some given cost or sacrifice, may be quite another thing. The judgments about what is good or worthwhile are not irrelevant to the scientist as scientist, although there may be differences about the precise obligations; for the latter involves scaling problems among competing goods as well as judgments of means.

But, fourth, there may be judgments of social obligation which a scientist could make as scientist, if the scaling and means components become clear. Here the emphasis on the modern scene often falls on the cooperation of different scientific disciplines in concerted social action. For the one science may supplement the gaps of knowledge which prevent another from turning judgments of good into either conditional or highly probable obligations. In such context there is not, then, an inherent barrier to obligation judgments, but simply a limitation of knowledge, or sometimes a difference in comparative values which further investigation may diminish. The scientist as scientist may thus find himself able to state contingent or hypothetical obligations—for example, "if such and such a country wants peace, it ought to abandon such and such attitudes." Sometimes, the if-clause drops away by common consent. Contemporary social scientists argue about the comparative social advantage of socialist and private enterprise in developing underdeveloped countries. But where is the social scientist who will sponsor the preservation of feudalism in Egypt or Iran or Saudi Arabia? This rejection is not just a value judgment about the intrinsic worth of the feudal way of life; it embodies a scientific thesis that whatever sets of values contemporary men may hold as basic, feudalism, if perpetuated, will thwart them.

Finally, there may be limiting points at which knowledge is insufficient, or conflict in purposes too great. Even here, it may be rather as a scientist offering an informed guess or a plausible hypothesis, or as a trained thinker clarifying alternatives, than as an ordinary citizen, that the scientist engages in social action.

In this domain, again, there need not be an all or nothing attitude. The gap between values that social scientists commonly agree on and the dominating policies of practical politics in our society is often so great that there is the most pressing need for the independent effort of the scientist in social action.

Research into ways in which social science enters value theory is doubly difficult, because it has been attacked from both sides. For a long time, the social scientists insisted values were not their business while the value theorists were busy widening the gap by arguing for the philosophical irrelevance of scientific-factual materials. Together they have gathered a formidable array of slogans:

> Science tells you the means, but not the end.
> Science tells you the cause of your choice, but not whether it is the right choice.
> Science may help you map the pattern of your past choices, but cannot tell you whether to choose to adhere to the pattern of the past.
> Science fashions beliefs, not attitudes.
> You can't get the "ought" from the "is."
> You can't get the "desirable" from the "desired."

You can't get the "prescriptive" from the "descriptive."
You can't get the "imperative" from the "indicative."

And so on, with considerable ingenuity in saying the same thing in different ways.

The philosophical arguments for maintaining the gap pose the issue of the relation of science and value in a deductive model: how to deduce value conclusions from scientific premises. What is thus demonstrated by the arguments is really not that science and value have no relation, but that such a model oversimplifies their relation to the point of irrelevance, that the relations are much more varyingly and complexly patterned. At the same time, a sociological analysis can readily discern that a grim battle is being fought. It appears to be a strange alliance between two quite disparate forces. One is the general resistance to those changes in traditional values which the growth of scientific knowledge might suggest. The other is the determination to keep value judgment open as a continuing human process with a major measure of autonomy. In this respect, it constitutes a modern resistance to the bureaucratization of men's choice of their lives, whether the bureaucracy be religious or political or scientific. It is thus a recall to responsible choice.

The path of solution I have suggested for ethical theory in other writings [2] is to distinguish four methodologies or enterprises— analytic, descriptive, causal-explanatory, and evaluative. Carried on as an activity, each enterprise is distinct from the others, having its own aims and forms of results. But this does not mean that they are dealing with distinct materials, nor that the results of one may not promote the carrying out of another. Each in itself has unlimited scope. Analysis may go after the concepts of science as well as those of value. Description may focus on the activity of men having a purpose, or making moral choices, or reflecting in ethical theorizing, just as it may focus on men moving or behaving. Causal explanation may be sought for any of these processes, although different philosophical outlooks may have different hopes concerning the outcome. Similarly, evaluation is a human enterprise appropriate to any field: it has but to render explicit the criteria and standards that are being invoked in the particular value process. On the whole, in scientific activity the descriptive and causal-explanatory aspects have stood out more prominently; in philosophical activity the analytic and evaluative. But each has some portion of the other two as well, at least in the background. The division here may be historically grounded, having no ultimate rationality once the relation of the enterprises is carefully worked out.

As to the mutual help of the enterprises, this, in turn, is a subject for careful study. It is by now commonplace that the extension of description into new areas forces the analytic construction of new concepts (as, for example, the minute study of abnormal behavior prompted concepts of repression and the unconscious; or the extended study of differences in group behavior prompted the development of the concept of culture). Causal explanation similiarly extends the range of phenomena under investigation. Cumulative scientific activity along all these lines restructures the field for investigation; new and more subtle questions are asked, new meanings found, new values fashioned or discerned.

It follows that the entry of social science into value requires the same type of extended and differentiated analysis as the entry of value into science demanded of us. In a full study, we would have to distinguish value theory, specific value judgments, and applications of value judgment in conduct, just as we distinguished pure science, applied science, and social action. Instead, let us deal briefly with having purposes and pro-or-con attitudes, on the one hand, and distinctively moral judgments of worthwhile (good) or obligation, on the other.

In the case of having purposes and having pro-or-con attitudes, the descriptive and explanatory scientific task coincides with a large part of social science itself. Such values are part of the very content of the psychological and social sciences. Anthropological mapping of cultures and patterns, sociological value study, and psychological attitude and personality study, are concentrated in great measure on this field. Similarly, they may study how changes take place in the existent value system of persons or groups, the conditions and theory of their transformation, whether from internal pressures or external encounters. In all this investigation, we see the external role of science in value.

At what points do we find science passing into an internal influence in having purposes or pro-*and*-con attitudes? This can mean at what points do we find the knowledge gained about human purposes and attitudes affecting or altering human purposes and attitudes. This again is clearly a research problem for social science, especially for the sociology of science (pure and applied) and the psychology of knowledge. There is no simple key to it; it cannot be settled by a philosophical formula or by deduction from a historical theory of determinants or a psychological theory of consciousness—though they are relevant. It requires careful distinction of types of purposes and attitudes, and special research for different types. Or again, the internal influence of science in this area may refer to the way scientific knowledge affects our ideas of purposes and attitudes. This leads to the third type of entry, through the existence of social science parameters in this segment of value theory.

The role of social science parameters in having purposes and pro-or-con attitudes can best be grasped by focusing on the very concepts of having a purpose and holding an attitude. Are these simply lines of direction in action and feeling? Or consolidated habits of reaction? Or deeper impulses and drives fashioned into an organization under specific familial and social relations? Or manifestations of a developed self with stabilized boundaries and internal dynamic patterns? And so on, for different approaches in the theory of psychological and social determinants of human action. Our problem here is not to settle what is not yet settled in these inquiries, but to recognize the sense in which the very understanding of human purpose and human attitude embodies within it social science answers to social science questions. For a scientifically-oriented outlook, it seems clearly established by this day that human purpose and human attitudes are thoroughly sociocultural phenomena. The attempt to pinpoint the social science parameters is simply the struggle to make one's factual presuppositions in this domain of value theory explicit and responsible.

So far, we have dealt only with the purpose and attitude subdomain of value. The more critical questions arise in the distinctively moral sphere where the focus is on judging good (worthwhile) and bad, or on assessing obligation. Here again, having reassured ourselves that no attack is intended on the enterprise of evaluation or the activity of responsible moral choice, we have to differentiate the types of scientific entry. The external role of science is granted in the slogans by surrendering the sphere of means to science while retaining ends for ethics. Even this surrender is over-hasty; means problems are permeated with evaluation which should also be rendered explicit.

The internal influence of science in morals is seen most dramatically in the effects of causal knowledge on evaluations, especially in the growth of psychological knowledge. Formally, one might be tempted to say that the influence has its impact not on the value, but on the relation of the men to the value in the given situation. It is their "holding" of the value which is scrutinized, and its relation to other values that they hold which proves to have a sizable component of factual "cement." Men may come to realize that their punishing or disciplining others contains a large component of aggressivity; the result, within the pattern of other accepted values, may be a humanization in the values assigned to judicial decision or discipline of the young. The technique of developing insight in the individual therapy situation is a model of the internal influence of science on value. Comparably in sociocultural patterns, the understanding of functional relations may affect the evaluation of institutions and social practices.

The social science parameters in moral choice and ethical theory also emerge in careful inquiry. One may expect that there will be some carryover from the subdomain of purposes and attitudes, but this raises the ethical theory question of how far ethical concepts of goodness and obligation are to be understood in terms of complexes of attitudes, purposes, and feelings. For example, can the ethical notion of an "ideal" be analyzed as a mode of functioning of major human purposes in the search for a form of organization that will advance the movement of men toward a solution of specific human problems, and at the same time, enlist deep feelings over a long time-span? We need not minimize the conflict that is to be found in ethical theory over such problems of meaning-analysis. In the long run, I think it can be settled only by analyses that take their point of departure in ethical theory, that map its phases fully and pinpoint its processes, and show precisely where alternative solutions or proposals take different form as one assumes different results in the psychological and social sciences.[3]

In general, a scientifically-oriented approach, mindful of the lessons of an evolutionary social theory about man and his works, will see the moral and ethical subdomains of value as an emergent level in the development and functioning of man. Such an emergence by no means rules out phenomenological qualities of a specifically moral sort in the field of awareness, nor unique conceptual constructs. It affirms, however, that this moral level arises, expresses, and functions with respect to the range of human needs and purposes, and that the meaning of these concepts is to be found in their systematic relations to purposes, attitudes, feelings (and complexes of these) in the wider value domain. Thus scientific study (psychological, cultural, social, and historical) of purpose, striving, and aspiration, means and ends in their interrelations, of pleasure and pain, sympathy, love, guilt and shame, of human development in familial and social milieu, and a whole host of human actions and reactions, including intelligence and creativity, throws light on the moral and ethical domain. Men can thus achieve a fuller understanding of their existent morality and of their own ethical reflection in guiding and reconstructing it.

A social science that sees its value bearings, and a value theory that sees its scientific linkage, need no longer seem a dream in the present state of man's development. It can instead become a powerful instrument in human growth.

NOTES

1. Interestingly enough, Mills at one point in *The Sociological Imagination*, p. 117, attacks the very ideal of prediction in social science as substituting for responsible choice. Perhaps this could be taken care of by specifying the form of prediction to be: "Under such-and-such conditions, an event of the class X will happen, unless some action of the class Y is taken."

2. Especially in my book *Method in Ethical Theory* (Indianapolis, 1963). Various phases of the problem of the relation of science and ethics are dealt with in: *Ethical Judgment: The Use of Science in Ethics* (Glencoe, 1955); *Anthropology and Ethics*, written in collaboration with May Edel (Springfield, Ill., 1959; rev. ed., New Brunswick,. N.J.: Transaction, 1970); and *Science and the Structure of Ethics* (Chicago, 1961).

3. For an investigation along these lines, see my *Science and the Structure of Ethics*, Part III.

13. Values and Political Science: Notes on the Strategy of Research

This paper was written for the first of a series of conferences held by the Department of Political Science at Northwestern University in 1966 on the general topic of "Social Scientists and the Normative Analysis of Political Life." The conferences were prompted by a growing cleavage in many political science departments at that time between those for whom normative questions were scientifically meaningful and many of those who pushed them aside in their attempt to attune research to the new instruments of group simulation for computer manipulation. (I trust that the situation has changed by this time, since there is no inherent contradiction between a concern with value and computer modeling.) I did not attempt to investigate the application of science to normative judgments, since I had dealt with this at length in previously published books. Instead, I tried out the program of chapter 12 above, of locating the entry points for values in the structure of research in political science, political theory, and political practice. One of the implications of the paper is that values play some role in the determination of categories employed in the very research that attempts to avoid values.

This paper has not been published previously.

Wider study by political scientists of the points at which values impinge on their discipline is something that a philosopher can only welcome. Too often in the past, it has fallen to the lot of the philosopher as outsider to track down value commitments operating surreptitiously in a political theory, a political description, or a proposed political policy. We pay a high price for the surreptitious, for when it is unmasked there is often a tendency to render all social theory suspect, to regard it as "ideological" in the older disparaging sense of the term, and so there arises either a general aversion to theorizing or else an arbitrary resort to values on the assumption that anything goes—if it goes. The present paper is part of the effort to render the role of values a responsible one.

THE PROBLEMS BEFORE US

Before plunging into our problems, a word on the term "value." It is a very broad term, often serving as a tag for a rather heterogeneous class. It is wise to distinguish at least four uses, since what is said about values in one of these senses may not always hold of values in another of the senses. A minimal sense of value is that of a *pro* or *anti* attitude to something, a being for or against it. A second sense is the ordinary one of purposes; men's aims or purposes are often spoken of as their values. A third sense carries the idea of judgment or evaluation—our values are what we judge *worthwhile* or *good,* and not all our aims or purposes, when reflected on, are judged to be values in this sense. A fourth sense is prescriptive, it specifies what we *ought to do.* This last sense is clearly stronger than even the third; for several competing aims may be all worthwhile—say, the different careers that face a college student—but only one of them may be so right under the conditions or in light of the whole picture that it ought to be pursued. We may note that what are ordinarily called moral values are more likely to be found in the third and fourth group, but by no means exhaust them. In any case, our concern in this study is not primarily with moral values, but with the different types, levels, and locations of values and value judgment in political science, political theory, and political policy.

The traditional view of the place of values in political science grants, of course, that they have a place as part of the phenomena the science studies. Men do have purposes, they line up for or against plans, they express preferences and make judgments, and they assign or shoulder obligations. And some of all these purposes, attitudes, judgments of preference, and obligations do enter into the political side of life. Thus there is no reason why political science, where it finds a knowledge of these values relevant to its tasks, should not employ or have employed all the sociological and anthropological techniques of investigation to determine the distribution of values in a given population or a given cultural tradition.

The traditional view, however, draws the line at the operations of the political scientist. He has, of course, the intellectual values of a scientist, but beyond that, values have no place in his operations. His mapping of the field is scientific description, his conceptualization of the material is guided by scientific criteria, his classifications are in terms of scientific fruitfulness, his definitions embody the lessons of history and social science and are not intended to be persuasive in the sense of imparting value attitudes, and so on.

Beyond political science lie two directions in the discipline—a theoretical one leading to political theory and a practical one leading to judgments of political and social policy. The traditional view again sees no place for values, other than the intellectual values, in political theory; it is a critical consideration of the concepts, methods, and laws of political science. The traditional view does, however, recognize—and indeed how could anyone fail to admit this—that values enter into determination of political policy. For policy means simply the path of action that will carry to fulfillment our basic purposes. What the traditional view does insist is that we separate in policy decisions the purely factual picture of the proposed path and its consequences—this is a scientifically determinable matter, if we have enough knowledge—and the separate value judgment which asserts that the consequences are desirable, that they are better than the consequences of alternative available paths, and finally, that we ought to follow the proposed path. Unlike the scientifically determined facts in the picture, the values are said to be *subjective*. Science can study the theory of social policy and see what aims, in fact, serve as standards, but it cannot furnish prescriptions. There was a time, it is true, when this was not recognized, because political science was enmeshed and smothered in ethics; that was in the days of Plato and Aristotle, and later among the theologians. But at the opening of the modern era, knight-errants Machiavelli and Hobbes came dashing in with a sword of realism and a lance of secularization and rescued political science, so that ever after—with a bit of help from Max Weber—it prospered by keeping ethics at a distance.

How shall we tackle the traditional picture of the place of values in political science? First we must reckon with the two myths—the historical myth of the detachment from ethics and the metaphysical myth of the subjectivity of value. Second, we shall look briefly at the kinds of locations at which values are admittedly found in the description of political phenomena or the analysis of political systems. Third, we shall propose some strategies for research into the location of values and consider in a preliminary way what we may expect them to accomplish and what are their limitations. Fourth, we shall apply them to various phases of the activity of the political scientist and the political theorist to determine whether there really are places where value commitments are highly relevant, probably occur, or are unavoidable. We can look at the activities of conceptualizing the field, marking out borders and making classifications, establishing definitions, analyzing basic concepts and special concepts, incorporating basic factual assumptions, and finally, formulating the concepts that enter into the theory of policy.

THE MYTHS OF A VALUE-FREE POLITICAL SCIENCE

The Historical Myth

It is true that Aristotle's *Politics*, the foundation treatise of Western political science, is continuous with his ethics, and that both of these are seen as divisions in the art of organizing the whole of life in the light of the discovered good. Ethics deals with the character side and the determination of the kinds of virtues to be established, politics with the kinds of institutions appropriate. But this broad perspective does not prevent Aristotle from examining—in fact it spurs him to it—the detailed phenomena of ruling in many societies, studying constitutions and their patterns, classifying on appropriate bases and revising classification in the light of causal exploration, examining the causes of revolution in various constitutions, projecting his own ideal organization and estimating the best approximations to it under different human conditions, giving advice to holders of different values in the light of their own aims in their own systems, and all of this without confusing where he is being descriptive, analytic, causal-explanatory, and evaluative. If his value attitudes sound dogmatic to historically sophisticated moderns, we can at least see the source of his dogmatism in his metaphysical teleology, his bland assumption that nature in human affairs, as well as in biology, follows a plan of striving for the good.

Again, it is true that there was in due course a secularizing of politics. But how was this a de-Aristotelianization, or a separating of politics from ethics? Take Hobbes as example—for what could be more secular than a system built on physiology, that encapsulates religion itself as a control mechanism in ensuring obedience of subjects. The *Leviathan* is a book on ethics and politics, it does not separate them. But because changes have taken place in the theory of metaphysics, in the conception of reason, and in the growth of the physical sciences, Hobbes gives different answers to the same questions that Aristotle asked and offers a different theory of ethics. He has abandoned the teleology of final causes as an explanatory schema, though he has much to tell us about purposive behavior and the strategy of plans. He has modified the concept of reason, changing it from the immediate grasping of ultimate truths (an "essence-realism") to a mode of operating with symbols, a reckoning of names; consequently, reason no longer furnishes a value content of its own, Instead of the Aristotelian good (which in any case was a wide notion of the direction of human striving and so included much that modern Kant-influenced ethics would regard as simply goal striving and not the "really moral"), Hobbes offered the mass of human desires. For the ethics proper, he offered a genetic conception of how the desires grow into plans and how the need for security grows into a paramount obligation to maintain a system for preserving law and order. This theme permeates his work, it enters into his very definition of ethics, his selection of moral rules (natural laws), his treatment of virtues—for example, he thinks of sobriety in drink as a natural law when he pictures the disorder to which intemperance leads, but he lists it as a private matter when disorder consequences do not come to mind. In general then, we have not an abandoning of ethics, but a quite different theory of what ethics is. A similar picture can perhaps be traced in the theological writings as well. The view of man as corrupt since his fall means that it is futile to think of social order in terms of pursuing the good; the best we can hope for is an order that restrains the disorderly in man. In short, the general swing is not from ethics to nonethics, but from a politics that sets its sights for the achievement of the good (happiness of man) to a politics that sets its sights for the necessary conditions for achieving the good. Of course within the general swing, there are different interpretations of the good itself. The power required for security may itself be to some men the very content of the good. But this is not something modern: in Plato's *Republic,* Thrasymachus is not denying a good for man, but asserting it to lie in the power that makes possible achievement of the Id values of aggressiveness, sexuality, and acquisitiveness.

The Myth That Values Are Subjective

This metaphysical myth cannot be so readily disposed of as historical myths about writers whose works can be more critically reassessed. For it simply echoes what has been a pervasive doctrine in traditional dualist philosophy since Descartes. It will perhaps suffice for our present purposes to make a number of comments on it.

1. It is not a doctrine that the political scientist or theorist establishes in his own work, but one that he imposes on his work as a philosophical importation. The phenomena he notes, in strictly scientific investigation, are that men's aims or purposes and pro-attitudes differ sharply and are productive of conflict, and that in terms of political science alone, he is unable to resolve differences in what men regard as desirable and obligatory. The best he seems able to do as descriptive scientist is to trace the configurations these values assume under different social and historical conditions.

2. If he limited himself to the presence of difference, conflict, and arbitrariness, he would find them also in men's views of what military policies will achieve permanent victory, what economic policies will bring dependable prosperity, and so on. But there he does not leap to a doctrine of subjectivity. Instead, he reports that the facts are unclear or the criteria not yet agreed on. Hence, again it is clear that in allegations of subjectivity a philosophical choice is being made, not a scientific discovery.

3. The normal assumption where the political scientist alone cannot settle a question relevant to his field is to enlist outside cooperation. He is not equipped to settle economic questions or military questions by himself. Similarly perhaps, an "ought" question requires cooperation of many disciplines, including ethics.

4. There is a long tradition of acceptance of the dogma that objective nature is measurable and confirmable while subjective spirit is arbitrary and incalculable. It finds varied expression in political theory. Sometimes, it imparts an all-pervading arbitrariness into political science; for example, R. M. MacIver in his *The Web of Government,* regards every society as held together by its

myth system, and asserts of the question how men *should* be governed that "the *should* is always expressive of the thinker's own myth complex, is always subject to his presuppositions and so lies outside the ambit of science . . . ." [1] Sometimes, there is a more persistent attempt to separate the strands that can be treated scientifically from those specific ones that are simply dependent on one's own values; for example, Robert A. Dahl suggests that, ultimately, no amount of factual knowledge will be sufficient to make the appraisals required for assigning a value to a given set of consequences in making a political analysis, or again in shaping one's orientation to risk and uncertainty.[2] Usually these statements can be tracked down to a current philosophical dualism. MacIver's account of myth as contrasted with technique is highly metaphysically-laden. It expresses in revised form the distinction he made in his earlier book, *Society*, between culture and civilization. Civilization consisted of techniques, physical and social, that were cumulative and served as means. Culture was tied to ends, to the inner noncumulative spiritual life of man. Behind this lay his philosophical dualism of nature and spirit, not merely as distinct phenomena, but as involving distinct explanatory principles. Dahl's conclusion reflects the modern sharp dualism of fact and value, cast in the positivist form of verifiable and nonverifiable.

5. Finally, it is worth reminding political science that the experience of many special fields—psychology is a good example—has been that they risk scientific frustration if they cling to abstract philosophical dogmas that have already cracked and are being discarded or questioned in philosophy itself. The dualisms of objective and subjective in general, and of fact and value in particular, are undergoing sharp criticism along many different paths.[3] It does not follow from this that the political scientist will wake up one day to find all value questions scientifically resolvable, but that the conditions that prevent resolution cut across many different kinds of material and are not ground for distinguishing generally facts and values. The sharp antithesis of fact and value may itself meet the same fate as did the contrast of measurable quantity and unmeasurable quality, which simply faded away as measurement became understood as a type of ordering, and studies of diverse forms of ordering went freely into every field without regard to metaphysical no-trespass signs.

It is important to stress that nothing said so far—nor anything to be said in the present study—denies a distinction between the

enterprise of describing and the enterprise of evaluating or pre-
scribing. What is denied is that there are different bodies of facts
or of propositions rather than different contexts of activity.

THE PLACE OF VALUES AMONG
POLITICAL PHENOMENA

The place of values among political phenomena can be sought
in two ways. We look on the object-level of phenomena, recognizing as an identifying mark of the political that it is concerned
with, broadly speaking, phenomena of the regulation of human
behavior. (A more precise identification involves already the scientific conceptualization of the field.) Or else we look on the
formal level and see how the concept of a political system is
articulated for descriptive purposes. Let us briefly follow each of
these paths.

On the object-level let us begin at the bottom by looking for the
purposes which support either the establishment or the maintenance of regulatory systems. We expect to find some purposes or
value-attitudes with respect to orderly life which are presupposed
by the existence of a political system. In human history, they
prove to be more specific than the general appeal of the need for
security, since order can be found on simple social levels without
distinctive political mechanisms. Inquiries concerning the origin of
the state on the historical scene sometimes help pinpoint the more
definite human purposes under specific conditions. For example,
R. H. Lowie, in his *The Origin of the State*,[4] gives the example of
the Plains Indians who have no concentration of power over men
in their society most of the year, but give commanders power of
life and death during the short period of the buffalo hunt, because
the year's food supply depends on precision during this expedi-
tion, so that absolute obedience is demanded. Here we see a kind
of part-time state in the making to serve special needs. Irrigation
needs seem to have played a comparable role, but more permanently demanding organization, in parts of Asia. In his argument
that the state originates in exploitation, Franz Oppenheimer [5]
discusses the attitudes of herders to farmers which led them,
when they conquered a farming area, to regularize a partial
confiscation of produce as a tax. When states become prevalent,
we tend to ignore the dimension of their supporting value-base.
But in our own century, we become conscious again of the need
for special attitudes underlying political organization when we

attend to the experiences of colonial powers in relation to peoples whose ways did not fit into the requirements of a Western state form. We see, for example, how the colonial power could not count on a labor supply for economic development, how it had to command labor and introduce a head tax to compel people to work for money, and how often people worked just enough to pay the tax and then stopped. In general, there is a whole dimension of values worth exploring in the sociocultural matrix, bearing on this question of attitudes to the state as a whole. (In some communities, attitudes to police may serve as a diagnostic index.) Many of the different theories of the nature of the state also embody conflicting views of the purposes underlying the existence of political phenomena. It is not necessary for value exploration to settle these theoretical differences; instead, each theory can add to the inventory of possible values affecting political institutions.

We need not work our way up here through the various ranges of political phenomena, for we are there in more familiar terrain. Obviously, the comparison of different political systems will be fruitful in locating different values impinging at critical points. The kind of values, expectations, and purposes supporting a democratic system in which there is widespread political activity will be likely to differ considerably from those in an autocratic or authoritarian form. And so on. As we have suggested, there is noting to bar the most intensive scientific study of the different kinds of values in this whole domain. Even so subtle a point as the values that enter into recognition of authority in different systems and the bases on which people, in fact, feel themselves bound could, while difficult, be investigated with some hope of success.

If we start along the second path, the formal level, we want to find ways of pinpointing the places in an outline sketch of a political system where values are likely to appear. This presupposes a fully articulated analysis of a political system. It is likely that we shall find in such a sketch very definite places left blank to be filled in for different political systems by different values. We may regard these as value places, or value placeholders, or value parameters. Take as an exmple a sketch of a political system like David Easton's in *A Framework for Political Analysis*.[6] As we shall see later, he takes a central mark of the political system to be that it allocates, in effect, scarce goods. It follows that a sketch of any political system will have a place to be filled in answering the question, "What type of allocation is there?" There is no escaping having an answer, since to say that a given system does not interfere will be equivalent to answering that it allows each man to keep what he can get within the law. Now a rule of allocation is, in effect, what in the history of ethics has been called a principle of distributive justice. And so we find that, at this point in a political system, one has to answer by indicating the conception of distributive justice in the community. There are, no doubt, many other comparable value placeholders in the sketch of a political system. For example, there will be points at which the power of the state will be used to support agreements that men make, and definite sanctions for various types of acts. In a developed political system with a systematized law, such values can be studied in the law of contracts, the criminal law, and so on,

An especially important location for basic values is to be found in the conceptions of the functions of the state. Here values get built into the conception of functions. A political system in which the functions of the state include explicitly the regulation of religions and publications is likely to have a quite different value configuration from one which explicitly forbids such state actions.

Finally, we will have to face, both in the examination of values among the phenomena and the place of values in the articulated political system, all the methodological questions of value inquiry, such as careful distinctions of means and ends, multiple descriptions of the same behavioral act, varying justifications for the same act, and so on. For example, suppose two states both intervene to settle strikes. One does so on the ground that the strike has issued in violent disorder, but with the implication that if it had not, the state would not have interfered. The other intervenes on the ground that it is the function of the state to harmonize classes (as in the organic conception of Italian fascism). The specific value—settle class disputes—is built into the role of the state in the latter, but not in the former. An intermediate system might have advisory mediation services.

Let this suffice for suggestions on the systematic search for values among the political phenomena. After all, we are dealing with an area in which it is agreed that values are to be found. Let us, therefore, go on to more debated ground—questions of values in political science and political theory.

STRATEGIES OF RESEARCH IN VALUE LOCATION

When we move from discerning values in political phenomena to pinpointing them in the operations of the political scientist and the political theorist, our difficulties are enormously increased. For we are working against the traditional interpretations of a value-free political science. We, therefore, require explicit strategies of research and a consciousness of their possibilities and limits. The difficulties will be diminished once more later on when we deal with social policy, for there again it is conceded that values are to be found and the task is merely to analyze types and specify locations. But in the intervening area which constitutes the larger part of our study, there is debate over almost every inch of the ground.

The Strategy of Alternative Possibilities

This consists in fixing on some point in the operations of political science, comparing different treatments or else elaborating alternative ones speculatively, and then considering whether there are kinds of values which might justify inclining to one rather than another alternative. The results are usually suggestive rather than decisive, since only fuller examination of the alternative systems as a whole, and a better understanding of criteria, could bring out definite answers. But the tentative character of this method is inherent in it. For it consists in showing that selection has taken place, whether explicitly or tacitly. Yet obviously any determinate conceptual apparatus in the operations of the science involves an act of selection, so that the fact of selection is not enough. If it alone indicated the presence of values, we would have to conclude that there are always values present. Hence, it is the specific content and the specific alternatives that are significant, and whether there are simply general aims such as securing a more fruitful scientific explanation which are sufficient to account for the selection. Yet in spite of all these tentative elements, we shall see that the method can be extraordinarily suggestive.

The Strategy of Historical Correlates

This would consist in comparing trends in political science with historical trends in social policy. If an adequate congruence is found, it might suggest that the trends in political science or political theory constituted, in some sense, value responses to trends in social policy and, therefore, embodied the specific values present in the latter. The strength of such a method lies largely in any historical richness it is able to muster. We shall consider changing twentieth century conceptions of democracy as an illustration.

The Strategy of Model Extraction

This is a very different kind of method and will not be employed much in what follows because it is oriented especially to dealing with full-length political theories and attempting to locate their embedded values. For example, in analyzing theories like those of Hobbes, Locke, Rousseau, Marx, and others, it would not get into debates about correctness, but would first try to fashion out of each theory a model of a type of society. What would a pure Hobbesian organization be like, a Lockean, and so on? A full analysis would give its types of men, their typical interrelations and organization, and so on. The finished models would be regarded as models of possible societies. Short of discovered inconsistencies, we could then look for interpretations, not necessarily in whole societies alone, but also in specific organizations. Thus Laski suggested that, in effect, the Lockean model would fit a limited liability corporation. Similarly, we might find the Rousseau model fitting some types of familial structure. And so on. It is likely that such a procedure, whatever its other uses—and I think it could be used to transform the traditional ways of evaluating political theories, but this is not our present concern—would help us pinpoint the values in the theory, for example, the values of community, individual independence, security, and so on.

Now suppose our strategies discover values for us—of one or another of the four types—embedded or built in theoretical conceptions and processes. The initial gain is one of awareness. But beyond this lie several types of further study and recommendation. One study would be historical and might suggest why some values rather than other values were found in the political science and theory of a given period. This would be akin to the familiar theory of ideology in the social sciences. A second study might be analytic and seek to determine which values were unavoidable and which could be expunged. If there were many of the former, a conclusion might be reached that there are no sharp lines between political science and normative political philosophy, or perhaps that political theory is irretrievably an instrument of political policy. A possible recommendation for intellectual policy in political science might still be to establish scrupulously a value-free science, to expel all but intellectual-scientific values. This would no longer be taken as an inherent character of the science, but as a policy decision about the desirable character of the enterprise to be carried on. It would, therefore, require a justification—for example, the belief that neutrality will achieve greater scientific progress, or that if values are embedded in the conceptual apparatus of the science, it will weaken the commitment of the investigator to the one value of truth, and so on. Very probably, the question will turn out to be extremely complex, rather than of a single or a unified type.

I shall suggest in what follows that there is no wholesale solution to the problem, that what is desirable as intellectual-scientific policy varies with different parts of the field or system and depends, in part, on the state of development of the science and the institutions which demarcate its subject matter. Hence, I propose that values be rendered explicit everywhere and that we see where they can be set aside, where they have a desirable role to play in the inner operation of the sciences, and where they are altogether unavoidable, so that one or another value has to be selected. The exact form in which values rendered explicit and not to be expelled would then appear in the systematizations of the science is a further question that would require full logical consideration. There need be no single or uniform answer. For example, we shall see that values may be given a place among criteria in a classification, or incorporated into definitions, or constitute some of the justifying reasons for choice among alternative conceptual schemes, and so on.

VALUES IN CONCEPTUALIZATION OF THE FIELD

Under the notion of conceptualizing the field, I shall consider characterization of central phenomena (first selection of the generic mark of the political, then selection of the differentiating mark), marking out boundaries of the field, and classification of political forms.

The General Mark of the Political

Does it make much difference to the science if its phenomena are characterized as organized pursuit of the good (Aristotle), authoritative allocation (Easton), power (Lasswell), pressure (A. F. Bentley), or decision (Herbert Simon)? Obviously on some of these, the field becomes wider than on others. And in principle, as a result, some kinds of phenomena may be pushed out of view, and others brought into central focus. Or again, some category of social life—say ideals—may find itself more at home or less at home within the political field. If politics is the organized pursuit of the good, then ideals have a special locus in the science. If politics is cast as a mass of pressures, then ideals are part of the causes of motion, though not very powerful, as Bentley sees them. If politics is power, then ideals are part of the bases by which the ruling elites hold on to their followers. And so on. The treatment of ideals especially, in political theories, seems to carry pro or anti attitudes, with overtones of "idealism" or "cynicism." Whether the connections are necessary or contingent, the value tone is often very marked.

The Differentiating Mark of the Political

A generic mark calls attention to a central phenomenon, but invariably it applies also to other organizations than the state. Aristotle, having used the mark of ruling, has to distinguish the rule of governor over subjects from that of father over children, husband over wife, master over slaves. Easton, to avoid finding private government everywhere, calls the others "parapolitical systems." [7]

One differentiating mark often used is the fact that the state has a wider extent or scope, covering the whole country, whereas private associations and organizations may be authoritative only for their members. This might not seem to embody any concrete values, until we recall that there have been political philosophies that challenged whether this makes a really significant difference. Political pluralism saw power, in fact, dispersed among all sorts of groups, with the state only a limited-purpose organization. Guild socialism would have given power to economic groups, with the state as merely a harmonizing mechanism. These views did not achieve marked success, not because they may not represent logical possibilities, but because the integrated character of modern social problems, requiring a unified or centrally organized

approach, militated against them. This suggests that the differentiating mark of all-inclusiveness for the political group itself may
convey the demand for unity, as a positive or pro-attitude. Quite
explicitly in the procedure of the science, one might include the
value ground—what is desirable in the light of the character of
modern problems—among the grounds for selection of the mark.

The second and perhaps more important differentiating mark is
that the government has *authority* in a special sense, that officials
of limited groups derive their authority from the status of that
group given it by the state. If the generic mark of the political is
power, for example, then the differentiating mark—authority—is
what differentiates the governor from the corporation executive or
the college president. More dramatically, it is what differentiates
the governor from the rebel, the policeman from the gangster.
Does the concept of authority carry with it any values? One might
suspect it does, from the almost hushed awe which its discussion
often invites. Yves Simon writes as follows about the difference
between violence and coercion: " 'Violence' is sometimes used as
a synonym of 'coercion.' In this sense the arrest of a burglar by a
police officer is an act of violence. Anybody can see that this is
loose language, to be prohibited whenever scientific rigor is
needed. Not the policeman, but the burglar, is violent." [8] Compare
it with the remark on the conservative's abhorrence of violence—I
think it is Dewey's somewhere—that those in power always con-
demn violence against them but have their own violence safely
stowed within the legal system. These are quite contrasting value
attitudes. But it is not simply a question of having different
attitudes, but whether when we become conscious of them the
political theorist should choose his differentiating mark of the
political *in such a way as to build in a justification or legitimacy
for the governing power,* or so neutralize his concepts that *legitimacy shall depend on how the governing power acts.* In any
case, even apart from this more general issue, specific values
emerge when the grounds for authority are discussed. For the
range of hypotheses goes from the mantle conferred by the divine
power to the free consent of the subject. The analysis of the
concept of authority would thus seem to express a veritable
program for the desirable form of obedience or loyalty in political
organization.

A concept of authority would thus seem to be unavoidably
value-laden, with values in the fourth sense of obligation rather
than merely pro-attitudes or purposes or worthwhile objects.

Hence, it might be best intellectual policy to gear the concept of authority explicitly to the analysis of the total sociopolitical scene, building in consciously the values that can be justified as desirable. For example, in the present age with its strong dangers of authoritarian rule, its intense need for individual creativity and new ideas, often with new moral claims being made for civil disobedience as a means of breaking through hardened institutional injustices and, in any case, a growing moral emphasis on sensitive conscience in social matters, a theory of authority becomes a complex value-pattern instead of a single slogan or axiomatic principle. The job of analyzing authority has, therefore, to be explicitly and self-consciously normative, if it is to avoid either emptiness or surreptitious value dogmatism.[9]

Boundaries Between Political and Nonpolitical

The setting up of boundaries also clearly involves value considerations. The best illustration is the sharp separation that has existed between the political and the economic. On the conceptual side this has involved, in legal philosophy, a sharp distinction between sovereignty as rule over persons and property as control over things. Morris R. Cohen strongly attacks this distinction. He argues that the essence of property is not a relation between persons and things, but a relation between persons with respect to things. The law of property, by enabling one man to exclude others from resources, in effect confers sovereignty on him, enabling him to decide the character of other people's lives.[10] In effect, the sharp distinction of concepts and the sharp separation of fields is part of the ideological complex by which the laissez-faire tradition saw the activity of business as part of the natural order, whereas that of law was an artificial addition for limited purposes.

Such ideological components in fixing the boundaries between the political and the economic can, no doubt, be scientifically discounted. But both methodological issues and value issues remain to be frankly faced, and neither is readily resolvable. Can political science operate as a separate science with laws relating purely political terms, or are its laws best understood and political predictions best made in a science which employs socio-political-economic variables, as for example Marxist historical materialism contends? This is a methodological issue of broad scope in border relations. And again, what are the desirable relations of state and economy in social policy? This is a value issue of tremendous scope, some answer to which almost inevitably gets built into concepts of the political. Explicit recognition of value content and commitment is therefore essential. Perhaps this area of analysis would be helped by using the Strategy of Historical Correlates and tracing the changing theoretical borders of political and economic in the changing socioeconomic systems of historical development.

Classification of Political Forms

As logicians frequently point out, logical classes can be formed with any identifying mark. Therefore, the responsibility of justifying a particular scientific classification lies with the scientist. He has to show why one rather than another path of classifying should be followed. The mere invention of a name for the group is not enough. It is sometimes very easy to spot the values that determine a mode of classification in the political field. When Herbert Hoover uses a concept of *statism* to embrace in a single class all of fascism, nazism, communism, socialism, and new dealism, just because they all make inroads on the "fifth freedom" of free enterprise, he is clearly conveying the value attitude that any state regulation over business for social purposes is undesirable.[11] The concept of "totalitarianism" which has achieved considerable vogue functioned first, so far as I can see, to put fascism and communism within a single rubric, as against a conception which had fascism and nazism outside the rationalist tradition, but had communism and liberalism within it differing sharply on empirical assumptions about the ways of achieving a utilitarian well-being. By taking the economic similarity as classifying mark, the Marxists were able to put liberalism and nazism in the same group, as contrasted with socialism. By using the classifying mark of the attempt to control the totality of the life of the people, some liberal philosophers saw Catholicism as a totalitarian outlook, in spite of its view of the dignity of every man. A Catholic philosopher like Maritain, on the other hand, could group totalitarianism and liberalism together, as against Catholicism, as embodying, respectively, abstract totality and abstract individualism—totality and individual being polar opposites within an identical concentration on the individual—whereas Catholic doctrine exalts the spiritual person over the material individual.[12] In general, political scientists assimilating their classifications to the dominant we-they pattern of recent years found the "they" extremely heterogeneous. For example, David Spitz, in his *Patterns of Anti-Democratic Thought,*[13] puts under the rubric of "class-authority" all of Plato and Calhoun, reactionary theorists of the extreme right and doctrinaire theorists of the extreme left.

Strangely enough, Aristotle, who includes an explicit ethical criterion in his classifications of political forms, shows us the most sober scientific approach. He starts out with two criteria—how big is the ruling group (one, a few, many), and are they pursuing the common good or their own interests. After examining the various forms that result, and the way they function, he shifts the classification, in part, to an economic basis, which includes wealth and poverty in dealing with oligarcy and democracy, and type of economy in working out subclasses within each group. The result may not be satisfactory—perhaps in part because the concept of the common good is too taken for granted—but at least he sticks close to the evidence, refines his classification for explanatory purposes, and states his values separately though emphatically. It may be that precisely because contemporary classifications purport to be without values that they are too fertile a location for finding values!

While it is logically possible that classification of political forms proceeds on the purely scientific aim of yielding the most fruitful ordering, I suspect that a study of the classifications found in political science texts of recent decades, along the lines of the Strategy of Historical Correlates, would show that modes of classification have served to a marked degree as instruments of politico-social policy. If this prove to be the case, perhaps the best recommendation at the present time would be to suspend classification for a decade or two! If not, then at least one might insist that every proposed classification come with a fully articulated justification-theory.

VALUES IN BASIC DEFINITIONS

I should like to consider the location of values in basic definition in two illustrations which have been highly controversial and produced many competing proposals—that of the state in general, and democracy in particular. The fact of controversy makes easy the application of the Strategy of Alternative Possibilities, which will suffice in the case of the state; the marked historical change in conceptions that has characterized the idea of democracy tempts one into the Strategy of Historical Correlates.

The general perspective of a political scientist is often crystallized—or at least it used to be—in some definition of the state. To answer the question "What is the state?" was long regarded as the pinnacle of theoretical wisdom. Now a definition, if it is not just a stipulation but a real or structural or theoretical definition, purports to embody a correct account of the subject matter. It reflects the results of the science at that stage of development. The only values that are supposed to enter are the purely scientific values of consistency, clarity, and fruitfulness. What makes one look for further values in the definitions of the state is their very number and the heat of controversy about them. If gathered, they would probably run a close second to Gordon Allport's assembly of fifty-odd definitions of "personality." [14]

Take, for example, the definition given in MacIver's *The Modern State*:[15] "The state is an association which, acting through law as promulgated by a government endowed to this with coercive power, maintains within a community territorially demarcated the universal external conditions of social order." Now why the *external* conditions? Why not any conditions that it decides to maintain? Clearly, MacIver is saying that the state should keep its hands off art and religion and philosophy and some part of morality. This prescriptive value component in the definition—the familiar value judgment of a liberal outlook—is somewhat obscured by an attempted historical justification and a definitional policy. The policy is to define the state by the form it takes when fully evolved, and the historical claim is that the liberal democratic state is increasingly that form. We need not enter into the dubious concept of a completed evolution, nor the features ascribed to it. But we may note that it leads MacIver to treat any taking over of functions by the state, when these have been previously separated, as a rollback of history bound to be a temporary episode—he illustrates with fascist and communist forms. The difficulties in maintaining the historical picture suggest strongly the centrality of the value component.

MacIver quotes a letter from Bosanquet which illustrates a contrary evaluation. "Take the relation of the State to Art and Religion—the things most out of its apparent sphere. *How* it ought to deal with them for the best at any given epoch is a fearful problem; but if it, *prima facie,* lets them alone it is none the less dealing with them. It only lets them alone in a certain way and on certain terms, conceived in the interest of the best life" (p. 219).

Bosanquet is thus taking it for granted that the State encompasses all human life—his Hegelian conception is familiar enough. So that even if it does nothing, what is more, even if at the given stage it is incapable of doing anything, it is still rightfully exercising its judgment in refraining in that area.

In some conceptions of the state which carry a value attitude, the historical component may be dominant. For example, the Marxian view of the state certainly breathes a hatred of exploitation in its definition of the state as the executive arm of the dominant class. But its attempt to justify this definition would clearly rest on its historical claim that states have arisen and existed only in class societies and have invariably served dominant class functions. However, it is possible to have a definition of the state which excludes both historical and valuational components and forces them to be separate historical and moral judgments. It is possible to define the state by stipulation as Harold Laski does in his *The State in Theory and Practice* [16]—that we have a state in a given country when we have an organization that has a monopoly of coercive power. It would then be open for the historically-minded to assert how that power has always been used, and for the morally-minded to judge how it should always be used. But once we adopt such a procedure, the most interesting things in political theory will no longer take the form of definitions. They will have to embody hard work. We may recall Bertrand Russell's remark somewhere that the advantage of stipulative definition over empirical statements is like that of theft over honest labor. But perhaps this is unfair. A serious definition in any science already builds in the product of hard labor. But we ought always to recognize what is built in, whether it be history, social theory, psychological assumptions, or value contentions.

In the case of *democracy,* the history of its theory in modern times is fairly clear. It developed in successive strata. A concept of liberty came first, and in its seventeenth century form (e.g., Milton or Locke) by no means included political democracy in the minimal sense of giving every man a vote. Political democracy grew in theory (and the Leveller dream eventually came true in practice), but by that time, concepts of social equality and social democracy were on the scene. Thus the twentieth century inherited the three layers, with strong pressures from socialism to focus its theory on the economic a ena. There was considerable expansion of the conception of democracy as embracing wider social controls of economic life, and as permeating a wider range of social relationships.

Of course, antidemocratic theory maintained itself throughout this whole period. But more significant for political science was the growing power analysis. It did not so much take an anti-democratic stand as refuse to consider seriously the concepts of democracy. Mosca, for example, had earlier treated democracy as simply the name for a type of ruling class that was open from below, not as government by the consent of the governed, and certainly not government by the people! [17] In the 1940s and 1950s, the economic aspects of democratic theory seem to have dropped out. Democracy became conceived in almost wholly pure-political terms; its core is seen in political rights, with strong emphasis on the right to opposition.

A Strategy of Historical Correlates would investigate how far these trends paralleled the relations of the capitalist and communist world, whether the contractions in the democratic concept were functionally related to the increase of hostility in the cold war period. Of course, if such correlations are found, there still remains the question of interpretation. I think it is of the utmost importance for political scientists of the present day in America to ask themselves whether the particular form that democratic theory takes today, and has taken for the past two decades, represents genuine lessons of traumatic historical experience, or whether it is an ideational response to capitalist-communist conflict and the cold war; and if both, in what respects each. It is interesting to note that an international symposium prepared by UNESCO and published in 1951 [18] asked specifically about the different concepts of democracy. While the expected differences of interpretation between the Marxist political theorists and the theorists from capitalist countries are to be found, there are a number of variations. It is perhaps not without social implications that expressions of hope for a synthesis come from those caught in between. Thus a Latin-American representative, Risieri Frondizi, writes: "That is the ideal: a political democracy that is not supported by social injustice; or a social democracy that is not built up at the cost of lack of freedom and human dignity." [19]

Whatever the actual interpretation of the correlates, if they are established, it would seem to warrant the view that in some sense or other, the values embedded in the social policy are also embedded in the analysis of the concept. And the special significance of this strategy of inquiry, as compared to the more minimal Strategy of Alternative Possibilities, would be that in relating to social policies it sees the conceptual analysis as carrying not merely values in the sense of what is thought good or worthwhile, but values in the stronger sense of prescriptive obligation. In this sense, a special definition of democracy is more explicitly urging a special way of life and action. Formulations of the democratic concept thus require as part of their justification specific normative considerations.

VALUES IN THE USE OF BASIC CONCEPTS AND THE ASSUMPTION OF BASIC AIMS

In considering the generic mark of the political, as part of conceptualizing the field, I asked whether it made much difference how the central phenomena were conceived, and whether that difference had a value character. I should now like to explore this further, beginning with two illustrations and then reflecting on the nature of the attempt to set up some concepts as basic. In these reflections, we shall find the Strategy of Model Extraction to be of some help. The two illustrations are Easton's view that the identifying mark of the political is authoritative allocation, and Lasswell's view that power is the central concern of political science. Easton is setting up a basic concept for political science. In the case of power conceptions, there is a possible ambiguity. They may be asserting that the actual phenomena of politics are men exercising power over others. If so, it comes close to Bentley's classic picture of pressure phenomena; [20] it is not implied that power is the goal or the aim, just that pressure is going on, for many different aims. On the other hand, many of the power theorists speak as if a power approach in politics means that power is the goal, the actual aim in political phenomena. Thus power theory makes the assumption of a basic aim of men in the field, not just the assignment of a basic concept for analysis in the field. When Hobbes ascribed to men a restless desire for power as the veritable center of their natures, there was the same ambiguity. He goes on to say that they have to keep on pursuing power because otherwise they will be insecure in what they have; on this assumption an achieved security, if it were possible, would obviate the need for this restless striving. On the other hand, Hobbes sometimes speaks as if the desire to accumulate power and outdo others were the end itself. This is a quite different picture.

David Easton, in his *A Framework for Political Analysis,* offers his basic concept as an identifying criterion: "What distinguishes political interactions from all other kinds of social interactions is that they are predominantly oriented toward the authoritative allocation of values for a society." [21] He adds that the allocations among persons or groups are of three kinds: "An allocation may deprive a person of a valued thing already possessed; it may obstruct the attainment of values which would have otherwise been obtained; or it may give some persons access to values and deny them to others." However the decision to accept authoritative allocations as obligatory may arise, its occurrence is taken by Easton as the distinguishing mark of the political. Now what strikes one immediately in reading this is the assumption of scarce goods as defining the political situation. There is no mode of allocation that consists in increasing the supply or helping raise productivity to ensure wider securing of the goods in question. Easton points out shortly after that the political system does not do all the allocating, that "the fundamental fact confronting all societies is that scarcity of some valued things prevails," [22] but that many conflicts are settled by autonomous interaction, yet where differences unresolved become disruptive of prevailing ideas of order and justice, "every society provides for processes through which special structures either aid in achieving some regulation of the differences or imposes a settlement. These differentiated roles we identify through such concepts as rulers, government, authorities, chiefs, and clan elders."

Note that Easton is not merely saying that governments have dispute-settling functions which, in effect, allocate scarce values. He is using authoritative allocation as prime identification of political systems. Now it may be historically correct that political systems crystallized with the exercise of such functions. But in giving them a definitory role, something has been added. Some set of values has been given an internal influence within the very concept of a political system. What these values are is a more difficult question. Scarcity has been enshrined, with a value attitude of acceptance or resignation toward its unavoidability—for you do not fashion defining criteria by transient features. Or else it may embody the value assumption that governments should not produce but only influence distribution—an assumption surely being transformed in the growth of welfare states and socialist states, or even in capitalist states that play a large part in encouraging productivity. I am not wholly sure that this treatment is fair to Easton. He seems more to be seeking the widest general function, and it may be that the values lie in his limitation of types. But let this serve as a warning to look for the value impact of basic concepts in political science, no matter how abstract they may seem.

Now about power theory. Power theory tends to be a natural carrier for value attitudes. But the value is not always the same. Perhaps that is because some theorists seem to identify with the wielder of power, others with the subject who obeys or yields. Bertrand Russell, in his *Power, A New Social Analysis*,[23] tries to see power in political science as the analogue of energy in physics; a science of power maps its forms and sources. He quips, "Every man would like to be God, if it were possible; some few find it difficult to admit the impossibility." [24] But his values are perfectly clear—he wants power tamed in the interest of human values. On the other hand, a writer like James Burnham, offering a power interpretation of politics in his *The Machiavellians*,[25] clearly identifies with the manipulators and gives a picture of men as dupes led by meaningless ideals.

The bulk of power theory is, of course, more soberly concerned with mapping distributions and studying actual political phenomena. We are not dealing with these studies or their merit, nor even with raising the question whether other organizational categories could do the job with greater depth. We are concerned solely with the question whether the conceptualization in terms of power builds in value-attitudes of one or another kind. This would have to be worked through quite concretely by examining the scientific operation of the conceptual apparatus of power theory where it is applied in concrete studies. Thus it would have to evaluate the concepts of an influential theory like Lasswell's— its distinction of elite and mass in terms of what they get; its classification of values as deference, income, safety; its treatment of symbols ("By the use of sanctioned words and gestures the elite elicits blood, work, taxes, applause, from the masses"); [26] its treatment of interests and change. This is no small task, especially as Lasswell and Kaplan, in their *Power and Society*[27] seriously attempt to work out a neutral conceptual framework for political inquiry which will not beg questions of fact or of value. The Lasswellian categories do have an initial plausibility; but I think it comes from the fact that they are the categories of our present middle-class culture in the present state of the Western world and its problems, and they reflect the present character of the state and the present balance of basic classes and interests. But we live in a changing world, and Lasswell has no real theory of the dynamics of change. Accordingly, the use of his categories imposes permanently a special pattern upon political process. To take one example, Lasswell and Kaplan insist that equality must never be defined so as to exclude the existence of an elite; [28] it is access to power that admits of equality, not its distribution. Yet power carries its value rewards, and so inequality is enshrined perpetually. Now this is quite different from saying that there will always be differences; it introduces a consolidated hierarchical principle for ever after. On the whole, I should like to offer the hypothesis that the power categories of this type fail of scientific neutrality. Because they fundamentally divert attention from men's concrete needs and purposes and their sociohistorical interaction, they do two things. They transmute men's aims into a generalized pursuit of power and so impose a psychology of domination-submission on human relations, to the neglect of the bulk of human strivings. And they look upon all human processes from the point of view of the attempt to dominate—the upper point of view. They thus interpret ideals, as I have suggested above, more as instruments of controlling subjects than as expressing the aims, needs, hopes of the mass of men. This is no small hypothesis and all I have tried to do here is to suggest its outlines for research. But if it has only partial truth, it is very important for understanding, for example, the constant political miscalculation of the military mind in the modern world, the basic mistrust of any movement toward social revolution in dealing with countries that are still, in effect, semifeudal, and the equation of demands for social change and development with communist conspiracy, on the part of many who are concerned with determining foreign policy.

The multiplication of basic concepts proposed for political science and the complexity of justifying selection of one of them raises the general question whether such an enterprise is really required for the science at its present stage of development. If each basic concept selects a range of phenomena, builds methods of inquiry and a theory-schema around itself, and furthermore, possibly embodies central assumptions about the character of human striving as well as about desirable human attitudes, then it may be far too early to try to do for political science what a physicist does in a well-developed field with much more refined and established data and method. Perhaps the competition of theoretical formulations may more fruitfully be subjected to the Strategy of Model Extraction. Let me compare what I have in mind with Joseph Tussman's discussion in the early part of his *Obligation and the Body Politic* [29] of interpretations of political phenomena in terms of *power, habit, and agreement*. Tussman is interested in the problem of maintaining certain significance of normative concepts of right, duty, common good, and so on. But he does suggest, in effect, three models which correspond to the interpretations—the slave-like model for power, the language model for habit, and the voluntary group model for agreement. Our strategy would start rather with the theories, extract general models of domination-subordination, habit institution, and contractual relation; and then see the more special examples as interpretations of the general models in specific human institutions. The outcome, in any case, is a transformation of the initial inquiry. Instead of asking which is the correct basic concept for political theory, we are led to three different questions.

1. How far are particular given political systems in their social context, in fact, illustrative of each of these (and other) models? This is a descriptive question, and the answer for a particular society would probably be that it is in such and such degrees slavish, habit operating, and contractual.

2. By organizing our inquiry in terms of any one, can we explain more of the rest, whether the explicandum be behavior, linguistic usage, or achievement of goals sought? This is a methodological issue, and I have suggested there is no available answer that is decisive.

3. How far is it desirable that a given society be more or less slavish, operate more or less habitually, widen or narrow the range of contractual relations or opportunities for individual commitment? This is clearly a normative question and the answer is a function of values that should be rendered explicit.

By such an analysis of attempts to assign basic concepts for political science, the very inquiry is reorganized. A central gain is the removal of theories that disguise answers to (3) under the assumption of answers to (2).

VALUES IN THE USE OF SPECIAL
CONCEPTS

Let us turn next from basic concepts to the many special concepts that have to be employed in political science. Let me take as an illustration some controversies over the correct analysis of the concept of freedom. In his *Dimensions of Freedom*, Felix E. Oppenheim carries out a refined analysis of freedom and related concepts.[30] I cannot, of course, present it formally here, but I am interested in looking at one of the consequences that follows quite logically in his framework. It is that certain common uses of the term "free" become incorrect; for example, he says: "By organizing a 'free' public school system, government made it possible for all children to go to school, which many were previously unable to do. But government did not make them free to get an education; this they were free to do before. With compulsory education, they became now, on the contrary, unfree to stay out of school. 'Economic freedom' may refer either to social freedom, namely to noninterference by government with private economic activities, or to economic security which has to do, not with social freedom, but with the fact that government makes it possible for all to attain a certain living standard; and this requires government on the contrary to limit their freedom in economic matters." [31] In short, if I understand him aright, we are forbidden to say that social legislation increased our freedom, but must say instead that it cut our freedom in the interest of our security.

Why, however, must we say this? We do find the forbidden formulation used. For example, toward the end of World War II it found frequent expression. The Four Freedoms included freedom from want. Franklin D. Roosevelt's message to Congress in January 1944 embodied an Economic Bill of Rights in which it was said that all businessmen should have the right "to trade in an atmosphere of freedom from unfair competition and domination by monopolies at home or abroad." Thus social security and restraint on monopolies were seen as increasing freedom from want and economic freeodm, not cutting it down in the interests of security or opportunity. In an interesting pamphlet issued by the Office of War Information in August 1942 on the Four Freedoms, it was even said that guaranteeing freedom of speech carried with it the right to education to have something worth saying, as well as the traditional absence of governmental and nongovernmental penalties on expression of opinion.

Obviously if Oppenheim's definitions are to prevail, we cannot say such things. But why cannot we work out an analysis of freedom in terms of which these modes of speech will be possible? For example, we might say that freedom is a concept used by men in any age to mean the removal of the major typical obstacles to the major typical and approved aims of the mass of men of that age. When the political state constituted the major obstacle—probably because it expressed the entrenched interests of a previous mode of life—men thought of freedom as preventing state interference in their activity. In the modern world, if it is true that state action is necessary to help achievement of their approved major aims, and the chief obstacle comes from entrenched economic interests, then checking those entrenched interests and even strengthening certain powers of the state can consistently be regarded as increasing freedom.

The point of this illustration is simply to show that even what appears to be a matter of conceptual analysis may be shown—by expanding the domain of possibilities and working out alternative conceptual schemes—to embody or have already built-in values. In this struggle over the meaning of freedom, two quite opposing social outlooks are involved, and neither should be allowed to entrench itself surreptitiously, that is, posing as pure conceptual analysis. And no doubt, similar analyses can be made for the use of concepts of equality, justice, impartiality, and hosts of others in political theory.

An objection may, however, be raised at this point. Perhaps it can best be considered by continuing one of the examples above. Suppose someone introduced a bill to guarantee libraries throughout the country in every town and argued that he was doing it to extend freedom of speech, since such freedom required information. Is there really a difference of values in the Oppenheim scheme when the same bill could be supported in that framework by seeing, for example, an economic need for libraries as part of increased education for a more skilled labor force? Does the abstract schema really carry the values, or may one simply use it with varying reliability as a diagnostic feature of conservatism or liberalism? Perhaps, we might object, if the library bill were passed on economic grounds, the result might be a preponderance of technical books in the library. Well, it might be replied, an additional justification in terms of the values of the humanities could be included, once the libraries were to exist on economic grounds. Now obviously, if one keeps adding premises to make sure that the same conclusion is reached, the same conclusion will be reached. If all the facts and all the values are the same, then looking backwards, it may not matter what conceptual scheme was used. The underlying philosophical issue is how the mode of justification affects policy in the period in which policy is being decided; that is, which kind of conceptual scheme most effectively clarifies issues, breaks through barriers, speeds up action, and in other ways best furthers achievement. Philosophers today, in discussing scientific method, sometimes distinguish a process analysis from a product analysis; the former is concerned with concepts as they help inquiry, the latter with the role of concepts in a finished analysis. Our inquiry into theoretical concepts in political science is a process inquiry, and in this sense, it looks to me as if one kind of conceptual scheme can further adoption of policy along particular lines, and another can hinder it. It is never an a priori question, but always a matter of the cultural-ideational climate. And therefore, the pinpointing of the value requires detailed historical consideration.

VALUES IN THE INCORPORATION OF
BASIC FACTUAL COMMITMENTS

There is another place in the work of the political scientist where value commitments may be found. This is, surprisingly, in the acceptance of basic factual assumptions, where the evidence for the facts is insufficient or inconclusive. In an ideally finished science this could not happen; no further value other than any involved in establishing the facts could come riding, as it were, on the back of the facts. We would know what is the case, and this distinct from any consequences the truth might have on our values. But political science, unfortunately, deals with factual materials that are often themselves the subject of controversy, so that in a process analysis, not a product analysis, it is very likely that we will find values attached to different proposed factual assumptions, and sometimes even stimulating the adoption of the assumption to which they are attached.

The clearest example is the role played by assumptions about human nature in political science. Some assumption about human nature is unavoidable, because political science has to know what motives, sanctions, dispositions, and so forth it can count on or has to face in explaining or in predicting the political behavior of man. This psychological part of its framework of analysis has to be filled in somehow or other. If it is left wholly blank, it is being filled, in effect, by the assumption that anything may happen, or that man is completely plastic. Now the assumptions of what man is like basically and unalterably are bound to influence the character of government and law. If man is as Hobbes pictured him in the state of nature, then a strong government is required at least as insurance—unless man is such that the growing knowledge of his Hobbesian nature leads him to act so as to restrain it! If man is basically rational, then the more optimistic democratic procedures are better warranted. If man is thoroughly affiliative, mutually-aiding and other-loving, than an anarchism of Kropotkin's type may be feasible. And so on. It is a historical fact that from Plato's treatment of the masses as the dragon that has to be repressed, down to the present day, the psychologies of man seem so often to correspond precisely to what would be required by the type of political system that is being advocated. Both are the product of a particular cultural milieu with a particular context of problems.[32]

Under these conditions, the acceptance of a particular psychology of man will have a value-attitude alongside it. For our present purpose we need not go beyond this. Any suggestion that the assumption of fact is determined by the desire to support the value must be tested by the evidence for the particular theorist.

We may also note that many special political generalizations may be tied to as yet inconclusive psychological assumptions, and so admit of special value attitudes. Michels' iron law of oligarchy carries a skeptical evaluation of the possible achievement of continuous democracy, on the basis of a man-is-like-that assumption. Again, if we take the psychological view that every activity expresses some specific instinctual energies, it will make considerable difference to our attitude, say to punishment, whether we construe it as realistic protective deterrence, or as fighting the inner temptation to commit the crime in question. Or whether the desire for equality be conceived as a realistic battle against discrimination, or as an expression of envy and weakness as Nietzsche saw it.

VALUES IN POLICY JUDGMENT

We turn finally from the values in the scientific activities of the political scientist and the theoretical activities of the political theorist, to the political science problems in the determination of policy. Here, as we saw at the outset, the political scientist recognizes that values are necessary—and what is more, not merely values that constitute general attitudes or purposes, but judgments of what is worthwhile and even prescriptions of what ought to be done. In this domain, we can look for values on the part of the political scientist concerned either with policy formation or with the theory of policy formation (it does not matter here whether we look at the object-level or the meta-level), in at least four respects. What are the standards used? How is the standard explicated? How is the standard justified? How is the standard applied—and especially, how is the situation structured for application of the standard?

Selection of the Standard.

There is quite a repertoire of standards found in the history of policy decisions. Often they are epitomized in the slogans of movements and countries in ferment. There are ideal ones, such as Liberty, Equality, Fraternity. There are concrete goals, such as Bread, Land, Peace, sometimes with Freedom added. There are general economic ones such as Maintaining a High Level of Prosperity. There are military ones of Victory, patriotic ones of Independence, or the Fatherland, or Religion, Morality, and Country. There are global ones of One World, with some attributes indicating its character. There are national ones expressed simply as The National Interest. There are political ones such as Making Democracy Work. There are calls for achievement, such as To Solve the Problems Now Facing Us. And so on. It need scarcely be argued that when a policy maker or a political scientist acting as advisor selects a standard, he is exhibiting or expressing some values, and it is of the greatest practical importance what these values are.

How Is the Standard Explicated?

This is not as simple as it seems, and in seeing the explication of a standard, we may discover specific value commitments. Take, for example, the standard of the *national interest* advanced by Morgenthau and Kennan for foreign policy.[33] What is the national interest? It tends to be assimilated to the maintenance of power and prestige. But perhaps it ought to consist in a correct reputation for some kind of character (e.g., a land of liberty or of opportunity). Is it a logical contradiction to say that the national interest may sometimes consist in being conquered by another country? One is reminded of the delightful movie, *The Mouse that Roared,* in which an impoverished small kingdom wants to solve its problems by being conquered by the United States. A serious example would be the underground in Nazi Germany pinpointing targets for British bombing. Were they furthering the German national interest under difficult and self-sacrificing conditions? Again, is there a tacit premise in the concept of the national interest that if something is for our interest it cannot be for the interest of Russia or China, or if it is for their interest it cannot be for ours? Or are there assumed common interests? But if there are many such, why should we not be governed in one class of matters by global interest, in another class by national interests? If we do not have a clarified conception, how shall we be able to judge whether land reform in Guatemala is inimical to our national interest if it threatens the profits of the United Fruit Company? We need not reject offhand such an index as the notorious "what is good for General Motors is good for America." We would have to find out what good is intended. It will make a considerable difference whether it is profits for investors, jobs in Detroit, prosperity for merchants, crowded cars on the highway in intermittent perpetual motion, or a suburban way of life for corporate vice-presidents stamped in an organization-man mold. Similarly, is what is in our national interest capitalism, or a higher material standard of living, or some particular form of freedom, or democracy, or what? I think I have suggested enough to indicate that the explication is bound to include very specific values, and that to make them clear and focus on them in the consideration of a proposed standard for forming policy is of the highest practical importance.

How Is the Standard Justified?

Precisely because the standard offered is one out of many possibilities, the problem of its justification unavoidably arises. Now it is precisely here that the way gets blocked by the assumption of the subjectivity of value. This is equivalent to saying that, ultimately, the basic values are arbitrary. Its practical meaning is that we stop where we are. We assert our basic value as a matter of fiat. No standard is better than any other, for no criterion for "better" is available. This means the exaltation of individual will, a not unfamiliar voluntarism in the history of ethics.

Actually, of course, we do not stop trying to justify our selection of standard. For example, on the standard of national interest, if we ask why not global interest or the interest of mankind, we find Kennan assuming that decent purposes and undertakings in the national interest will be conducive to a better world.[34] Or the assumption that an over-moralistic pursuit of global welfare under conditions we cannot control is sure to go astray and lead to greater trouble. These are justifications that can be investigated for the probable truth of their assumptions. In fact, in recent decades in the United States, we had a strange pattern of justification for much of basic policy. We were appearently unable to justify the state's doing something good because it is good, but only because not to do it would play into the hands of communism! Removal of racial discrimination was justified because it would win us allies in Africa, good education lest we fall behind the Russians, and so on.

The theory of justification of standards is a technical part of philosophical ethics and, as we suggested earlier, a very controversial one. But it is advanced enough to see that a sheer arbitrary voluntarism will not do, since it operates with an unanalyzed notion of an individual, and the same would hold for a group like the nation. There is probably no one mode of justifying all types of standards, and there are several modes that may prove particularly relevant to political standards. For political standards are of a special type—they are group-oriented, they refer to longer time spans than choices within the life of a single individual, and they can exhibit all sorts of overlapping of interests. Very prominent in political standards are those derived from pervasive necessary conditions to a wide variety of ends, so that the strength of those different goals is a kind of consolidated bank account on which those means may draw. Law and order, peace in international relations, a functioning economy, are familiar instances of this type of standard. The significant point is that some ends are even ruled out because they are incompatible with the means that support the variety of other ends.[35] I have carried this analysis farther here than is required simply to show that the justification of standards is a place in the theory of policy that is intimately value-laden. And in doing so, I have suggested that the traditional conception of subjectivity is far from the last word on the ethical frontier.

Structuring the Situation for Application of the Standard

Even where the standard is agreed upon, specific values may be discovered in the way the situation is structured for application of the standard. Obviously, there must be some formulation of the problem which generates the inquiry, and different formulations—different descriptions of the situation—are possible with far-reaching consequences. There is the story of the young boy whose parents showed him a picture of the Christian martyrs being thrown to the lions. The little lad burst into tears. Marvelling at his sensitivity, the parents asked him why he wept. He pointed to a scrawny lion and sobbed: "This poor lion hasn't got a Christian." He certainly had a sense of unfairness, but you would hardly call it the correct moral structuring of the problem depicted in the picture. If I remember aright, R. P. Dutt tells this story in his book, *Fascism and Social Revolution,*[36] to evaluate Mussolini's claim that Italy ought to have Ethiopia because she alone among the powers at that time had no colonies. Now whether we structure most national and international issues as how our side can win over communism, or how we can best overcome poverty and starvation throughout the globe, will make a tremendous difference in the policies we adopt. It will also reveal a great deal about our operative values.

In these few topics, I have only suggested how the analysis of value commitments in policy decision might be begun. A full study would require an articulation of the decision process comparable to our previous notion of a sketch of a political system. And the search for value commitments throughout it would be correspondingly detailed.

I have no doubt that concerted work on the location of values in political science will produce other strategies than the ones I have offered, and at the hands of political scientists will yield much richer case studies. But I think that the treatment I have suggested throughout makes at least three points clear: that the role of values in political science is a pervasive one, that laying bare their location and role is an indispensable part of political theory, and that once this is done it is possible to reckon responsibly with the many ways in which different types of value may play a part that is consistent with the scientific enterprise.

NOTES

1. R. M. MacIver, *The Web of Government* (New York: Macmillan, 1948), pp. 4, 8.
2. Robert A. Dahl, *Modern Political Analysis* (Englewood, Cliffs, N.J.: Prentice-Hall, 1963), p. 99.

3. I have elsewhere suggested [*The Theory and Practice of Philosophy* (New York: Harcourt Brace, 1946), pp. 175-86] that a naturalistic theory of man might want to throw overboard the whole subjective-objective terminology and replace it with the categories of events and qualities in the world that (1) can take place only with the presence of my organism, (2) can take place only with the presence of some organism, (3) can take place without the presence of any organism. The usual attributes of variability and invariability, shifting or constant, private or public, difficult or easy for others to verify, etc. cut across all of these and are not consolidated in any one of the three.

4. R. H. Lowie, *The Origin of the State* (New York: Harcourt Brace, c.1927).

5. Franz Oppenheimer, *The State, Its History and Development Viewed Sociologically* (Indianapolis, Ind.: Bobbs-Merrill, 1914).

6. David Easton, *A Framework for Political Analysis* (Englewood Cliffs, N.J.: Prentice-Hall, 1965).

7. Ibid., p. 50 ff.

8. Yves R. Simon, *Philosophy of Democratic Government* (Chicago: Phoenix, University of Chicago Press, 1961), p. 113.

9. The analysis of authority overlaps that of the concept of loyalty. For an interesting interplay of philosophical analysis with practical politics, see Francis B. Biddle, *The Fear of Freedom* (Garden City, N. Y.: Doubleday, 1951). Biddle, taking stock of the impact of the McCarthy period in the United States, raises such questions as whether the citizens who are sovereign should be expected to be loyal to a government, when government is understood as the servant of the people—should the master be loyal to the servant? Invoking Josiah Royce's conception in his *The Philosophy of Loyalty,* Biddle wonders whether ultimately a man's loyalty is not to his ideals, and whether society should not recognize and make room for such a conception.

10. M. R. Cohen, *Law and the Social Order* (New York: Harcourt Brace, 1933), essay on Property and Sovereignty. Cf. Robert L. Hale, *Freedom Through Law* (New York: Columbia University Press, 1952). Similar lessons emerge when one looks closely at the modern corporation and sees the changes it brought about in the very logic of private property. Cf. A. A. Berle and G. Means, *The Modern Corporation and Private Property* (New York: Commerce Clearing House, 1932), especially Book 4.

11. Herbert Hoover and Hugh Gibson, *The Problems of Lasting Peace* (Garden City, N. Y.: Doubleday, Doran, 1943).

12. Jacques Maritain, *The Person and the Common Good* (New York: Scribner, 1947).

13. David Spitz, *Patterns of Anti-Democratic Thought* (New York: Macmillan, 1949), p. 224.

14. Gordon Allport, *Personality: A Psychological Interpretation* (New York: Holt, 1945).

15. R. M. MacIver, *The Modern State* (Oxford: Clarendon Press, 1926), p. 22.

16. Harold Laski, *The State in Theory and Practice* (New York: Viking Press, 1935).

17. G. Mosca, *The Ruling Class* (New York: McGraw-Hill, 1939).

18. Richard McKeon, ed., *Democracy in a World of Tensions* (Chicago: University of Chicago Press, International Symposium prepared by UNESCO, 1951).

19. Ibid., p. 94.

20. Arthur F. Bentley, *The Process of Government* (Bloomington, Indiana: The Principia Press, 1949; first published 1908).

21. Easton, *A Framework for Political Analysis,* p. 50.

22. Ibid., p. 53.

23. Bertrand Russell, *Power, A New Social Analysis* (New York: Norton, 1938).

24. Ibid., p. 9.

25. James Burnham, *The Machiavellians* (New York: Day, 1943).

26. Harold D. Lasswell, *Politics: Who Gets What, When, How* (Meridian, 1958), p. 31.

27. Harold D. Lasswell and Abraham Kaplan, *Power and Society* (New Haven, Conn.: Yale University Press, 1950).

28. Ibid., p. 226.

29. Joseph Tussman, *Obligation and the Body Politic* (New York: Oxford Press, 1960).

30. Felix E. Oppenheim, *Dimensions of Freedom* (New York: St. Martin's Press, 1961).

31. Ibid., p. 123.

32. Cf. John Dewey, *Freedom and Culture* (New York, Capricorn, 1963), ch. 2, esp. p. 29.

33. Hans J. Morgenthau, *In Defense of the National Interest, A Critical Examination of American Foreign Policy* (New York: Knopf, 1951); and George Kennan, *American Diplomacy,* 1900-1950 (Chicago: University of Chicago Press, 1951).

34. Kennan, p. 103.

35. For a brief survey of types of standards in ethical theory, see Abraham Edel, *Science and the Structure of Ethics* (Chicago: University of Chicago Press, 1961), pp. 75-76.

36. R. P. Dutt, *Fascism and Social Revolution* (New York: International Publishers, 1935)

14. On Locating Values in Judicial Inference

Like chapter 13, this chapter continues the program of chapter 12, extending it to the central legal area of judicial process. It was presented at the World Congress of the International Association for Philosophy of Law and Social Philosophy in Brussels in 1971, and it was published in its Proceedings.

Such a program for research was an obvious next step for the theory of judicial decision. Both legal philosophy and judicial experience in the United States have already made it clear that legal interpretation is often more like judicial legislation than unavoidable deductions from the Constitution. For example, on the theoretical side we have legal realism and sociological jurisprudence. On the practical side there were the conservative values of the Supreme Court in the 1930s, when it sought to stem Roosevelt's New Deal, or the liberal values of the Supreme Court in the 1950s, when it opened the doors to school integration. It seemed time, therefore, in the philosophical exploration of judicial decision, to go beyond the reiteration of value content to pinpointing exactly where values entered and where some value judgments were unavoidable. As this brief paper shows, the question proved to be more complex than anticipated, because value judgment enters into the very determination of what a judicial process is. The scope and complexity of the problem should not incline us to abandon the task that is mapped in the paper. It rather emphasizes the point that problems of institutional reconstruction in line with the value judgments arise in the outcome.

By values or value-judgments, I shall mean here primarily judgments of what is good, worthwhile, or desirable. In legal

333

matters, the question of value judgments concerns, in effect, the adoption of social policies or decision along the lines indicated by them. In traditional accounts of judicial inference—construed as the process of reasoning by which the judge reaches a justifiable decision—it has often been maintained that value-judgments can only constitute an unwarranted intrusion. The judge's business is to declare, not to make the law. (Such arguments rise to critical proportions when a social crisis is imminent and the courts are praised or blamed for their role—as for example in the United States when in the 1930s a conservative Supreme Court majority held back the New Deal, or in the 1950s when a liberal majority precipitated a dynamic thrust for racial integration in schools.) It is assumed that the only justifiable way for values to enter judicial inference is in premises or legal conceptions or directives that come from the basic law or constitution (including the established character of the judge's role) or through legislation. A judicial inference that inserted premises about the country's need, or engaged in subtle utilitarianisms, would be engaged in normative trespass. For example, a court that decided to cut down constitutionally guaranteed freedom of speech because the country was at war and so national security should be placed higher in the social purpose scale would, in the absence of special restrictive legislation, be going beyond its appropriate role. (Compare the Frankfurter decision in the Jehovah Witness flag-salute case, at the beginning of World War II[1] and the court's subsequent reversal of this.)

This brief picture of the traditional view needs little comment. Legislatures are constantly changing laws or introducing new ones to give effect to social purposes. Legal concepts, such as theft or trespass, do embody a special valuation (of private property). Constitutions and legal systems do embody the broad purposes of peace, order, and particular conceptions of justice that are taken to give a coherence to the law. That values enter into the character of the judicial process itself may best be seen either in comparing different legal systems (for example, the French emphasis on inference from the code as against the British use of precedent in the common law) or even better, at points where a call arises for changes in the role of the judge. Take, for example, the movement in legal philosophy in the early decades of our century that called for greater freedom in judicial decision (freie Rechtsfindung).[2] In effect, it rested on the recognition that industrialization was bringing innumerable problems into all branches of law, that social needs were rapidly changing, that current methods of judicial decision imposed too great a rigidity, that the judges immersed in the detail of application in concrete cases were in an excellent position to sense the needs and new directions, and that older methods of judicial decision should be relaxed to give them greater scope. Now many parts of this picture rest on factual assumptions, such as the degree of rapidity of change, and the capabilities of judges to sense the new rather than to be typically encrustations of the old. But penetrating it all are the values of new forms of life coming into being, and the call on the law to help solve the problems generated, not to side with the old against the new. If we grant this fact-value configuration, then the values do exert an influence on the character of the judicial process. Of course, the specification of the character of that process may itself be a matter of constitution or of legislation, or an informal matter of the causal influence of growing social purposes. A similar perennial issue is the debate over the merits and demerits of *stare decisis*. Concepts of "revolutionary legality" may call on the judge to decide in the light of the changed purposes of the revolution. So too, a rapidly changing society might conceivably decide to give a maximum ten-year weight to precedents, forbidding them to be cited thereafter. In all such cases, values have a meta-theoretical role on the nature of the judicial process.

In spite of the traditional picture, it is recognized that, sometimes, the work of the law becomes so complex that the value-neutral character of the courts is strained to the limit. The judges seem in danger of turning into administrators setting social policy in detailed application. When this happens, it may still be possible to restore the traditional picture by, as it were, diverting the value pressure from the judicial to the legislative or executive branches of government. For example, one might regularize the judicial referral of large-scale policy decision to legislative commissions in institutional form. More often, the question is argued out (in the United States Supreme Court) in terms of the doctrine of judicial self-restraint. For administrative diversion of social value pressures when demands for change and the complexity of detail become overwhelming, there is the whole development of administrative law. The judicial process is thus left to operate within its traditional modes of inference.[3] But of course the question of modes of inference in administrative law then arises. Thus the procedure of an administrative hearing would have to decide how far it was to employ a juridical model, and how far it was frankly to operate with a means-end or teleological mode.

In all these cases, we have worked within the dominant traditional picture which keeps judicial inference relatively value-free. There is, however, a deviant tradition which is more skeptical about the value-aseptic character of judicial inference. It may pinpoint the place of values in two different ways. One is to assign them a limited role as an exceptional or occasional resort in the method of reaching a justifiable decision. The other claims for values a pervasive internal role which is necessary and unavoidable: no model of judicial inference is complete unless it has a place for value-variables.

As an example of the first, take Cardozo's exploration of the judicial process. He distinguishes several methods: the method of philosophy which engages in the analysis of cases with logical criteria, the method of history which traces an evolutionary development, the method of tradition which appeals to custom, and the method of sociology, which, in effect, uses conceptions of social welfare.[4] The method of sociology, inherently value-laden, is employed where the others are insufficient and leave gaps. The outcome would then be the maxim for a model of judicial inference: if nothing else works, go in for direct value-judgment.

An excellent example of the second alternative is the position proposed by Wurzel in the early part of this century that a category of *projection* be recognized as constitutive in judicial inference alongside the more traditional logical ideas of subsumption and analogy.[5] Wurzel's concept seems intended to be of the same logical type as subsumption and analogy. He says: "The process by which the concept is applied to the boundary case is not one of analysis, of separating the component parts of the concept and seeing which of the parts covers the case, but one of synthesis, by connecting the original concept with a new phenomenon and extending the concept so as to cover the latter." And again, "Projection is the extension of a concept found in formulated law to phenomena which were not originally contained in the concept, or at least were not demonstrably a part of the group of images forming the concept, without at the same time changing the nature of the concept as such." The connecting link in such a process is an experience or a state of feeling. The experience may be of economic and technological changes or a consciousness of injuries brought about in new ways, and the feelings may be values (e.g., familial) that steer the interpretation of a concept in one direction rather than another. That psychological elements enter into the process does not mean that Wurzel is guilty of "psychologism." Psychological elements enter into subsumption and analogy too—consciousness of an instance and grasping of a similarity. We can distinguish between the two aspects: recognizing the place of values *in* an adequate model of judicial inference, and offering psychological or economic hypotheses about the sources of the substitution-instances for the value variable.

The program posed by this possibility is to work out a model of judicial inference which will (ideally) show all the points at which, if no values are inserted, no definite decision will be reached. These are the points of choice where going ahead in the process will be held up unless we move one way or the other, and the way we move reflects a value-selection. If we follow traditional analysis of the constituent processes in judicial inference, the points of selection in the model may be identified as follows.[6]

Structuring the case. The problem in human behavior and relations that generated the legal case has to be brought within the ambit of the legal system. It has to be routed to some broad dimension of familiar problems, for example, violation of contract, criminal offense, disputed onwership. This selection, carried out by instigators and hammered into shape in pretrial procedures, is equivalent to seeing the situation under a given description, and it is clearly geared to the practical aim of steering the case into the direction most likely to bring a particular result. For example, in the 1930s, when workers stopped work but stayed at their places in the factory day and night until their grievances should be settled, was this to be seen as a form of strike ("sit-down") in the field of labor law, or as trespass in connection with property law, or as running an inn without a license and so going counter to municipal ordinance? That the trespass description was dominant expressed the traditional value emphasis on property rights. The treatment as a novel form of strike took chiefly a moral and sociological turn (e.g., that such strikes provoked less violence than picketing, or were more effective). The invocation of the municipal ordinance came only as a hasty effort to grasp a handy weapon.

Finding the law. Once the general description is clear and the case structured, what specific law is relevant? The selection among possibilities is often value-laden. This is clearest where there is no ready law to hand, and analogies are invoked. There are, of course, competing analogies, and the choice is guided by its anticipated results. To mention familiar historical examples, will it be one that extends the range of compensation for accidents or restricts it, and similarly for accidents due to defective industrial products? Or a contemporary example in the making: will it extend responsibility for industrial pollution or limit it?

Interpreting the law. It would be carrying coals to Newcastle to repeat the familiar story of the way in which judicial interpretation of the meaning of terms—Wurzel goes into grammatical and systematic and historical interpretation—carries whole social philosophies (as in the American experience with "due process" or "liberty") that in a particular age shape the distribution of wealth and resources (principles of distributive justice), the extent of burdens, the range of opportunities, and so on.

Applying the law. It is also well known that applying the law to given facts of the case often involves value-judgments, for example, about what is reasonable behavior or reasonable caution or limits of trust. Such judgments are setting standards for desirable human attitudes.

Reaching a decision. After all the previous phases, there is still the actual putting together in a decision. Here the comparative weight of different factors is a value problem. And the very pattern of the decision mode is, as we saw above, an implicit value-judgment about how a judge ought to decide. The law of evidence itself could well be studied for pinpointing the embedded values. So too, the general attitude to the legal struggle as a whole—to take extreme formulations, whether it embodies opposing scientific hypotheses to be judged, or a ceremonial duel whose rules of combat are to be maintained—itself is laden with large-scale value orientations.

We have thus essentially three positions about the place of values in judicial inference. One is a model which keeps them out, except as initially given in one of the several ways listed above. The second is a model of the method of decision which gives values a separate and limited place. The third, explored in greater detail, furnishes a pervasive role. Is it possible, at this late date in the twentieth-century history of controversy about the place of values in judicial inference, to adjudicate among these possibilities? I think it is, and I think that a full treatment could show how some of the older difficulties and objections to a recognition of the place of values have been dissolved by philosophical developments on the relation of fact and value, the relation of formal schemes and their interpretation, the relation of pragmatic to other elements in semiotic, the relation of context to content of ideas, and other advances that have relaxed traditional dogmatisms and over-sharp conceptual cuts. Obviously, this is not the occasion for the study of such preliminaries.

The attempt to compare the three positions necessitates a greater precision in the idea of judicial inference if confusion is to be avoided. The historical use of the term has a varying scope. In the narrowest sense, judicial inference covers only a purely logical notion of legal reasoning—for example whether it is deductive or inductive. But there is no guarantee of this narrow scope even in logic. Conceptions of "informal reasoning" as patterns of premise-conclusion relation that are definite but varied, and not reducible to the traditional two major forms, have been offered in contemporary British analytic ethics.[7] And claims for "practical reasoning" as not reducible to the other types have been offered in the whole history of logic. It is sometimes possible to pinpoint the additional elements in the character of the premises employed. For example, Aristotle distinguishes demonstrative from dialectical reasoning by the type of premises—the former uses primary and necessarily true premises, the latter uses premises that are commonly held. Similarly, one could see in concept of methods of judicial inference, such as Cardozo's, further rules about the source of the premises—whether they are to be sought in precedents, in history, in custom, or in judgments of social welfare. All such notions are to be carefully distinguished from genetic accounts of causal influence in the decision process; they are part of the analysis of the method of decision, as rules or instructions, and they are also analyzing the mode of justification, since they tell you where to appeal to justify your decision. In the long run, I believe that the notion of practical reasoning will have to be analyzed as a configuration of such elements as transformation rules, types of definitions employed, character and locus of premises (in well-distinguished dimensions), and so forth. In such a configuration, the place of values will no longer be regarded as intrusive.

The comparison of the models is more complex than at first might seem to be the case. It is not wholly clear what are the terms of their competition. On the face of it, they seem to be different analyses of the place of values in judicial inference. But they are not all distinct; some of them may cover a part-whole relation. Again, how well-defined is the subject-matter of which they are asserted? Is there only one real judicial inference for which they are competing analyses? Or does judicial inference contain several possibilities with respect to its form, so that they are different models which might conceivably fit the judicial process in different legal systems? Or again, may they not in some respects be models offered in a normative way, for how judicial inference *should* be carried on? These several alternatives do not fit neatly into anthropological description versus logical analysis, or psychology versus logic. It is rather that the context of the inquiry and the terms of its solution have not always been sufficiently determinate. In some respects, it is like the traditional approach over the deductive versus the inductive model. There arise initial arguments over whether induction is different from deduction, or whether it can be construed as a special case in which some general premise is suppressed. Even if they are different, there can be a controversy over which model correctly describes what is going on in the development of a certain field; it may be readily settled in mathematics but be controversial (at some periods) in physics, or in learning theory in psychology. And it may merge with the normative issue of which model should be used in a given field, for example, in law or history.

Almost all these kinds of problems arise with our three positions. It can be argued that each provides a model for the analysis of judicial inference with respect to the place of values, that one may be more basic than another by being a form of which that other is a special case, that one is correct as an account of how judicial inference, in fact, takes place while the other is incorrect at least in the sense of glossing over what actually happens or unavoidably happens, that the possibilities are normative models offering different ways of locating the impact of values which are genuine alternatives so that issues of the advantages and disadvantages of each possibility are paramount.

With respect to these various questions, I want to suggest next that the third possibility regarded as a model for judicial inference is, in one sense, at least the most basic. It enables us to develop the richest and most general model, and to see the other patterns as special cases of it under special conditions of stability and change, of simplicity and complexity, in the human sociohistorical field in which the law operates and to which it is applied. The third position—if it carries out its program—will furnish us with an inference-schema or inference-model in which the points where values enter are more or less clearly marked. To generate the other possibilities as special cases, we have only to cross out some of the occurrences of the value-variables. This can happen under two conditions. One is to ignore a variable, which is possible where the value-content is so established and permanent as to be taken for granted. That is, there is no social change which brings it into question, and there are no complexities in application which generate controversy. The second condition is to move its content systematically somewhere else, when value pressure cannot be ignored. The example from Cardozo illustrates the first of these—since it ignores the value elements in the traditional methods that manage to work, presumably because of the relative stability of the embedded values and moderate simplicity of the situations. The case of administrative law illustrates the second, where a field that "intrudes" values is transferred to the administrative process. The first of our three positions represent an even more restricted case. A society would have to be so stable and simple that its aims for the law and for legal method could be stated separately and antecedently, and thereafter the law set on its independent nonvalue course.

The tolerance in this approach to the models is a calculated one. It recognizes the multiplicity of perspectives from which such inquiries as we have been considering have been engaged in. Indeed, the picture does vary from the position of judge, lawyer, client, law professor, general public, and philosopher. Conceivably, one of the models might be a better working approximation for the lawyer, another a more profound framework for the philosopher. Presumably, Cardozo's description may be correct for Cardozo's practice, but may be analytically limited for the historian of social change. Whether it is normatively too restricted for Cardozo's own time depends on the sociohistorical analysis of Cardozo's time.

In general, it may very well be that nothing short of the fully conscious third model is appropriate for our time. For given the high complexity and the rapidity of social change, the field conditions appropriate to the other models simply do not hold. We require a consciousness of the full schema without ignoring any of the value-places, because we cannot be sure in almost any question that we are not faced with the need for a far-reaching reconstruction of the desirable rules and procedures of the law, and even where no changes are required, there may have to be a conscious reaffirmation of keeping things as they are. The burden of proof used to be on proposals of change; nowadays, it is equally on the maintenance of the existing ways.

This does not mean that within some limited domains other possibilities may not be applicable—but as deliberate decision. For example, even the old-fashioned deductive model is not ruled out in this way. It is simply recognized that it is useful only where there are no difficulties in a rather automatic structuring of the case, finding the law, interpreting and applying it, and so on. This is rarely so, but there may be restricted areas—automobile accident liability, for example—in which we may want deliberately to automatize and computerize decision.

These comments have been concerned with the type of inquiry and a program for evaluation. The actual evaluation is a much larger task. And there are many aspects which have not been raised. For example, there are the logical questions of the systematization of values and its impact in the map of value-places, how much redundancy there may be, what logical simplifications may be possible, and so on. In general, there has to be a greater coordination of what is going on in ethical theory with the analysis of values from the point of view of legal philosophy.

NOTES

1. Minersville School District v. Gobitis, 310 U.S. 586 (1939).
2. See volume 9 of The Modern Legal Philosophy Series, *Science of Legal Method* (Boston: Boston Book Company, 1917), especially the selections from Geny, Ehrlich, and Berolzheimer.
3. Cf. James M. Landis, *The Administrative Process* (New Haven: Yale University Press, 1938), especially ch. 4.
4. Benjamin Cardozo, *The Nature of the Judicial Process* (New Haven: Yale University Press, 1921; paperback, 1960). Professor Beryl Levy, in his *Cardozo and Frontiers of Legal Thinking*, rev. ed., (Cleveland: Press of Case Western Reserve University, 1969), p. 60, equates the method of sociology with the method of ethics.
5. See Karl Georg Wurzel, chapter on "Methods of Juridical Thinking" in The Modern Legal Philosophy Series, vol. op. cit., especially pp. 342-49.
6. Cf. Morris R. Cohen, "The Process of Judicial Legislation" in his *Law and the Social Order,* (New York: Harcourt Brace, 1933).
7. Cf. Gilbert Ryle, "Formal and Informal Logic," in *Dilemmas* (Cambridge: Cambridge University Press, 1956).

INDEX